THE ROMANTIC POETS
BYRON, SHELLEY, AND KEATS

The Romantic Poets II
Byron, Shelley, and Keats

With an Introduction and Contemporary Criticism

Edited by JOSEPH PEARCE
and ROBERT ASCH

IGNATIUS PRESS   SAN FRANCISCO

Cover art:
Illustration for *La Belle Dame sans Merci* by John Keats
Walter Crane, 1865
Photo © Fine Art Images/Bridgeman Images

Cover design by John Herreid

Dedicated to Stratford and Leonie Caldecott

Tradition is the extension of Democracy through time; it is the proxy of the dead and the enfranchisement of the unborn.

Tradition may be defined as the extension of the franchise. Tradition means giving votes to the most obscure of all classes, our ancestors. It is the democracy of the dead. Tradition refuses to submit to the small and arrogant oligarchy of those who merely happen to be walking about. All democrats object to men being disqualified by the accident of birth; tradition objects to their being disqualified by the accident of death. Democracy tells us not to neglect a good man's opinion, even if he is our groom; tradition asks us not to neglect a good man's opinion, even if he is our father. I, at any rate, cannot separate the two ideas of democracy and tradition.

—G. K. Chesterton

Ignatius Critical Editions—Tradition-Oriented Criticism for a new generation

CONTENTS

John Keats (1795–1821)

Contemporary Criticisms

INTRODUCTION

Lord Byron (1788–1824), Percy Bysshe Shelley (1792–1822), and John Keats (1795–1821) are the second generation of Romantic poets, distinguishing them from the early Romantic poets—William Blake (1757–1827), William Wordsworth (1770–1850), and Samuel Taylor Coleridge (1772–1834). In order to understand the importance of these hugely influential poets, we need to know something about Romanticism itself. What is Romanticism? Is it right or wrong? Is it right or left? Is it revolutionary or reactionary? What *is* it? Such questions are not academic, nor are they unimportant. On the contrary, they help us to understand the world in which we live.

In the afterword to the third edition of *The Pilgrim's Regress*, C. S. Lewis complained that "romanticism" had acquired so many different meanings that, as a word, it had become meaningless. "I would not now use this word … to describe anything," he complained, "for I now believe it to be a word of such varying senses that it has become useless and should be banished from our vocabulary."[1] *Pace* Lewis, if we banished words because they have multifarious meanings or because their meanings are abused or debased by maladroit malapropism, we should soon find it impossible to say *anything* at all. Take, for example, the word "love". Few words are more abused, yet few words are more axiomatic to an understanding of ourselves. John Lennon and Jesus Christ do not have the same thing in mind when they speak of love. C. S. Lewis understood this, of

[1] C. S. Lewis, afterword to *The Pilgrim's Regress: An Allegorical Apology for Christianity, Reason, and Romanticism*, 3rd ed. (Grand Rapids, Mich.: William B. Eerdmans, 1992), p. 200.

course. He understood it so well that he wrote a whole book on the subject. In *The Four Loves* he sought to *define* "love". And what is true of a word such as "love" is equally true of a word like "Romanticism". If we are to advance in understanding, we must abandon the notion of abolishing the word and commence instead with a definition of our terms. Lewis, in spite of his protestations, understood this also, proceeding from his plaintive call for the abolition of the word to the enumerating of various definitions of it, claiming that "we can distinguish at least seven kinds of things which are called 'romantic'."[2] From four loves to seven Romanticisms, Lewis was not about to abandon meaning, or the *mens sana*, to men without minds or chests.

Since Lewis' seven separate definitions of Romanticism are a little unwieldy, it is necessary to hone our definition of Romanticism into an encompassing unity within which the other definitions can be said to subsist. What makes Romanticism distinct, or, to return to our initial question, what *is* it? According to the *Collins Dictionary of Philosophy*, Romanticism is "a style of thinking and looking at the world that dominated 19th century Europe".[3] Arising in early medieval culture, it referred originally to tales in the Romance language about courtly love and other sentimental topics, as distinct from works in classical Latin. From the beginning, therefore, "Romanticism" stood in contradistinction to "classicism". The former referred to an outlook marked by refined and responsive *feelings* and thus could be said to be inward-looking, subjective, "sensitive", and given to noble dreams; the latter was marked by empiricism, governed by science and precise measures, and could be said to be outward-looking.

Having defined our terms, albeit in the broadest and most sweeping sense, we can proceed to a discussion of the ways in which human society has oscillated between the two alternative visions of reality represented by classicism and

---

[2] Ibid.
[3] *Collins Dictionary of Philosophy* (London: Collins, 1990).

Romanticism. First, however, we must insist that the oscillation is itself an aberration. It is a product of modernity. In the Middle Ages there was no such oscillation between these two extremes of perception. On the contrary, the medieval world was characterized by, indeed it was defined by, a theological and philosophical unity that transcended the division between Romanticism and classicism. The nexus of philosophy and theology in the Platonic-Augustinian and Aristotelian-Thomistic view of man represented the fusion of *fides et ratio*, the uniting of faith and reason. Take, for example, the use of the figurative or the allegorical in medieval literature, or the use of symbolism in medieval art. The function of the figurative in medieval art and literature was not intended primarily to arouse spontaneous *feelings* in the observer or reader, but to encourage the observer or reader to see the philosophical or theological significance beneath the symbolic configuration. In this sense, medieval art, informed by medieval philosophy and theology, is much more objective and outward-looking than the most "realistic" examples of modern art. The former points to abstract ideas that are the fruits of a philosophical tradition existing independently of either the artist or the observer; the latter derives its "realism" solely from the feelings and emotions of those "experiencing" it. One demands that the artist or the observer reach beyond himself to the transcendent truth that is out there; the other recedes into the transient feelings of subjective experience. The surrender of the transcendental to the transient, the perennial to the ephemeral, is the mark of "post-Christian", and postrational, society. It is also a consequence of the triumph of the subjectivism of a certain type of Romanticism.

The medieval fusion of faith and reason was fragmented, theologically, by the Reformation, and, philosophically, by the secularizing humanism of the Late Renaissance. Romanticism and classicism can be said to represent attempts to put the fragments of post-Christian Humpty-Dumptydom together again. They are attempts to make sense of the senselessness of fragmented *fides et ratio*.

The so-called "Enlightenment" was the philosophical phoenix-Frankenstein that rose from the ashes of this fragmented unity. It represented faithless "reason", or, more correctly, a blind faith in "reason" alone. In much the same way that the theological fragmentation of the Protestant Reformation had led to a rejection of scholastic *ratio* in its enshrining of *fides* alone, so the philosophical fragmentation of the Renaissance-Enlightenment had led to a rejection of *fides*, enshrining *ratio* alone. A belief that man had dethroned the gods of superstition led very quickly to the superstitious elevation of man into a self-worshipping deity. Eventually it led to the worship of the goddess Reason at Notre Dame Cathedral in Paris during the Reign of Terror that followed the French Revolution, the first manifestation of rationalist totalitarianism.

If the Enlightenment was characterized by scientism and skepticism, that is, the worship of science and the denigration of religion, the Romantic reaction against the Enlightenment would be characterized by skepticism about science and by the resurrection of religion. Romanticism would emerge, in fact, as the reaction of inarticulate "faith" against inarticulate "reason": heart worship at war with head worship. It was all a far cry from the unity of heart and head that had characterized Christian civilization. Paradoxically, however, and perhaps ironically, the Romantic reaction would lead many heart-searching Romantics to the heart of Rome. This was, at least, the case in England and France; though in Germany it led, via the genius of Wagner and the madness of Nietzsche, to the psychosis of Hitler. Even in England and France, the consequences of Romanticism were multifarious, leading Romantics in many different directions. Whereas the work of the early Romantics, especially Wordsworth and Coleridge, led many toward conversion to Christianity and particularly to Catholicism, the influence of the second generation of Romantics—Byron, Shelley, and Keats—led others toward an egocentric subjectivism that would spawn the postmodernism that dominated art and criticism in the latter half of the twentieth century.

The Romantic reaction in England could be said to have had its genesis in 1798 with the publication of *Lyrical Ballads* by Wordsworth and Coleridge. Published only nine years after the French Revolution, the poems in *Lyrical Ballads* represented the poets' recoil from the rationalism that had led to the Reign of Terror. Wordsworth would pass beyond the "serene and blessed mood"[4] of optimistic pantheism displayed in his "Lines composed a few miles above Tintern Abbey" to a full embrace of Anglican Christianity as exhibited in the allegorical depiction of Christ in "Resolution and Independence". Coleridge threw down the allegorical gauntlet of Christianity in "The Rime of the Ancient Mariner", and, in his "Hymn before Sunrise in the Vale of Chamouni", he saw beyond majestic nature ("O sovran BLANC!"[5]) to the majesty of the God of nature:

> Who made you glorious as the Gates of Heaven
> Beneath the keen full moon? Who bade the sun
> Clothe you with rainbows? Who, with living flowers
> Of loveliest blue, spread garlands at your feet?—
> GOD! let the torrents, like a shout of nations,
> Answer! and let the ice-plains echo, GOD!
> GOD! sing ye meadow-streams with gladsome voice!
> Ye pine-groves, with your soft and soul-like sounds!
> And they too have a voice, yon piles of snow,
> And in their perilous fall shall thunder, GOD![6]

In their reaction against the Enlightenment, Wordsworth and Coleridge had rediscovered the purity and passion of Christianity. In his own quixotically eccentric way, William Blake was also reacting against the Enlightenment, lamenting the

---

[4] William Wordsworth, "Lines composed a few miles above Tintern Abbey, on revisiting the banks of the Wye during a Tour, July 13, 1798", in *The Romantic Poets*, ed. Joseph Pearce and Robert Asch, vol. 1, *Blake, Wordsworth, and Coleridge*, Ignatius Critical Editions (San Francisco: Ignatius Press, 2014), p. 126, line 41.

[5] Samuel Taylor Coleridge, "Hymn before Sunrise in the Vale of Chamouni", in *Romantic Poets*, vol. 1, p. 391, line 3.

[6] Ibid., pp. 393–94, lines 54–63.

"dark Satanic Mills"[7] of industrialism. Although he shared the desire of Wordsworth and Coleridge for a purer vision untainted by Enlightenment rationalism, his dabbling in theology was singularly peculiar and ultimately heterodox.

The pattern of reaction initiated by the first wave of Romantic poets would be repeated in the various manifestations of neo-medievalism that would follow in its wake and that were a consequence of its influence. The Gothic Revival—heralded by the architect Augustus Pugin in the 1830s and championed by the art critic John Ruskin twenty years later—sought to discover a purer aesthetic through a return to medieval notions of beauty. The Oxford Movement—spearheaded by John Henry Newman, Edward Pusey, and John Keble—sought a return to a purer Catholic vision for the Church of England, leapfrogging the Reformation in an attempt to graft the Victorian Anglican church onto the Catholic Church of medieval England through the promotion of Catholic liturgy and a Catholic understanding of ecclesiology and the sacraments. The pre-Raphaelite Brotherhood—formed sometime around 1850 by Dante Gabriel Rossetti, John Everett Millais, William Holman Hunt, and others—sought a purer vision of art by leapfrogging the art of the Late Renaissance in pursuit of the clarity of medieval and Early Renaissance painting that existed, so the pre-Raphaelites believed and as their name implied, prior to the innovations of Raphael.

Perhaps the most important poetic voice to emerge from the Romantic reaction is that of Gerard Manley Hopkins, who was received into the Catholic Church by John Henry Newman in 1866, twenty-one years after Newman's own conversion. Influenced by the pre-Reformation figures of Saint Francis of Assisi and Duns Scotus, and by the Counter-Reformation rigor and vigor of Saint Ignatius Loyola, Hopkins wrote poetry filled with the dynamism of religious orthodoxy. Unpublished in his own lifetime, Hopkins was destined to emerge as one of the

---

[7] William Blake, "And did those feet in ancient time", in his Preface to *Milton*, in *Romantic Poets*, vol. 1, p. 79, line 8.

most influential poets of the twentieth century following the first publication of his verse in 1918, almost thirty years after his death.

Although these manifestations of Romantic neo-medievalism transformed nineteenth-century culture, countering the optimistic and triumphalistic scientism of the Victorian imperial psyche, it would be wrong to imply that Romanticism always led to medievalism. The neo-medieval tendencies of what might be termed light Romanticism were paralleled by a dark Romanticism, epitomized by the life and work of Byron and Shelley, which tended toward subjectivism and introspective self-indulgence.

If Wordsworth and Coleridge were reacting against the rationalist iconoclasm of the French Revolution, Byron and Shelley seemed to be reacting *against* Wordsworth's and Coleridge's reaction. Greatly influenced by *Lyrical Ballads*, Byron and Shelley were nonetheless uncomfortable with the Christian traditionalism that Wordsworth and Coleridge began to embrace. Byron devoted a great deal of the Preface to *Childe Harold's Pilgrimage* to attacking the "monstrous mummeries of the middle ages",[8] and Shelley, in his "Defense of Poetry", anathematized tradition by insisting that poets were slaves to the zeitgeist and that they were "the mirrors of the gigantic shadows which futurity casts upon the present".[9] Slaves of the spirit of the present, and mirrors of the giant presence of the future, poets were warriors of progress intent on vanquishing the superstitious remnants of tradition. Perhaps these iconoclastic musings could be seen as transient youthful idealism, especially as there appeared to be signs that Byron yearned for something more solid than the inarticulate creedless deism espoused in "The Prayer of Nature", and signs also that Shelley's militant atheism was softening into skylarking pantheism. Their

---

[8] George Gordon Byron, *The Poetical Works of Lord Byron*, ed. Henry Frowde (New York: Macmillan, 1907), p. 168.

[9] Percy Bysshe Shelley, *The Selected Poetry and Prose of Shelley* (Ware, Hertfordshire, U.K.: Wordsworth Poetry Library, 2002), p. 660.

early deaths, and the early death of their confrère, Keats, has preserved them forever as icons of youth whose poetry often attained heights of beauty and perception that transcended the incoherence of their philosophy.

The Byronic aura of the second generation of Romantics crossed the Channel and metamorphosed into the Decadence of Baudelaire, Verlaine, and Huysmans, all of whom plumbed the depths of despair before recoiling in horror into the arms of the Catholic Church. The symbolism of the French Decadence recrossed the Channel under the patronage of Oscar Wilde, who was an aficionado of Baudelaire, Verlaine, and Huysmans.

From the publication of *Lyrical Ballads* in 1798 to the death of Oscar Wilde in 1900, Romanticism could be seen, in large part, to be a reaction against the rationalism of the Enlightenment. It was, however, schizophrenic. The light Romanticism of Wordsworth and Coleridge staggered falteringly in the direction of a revitalized Christianity; the dark Romanticism of Byron, Shelley, and Keats led eventually to subjectivism, nihilism, and postmodernism.

Let's conclude by returning to our original questions. What is Romanticism? At its best, it is the generally healthy reaction of the heart to the hardness of the head. Is it right or wrong? It is often brilliantly right and sometimes disastrously wrong, but, in the words of the greatly misunderstood Romantic King Lear, it is perhaps "more sinned against than sinning" (Act 3, scene 2, line 60).[10] Is it right or left? It is neither and defies all efforts to be classified thus. Is it revolutionary or reactionary? It depends, of course, on how we are defining our terms. If, however, we are referring to political revolutions of the ilk of 1789 and 1917, it is counterrevolutionary and reactionary, at least in its English manifestation. What *is* it? It is, at its best, an effort to rediscover what has been lost—a groping in the depths of experience and in the darkness of modernity for the light of truth that tradition preserves. For, as Oscar Wilde reminds us

---

[10] William Shakespeare, *King Lear*, ed. Joseph Pearce, Ignatius Critical Editions (San Francisco: Ignatius Press, 2008).

in his *Lady Windermere's Fan*, "We are all in the gutter but some of us are looking at the stars."[11]

Lord Byron

George Gordon Byron, 6th Baron Byron of Rochdale, to give him the full grandiloquence of his blue-blooded title, was born in London in 1788, the son of the reckless Captain John Byron and Catherine Gordon of Gight, a Scottish heiress.

If "the Child is Father of the Man", as Wordsworth maintained,[12] we can perhaps see the recklessness and fecklessness of the adult Byron as being rooted in the presence of those characteristics in his parents and in his suffering of the consequences of their reckless and feckless behavior as a child. His father had squandered the family fortune, and his mother, deserted by her husband, took her bitterness out on her son. According to one of Byron's biographers, "The violent temper of his foolish, vulgar and deserted mother produced a repression in him which explains many of his later actions."[13]

In 1798, at the age of ten, he succeeded to the title on the death of "the wicked lord", his great uncle. Educated at the finest schools—he went to school in Dulwich and Harrow and then went to Trinity College, Cambridge—his first book of verse, *Hours of Idleness*, appeared in 1807. It was, however, *Childe Harold's Pilgrimage* that established his reputation. Published in 1812, the poem dramatized and romanticized the poet's grand tour, during which he visited Spain, Malta, Albania, and Greece. From this time, he began to cultivate a self-image, an artfully and artificially constructed persona or mask with which to present himself to the world. Thus was born the "Byronic hero", the man of mystery and the gloomy Romantic loner who would beguile his contemporaries. This

---

[11] These words are spoken by Lord Darlington in act 3 of Wilde's play.

[12] William Wordsworth, "My heart leaps up when I behold", in *Romantic Poets*, vol. 1, p. 142, line 6.

[13] *Chambers Biographical Dictionary* (London: Chambers, 1990), p. 241.

elaborate masquerade, in which part of the mystery is trying to separate the "real man", if he exists, from the mask that he presents, could be considered Byron's greatest artistic achievement—for better or for worse, eclipsing the importance of his verse. It would inspire, via Byronic imitators, such as Oscar Wilde and his "truth of masks", the radical relativism of postmodernism, in which there is no truth beyond the masks. Whereas Wilde ultimately rejected the masquerade, as signified by his conversion to Catholicism, Byron's ultimate position remains a mystery. It is a mystery, or a puzzle, with which Louis Markos struggles manfully, artfully, and, *me judice*, successfully in his essay on Byron in this edition.

For a brief period, Byron was lionized and lauded by London society, but his suspected incestuous relationship with his half sister, Augusta Leigh, led to his being ostracized and effectively forced into exile to the Continent (parallels with the life of Wilde are palpable). He met Shelley in Switzerland and then proceeded to Venice and Rome, where he wrote the final canto of *Childe Harold's Pilgrimage*. Settling in Venice, he continued to write poetry whilst becoming involved in the revolutionary politics of the time. In 1823, he joined the Greek insurgents who had risen against the Turks, then died of trench fever at Missolonghi in western Greece.

Byron's reputation and influence declined in his native land following his death but endured on the Continent, where he would influence writers as disparate in style and philosophy as Hugo, Heine, and Baudelaire.

Percy Bysshe Shelley

Born in 1792 into a wealthy family, his father being a Member of Parliament and his mother a landowner, Shelley appears to have imbibed atheistic and revolutionary ideas from his earliest youth. He espoused such views during his time at Eton and continued to do so as an undergraduate at University College,

Oxford. His authorship of a pamphlet entitled *The Necessity of Atheism* led to his expulsion from the university in 1811. In August of the same year, the nineteen-year-old Shelley eloped with the sixteen-year-old Harriet Westbrook, marrying her in Edinburgh. In July 1814, after Harriet had insisted upon a Church remarriage, he deserted his pregnant wife and one-year-old child and fled to the Continent with the sixteen-year-old Mary Godwin, who was also pregnant. In November, Harriet Shelley gave birth to her second child; in the following February, Mary Godwin, daughter of the atheist philosopher William Godwin, gave birth, prematurely, to a daughter who died within a few days.

In the summer of 1816, Mary and Percy visited Lord Byron at the Villa Diodati by Lake Geneva in Switzerland, a meeting that has become a literary legend for its inspirational role in the spawning of the classic novel *Frankenstein*. In December 1816, the drowned body of the deserted Harriet Shelley was discovered in the Serpentine, in London's Hyde Park, some weeks after she had apparently committed suicide. On December 30, barely days after the discovery of Harriet's body, Mary and Percy were married. In the following March, Percy was denied custody of his two children by Harriet.

Amid the turbulent backdrop of his personal life, Shelley was beginning to write the poetry that would establish his posthumous reputation. He wrote long poems inspired by Godwin's philosophy of atheism, such as *Queen Mab*, but is best known for his lyric verse, of which "To a Skylark", "Ode to the West Wind", "Ozymandias", and "The Cloud" are perhaps the best known and most anthologized. His uncompleted *A Defence of Poetry* marked him as a "progressive" in its advocacy of the superiority of the future over the past and its insistence that the poet should serve the zeitgeist.

Shelley was drowned off the coast of Italy on July 8, 1822. He was twenty-nine years old.

Although Shelley's moral obliquity and atheism prevented the widespread acceptance of his work in his own lifetime, he has been lionized by many admirers in the two centuries since his death. His star was in the ascendant during the Victorian period, in which his poetic and political influence spread, and he has now been honored by the very pillars of the society that he openly despised. University College, Oxford, has erected a splendid Shelley Memorial, perhaps in penance for its embarrassing defense of Christianity, and he has been granted a place of honor, alongside Byron and Keats, at Poets' Corner in Westminster Abbey.

John Keats

Born in London in 1795, John Keats was three years younger than Shelley and seven years younger than Byron; dying in Rome in 1821, he predeceased Shelley by one year and Byron by two. As such, John Keats was the youngest of the second generation of Romantic poets, not only in his life but also in his death. Astonishingly for a poet of his importance, significance, and influence, he was only twenty-five when he died. Few poets, if any, bear such a weighty legacy on such immortally youthful shoulders.

Keats' origins were not as humble as his early biographers have suggested, even though it must be conceded that he was not of the highest echelons of society. He didn't have parents who were aristocrats or Members of Parliament, as had the blue-blooded Byron and Shelley, nor was he educated at Harrow and Cambridge, as was Byron, or Eton and Oxford, as was Shelley; nonetheless, his education at an obscure boarding school in Enfield in Middlesex was of a very high standard, indicative of the relative wealth of his father, who was a livery-stable keeper and later a prosperous innkeeper.

Keats' father died in a riding accident when Keats was only eight, and his mother of tuberculosis six years later. Though he was orphaned at the age of fourteen, his parents' wealth ensured the continuance of his education. He became a surgeon's and apothecary's apprentice and later a medical student at Guy's Hospital. His heart, however, was never in the medical career being carved out for him; rather, he desired to be a poet.

In May 1816, the sonnet "O Solitude" became the first of his poems to be published. The remainder of his corpus of work would be written over the next four years, before the onset of the tuberculosis that would kill him. His greatest achievement was the volume *Lamia, Isabella, The Eve of St. Agnes, and Other Poems*, published in 1820, which is perhaps the most important volume of Romantic verse, except for the earlier *Lyrical Ballads* of Wordsworth and Coleridge. He is best known today for his odes, particularly "On a Grecian Urn", "To a Nightingale", "On Melancholy", and "To Autumn", all of which are regularly anthologized and the last of which, "To Autumn", was voted sixth in a poll of "the nation's favourite poems" conducted by the BBC in 1995. The only poem by one of the Romantic poets to do better than Keats' ode was Wordsworth's "Daffodils", which was voted into fifth place. Since, however, Keats' "Nightingale" was also in the top ten, in ninth place, there was no denying Keats' triumph as champion of all the Romantic poets in a strictly populist sense. On the second centenary of his birth, Keats' emergence as the most popular of British poets served as a timely reminder of his enduringly youthful brilliance.

TEXTUAL NOTE

A word or two about the principle of selection. It has been our intention to be guided as far as possible by the intrinsic aesthetic merit of each poem and its representative character in the poet's oeuvre. It is important to recognize that we are hardly out of an era that was in revolt against the nineteenth century and the Romantic tradition generally—there is still nothing quite as firm a critical consensus of the achievement of the Romantics and the Victorians as there is of the Renaissance or the neo-classical period. Consequently, a certain deference to historical importance becomes an essential—albeit secondary—criterion.

Space has imposed its inevitable limitations. Even with the omission of Walter Savage Landor, John Clare, George Crabbe, Sir Walter Scott, and Leigh Hunt, no Romantic anthology can hope to do full justice to the achievement of the six most important Romantic poets. We have tried to avoid fragmenting texts, especially in narrative verse. The exceptions require some explanation.

Lord Byron's *Beppo* was omitted to make room for the whole of *The Vision of Judgment* because *The Vision* is less like *Don Juan* than *Beppo* is, and because truncating *Beppo* would deface it. Similarly, John Keats' *Isabella* was passed over in favor of *The Eve of St Agnes*. These omissions were painful, but the alternatives seemed worse. Lord Byron's and Percy Bysshe Shelley's plays, too, could not but be mangled by fragmentary representation and were consequently left out altogether.

Some could not be included complete but could not be excluded either—Byron's *Giaour* for the Byronic hero; Keats' *Endymion* because the passage in question contains some of the poet's most justly celebrated lines; Shelley's *Witch of Atlas* for its many beauties, for its comparative neglect, and for being the only thing of its kind in English.

Byron's *Childe Harold's Pilgrimage* and *Don Juan* as well as Shelley's *Prometheus Unbound* presented other difficulties. *Childe Harold* submits more readily to editing as its cantos are comparatively independent of one another and its narrative structure is loose; there are clusters of stanzas within a larger unity, not unlike Alfred Lord Tennyson's *In Memoriam*. We were generous with *Prometheus*, but had it been given complete it would have made it all but impossible to include as much Shelley as we did, including *Adonais*, *The Triumph of Life*, and *Epipsychidion* in their entirety. As for Byron's *Don Juan* (a poem longer than the anthology), it was decided to include one whole canto—an early one, to keep the reader from feeling disoriented, one sufficiently varied, powerful, and self-contained to impart a genuine sense of what the poem is like.

GEORGE GORDON, LORD BYRON
1788–1824

Lines to Mr. Hodgson[1]

WRITTEN ON BOARD THE LISBON PACKET[2] (1809)

Huzza! Hodgson, we are going,
    Our embargo's[3] off at last;
Favourable breezes blowing
    Bend the canvass[4] o'er the mast.
From aloft the signal's[5] streaming,   5
    Hark! the farewell gun is fired;
Women screeching, tars blaspheming,
    Tell us that our time's expired.
      Here's a rascal
      Come to task all,   10
    Prying from the custom-house;
      Trunks unpacking,
      Cases cracking,
    Not a corner for a mouse
'Scapes unsearch'd amid the racket,   15
Ere we sail on board the Packet.

Now our boatmen quit their mooring,
    And all hands must ply the oar;
Baggage from the quay is lowering,
    We're impatient—push from shore.   20
"Have a care! that case holds liquor—
    Stop the boat—I'm sick—oh Lord!"

---

[1] *Mr Hodgson:* Francis Hodgson (1781–1852), churchman and educator, was also a poet and close friend of Byron.

[2] *LISBON PACKET:* Lisbon is the capital of Portugal, and a packet is a regularly scheduled cargo ship.

[3] *embargo's:* An embargo is a prohibition or block to trade or movement.

[4] *canvass:* i.e., the sails.

[5] *signal's:* The signal is the ship's flag.

"Sick, ma'am, damme, you'll be sicker
  Ere you've been an hour on board."
    Thus are screaming 25
    Men and women,
  Gemmen, ladies, servants, Jacks;
    Here entangling,
    All are wrangling,
  Stuck together close as wax.— 30
Such the general noise and racket,
Ere we reach the Lisbon Packet.

Now we've reach'd her, lo! the captain,
  Gallant Kidd,[6] commands the crew;
Passengers their berths are clapt in, 35
  Some to grumble, some to spew.
"Hey day! call you that a cabin?
  Why 'tis hardly three feet square;
Not enough to stow Queen Mab in—
  Who the deuce can harbour there?" 40
    "Who, sir? plenty—
    Nobles twenty
Did at once my vessel fill."—
    —"Did they? Jesus,
    How you squeeze us! 45
  Would to God they did so still:
Then I'd scape the heat and racket
Of the good ship, Lisbon Packet."

Fletcher! Murray! Bob![7] where are you?
  Stretch'd along the deck like logs— 50
Bear a hand, you jolly tar, you!
  Here's a rope's end for the dogs.

[6] *Gallant Kidd*: perhaps a playful reference to the notorious pirate William "Captain" Kidd (c. 1645–1701).

[7] *Fletcher . . . Bob*: Byron's three loyal servants. "Joe" Murray was his ancient retainer, while Robert Rushton appears as the "little page" of "Childe Harold's Good Night".

Hobhouse muttering fearful curses,
   As the hatchway down he rolls,
Now his breakfast, now his verses,   55
    Vomits forth—and damns our souls.
     "Here's a stanza
     On Braganza—[8]
  Help!"—"A couplet?"[9]—"No, a cup
    Of warm water—"   60
    "What's the matter?"
  "Zounds! my liver's coming up;
I shall not survive the racket
Of this brutal Lisbon Packet."

Now at length we're off for Turkey,   65
   Lord knows when we shall come back!
Breezes foul and tempests murky
   May unship us in a crack.
But, since life at most a jest is,
   As philosophers allow,   70
Still to laugh by far the best is,
   Then laugh on—as I do now.
    Laugh at all things,
    Great and small things,
  Sick or well, at sea or shore;   75
    While we're quaffing,
    Let's have laughing—
  Who the devil cares for more?—
Some good wine! and who would lack it,
Ev'n on board the Lisbon Packet?   80
              Falmouth Roads, June 30, 1809.

---

[8] *Braganza*: The Most Serene House of Braganza was one of the primary households of the Portuguese nobility and formed the royal and imperial household from 1640 to 1910.

[9] *couplet*: two-line rhyming poetic form.

Written after Swimming from Sestos to Abydos[10] (1810)

If, in the month of dark December,
    Leander,[11] who was nightly wont
(What maid will not the tale remember?)
    To cross thy stream, broad Hellespont![12]

If, when the wintry tempest roar'd,   5
    He sped to Hero, nothing loth,
And thus of old thy current pour'd,
    Fair Venus![13] how I pity both!

For *me*, degenerate modern wretch,
    Though in the genial month of May,   10
My dripping limbs I faintly stretch,
    And think I've done a feat to-day.

But since he cross'd the rapid tide,
    According to the doubtful story,
To woo,—and—Lord knows what beside,   15
    And swam for Love, as I for Glory;
'Twere hard to say who fared the best:
    Sad mortals! thus the Gods still plague you!
He lost his labour, I my jest:
    For he was drown'd, and I've the ague.[14]   20

---

[10] *Written . . . Abydos*: This poem was written on May 9, 1810, shortly after Byron (an able swimmer) swam from Sestos (the Asian side) to Abydos (the European coast).

[11] *Leander*: in classical mythology, the lover of Hero, a priestess of Aphrodite, the goddess of love. Leander nightly swam the Hellespont to visit his love, until one night when he was drowned in a storm.

[12] *Hellespont*: the Dardanelles, the strait connecting the Aegean Sea to the Sea of Marmara.

[13] *Venus*: in classical mythology, the goddess of love (also known as Aphrodite).

[14] *ague*: illness involving fever and shivering (examples include malaria).

Remember Thee! Remember Thee![15] (1813)

Remember thee! Remember thee!
  Till Lethe[16] quench life's burning stream,
Remorse and shame shall cling to thee,
  And haunt thee like a feverish dream!

Remember thee! Ay, doubt it not;   5
  Thy husband too shall think of thee!
By neither shalt thou be forgot,
  Thou *false* to him, thou *fiend* to me!

The Giaour[17]

Written between 1812 and 1813. The first and probably the finest of Byron's Oriental Tales, *The Giaour* was almost as successful as *Childe Harold*, running through fifteen editions in two years.

The exotic décor of these tales, their rather sinister air of authenticity, and the urgency and excitement of the best of them confirmed the author's reputation throughout Europe. Above all, they are of permanent significance for giving us the first full portrait of the Byronic hero: a fearless man of action living beyond society's norms, thirsting for more than life has to offer; a fatal star to women, without sentiment; the bearer of crushing, secret guilt, impenitent, yet driven to confess, or at least record his tale; a pariah in revolt against the moral rabble; *the* anti-hero—an existential figure.

Childe Harold, the Oriental Tales, and plays such as *Manfred* decisively influenced such figures as Goethe, Berlioz, Pushkin,

---

[15] *Remember Thee! Remember Thee!* Byron wrote this stinging poem in response to a note left by his discarded lover, the married Lady Caroline Lamb (1785–1828).

[16] *Lethe*: the river of the dead (of the realm of Hades), the water of which, when drunk, causes dead souls to forget their lives on earth.

[17] *Giaour*: a non-Muslim, an "infidel". It is pronounced with a soft *g* and rhymes with "power".

Balzac, Delacroix, Turner, Stendhal, Schumann, Musset, Mickiewicz, the Brontës, Liszt, Lermontov, Dostoevsky, Baudelaire, Nietzsche, Wilde, and Joyce.

From *The Giaour: A Fragment of a Turkish Tale* (1812–1813)

   Who thundering comes on blackest steed,[18]   180
With slacken'd bit and hoof of speed?
Beneath the clattering iron's[19] sound
The cavern'd echoes wake around
In lash for lash, and bound for bound;
The foam that streaks the courser's[20] side   185
Seems gather'd from the ocean-tide:
Though weary waves are sunk to rest,
There's none within his rider's breast;
And though to-morrow's tempest lower,
'Tis calmer than thy heart, young Giaour!   190
I know thee not, I loathe thy race,
But in thy lineaments I trace
What time shall strengthen, not efface:
Though young and pale, that sallow front
Is scathed by fiery passion's brunt;   195
Though bent on earth thine evil eye,
As meteor-like thou glidest by,
Right well I view and deem thee one
Whom Othman's sons[21] should slay or shun.

   On—on he hasten'd, and he drew   200
My gaze of wonder as he flew:
Though like a demon of the night

---

[18] *Who ...:* This portion of the poem is narrated by an unnamed Turkish fisherman who lands at Port Leone and witnesses the arrival of the Giaour (and much of the subsequent action of the poem).

[19] *clattering iron's:* i.e., of horseshoes.

[20] *courser's:* swift, strong horse (probably a warhorse).

[21] *Othman's sons:* Turks. The Ottoman Empire took its name from its thirteenth-century founder, Sultan Osman (or Othman) I, who reigned 1356–1369.

He pass'd, and vanish'd from my sight,
His aspect and his air impress'd
A troubled memory on my breast,   205
And long upon my startled ear
Rung his dark courser's hoofs of fear.
He spurs his steed; he nears the steep,
That, jutting, shadows o'er the deep;
He winds around; he hurries by;   210
The rock relieves him from mine eye;
For well I ween[22] unwelcome he
Whose glance is fix'd on those that flee;
And not a star but shines too bright
On him who takes such timeless flight.   215
He wound along; but ere he pass'd
One glance he snatch'd, as if his last,
A moment check'd his wheeling steed,
A moment breathed him from his speed,
A moment on his stirrup stood—   220
Why looks he o'er the olive wood?
The crescent[23] glimmers on the hill,

The Mosque's[24] high lamps are quivering still:
Though too remote for sound to wake
In echoes of the far tophaike,[25]   225
The flashes of each joyous peal
Are seen to prove the Moslem's zeal,
To-night, set Rhamazani's[26] sun;
To-night, the Bairam feast's[27] begun;
To-night—but who and what art thou   230

---

[22] *ween*: believe, suppose.

[23] *crescent*: symbol of Islam.

[24] *Mosque's*: A mosque is the Islamic place of worship.

[25] *tophaike*: a Turkish musket.

[26] *Rhamazani's*: Ramadan, a month of expiation and fasting in the Muslim calendar.

[27] *Bairam feast's*: feast commemorating the end of Ramadan (beginning at sunset and celebrated all night by the lighting up of the mosque and the noise of small-arms fire).

Of foreign garb and fearful brow?
And what are these to thine or thee,
That thou should'st either pause or flee?

He stood—some dread was on his face,
Soon Hatred settled in its place: 235
It rose not with the reddening flush
Of transient Anger's hasty blush,
But pale as marble o'er the tomb,
Whose ghastly whiteness aids its gloom.
His brow was bent, his eye was glazed;   240
He raised his arm, and fiercely raised,
And sternly shook his hand on high,
As doubting to return or fly:
Impatient of his flight delay'd,
Here loud his raven charger[28] neigh'd—   245
Down glanced that hand, and grasp'd his blade;
That sound had burst his waking dream,
As Slumber starts at owlet's scream.
The spur hath lanced his courser's sides;
Away, away, for life he rides: 250
Swift as the hurl'd on high jerreed[29]
Springs to the touch his startled steed;
The rock is doubled, and the shore
Shakes with the clattering tramp no more;
The crag[30] is won, no more is seen   255
His Christian crest[31] and haughty mien.[32]
'Twas but an instant he restrain'd
That fiery barb[33] so sternly rein'd;
'Twas but a moment that he stood,

---

[28] *raven charger*: black horse.

[29] *jerreed*: a blunted Turkish javelin, usually thrown from horseback.

[30] *crag*: steep projecting rock.

[31] *Christian crest*: coat of arms or other symbol emblazoned on his helmet, differentiating him from his Islamic surroundings.

[32] *mien*: bearing.

[33] *fiery barb*: i.e., the horse (a Barbary or Arabian stallion).

Then sped as if by death pursued: 260
But in that instant o'er his soul
Winters of Memory seem'd to roll,
And gather in that drop of time
A life of pain, an age of crime.
O'er him who loves, or hates, or fears,   265
Such moment pours the grief of years:
What felt *he* then, at once opprest[34]
By all that most distracts the breast?
That pause, which ponder'd o'er his fate,
Oh, who its dreary length shall date!   270
Though in Time's record nearly nought,[35]
It was Eternity to Thought!
For infinite as boundless space
The thought that Conscience must embrace,
Which in itself can comprehend   275
Woe without name, or hope, or end.

* * * * *

The Mind, that broods o'er guilty woes,   422
    Is like the Scorpion[36] girt by fire,
In circle narrowing as it glows,
The flames around their captive close,   425
Till inly search'd by thousand throes,
    And maddening in her ire,
One sad and sole relief she knows,
The sting she nourish'd for her foes,
Whose venom never yet was vain,   430
Gives but one pang, and cures all pain,
And darts into her desperate brain;
So do the dark in soul expire,
Or live like Scorpion girt by fire;

[34] *opprest*: oppressed.

[35] *nearly nought*: almost nothing (i.e., no time at all).

[36] *Scorpion*: Ancient legend said that, brought to bay, the Scorpion would sting itself to death in a rage.

So writhes the mind Remorse hath riven,   435
Unfit for earth, undoom'd for heaven,
Darkness above, despair beneath,
Around it flame, within it death!

"She walks in beauty"[37] (1814)

I

She walks in beauty, like the night
    Of cloudless climes and starry skies;
And all that's best of dark and bright
    Meet in her aspect and her eyes:
Thus mellow'd to that tender light   5
    Which heaven to gaudy day denies.

II

One shade the more, one ray the less,
    Had half impair'd the nameless grace
Which waves in every raven tress,
    Or softly lightens o'er her face;   10
Where thoughts serenely sweet express
    How pure, how dear their dwelling-place.

III

And on that cheek, and o'er that brow,
    So soft, so calm, yet eloquent,
The smiles that win, the tints that glow,   15
    But tell of days in goodness spent,
A mind at peace with all below,
    A heart whose love is innocent!

---

[37] "*She walks in beauty*": On June 11, 1814, at an evening party, Byron saw his cousin Lady Wilmot Horton (then in mourning), and, struck by her beauty, he returned home and wrote this poem in a single night.

The Destruction of Sennacherib[38] (1815)

I

The Assyrian came down like the wolf on the fold,
And his cohorts were gleaming in purple and gold;
And the sheen of their spears was like stars on the sea,
When the blue wave rolls nightly on deep Galilee.

II

Like the leaves of the forest when Summer is green,   5
That host with their banners at sunset were seen:
Like the leaves of the forest when Autumn hath blown,
That host on the morrow lay wither'd and strown.

III

For the Angel of Death spread his wings on the blast,
And breathed in the face of the foe as he pass'd;   10
And the eyes of the sleepers wax'd deadly and chill,
And their hearts but once heaved, and for ever grew still!

IV

And there lay the steed with his nostril all wide,
But through it there roll'd not the breath of his pride:
And the foam of his gasping lay white on the turf,   15
And cold as the spray of the rock-beating surf.

V

And there lay the rider distorted and pale,
With the dew on his brow, and the rust on his mail;

---

[38] *Sennacherib*: an arrogant, all-conquering king of Assyria (705–681 B.C.)—
something of an Old World Napoleon—whose forces besieging Jerusalem
were destroyed in one night by the angel of the Lord, according to the biblical
account. He was later killed by his sons for his desecration of Babylon. Cf.
2 Kings 19.

And the tents were all silent, the banners alone,
The lances unlifted, the trumpet unblown.   20

VI

And the widows of Ashur[39] are loud in their wail,
And the idols are broke in the temple of Baal;[40]
And the might of the Gentile, unsmote by the sword,
Hath melted like snow in the glance of the Lord!

**Stanzas for Music: "THEY say that Hope is happiness"
(1814/1815)**

I

THEY say that Hope is happiness;
    But genuine Love must prize the past,
And Memory wakes the thoughts that bless:
    They rose the first—they set the last;

II

And all that Memory loves the most   5
    Was once our only Hope to be,
And all that Hope adored and lost
    Hath melted into Memory.

III

Alas! it is delusion all:
    The future cheats us from afar,   10
Nor can we be what we recall,
    Nor dare we think on what we are.

[39] *Ashur*: i.e., Assyria.
[40] *Baal*: Semitic word meaning "Lord" or "owner" and attached to or associated with a number of local gods, sometimes idolatrously worshipped by the Israelites (incurring the wrath of the Lord).

Fare thee well! (1816)

'Alas! they had been friends in Youth;
But whispering tongues can poison truth;
And constancy lives in realms above;
And Life is thorny; and youth is vain:
And to be wroth with one we love,
Doth work like madness in the brain;

* * * * *

But never either found another
To free the hollow heart from paining—
They stood aloof, the scars remaining,
Like cliffs, which had been rent asunder;
A dreary sea now flows between,
But neither heat, nor frost, nor thunder
Shall wholly do away, I ween,
The marks of that which once hath been.'

COLERIDGE'S *Christabel*[41]

Fare thee well! and if for ever,
    Still for ever, fare *thee well:*
Even though unforgiving, never
    'Gainst thee shall my heart rebel.

Would that breast were bared before thee   5
    Where thy head so oft hath lain,
While that placid sleep came o'er thee
    Which thou ne'er canst know again:

Would that breast, by thee glanced over,
    Every inmost thought could show!   10
Then thou would'st at last discover
    'Twas not well to spurn it so.

---

[41] COLERIDGE'S Christabel: Samuel Taylor Coleridge (1772–1834), one of the founding poets of the Romantic Movement, published his long but incomplete poem, *Christabel*, in 1816 at Byron's urging.

Though the world for this commend thee—
   Though it smile upon the blow,
Even its praises must offend thee,   15
   Founded on another's woe:

Though my many faults defaced me,
   Could no other arm be found,
Than the one which once embraced me,
   To inflict a cureless wound?   20

Yet, oh yet, thyself deceive not;
   Love may sink by slow decay,
But by sudden wrench, believe not
   Hearts can thus be torn away:

Still thine own its life retaineth—   25
   Still must mine, though bleeding, beat;
And the undying thought which paineth
   Is—that we no more may meet.

These are words of deeper sorrow
   Than the wail above the dead;   30
Both shall live, but every morrow
   Wake us from a widow'd bed.

And when thou would solace gather,
   When our child's first accents flow,
Wilt thou teach her to say 'Father!'   35
   Though his care she must forego?

When her little hands shall press thee,
   When her lip to thine is press'd,
Think of him whose prayer shall bless thee,
   Think of him thy love had bless'd!   40

Should her lineaments resemble
   Those thou never more may'st see,

Then thy heart will softly tremble
    With a pulse yet true to me.

All my faults perchance thou knowst,   45
    All my madness none can know;
All my hopes, where'er thou goest,
    Wither, yet with *thee* they go.

Every feeling hath been shaken;
    Pride, which not a world could bow,   50
Bows to thee—by thee forsaken,
    Even my soul forsakes me now:

But 'tis done—all words are idle—
    Words from me are vainer still;
But the thoughts we cannot bridle   55
    Force their way without the will.—

Fare thee well!—thus disunited,
    Torn from every nearer tie,
Sear'd in heart, and lone, and blighted,
    More than this I scarce can die.   60

March 17, 1816

Sonnet on Chillon[42] (1816)

Eternal Spirit of the chainless Mind!
    Brightest in dungeons, Liberty! thou art,
    For there thy habitation is the heart—
The heart which love of thee alone can bind;
And when thy sons to fetters are consign'd—   5
    To fetters, and the damp vault's dayless gloom,
    Their country conquers with their martyrdom,
And Freedom's fame finds wings on every wind.

---

[42] *Chillon*: The Château de Chillon, situated on Lake Geneva (also known as Lake Léman) in Switzerland, was Byron's inspiration.

Chillon! thy prison is a holy place,
   And thy sad floor an altar—for 'twas trod,   10
Until his very steps have left a trace
   Worn, as if thy cold pavement were a sod,
By Bonnivard![43]—May none those marks efface!
   For they appeal from tyranny to God.

Prometheus[44] (1816)

I

Titan![45] to whose immortal eyes
   The sufferings of mortality,
   Seen in their sad reality,
Were not as things that gods despise;
What was thy pity's[46] recompense?   5
A silent suffering, and intense;
The rock, the vulture, and the chain,
All that the proud can feel of pain,
The agony they do not show,
The suffocating sense of woe,   10
   Which speaks but in its loneliness,
And then is jealous lest the sky
Should have a listener, nor will sigh
   Until its voice is echoless.

---

[43] *Bonnivard* [*sic*]: François Bonivard/Bonnivard (1496–1570), a Swiss patriot and historian at one time imprisoned in the Castle of Chillon.

[44] *Prometheus*: in classical mythology, the Titan, gifted with forethought, who stole the fire of the gods to give to mortal man. In punishment, Zeus, the first of the gods, had him chained to Mount Kaukasos, where daily an eagle feasted upon his liver. The later Romantics, including Byron, Shelley, and Keats, all celebrated Prometheus as a revolutionary and a visionary (a prototype of their Romantic ideal).

[45] *Titan*: powerful race of deities in early mythology.

[46] *pity's*: i.e., toward mankind in giving them fire.

II

Titan! to thee the strife was given   15
   Between the suffering and the will,
   Which torture where they cannot kill;
And the inexorable Heaven,
And the deaf tyranny of Fate,
The ruling principle of Hate.   20
Which for its pleasure doth create
The things it may annihilate,
Refused thee even the boon to die:
The wretched gift eternity
Was thine—and thou hast borne it well.   25
All that the Thunderer[47] wrung from thee
Was but the menace which flung back
On him the torments of thy rack;
The fate thou didst so well foresee,
But would not to appease him tell;   30
And in thy Silence was his Sentence,
And in his Soul a vain repentance,
And evil dread so ill dissembled
That in his hand the lightnings trembled.

III

Thy Godlike crime was to be kind,   35
   To render with thy precepts less
   The sum of human wretchedness,
And strengthen Man with his own mind;
But baffled as thou wert from high,
Still in thy patient energy,   40
In the endurance, and repulse
   Of thine impenetrable Spirit,
Which Earth and Heaven could not convulse,
   A mighty lesson we inherit:
Thou art a symbol and a sign   45
   To Mortals of their fate and force;

---

[47] *Thunderer*: Zeus, who wielded a mighty thunderbolt.

Like thee, Man is in part divine,
   A troubled stream from a pure source;
And Man in portions can foresee
His own funereal destiny;   50
His wretchedness, and his resistance,
And his sad unallied existence:
To which his Spirit may oppose
Itself—and equal to all woes,
   And a firm will, and a deep sense,   55
Which even in torture can descry
   Its own concenter'd recompense,
Triumphant where it dares defy,
And making Death a Victory.

                       Diodati, July 1816

Childe Harold's Pilgrimage

The reputation of Byron's first great success, *Childe Harold*, has been overshadowed by the author's later comic masterpieces; it has, however, numbered Goethe, Newman,[48] Ruskin, Arnold, Charles Whibley, and Christopher Dawson among its admirers.

The first two cantos, recording the author's trip to Spain, Portugal, and the Levant during the Peninsular War, were published March 10, 1812. Its success was instant and explosive: the expensive edition of five hundred copies sold out in three days and went through another three editions by the end of the year. Even the author was taken aback: "I awoke one morning and found myself famous."[49]

---

[48] *Newman*: See Wilfred Ward, *The Life of John Henry Cardinal Newman: Based on His Private Journals and Correspondence*, vol. 2 (New York: Longmans, Green, 1912), p. 354.

[49] In Thomas Moore, *Letters and Journals of Lord Byron*, vol. 1 (New York: J. J. Harper, 1830), p. 255.

Canto 3 followed in 1816, in the wake of Byron's self-imposed exile from England and separation from his wife and daughter. The hero's route takes him from the Netherlands—and the field of Waterloo—along the Rhine, and into Switzerland. The poet broods on the downfall of Napoleon, and the age-old war of aggression and tyranny on patriotism and liberty. There is in this canto an interesting contest between masculine and feminine types that runs contrapuntally to the opposition of human will and Nature. The influence of Shelley, and above all Wordsworth, is particularly felt.

Byron closed his account in 1818 with canto 4. Harold—who has been reduced to a cameo appearance in canto 3—is definitively abandoned. The scene is Italy: Venice, Arqua, Ferrara, Florence, and Rome. Literature comes in strong here—Shakespeare, Dante, Petrarch, Boccaccio, Ariosto, and Tasso. However, it is perhaps architecture that is the most potent symbol of survival amid the ruins. Poised between permanence and transience, immortality and failure, the poet asserts the fragile triumph of art, of culture, of order, of himself. Byron brings his pilgrimage to a cautiously optimistic close, affirming the inextinguishable greatness of the human spirit, the enduring value of human achievement, and the abiding solace and wonder of Nature. According to Susan J. Wolfson and Peter J. Manning, "The concluding apostrophe to the ocean (lines 1603–56) marks a turn from the stability of sculpture and architecture to fluidity, and points towards *Don Juan*."[50]

How can we account for the enormous impact of *Childe Harold*? There is the originality of form—a travelogue-cum-topographical poem in Spenserian stanzas. In a period of upheaval, the poem's reflections on the "Spirit of the Age" and its relationship with the European tradition—the author's commitment to both radical and traditionalist values—made it an utterly modern, "relevant" poem, narrated by a man who was himself to become symbolic of both the culture and malaise of

---

[50] Lord Byron, *Selected Poems*, ed. Susan J. Wolfson and Peter J. Manning (Harmondsworth, U.K.: Penguin, 1996), p. 807.

modern Europe. Above all, perhaps, there was the power and fascination of the narrator's voice—always present in Byron.[51]

From *Childe Harold's Pilgrimage*: Canto the Third (1816)

I

Is thy face like thy mother's, my fair child!
ADA![52] sole daughter of my house and heart?
When last I saw thy young blue eyes they smiled,
And when we parted,—not as now we part,
But with a hope.[53]—   5
                    Awaking with a start,
The waters heave around me; and on high
The winds lift up their voices: I depart,
Whither I know not; but the hour's gone by,
When Albion's[54] lessening shores could grieve or glad
    mine eye.

II

Once more upon the waters! yet once more!   10
And the waves bound beneath me as a steed
That knows his rider. Welcome, to their roar!

---

[51] See, inter alia, Matthew Arnold: "A personality of Byron's force counts for so much in life." Matthew Arnold, "Byron", in *Essays in Criticism: Second Series* (London: Macmillan, 1958), p. 117, and W. H. Auden: "From the earliest years till the end, the tone of voice rings true and utterly unlike anybody else's." W. H. Auden, "Byron: The Making of a Comic Poet", in *The Dyer's Hand and Other Essays* (New York: Vintage, 1990). The blurring of the barrier between the man and his art in Byron anticipates Wilde.

[52] ADA: Augusta Ada Byron, the daughter of Lord and Lady Byron (December 10, 1815–November 27, 1852). She enjoyed a career as a brilliant mathematician and worked with Charles Babbage on what was effectively primitive computer science.

[53] *hope*: i.e., to be reunited with his wife and daughter (though the couple remained estranged).

[54] *Albion's*: Albion is the ancient name of England (from which Byron departed on April 25, 1816).

Swift be their guidance, wheresoe'er it lead!
Though the strain'd mast[55] should quiver as a reed,
And the rent canvass fluttering strew the gale,   15
Still must I on; for I am as a weed,
Flung from the rock, on Ocean's foam, to sail
Where'er the surge may sweep, the tempest's breath
     prevail.

III

In my youth's summer I did sing of One,[56]
The wandering outlaw of his own dark mind;   20
Again I seize the theme, then but begun,
And bear it with me, as the rushing wind
Bears the cloud onwards: in that Tale I find
The furrows of long thought, and dried-up tears,
Which, ebbing, leave a steril track behind,   25
O'er which all heavily the journeying years
Plod the last sands of life,—where not a flower appears.

IV

Since my young days of passion—joy, or pain,
Perchance my heart and harp have lost a string,
And both may jar:[57] it may be, that in vain   30
I would essay as I have sung to sing.
Yet, though a dreary strain, to this I cling
So that it wean me from the weary dream
Of selfish grief or gladness—so it fling
Forgetfulness around me—it shall seem   35
To me, though to none else, a not ungrateful theme.

[55] *mast*: i.e., the ship's mast.
[56] *One*: i.e., of Harold.
[57] *jar*: be out of tune.

V

He, who grown aged in this world of woe,
In deeds, not years, piercing the depths of life,
So that no wonder waits him; nor below
Can love, or sorrow, fame, ambition, strife,   40
Cut to his heart again with the keen knife
Of silent, sharp endurance: he can tell
Why thought seeks refuge in lone caves, yet rife
With airy images, and shapes which dwell
Still unimpair'd, though old, in the soul's haunted cell.   45

VI

'Tis to create, and in creating live
A being more intense, that we endow
With form our fancy, gaining as we give
The life we image, even as I do now.
What am I? Nothing: but not so art thou,   50
Soul of my thought![58] with whom I traverse earth,
Invisible but gazing, as I glow
Mix'd with thy spirit, blended with thy birth,
And feeling still with thee in my crush'd feelings' dearth.

VII

Yet must I think less wildly:—I *have* thought   55
Too long and darkly, till my brain became,
In its own eddy boiling and o'erwrought,
A whirling gulf of phantasy and flame:
And thus, untaught in youth my heart to tame,
My springs of life were poison'd. 'Tis too late!   60
Yet am I changed; though still enough the same
In strength to bear what time can not abate,
And feed on bitter fruits without accusing Fate.

[58] *Soul of my thought*: i.e., Harold.

VIII

Something too much of this:—but now 'tis past,
And the spell closes with its silent seal.[59]   65
Long absent HAROLD re-appears at last;
He of the breast which fain no more would feel,
Wrung with the wounds which kill not, but ne'er heal;
Yet Time, who changes all, had alter'd him
In soul and aspect as in age: years steal   70
Fire from the mind as vigour from the limb;
And life's enchanted cup but sparkles near the brim.

* * * * *

X

Secure in guarded coldness, he had mix'd
Again in fancied safety with his kind,
And deem'd his spirit now so firmly fix'd
And sheath'd with an invulnerable mind,   85
That, if no joy, no sorrow lurk'd behind;
And he, as one, might 'midst the many stand
Unheeded, searching through the crowd to find
Fit speculation; such as in strange land
He found in wonder-works of God and Nature's hand.   90

* * * * *

XVII

Stop!—for thy tread is on an Empire's dust![60]   145
An Earthquake's spoil is sepulchred[61] below!

---

[59] *Something . . . seal*: Byron will speak no longer of himself but only of (and through) the character of Harold (who largely personifies Byron).

[60] *Stop . . . dust*: This and the following stanza were written after Byron visited Waterloo, the location of the final defeat of the emperor Napoleon Bonaparte (1769–1821) by forces commanded by the Duke of Wellington (1769–1852).

[61] *sepulchred*: entombed.

Is the spot mark'd with no colossal bust?
Nor column trophied[62] for triumphal show?
None; but the moral's truth tells simpler so,
As the ground was before, thus let it be;—   150
How that red rain hath made the harvest grow!
And is this all the world has gain'd by thee,
Thou first and last of fields! king-making Victory?[63]

XVIII

And Harold stands upon this place of skulls,
The grave of France, the deadly Waterloo;   155
How in an hour the power which gave annuls
Its gifts, transferring fame as fleeting too!
In 'pride of place'[64] here last the eagle[65] flew,
Then tore with bloody talon the rent plain,
Pierced by the shaft of banded nations through;   160
Ambition's life and labours all were vain;
He wears the shatter'd links of the world's broken
    chain.[66]

* * * * *

XXI

There was a sound of revelry by night,[67]
And Belgium's capital[68] had gather'd then

---

[62] *column trophied*: i.e., triumphant column over the spot.

[63] *king-making Victory*: The defeat of Napoleon restored the Bourbon monarchy and simultaneously strengthened monarchies around Europe.

[64] *'pride of place'*: Byron himself defines this as a falconry term, meaning the highest pitch of flight.

[65] *eagle*: i.e., Napoleon.

[66] *He . . . chain*: The defeated Napoleon is imprisoned and in exile on the island of Saint Helena.

[67] *revelry by night*: The Duchess of Richmond held a glorious ball in Brussels shortly before Waterloo (on June 15, 1815, the eve of the Battle of Quatre Bras, which led up to Waterloo).

[68] *Belgium's capital*: i.e., Brussels.

Her Beauty and her Chivalry, and bright
The lamps shone o'er fair women and brave men;
A thousand hearts beat happily; and when   185
Music arose with its voluptuous swell,
Soft eyes look'd love to eyes which spake again,
And all went merry as a marriage-bell;
But hush! hark! a deep sound strikes like a rising knell!

XXII

Did ye not hear it?—No; 'twas but the wind,   190
Or the car rattling o'er the stony street;
On with the dance! let joy be unconfined;
No sleep till morn, when Youth and Pleasure meet
To chase the glowing Hours with flying feet—
But hark!—that heavy sound breaks in once more,   195
As if the clouds its echo would repeat;
And nearer, clearer, deadlier than before!
Arm! Arm! it is—it is—the cannon's opening roar!

XXIII

Within a window'd niche of that high hall
Sate Brunswick's fated chieftain;[69] he did hear   200
That sound the first amidst the festival,
And caught its tone with Death's prophetic ear;
And when they smiled because he deem'd it near,
His heart more truly knew that peal too well
Which stretch'd his father[70] on a bloody bier,   205
And roused the vengeance blood alone could quell:
He rush'd into the field, and, foremost fighting, fell.

[69] *Brunswick's fated chieftain*: Frederick William, Duke of Brunswick (1771–1815), who was killed at Quatre Bras.

[70] *father*: i.e., Duke of Brunswick's father, Charles William Ferdinand, a passionate opponent of the ambitions of Napoleon; he was mortally wounded in 1806 at the Battle of Auerstedt.

XXIV

Ah! then and there was hurrying to and fro,
And gathering tears, and tremblings of distress,
And cheeks all pale, which but an hour ago   210
Blush'd at the praise of their own lovliness;
And there were sudden partings, such as press
The life from out young hearts, and choking sighs
Which ne'er might be repeated; who could guess
If ever more should meet those mutual eyes,   215
Since upon night so sweet such awful morn could rise!

XXV

And there was mounting in hot haste: the steed,
The mustering squadron, and the clattering car,
Went pouring forward with impetuous speed,
And swiftly forming in the ranks of war;   220
And the deep thunder peal on peal afar;
And near, the beat of the alarming drum
Roused up the soldier ere the morning star;
While throng'd the citizens with terror dumb,
Or whispering, with white lips—'The foe! they come!
they come!'   225

XXVI

And wild and high the 'Cameron's gathering'[71] rose!
The war-note of Lochiel, which Albyn's[72] hills
Have heard, and heard, too, have her Saxon foes:—
How in the noon of night that pibroch[73] thrills,
Savage and shrill! But with the breath which fills   230

---

[71] *'Cameron's gathering'*: the song of the Cameron clan of Scotland, calling them to battle.

[72] *Albyn's*: Scotland's.

[73] *pibroch*: bagpipe military cadences.

Their mountain-pipe, so fill the mountaineers
With the fierce native daring which instils
The stirring memory of a thousand years,
And Evan's, Donald's[74] fame rings in each clansman's
    ears!

XXVII

And Ardennes[75] waves above them her green leaves,   235
Dewy with nature's tear-drops, as they pass
Grieving, if aught inanimate e'er grieves,
Over the unreturning brave,—alas!
Ere evening to be trodden like the grass
Which now beneath them, but above shall grow   240
In its next verdure, when this fiery mass
Of living valour, rolling on the foe
And burning with high hope, shall moulder cold and low.

XXVIII

Last noon beheld them full of lusty life,
Last eve in Beauty's circle proudly gay,   245
The midnight brought the signal-sound of strife,
The morn the marshalling in arms,—the day
Battle's magnificently-stern array!
The thunder-clouds close o'er it, which when rent
The earth is cover'd thick with other clay,   250
Which her own clay shall cover, heap'd and pent,
Rider and horse,—friend, foe,—in one red burial blent!

---

[74] *Evan's, Donald's*: referring to two Cameron heroes: Sir Evan Cameron (1629–1719), who fought against Cromwell, and Donald Cameron (1695–1748), who supported James Stuart ("the Young Pretender").

[75] *Ardennes*: The Ardennes are forests stretching from Belgium to France and through Luxembourg; Byron conflated his knowledge of this forest with the wood of Soignies (in western Belgium), the location of a famous battle of German rebels against Roman forces, and the imagined Forest of Arden, featured most famously in Shakespeare's *As You Like It*.

XXIX

Their praise is hymn'd by loftier harps than mine;
Yet one[76] I would select from that proud throng,
Partly because they blend me with his line,   255
And partly that I did his sire some wrong,
And partly that bright names will hallow song;
And his was of the bravest, and when shower'd
The death-bolts deadliest the thinn'd files along,
Even where the thickest of war's tempest lower'd,   260
They reach'd no nobler breast than thine, young,
    gallant Howard!

XXX

There have been tears and breaking hearts for thee,
And mine were nothing, had I such to give;
But when I stood beneath the fresh green tree,
Which living waves where thou didst cease to live,   265
And saw around me the wide field revive
With fruits and fertile promise, and the Spring
Come forth her work of gladness to contrive,
With all her reckless birds upon the wing,
I turn'd from all she brought to those she could not
    bring.   270

XXXI

I turn'd to thee, to thousands, of whom each
And one as all a ghastly gap did make
In his own kind and kindred, whom to teach
Forgetfulness were mercy for their sake;
The Archangel's trump,[77] not Glory's, must awake   275

---

[76] *one*: Frederick Howard (1785–1815), son of the Earl of Carlisle, who died at
the Battle of Waterloo and was commemorated by Southey in his *Poet's Pilgrimage*.

[77] *Archangel's trump*: the trumpet blast of the Archangel Gabriel, announcing
the end of the world and the resurrection of the dead.

Those whom they thirst for; though the sound of
    Fame
May for a moment soothe, it cannot slake
The fever of vain longing, and the name
So honour'd but assumes a stronger, bitterer claim.

XXXII

They mourn, but smile at length; and, smiling,
    mourn: 280
The tree will wither long before it fall;
The hull drives on, though mast and sail be torn;
The roof-tree sinks, but moulders on the hall
In massy hoariness; the ruin'd wall
Stands when its wind-worn battlements are gone;   285
The bars survive the captive they enthral;
The day drags through though storms keep out the
    sun;
And thus the heart will break, yet brokenly live on:

XXXIII

Even as a broken mirror, which the glass
In every fragment multiplies; and makes   290
A thousand images of one that was,
The same, and still the more, the more it breaks;
And thus the heart will do which not forsakes,
Living in shatter'd guise, and still, and cold,
And bloodless, with its sleepless sorrow aches,   295
Yet withers on till all without is old,
Showing no visible sign, for such things are untold.

XXXIV

There is a very life in our despair,
Vitality of poison,—a quick root
Which feeds these deadly branches; for it were   300
As nothing did we die; but Life will suit

Itself to Sorrow's most detested fruit,
Like to the apples on the Dead Sea's shore,[78]
All ashes to the taste: Did man compute
Existence by enjoyment, and count o'er   305
Such hours 'gainst years of life,—say, would he name
    threescore?

* * * * *

XXXVIII

Oh, more or less than man—in high or low,
Battling with nations, flying from the field;   335
Now making monarchs' necks thy footstool, now
More than thy meanest soldier taught to yield;
An empire thou couldst crush, command, rebuild,
But govern not thy pettiest passion, nor,
However deeply in men's spirits skill'd,   340
    Look through thine own, nor curb the lust of war,
Nor learn that tempted Fate will leave the loftiest star.

XXXIX

Yet well thy soul hath brook'd the turning tide
With that untaught innate philosophy,
Which, be it wisdom, coldness, or deep pride,   345
Is gall and wormwood to an enemy.
When the whole host of hatred stood hard by,
To watch and mock thee shrinking, thou hast smiled
With a sedate and all-enduring eye;—
    When Fortune fled her spoil'd and favourite child,   350
He stood unbow'd beneath the ills upon him piled.

* * * * *

[78] *apples . . . shore*: According to Byron's own note, "The (fabled) apples on
the brink of the lake Asphaltites were said to be fair without, and, within, ashes."
These "apples" have been identified as a species of gallnut (accounting for their
dry, dusty interior).

XLII

But quiet to quick bosoms is a hell,   370
And *there* hath been thy bane; there is a fire
And motion of the soul which will not dwell
In its own narrow being, but aspire
Beyond the fitting medium of desire;
And, but once kindled, quenchless evermore,   375
Preys upon high adventure, nor can tire
Of aught but rest; a fever at the core,
Fatal to him who bears, to all who ever bore.

XLIII

This makes the madmen who have made men mad
By their contagion; Conquerors and Kings,   380
Founders of sects and systems, to whom add
Sophists, Bards, Statesmen, all unquiet things
Which stir too strongly the soul's secret springs,
And are themselves the fools to those they fool;
Envied, yet how unenviable! what stings   385
Are theirs! One breast laid open were a school
Which would unteach mankind the lust to shine or rule:

XLIV

Their breath is agitation, and their life
A storm whereon they ride, to sink at last,
And yet so nursed and bigoted to strife,   390
That should their days, surviving perils past,
Melt to calm twilight, they feel overcast
With sorrow and supineness, and so die;
Even as a flame unfed, which runs to waste
With its own flickering, or a sword laid by,   395
Which eats into itself, and rusts ingloriously.

XLV

He who ascends to mountain-tops, shall find
The loftiest peaks most wrapt in clouds and snow;
He who surpasses or subdues mankind,
Must look down on the hate of those below.   400
Though high *above* the sun of glory glow,
And far *beneath* the earth and ocean spread,
Round him are icy rocks, and loudly blow
Contending tempests on his naked head,
And thus reward the toils which to those summits led.   405

XLVI

Away with these! true Wisdom's world will be
Within its own creation, or in thine,
Maternal Nature! for who teems like thee,
Thus on the banks of thy majestic Rhine?[79]
There Harold gazes on a work divine,   410
A blending of all beauties; streams and dells,
Fruit, foliage, crag, wood, cornfield, mountain vine,
And chiefless castles breathing stern farewells
From gray but leafy walls, where Ruin greenly dwells.[80]

XLVII

And there they stand, as stands a lofty mind,   415
Worn, but unstooping to the baser crowd,
All tenantless, save to the crannying wind,
Or holding dark communion with the cloud.
There was a day when they were young and proud,
Banners on high, and battles[81] pass'd below;   420

---

[79] *Rhine*: one of the most famous and important rivers in Europe, stretching from the Swiss Alps to the North Sea coast in the Netherlands.

[80] *Chiefless castles . . . dwells*: This does not refer necessarily to specific castles but gestures toward the enduring "antiquity" of Europe (and additionally indulges the Romantic poet's fascination with ruins).

[81] *battles*: i.e., battalions.

But they who fought are in a bloody shroud,
And those which waved are shredless dust ere now,
And the bleak battlements shall bear no future blow.

* * * * *

XLIX

In their baronial feuds and single fields,
What deeds of prowess unrecorded died!
And Love, which lent a blazon to their shields,[82]   435
With emblems well devised by amorous pride,
Through all the mail of iron hearts would glide;
But still their flame was fierceness, and drew on
Keen contest and destruction near allied,
And many a tower for some fair mischief won,   440
Saw the discolour'd Rhine beneath its ruin run.

* * * * *

LI

A thousand battles have assail'd thy banks,
But these and half their fame have pass'd away,
And Slaughter heap'd on high his weltering ranks;
Their very graves are gone, and what are they?
Thy tide wash'd down the blood of yesterday,   455
And all was stainless, and on thy clear stream
Glass'd with its dancing light the sunny ray;
But o'er the blacken'd memory's blighting dream
Thy waves would vainly roll, all sweeping as they seem.

* * * * *

[82] *blazon . . . shields*: A blazon is a formal description of a coat of arms or other emblem, as would be displayed on the shields of warriors.

LVIII

Here Ehrenbreitstein,[83] with her shatter'd wall
Black with the miner's blast, upon her height   555
Yet shows of what she was, when shell and ball
Rebounding idly on her strength did light:
A tower of victory! from whence the flight
Of baffled foes was watch'd along the plain:
But Peace destroy'd what War could never blight,   560
And laid those proud roofs bare to Summer's rain—
On which the iron shower for years had pour'd in vain.

LIX

Adieu to thee, fair Rhine! How long delighted
The stranger fain would linger on his way!
Thine is a scene alike where souls united   565
Or lonely Contemplation thus might stray;
And could the ceaseless vultures cease to prey
On self-condemning bosoms, it were here,
Where Nature, nor too somber nor too gay,
Wild but not rude, awful yet not austere,   570
Is to the mellow Earth as Autumn to the year.

* * * * *

LXI

The negligently grand, the fruitful bloom
Of coming ripeness, the white city's sheen,
The rolling stream, the precipice's gloom,
The forest's growth, and Gothic walls between,
The wild rocks shaped as they had turrets been   585
In mockery of man's art; and these withal

---

[83] *Ehrenbreitstein*: magnificent fortress on the Rhine, purportedly one of the strongest in Europe, destroyed by the French at the end of the eighteenth century.

A race of faces happy as the scene,
Whose fertile bounties here extend to all,
Still springing o'er thy banks, though Empires near them fall.

LXII

But these recede. Above me are the Alps,[84]   590
The palaces of Nature, whose vast walls
Have pinnacled in clouds their snowy scalps,
And throned Eternity in icy halls
Of cold sublimity, where forms and falls
The avalanche—the thunderbolt of snow!   595
All that expands the spirit, yet appals,
Gather around these summits, as to show
How Earth may pierce to Heaven, yet leave vain man
    below.

* * * * *

LXV

By a lone wall a lonelier column rears
A gray and grief-worn aspect of old days;
'Tis the last remnant of the wreck of years,
And looks as with the wild-bewilder'd gaze   620
Of one to stone converted by amaze,
Yet still with consciousness; and there it stands
Making a marvel that it not decays,
When the coeval[85] pride of human hands,
Levell'd Aventicum,[86] hath strew'd her subject lands.   625

---

[84] *Alps:* The most famous and one of the grandest mountain ranges of Europe,
the highest point of which is Mont Blanc, standing between Italy and France.

[85] *coeval:* built at the same time.

[86] *Aventicum:* an ancient Roman colony in Switzerland (the ruins of the city
are near the city of Avenches), destroyed first by the Alamanni (rebellious
German tribes) and later by the warrior ruler Attila the Hun (died 453).

LXVI

And there—oh! sweet and sacred be the name!—
Julia[87]—the daughter, the devoted—gave
Her youth to Heaven; her heart, beneath a claim
Nearest to Heaven's, broke o'er a father's grave.
Justice is sworn 'gainst tears, and hers would crave   630
The life she lived in; but the judge was just,
And then she died on him she could not save.
Their tomb was simple, and without a bust,
And held within their urn one mind, one heart, one
    dust.

* * * * *

LXIX

To fly from, need not be to hate, mankind:
All are not fit with them to stir and toil,
Nor is it discontent to keep the mind   655
Deep in its fountain, lest it overboil[88]
In the hot throng, where we become the spoil
Of our infection, till too late and long
We may deplore and struggle with the coil,[89]
In wretched interchange of wrong for wrong   660
Midst contentious world, striving where none are
    strong.

[87] *Julia*: According to popular legend, the priestess Julia Alpinus died of grief when her father, Julius Alpinus, was executed in 69 A.D. for rebelling against the emperor, and her ashes were interred together with her father's. Scholars of the mid-nineteenth century established that Julia Alpinus and her tragic death were invented by a sixteenth-century scholar.

[88] *Deep . . . overboil*: Hot springs (natural fountains), on the brink of rising to the surface, appear to boil over. The metaphor is derived from a hot spring that appears to boil over at the moment of its coming to the surface. As the particles of water, when they emerge into the light, break and bubble into a seething mass, so, too, does passion chase and beget passion in the "hot throng" of general interests and individual desires.

[89] *coil*: mortal body.

LXX

There, in a moment, we may plunge our years
In fatal penitence, and in the blight
Of our own soul turn all our blood to tears,
And colour things to come with hues of Night;   665
The race of life becomes a hopeless flight
To those that walk in darkness: on the sea,
The boldest steer but where their ports invite,
But there are wanderers o'er Eternity
Whose bark drives on and on, and anchor'd ne'er
     shall be.   670

* * * * *

LXXXVI

It is the hush of night, and all between
Thy margin and the mountains, dusk, yet clear,
Mellow'd and mingling, yet distinctly seen,
Save darken'd Jura,[90] whose capt[91] heights appear
Precipitously steep; and drawing near,   810
There breathes a living fragrance from the shore,
Of flowers yet fresh with childhood; on the ear
Drops the light drip of the suspended oar,
Or chirps the grasshopper one good-night carol more;

LXXXVII

He is an evening reveller, who makes   815
His life an infancy, and sings his fill;
At intervals, some bird from out the brakes[92]
Starts into voice a moment, then is still.
There seems a floating whisper on the hill,

---

[90] *Jura*: a mountain range between Switzerland and France (west of the lake
and consequently appearing "darkened" against the western sky).

[91] *capt*: capped (i.e., snow-capped).

[92] *brakes*: thicket, area overgrown densely with briars.

But that is fancy, for the starlight dews   820
All silently their tears of love instil,
Weeping themselves away, till they infuse
Deep into Nature's breast the spirit of her hues.

LXXXVIII

Ye stars! which are the poetry of heaven!
If in your bright leaves we would read the fate   825
Of men and empires,—'tis to be forgiven,
That in our aspirations to be great,
Our destinies o'erleap their mortal state,
And claim a kindred with you; for ye are
A beauty and a mystery, and create   830
In us such love and reverence from afar,
That fortune, fame, power, life, have named themselves
    a star.

* * * * *

XCII

The sky is changed!—and such a change! Oh night,[93]   860
And storm, and darkness, ye are wondrous strong,
Yet lovely in your strength, as is the light
Of a dark eye in woman! Far along,
From peak to peak, the rattling crags among
Leaps the live thunder! Not from one lone cloud,   865
But every mountain now hath found a tongue,
And Jura answers, through her misty shroud,
Back to the joyous Alps, who call to her aloud!

XCIII

And this is in the night:—Most glorious night!
Thou wert not sent for slumber! let me be   870

---

[93] *The sky . . . night*: Byron is reflecting upon a thunderstorm that occurred on
June 13, 1816.

A sharer in thy fierce and far delight,—
A portion[94] of the tempest and of thee!
How the lit lake shines, a phosphoric sea,
And the big rain comes dancing to the earth!
And now again 'tis black,—and now, the glee   875
Of the loud hills shakes with its mountain-mirth,
As if they did rejoice o'er a young earthquake's birth.

XCIV

Now, where the swift Rhone[95] cleaves his way
    between
Heights which appear as lovers who have parted
In hate, whose mining depths so intervene,   880
That they can meet no more, though brokenhearted!
Though in their souls, which thus each other
    thwarted,
Love was the very root of the fond rage
Which blighted their life's bloom, and then departed:
Itself expired, but leaving them an age   885
Of years all winters,—war within themselves to wage.

XCV

Now, where the quick Rhone thus hath cleft his way,
The mightiest of the storms hath ta'en his stand:
For here, not one, but many, make their play,
And fling their thunder-bolts from hand to hand,   890
Flashing and cast around: of all the band,
The brightest through these parted hills hath fork'd
His lightings,—as if he did understand,
That in such gaps as desolation work'd,
There the hot shaft should blast whatever therein
    lurk'd.   895

---

[94] *portion*: part.
[95] *Rhone*: one of the major rivers of Europe, running from Switzerland into France.

XCVI

Sky, mountains, river, winds, lake, lightnings! ye!
With night, and clouds, and thunder, and a soul
To make these felt and feeling, well may be
Things that have made me watchful; the far roll
Of your departing voices, is the knoll[96]   900
Of what in me is sleepless,—if I rest.
But where of ye, oh tempests! is the goal?
Are ye like those within the human breast,
Or do ye find, at length, like eagles, some high nest?

XCVII

Could I embody and unbosom now   905
That which is most within me,—could I wreak
My thoughts upon expression, and thus throw
Soul, heart, mind, passions, feelings, strong or weak,
All that I would have sought, and all I seek,
Bear, know, feel, and yet breathe—into *one* word,   910
And that one word were Lightning, I would speak;
But as it is, I live and die unheard,
With a most voiceless thought, sheathing it as a sword.

* * * * *

C

Clarens![97] by heavenly feet thy paths are trod,—
Undying Love's, who here ascends a throne
To which the steps are mountains; where the god
Is a pervading life and light,—so shown   935
Not on those summits solely, nor alone
In the still cave and forest; o'er the flower
His eye is sparkling, and his breath hath blown,
His soft and summer breath, whose tender power
Passes the strength of storms in their most desolate hour. 940

[96] *knoll*: knell (tolling of bells).
[97] *Clarens*: a town beside Lake Geneva.

CI

All things are here of *him*; from the black pines,
Which are his shade on high, and the loud roar
Of torrents, where he listeneth, to the vines
Which slope his green path downward to the shore,
Where the bow'd waters meet him, and adore,   945
Kissing his feet with murmurs; and the wood,
The covert of old trees, with trunks all hoar,
But light leaves, young as joy, stands where it stood,
Offering to him, and his, a populous solitude.

CII

A populous solitude of bees and birds,   950
And fairy-formed and many-colour'd things,
Who worship him with notes more sweet than words,
And innocently open their glad wings,
Fearless and full of life: the gush of springs,
And fall of lofty fountains, and the bend   955
If stirring branches, and the bud which brings
The swiftest thought of beauty, here extend,
Mingling, and made by Love, unto one mighty end.

CIII

He who hath loved not, here would learn that lore,
And make his heart a spirit; he who knows   960
That tender mystery, will love the more,
For this is Love's recess, where vain men's woes,
And the world's waste, have driven him far from
    those,
For 'tis his nature to advance or die;
He stands not still, but or decays, or grows   965
Into a boundless blessing, which may vie
With the immortal lights, in its eternity!

* * * * *

CV

Lausanne! and Ferney![98] ye have been the abodes
Of names which unto you bequeath'd a name;
Mortals, who sought and found, by dangerous roads,
A path to perpetuity of fame: 980
They were gigantic minds, and their steep aim
Was, Titan-like, on daring doubts to pile
Thoughts which should call down thunder, and the
    flame
Of Heaven, again assail'd, if Heaven the while
On man and man's research could deign do more than
    smile.   985

CVI

The one[99] was fire and fickleness, a child,
Most mutable in wishes, but in mind,
A wit as various,—gay, grave, sage, or wild,—
Historian, bard, philosopher, combined;
He multiplied himself among mankind,   990
The Proteus[100] of their talents: But his own
Breathed most in ridicule,—which, as the wind,
Blew where it listed, laying all things prone,—
Now to o'erthrow a fool, and now to shake a throne.[101]

[98] *Lausanne! and Ferney!* The English historian Edward Gibbon (1737–1794) completed his famous *Decline and Fall of the Roman Empire* in 1788 while visiting Lausanne. François-Marie Arouet de Voltaire (1694–1778), French Enlightenment thinker and writer, lived at his estate at Ferney, near Geneva, and lived for a time at Lausanne as well.

[99] *one:* i.e., Voltaire.

[100] *Proteus:* in classical mythology, an ancient sea god (the "old man of the sea") who can tell the future but will change his shape to avoid being forced to do so.

[101] *Now . . . throne:* In fact, though Voltaire frequently lampooned public figures in his writings, he at the same time frequently worked to gain the patronage and esteem of monarchs and other important figures including Louis XV of France, George II of England, Frederick II of Germany, Catherine of Russia, and Pope Benedict XIV. At the same time, however, his writings helped lay the foundation for the eruption of the French Revolution.

CVII

The other,[102] deep and slow, exhausting thought,   995
And hiving wisdom with each studious year,
In meditation dwelt, with learning wrought,
And shaped his weapon with an edge severe,
Sapping a solemn creed[103] with solemn sneer;
The lord of irony,—that master-spell,   1000
Which stung his foes to wrath, which grew from
    fear,[104]
And doom'd him to the zealot's ready Hell,
Which answers to all doubts so eloquently well.

CVIII

Yet, peace be with their ashes,—for by them,
If merited, the penalty is paid;   1005
It is not ours to judge,—far less condemn;
The hour must come when such things shall be made
Known unto all,—or hope and dread allay'd
By slumber, on one pillow,—in the dust,
Which, thus much we are sure, must lie decay'd;   1010
And when it shall revive, as is our trust,[105]
'Twill be to be forgiven, or suffer what is just.

* * * * *

CXIV

I have not loved the world, nor the world me,—
But let us part fair foes; I do believe,
Though I have found them not, that there may be   1060

---

[102] *other*: i.e., Gibbon.

[103] *solemn creed*: i.e., Christianity (despised by both Voltaire and Gibbon).

[104] *foes . . . fear*: Gibbon's *Decline and Fall* provoked criticism, particularly from Church of England clerics and members of the church hierarchy.

[105] *as is our trust*: Byron's religious opinions fluctuated, but he did tend to believe in an afterlife and the superiority of mind over matter. See, for example, his "Detached Thoughts", 1821–1822, especially nos. 96–98.

Words which are things,—hopes which will not
    deceive,
And virtues which are merciful, nor weave
Snares for the failing: I would also deem
O'er others' griefs that some sincerely grieve;
That two, or one, are almost what they seem,   1065
That goodness is no name, and happiness no dream.

CXV[106]

My daughter![107] with thy name this song begun—
My daughter! with thy name thus much shall end—
I see thee not,—I hear thee not,—but none
Can be so wrapt in thee; thou art the friend   1070
To whom the shadows of far years extend:
Albeit my brow thou never should'st behold,
My voice shall with thy future visions blend,
And reach into thy heart,—when mine is cold,—
A token and a tone, even from thy father's mould.   1075

CXVI

To aid thy mind's developement, to watch
Thy dawn of little joys,—to sit and see
Almost thy very growth,—to view thee catch
Knowledge of objects,—wonders yet to thee!
To hold thee lightly on a gentle knee,   1080
And print on thy soft cheek a parent's kiss,—
This, it should seem, was not reserved for me;
Yet this was in my nature:—as it is,
I know not what is there, yet something like to this.

---

[106] CXV: Byron was at one time uncertain whether he ought to publish the final stanzas of the poem (referring to his daughter Ada).

[107] *daughter*: i.e., Ada.

CXVII

Yet, though dull Hate as duty should be taught,[108]   1085
I know that thou wilt love me; though my name
Should be shut from thee, as a spell still fraught
With desolation,—and a broken claim:
Though the grave closed between us,—'twere the same,
I know that thou wilt love me;[109] though to drain   1090
My blood from out thy being were an aim,
And an attainment,—all would be in vain,—
Still thou would'st love me, still that more than life retain.

CXVIII

The child of love,—though born in bitterness
And nurtured in convulsion,—of thy sire   1095
These were the elements,—and thine no less.
As yet such are around thee,—but thy fire
Shall be more temper'd, and thy hope far higher.
Sweet be thy cradled slumbers! O'er the sea,
And from the mountains where I now respire,   1100
Fain would I waft such blessing upon thee,
As, with a sigh, I deem thou might'st have been to me!

[108] *though dull ... taught*: i.e., even if Ada be brought up dutifully to hate her father.

[109] *thou wilt love me*: Byron expects his daughter, the "child of love" (line 1094), to come to love him through reading his works. She did, even choosing to be buried next to him.

To Thomas Moore: "What are you doing now"[110] (Late 1816)

What are you doing now,
   Oh Thomas Moore?
What are you doing now,
   Oh Thomas Moore?
Sighing or suing now,   5
Rhyming or wooing now,
Billing or cooing now,
   Which, Thomas Moore?

But the Carnival's coming,
   Oh Thomas Moore,   10
The Carnival's coming,
   Oh Thomas Moore,
Masking and humming,
Fifing and drumming,
Guitarring and strumming,   15
   Oh Thomas Moore.

To Thomas Moore: "My boat is on shore" (1817)

I

MY boat is on the shore,
   And my bark is on the sea;
But, before I go, Tom Moore,
   Here's a double health to thee!

II

Here's a sigh to those who love me,   5
   And a smile to those who hate;
And, whatever sky's above me,
   Here's a heart for every fate.

---

[110] *Thomas Moore*: Thomas Moore (1779–1852), Irish poet and songwriter and a close friend of Byron.

III

Though the Ocean roar around me,
   Yet it still shall bear me on;   10
Though a desert should surround me,
   It hath springs that may be won.

IV

Were't the last drop in the well,
   As I gasped upon the brink,
Ere my fainting spirit fell,   15
   'T is to thee that I would drink.

V

With that water, as this wine,
   The libation I would pour
Should be—peace with thine and mine,
   And a health to thee, Tom Moore.   20

"So, we'll go no more a roving"[111] (1817)

I

So, we'll go no more a roving
   So late into the night,
Though the heart be still as loving,
   And the moon be still as bright.

---

[111] *"So . . . a roving"*: This hangover poem was written in a letter to Thomas Moore on February 28, 1817, after Byron's participation in the riotous Mardi Gras revelries of Venice. "One evening [Beerbohm] walked unannounced into Ted Craig's cottage declaiming Byron's song 'So, we'll go no more a roving.' At the end, 'Surely the most beautiful lyric in English!' cried Max enthusiastically." Lord David Cecil, *Max: A Biography* (Boston: Riverside Press of Houghton Mifflin, 1965), p. 364.

II

For the sword outwears its sheath,   5
  And the soul wears out the breast,
And the heart must pause to breathe,
  And love itself have rest.

III

Though the night was made for loving,
  And the day returns too soon,   10
Yet we'll go no more a roving
  By the light of the moon.

From *Childe Harold's Pilgrimage*:
Canto the Fourth[112] **(1817)**

I

I stood in Venice, on the Bridge of Sighs;[113]
A palace and a prison on each hand:
I saw from out the wave her structures rise
As from the stroke of the enchanter's wand:
A thousand years their cloudy wings expand   5
Around me, and a dying Glory smiles
O'er the far times, when many a subject land
Look'd to the winged Lion's[114] marble piles,
Where Venice sate in state, throned on her hundred
  isles!

---

[112] For information on this Canto and *Childe Harold* as a whole, see the introduction to Canto the Third above.

[113] *Bridge of Sighs*: a famous covered bridge in Venice between Doge's Palace and the Prison of San Marco.

[114] *winged Lion's*: symbol of Saint Mark the Evangelist, patron of Venice.

II

She looks a sea Cybele,[115] fresh from ocean,   10
Rising with her tiara of proud towers
At airy distance, with majestic motion,
A ruler of the waters and their powers:
And such she was;—her daughters had their dowers
From spoils of nations, and the exaustless East   15
Pour'd in her lap all gems in sparkling showers.[116]
In purple was she robed,[117] and of her feast
Monarchs partook, and deem'd their dignity increased.

III

In Venice Tasso's[118] echoes are no more,
And silent rows the songless gondolier;   20
Her palaces are crumbling to the shore,
And music meets not always now the ear:
Those days are gone—but Beauty still is here.
States fall, arts fade—but Nature doth not die,
Nor yet forget how Venice once was dear,   25
The pleasant place of all festivity,
The revel of the earth, the masque[119] of Italy!

---

[115] *Cybele*: in classical mythology, mother of all the gods; she who wore a turreted tiara.

[116] *all gems . . . showers*: The wealth of Venice was popularly recognized in the wide display of gems throughout the city, from the Church of Saint Mark to the drinking vessels and necklaces seen among the nobility.

[117] *In purple . . . robed*: After the sack of Constantinople, in 1204, the Doge of Venice gained an imperial status.

[118] *Tasso's*: Stanzas of *Jerusalem Delivered*, an epic by the Venetian poet Torquato Tasso (1544–1595), were widely sung by gondoliers for several centuries after his death, but this custom had largely fallen out of practice by Byron's day.

[119] *masque*: a form of elaborate masked ball, revelry, and court pageantry, popular especially in the seventeenth century and continuing intermittently until the 1950s (Carlos de Beistegui's at the Palazzo Labia in 1951, for example).

IV

But unto us she hath a spell beyond
Her name in story, and her long array
Of mighty shadows, whose dim forms despond   30
Above the dogeless city's[120] vanish'd sway;
Ours is a trophy which will not decay
With the Rialto;[121] Shylock and the Moor,[122]
And Pierre,[123] can not be swept or worn away—
The keystones of the arch! though all were o'er,   35
For us repeopled were the solitary shore.

V

The beings of the mind are not of clay;
Essentially immortal, they create
And multiply in us a brighter ray
And more beloved existence: that which Fate   40
Prohibits to dull life, in this our state
Of mortal bondage, by these spirits supplied
First exiles, then replaces what we hate;
Watering the heart whose early flowers have died,
And with a fresher growth replenishing the void.   45

* * * * *

VIII

I've taught me other tongues—and in strange eyes
Have made me not a stranger; to the mind   65
Which is itself, no changes bring surprise;

---

[120] *dogeless city's*: Napoleon deposed the last Doge of Venice in 1797 (by 1817, when Byron visited and wrote his poem, the city was under Austrian rule).

[121] *Rialto*: the middle islands and commercial center of Venice.

[122] *Shylock and the Moor*: the Jewish moneylender and titular protagonist of William Shakespeare's *Merchant of Venice* and *Othello*, respectively.

[123] *Pierre*: a character in the play *Venice Preserved* (1682) by Thomas Otway (1652–1685).

Nor is it harsh to make, nor hard to find
A country with—ay, or without mankind;
Yet was I born where men are proud to be,
Not without cause; and should I leave behind   70
The inviolate island of the sage and free,
And seek me out a home by a remoter sea.

IX

Perhaps I loved it well; and should I lay
My ashes in a soil which is not mine,
My spirit shall resume it—if we may   75
Unbodied choose a sanctuary.[124] I twine
My hopes of being remember'd in my line
With my land's language: if too fond and far
These aspirations in their scope incline,—
If my fame should be, as my fortunes are,   80
Of hasty growth and blight, and dull Oblivion bar

X

My name from out the temple where the dead
Are honour'd by the nations—let it be—
And light the laurels on a loftier head!
And be the Spartan's epitaph[125] on me—   85
'Sparta hath many a worthier son than he.'
Meantime I seek no sympathies, nor need;
The thorns which I have reap'd are of the tree
I planted,—they have torn me,—and I bleed:
I should have known what fruit would spring from such
    a seed.   90

---

[124] *Unbodied . . . sanctuary*: i.e., choose our own resting place after death.

[125] *Spartan's epitaph*: the response of the mother of the general Brasidas to praise of her dead son, as reported by the Greek biographer-historian Plutarch (c. 46–120).

XI

The spouseless Adriatic[126] mourns her lord;
And, annual marriage, now no more renew'd,
The Bucentaur[127] lies rotting unrestored,
Neglected garment of her widowhood!
St Mark yet sees his lion where he stood,   95
Stand, but in mockery of his wither'd power,
Over the proud Place where an Emperor sued,[128]
And monarchs gazed and envied in the hour
When Venice was a queen with an unequall'd dower.

* * * * *

XV

Statues of glass—all shiver'd—the long file
Of her dead Doges are declined to dust;
But where they dwelt, the vast and sumptuous pile
Bespeaks the pageant of their splendid trust;   130
Their sceptre broken, and their sword in rust,
Have yielded to the stranger: empty halls,
Thin streets, and foreign aspects, such as must
Too oft remind her who and what enthrals,
Have flung a desolate cloud o'er Venice' lovely walls.   135

* * * * *

XVIII

I loved her from my boyhood—she to me
Was as a fairy city of the heart,   155

---

[126] *spouseless Adriatic*: Venice was known as the Queen of the Adriatic, therefore the loss of her doge leaves the ocean spouseless.

[127] *Bucentaur*: state galley of the Doges of Venice, from which the doge traditionally dropped a ring into the Adriatic to "wed" it. Napoleon ordered it destroyed in 1798.

[128] *proud . . . sued*: St. Mark's Basilica is the place where the emperor Frederick Barbarossa submitted to the authority of Pope Alexander III.

Rising like water-columns from the sea,
Of joy the sojourn, and of wealth the mart;
And Otway, Radcliffe, Schiller, Shakespeare's art, [129]
Had stamp'd her image in me, and even so,
Although I found her thus, we did not part,   160
Perchance even dearer in her day of woe,
Than when she was a boast, a marvel, and a show.

* * * * *

XLVII

Yet, Italy! through every other land   415
Thy wrongs should ring, and shall, from side to side;
Mother of Arts! as once of arms; they hand
Was then our guardian, and is still our guide;
Parent of our Religion! whom the wide
Nations have knelt to for the keys of heaven!   420
Europe, repentant of her parricide,
Shall yet redeem thee, and, all backward driven,
Roll the barbarian tide, and sue to be forgiven.

* * * * *

XLIX

There, too, the Goddess loves in stone,[130] and fills
The air around with beauty; we inhale
The ambrosial aspect, which, beheld, instils   435
Part of its immortality; the veil
Of heaven is half undrawn; within the pale

---

[129] *Otway, Radcliffe, Schiller, Shakespeare's art*: *Venice Preserved* (1682) by Thomas Otway (1652–1685), *The Mysteries of Udolpho* (1794) by Mrs. Ann Radcliffe (1764–1823), *Der Geisterseher* (*The Ghost-Seer*) (1787–1789) by Friedrich von Schiller (1759–1805), and both Shakespeare's *Merchant of Venice* and *Othello* are at least partially set in Venice.

[130] *Goddess . . . stone*: The statue of Venus de' Medici, depicting the classical goddess of love, was then enshrined in the Uffizi Gallery at Florence.

We stand, and in that form and face behold
What mind can make, when Nature's self would fail;
And to the fond idolaters of old   440
Envy the innate flash which such a soul could mould:

* * * * *

LI

Appear'dst thou not to Paris in this guise?
Or to more deeply blest Anchises? or,
In all thy perfect goddess-ship, when lies
Before thee thy own vanquish'd Lord of War?
And gazing in thy face as toward a star,   455
Laid on thy lap, his eyes to thee upturn,
Feeding on thy sweet cheek! while thy lips are
With lava kisses melting while they burn,
Shower'd on his eyelids, brow, and mouth, as from
    an urn!

LII

Glowing, and circumfused in speechless love,   460
Their full divinity inadequate
That feeling to express, or to improve,
The gods become as mortals, and man's fate
Has moments like their brightest; but the weight
Of earth recoils upon us;—let it go!   465
We can recal such visions, and create,
    From what has been, or might be, things which grow
Into thy statue's form, and look like gods below.

LIII

I leave to learned fingers, and wise hands,
The artist and his ape, to teach and tell   470
How well his connoisseurship understands

The graceful bend, and the voluptuous swell:
Let these describe the undescribable:
I would not their vile breath should crisp the stream
Wherein that image shall for ever dwell;   475
The unruffled mirror of the loveliest dream
That ever left the sky on the deep soul to beam.

* * * * *

LXIX

The roar of waters!—from the headlong height
Velino[131] cleaves the wave-worn precipice;
The fall of waters! rapid as the light   615
The flashing mass foams shaking the abyss;
The hell of waters! where they howl and hiss,
And boil in endless torture; while the sweat
Of their great agony, wrung out from this
Their Phlegethon,[132] curls round the rocks of jet   620
That gird the gulf around, in pitiless horror set,

LXX

And mounts in spray the skies, and thence again
Returns in an unceasing shower, which round,
With its unemptied cloud of gentle rain,
Is an eternal April to the ground,   625
Making it all one emerald:—how profound
The gulf! and how the giant element
From rock to rock leaps with delirious bound,
Crushing the cliffs, which, downward worn and rent
With his fierce footsteps, yield in chasms a fearful vent! 630

---

[131] *Velino*: river in central Italy.
[132] *Phlegethon*: one of the rivers of Hell that burns with fire but is not consumed.

LXXI

To the broad column which rolls on, and shows
More like the fountain of an infant sea
Torn from the womb of mountains by the throes
Of a new world, than only thus to be
Parent of rivers, which flow gushingly,   635
With many windings, through the vale:—Look back!
Lo, where it comes like an eternity,
As if to sweep down all things in its track,
Charming the eye with dread,—a matchless cataract,[133]

LXXII

Horribly beautiful! but on the verge,   640
From side to side, beneath the glittering morn,
An Iris sits, amidst the infernal surge,
Like Hope upon a death-bed, and, unworn
Its steady dyes, while all around is torn
By the distracted waters, bears serene   645
Its brilliant hues with all their beams unshorn:
Resembling, 'mid the torture of the scene,
Love watching Madness with unalterable mien.

* * * * *

LXXVII

Then farewell, Horace; whom I hated so,   685
Not for thy faults, but mine; it is a curse
To understand, not feel thy lyric flow,
To comprehend, but never love thy verse,
Although no deeper Moralist rehearse
Our little life, nor Bard prescribe his art,   690

---

[133] *matchless cataract*: Cascata del Marmore of Terni, Italy, a man-made waterfall.

Nor livelier Satirist the conscience pierce,
   Awakening without wounding the touch'd heart,
Yet fare thee well—upon Soracte's[134] ridge we part.

LXXVIII

Oh Rome! my country! city of the soul!
   The orphans of the heart must turn to thee,   695
Lone mother of dead empires! and control
   In their shut breasts their petty misery.
   What are our woes and sufferance? Come and see
The cypress, hear the owl, and plod your way
   O'er steps of broken thrones and temples, Ye!   700
   Whose agonies are evils of a day—
A world is at our feet as fragile as our clay.

LXXIX

The Niobe[135] of nations! there she stands,
   Childless and crownless, in her voiceless woe;
An empty urn within her wither'd hands,   705
   Whose holy dust was scatter'd long ago;
   The Scipios'[136] tomb contains no ashes now;
The very sepulchres lie tenantless
   Of their heroic dwellers: dost thou flow,
   Old Tiber![137] through a marble wilderness?   710
Rise, with thy yellow waves, and mantle her distress.

---

[134] *Soracte's*: Mount Soracte is a mountain ridge near Rome, Italy.

[135] *Niobe*: Greek mythological figure who boasted of her fourteen children to Leto, who had only two, the deities Apollo and Artemis. The latter punished Niobe for her pride by slaughtering all her children. She wept ceaselessly and was turned into a weeping rock (identified with Mount Sipylus).

[136] *Scipios'*: Scipio Africanus (236–183 B.C.) and Scipio Aemilianus, or Scipio Africanus the Younger (185–129 B.C.), his grandson by adoption—among the greatest of Roman generals, conquerors of Hannibal and Carthage.

[137] *Tiber*: the river that runs through Rome to the Tyrrhenian Sea.

LXXX

The Goth, the Christian, Time, War, Flood, and
    Fire,[138]
Have dealt upon the seven-hill'd[139] city's pride;
She saw her glories star by star expire,
And up the steep barbarian monarchs ride,   715
Where the car[140] climb'd the capitol;[141] far and wide
Temple and tower went down, nor left a site:—
Chaos of ruins! who shall trace the void,
O'er the dim fragments cast a lunar light,
And say, 'here was, or is,' where all is doubly night?   720

LXXXI

The double night of ages, and of her,
Night's daughter, Ignorance, hath wrapt and wrap
All round us; we but feel our way to err:
The ocean hath his chart, the stars their map,
And Knowledge spreads them on her ample lap;   725
But Rome is as the desert, where we steer
Stumbling o'er recollections; now we clap
Our hands, and cry 'Eureka!' it is clear—
When but some false mirage of ruin rises near.

[138] *Goth . . . Fire*: Throughout history, Rome has been destroyed by many forces, including multiple sackings by the Goths and other barbarian tribes. Flood, fire, time, and war are also obvious causes for the decay of the ancient city. This volley against the Christians, however, probably refers more to the occasional practice of popes and prelates to recycle the building materials of collapsed antiquity and resurrect them in the form of churches, for example.

[139] *seven-hill'd*: The ancient city of Rome was famously constructed upon seven hills: Palatine (the legendary origin of the city), Capitoline (where the government is seated), Quirinal, Viminal, Esquiline, Caelian, and Aventine.

[140] *car*: chariot (of warriors riding triumphantly into Rome).

[141] *capitol*: i.e., the Capitoline hill.

LXXXII

Alas! the lofty city! and alas!   730
The trebly hundred triumphs![142] and the day
When Brutus made the dagger's edge[143] surpass
The conqueror's sword in bearing fame away!
Alas, for Tully's[144] voice, and Virgil's[145] lay,
And Livy's[146] pictured page!—but these shall be   735
Her resurrection; all beside—decay.
Alas, for Earth, for never shall we see
That brightness in her eye she bore when Rome was free!

LXXXIII

Oh thou, whose chariot roll'd on Fortune's wheel,
Triumphant Sylla![147] Thou, who didst subdue   740
Thy country's foes ere thou wouldst pause to feel
The wrath of thy own wrongs, or reap the due
Of hoarded vengeance till thine eagles flew
O'er prostrate Asia;—thou, who with thy frown
Annihilated senates—Roman, too,   745
With all thy vices, for thou didst lay down
With an atoning smile a more than earthly crown—

[142] *triumphs*: (1) triumphal procession; (2) military victory. The established number of triumphal processions into Rome is approximately 320.

[143] *Brutus . . . edge*: Marcus Junius Brutus (85–42 B.C.), a politician of the Roman Republic, is principally known as one of the conspirators in the assassination of Gaius Julius Caesar (100–44 B.C.), his onetime friend.

[144] *Tully's*: Marcus Tullius Cicero (106–43 B.C.), orator and philosopher of the Roman Republic.

[145] *Virgil's*: Publius Vergilius Maro (70–19 B.C.), one of the primary poets of classical Rome, author of the *Aeneid*.

[146] *Livy's*: Titus Livius (59 B.C.–A.D. 17), Roman historian.

[147] *Sylla*: Lucius Cornelius Sulla Felix (c. 138–78 B.C.), cruel, dissipated Roman general, considered one of the greatest men of Roman history, principally for the fact that he wielded great power both as a consul and as a dictator, but renounced all of it and retired into public life.

LXXXIV

The dictatorial wreath—couldst thou divine
To what would one day dwindle that which made
Thee more than mortal? and that so supine   750
By aught than Romans Rome should thus be laid?
She who was named Eternal, and array'd
Her warriors but to conquer—she who veil'd
Earth with her haughty shadow, and display'd,
Until the o'er-canopied horizon fail'd,   755
Her rushing wings—Oh, she who was Almighty hail'd!

* * * * *

LXXXVIII

And thou, the thunder-stricken nurse of Rome![148]
She-wolf! whose brazen-imaged dugs impart   785
The milk of conquest yet within the dome
Where, as a monument of antique art,
Thou standest:—Mother of the mighty heart,
Which the great founder suck'd from thy wild teat,
Scorch'd by the Roman Jove's etherial dart,[149]   790
And thy limbs black with lightning—dost thou yet
Guard thine immortal cubs,[150] nor thy fond charge forget?

LXXXIX

Thou dost;—but all thy foster-babes are dead—
The men of iron; and the world hath rear'd
Cities from out their sepulchres: men bled   795
In imitation of the things they fear'd,

---

[148] *thunder-striken ... Rome!* Although there were many statues depicting the she-wolf who suckled the legendary founders of Rome, this probably refers to the bronze figure known as the Capitoline Wolf, attributed traditionally to Etruscan craftsmanship of the fifth century B.C.

[149] *Roman ... dart:* i.e., Jove (or Zeus), the king of the gods, and his thunderbolt.

[150] *immortal cubs:* Romulus and Remus, the legendary twin founders of Rome, were suckled by a she-wolf in their infancy.

And fought and conquer'd, and the same course steer'd,
At apish distance; but as yet none have,
Nor could, the same supremacy have near'd,
Save one vain man,[151] who is not in the grave,   800
But, vanquish'd by himself, to his own slaves a slave—

XC

The fool of false dominion—and a kind
Of bastard Cæsar, following him of old
With steps unequal; for the Roman's mind
Was modell'd in a less terrestrial mould,   805
With passions fiercer, yet a judgment cold,
And an immortal instinct which redeem'd
The frailties of a heart so soft, yet bold,
Alcides[152] with the distaff now he seem'd
At Cleopatra's[153] feet,—and now himself he beam'd.   810

XCI

And came—and saw—and conquer'd![154] But the man
Who would have tamed his eagles[155] down to flee,
Like a train'd falcon, in the Gallic van,[156]
Which he, in sooth, long led to victory,
With a deaf heart which never seem'd to be   815
A listener to itself, was strangely framed;
With but one weakest weakness—vanity,
Coquettish in ambition—still he aim'd—
At what? can he avouch—or answer what he claim'd?

---

[151] *one vain man*: Napoleon Bonaparte (1769–1821).

[152] *Alcides*: Hercules.

[153] *Cæsar . . . Cleopatra's*: Julius Caesar and Cleopatra (69–30 B.C.) were lovers.

[154] *came . . . conquer'd*: According to Suetonius, Caesar's report of his lightning-fast victory over Pharnaces of Pontus was "Veni, vidi, vici"—"I came, I saw, I conquered."

[155] *tamed his eagles*: Napoleon introduced bronze eagles on poles to serve as battle standards in emulation of the Romans.

[156] *Gallic van*: the forefront of the army.

XCII

And would be all or nothing—nor could wait   820
For the sure grave to level him; few years
Had fix'd him with the Cæsars in his fate,
On whom we tread: For *this* the conqueror rears
The arch of triumph!¹⁵⁷ and for this the tears
And blood of earth flow on as they have flow'd,   825
An universal deluge, which appears
Without an ark for wretched man's abode,
And ebbs but to reflow!—Renew thy rainbow, God!¹⁵⁸

XCIII

What from this barren being do we reap?
Our senses narrow, and our reason frail,   830
Life short, and truth a gem which loves the deep,
And all things weigh'd in custom's falsest scale:
Opinion an omnipotence,—whose veil
Mantles the earth with darkness, until right
And wrong are accidents, and men grow pale   835
Lest their own judgements should become too bright,
And their free thoughts be crimes, and earth have too
    much light.

* * * * *

XCVIII

Yet, Freedom! yet thy banner, torn, but flying
Streams like the thunder-storm *against* the wind;¹⁵⁹   875
Thy trumpet voice, though broken now and dying,
The loudest still the tempest leaves behind:

¹⁵⁷ *arch of triumph*: Napoleon commissioned the huge Arc de Triomphe after the victory of Austerlitz in 1806. It is modeled on the Arch of Titus in Rome.

¹⁵⁸ *deluge . . . God!* A reference to the Flood sent by God to cleanse the earth of evil men; Noah's ark, and the covenant between God and the descendants of Noah; including the guarantee that there would be no second Flood. The sign of this covenant was the rainbow. See Genesis 6–9.

¹⁵⁹ *Yet . . . wind*: Percy Bysshe Shelley placed these two lines at the beginning of his "Ode to Liberty" (cf. p. XX).

Thy tree hath lost its blossoms, and the rind,
  Chopp'd by the axe, looks rough and little worth,
  But the sap lasts, and still the seed we find   880
  Sown deep, even in the bosom of the North;
So shall a better spring less bitter fruit bring forth.

* * * * *

CVI

Then let the winds howl on! their harmony
  Shall henceforth be my music, and the night
  The sound shall temper with the owlets' cry,[160]
  As I now hear them, in the fading light
  Dim o'er the bird of darkness' native site,   950
  Answering each other on the Palatine,[161]
  With their large eyes, all glistening gray and bright,
  And sailing pinions.[162]—Upon such a shrine
What are our petty griefs?—let me not number mine.

CVII

Cypress and ivy, weed and wallflower grown   955
  Matted and mass'd together, hillocks heap'd
  On what were chambers, arch crush'd, column strown
  In fragments, choked up vaults, and frescos steep'd
  In subterranean damps, where the owl peep'd,
  Deeming it midnight:—Temples, baths, or halls?   960
  Pronounce who can; for all that Learning reap'd
  From her research hath been, that these are walls—[163]
Behold the Imperial Mount![164] 'tis thus the mighty falls.

---

[160] *owlets' cry*: considered, in ancient civilizations (particularly the Roman), as a bad omen.

[161] *Palatine*: the Palatine hill.

[162] *pinions*: wings.

[163] *what were . . . walls*: "Learning" and scholarship cannot properly clarify or delineate what the ruins of the past once were.

[164] *Imperial Mount*: i.e., the Palatine (centermost of the seven hills, and one of the most ancient parts of Rome).

CVIII

There is the moral of all human tales;
 'Tis but the same rehearsal of the past,   965
First Freedom and then Glory—when that fails,
Wealth, vice, corruption,—barbarism at last.
And History, with all her volumes vast,
Hath but *one* page,—'tis better written here,
Where gorgeous Tyranny hath thus amass'd   970
All treasures, all delights, that eye or ear,
Heart, soul could seek, tongue ask—Away with words!
 draw near,

CIX

Admire, exult—despise—laugh, weep,—for here
There is such matter for all feeling:—Man!
Thou pendulum betwixt a smile and tear,   975
Ages and realms are crowded in this span,
This mountain, whose obliterated plan
The pyramid of empires pinnacled,
Till the sun's rays with added flame were fill'd!   980
Where are its golden roofs?[165] where those who dared
 to build?

CX

Tully was not so eloquent as thou,
Thou nameless column[166] with the buried base!
What are the laurels of the Cæsar's brow?
Crown me with ivy from his dwelling-place.   985
Whose arch or pillar meets me in the face,

[165] *golden roofs*: The Domus Aurea (the "Golden House") was built at the command of the emperor Nero upon the Palatine after a vast fire had destroyed all the houses of affluent Romans on that hill in 64 A.D.

[166] *nameless column*: The column of Phocas, built by order of the Byzantine emperor Phocas (c. 580–610), was not "nameless" when Byron wrote, since the base of the column was excavated in 1813, revealing its origin.

Titus or Trajan's?[167] No—'tis that of Time:
Triumph, arch, pillar, all he doth displace
Scoffing; and apostolic statues climb
To crush the imperial urn,[168] whose ashes slept sublime,   990

* * * * *

CXXVI

Our life is a false nature—'tis not in
The harmony of things,—this hard decree,
This uneradicable taint of sin,
This boundless upas,[169] this all-blasting tree,
Whose root is earth, whose leaves and branches be   1130
The skies which rain their plagues on men like dew—
Disease, death, bondage—all the woes we see—
And worse, the woes we see not—which throb
    through
The immedicable[170] soul, with heart-aches ever new.

* * * * *

CXXX

Oh Time! the beautifier of the dead,
Adorner of the ruin,[171] comforter
And only healer when the heart hath bled—
Time! the corrector where our judgements err,   1165
The test of truth, love,—sole philosopher,

---

[167] *Titus or Trajan's*: Titus Flavius Vespasianus (39–81) and Marcus Ulpius Nerva Traianus Augustus (53–117) were both Roman emperors.

[168] *apostolic . . . urn*: The statue of Trajan placed atop his column (which traditionally was believed to hold the emperor's ashes but was found empty by medieval excavators) was replaced with a statue of Saint Peter by order of Pope Sixtus V in 1588.

[169] *upas*: a deciduous tree, common to tropical Africa and Asia, from which poison is extracted for arrows.

[170] *immedicable*: i.e., beyond the soothing power of medicine.

[171] *Adorner of the ruin*: i.e., with the overgrowth of shrubs and wildflowers.

For all beside are sophists, from thy thrift,
Which never loses though it doth defer—
Time, the avenger! unto thee I lift
My hands, and eyes, and heart, and crave of thee a gift: 1170

CXXXI

Amidst this wreck, where thou hast made a shrine
And temple more divinely desolate,
Among thy mightier offerings here are mine,
Ruins of years—though few, yet full of fate:—
If thou hast ever seen me too elate,   1175
Hear me not; but if calmly I have borne
Good, and reserved my pride against the hate
Which shall not whelm me, let me not have worn
This iron in my soul in vain—shall *they* not mourn?

* * * * *

CXXXIV

And if my voice break forth, 'tis not that now
I shrink from what is suffer'd: let him speak
Who hath beheld decline upon my brow,   1200
Or seen my mind's convulsion leave it weak;
But in this page a record will I seek.
Not in the air shall these my words disperse,
Though I be ashes; a far hour shall wreak
The deep prophetic fulness of this verse,   1205
And pile on human heads the mountain of my curse!

CXXXV

That curse shall be Forgiveness.—Have I not—
Hear me, my mother Earth! behold it, Heaven!—
Have I not had to wrestle with my lot?
Have I not suffer'd things to be forgiven?   1210
Have I not had my brain sear'd, my heart riven,
Hopes sapp'd, name blighted, Life's life lied away?

And only not to desperation driven,
  Because not altogether of such clay
As rots into the souls of those whom I survey.   1215

CXXXVI

From mighty wrongs to petty perfidy
Have I not seen what human things could do?
From the loud roar of foaming calumny
  To the small whisper of the'as paltry few,
  And subtler venom of the reptile crew,   1220
The Janus[172] glance of whose significant eye,
  Learning to lie with silence, would *seem* true,
  And without utterance, save the shrug or sigh,
Deal round to happy fools its speechless obloquy.

CXXXVII

But I have lived, and have not lived in vain: 1225
  My mind may lose its force, my blood its fire,
And my frame perish even in conquering pain;
  But there is that within me which shall tire
  Torture and Time, and breathe when I expire;
Something unearthly, which they deem not of,   1230
  Like the remember'd tone of a mute lyre,
  Shall on their soften'd spirits sink, and move
In hearts all rocky now the late remorse of love.

* * * * *

CXL

I see before me the Gladiator[173] lie:
He leans upon his hand—his manly brow

---

[172] *Janus*: in classical mythology, the two- or four-faced Roman god of doorways and beginnings (from whose name the month of January is derived).

[173] *Gladiator*: The classical marble statue of the "Dying Gaul" (which is believed to be a copy of a lost bronze Hellenistic sculpture) was formerly known as the "Dying Gladiator", believed to depict a warrior who would battle to the death for the entertainment of Roman audiences.

Consents to death, but conquers agony,
And his droop'd head sinks gradually low—   1255
And through his side the last drops, ebbing slow
From the red gash, fall heavy, one by one,
Like the first of a thunder-shower; and now
The arena swims around him—he is gone,
Ere ceased the inhuman shout which hail'd the wretch
    who won.   1260

CXLI

He heard it, but he heeded not—his eyes
Were with his heart, and that was far away:
He reck'd not of the life he lost nor prize,
But where his rude hut by the Danube[174] lay,
There were his young barbarians all at play,   1265
There was their Dacian[175] mother—he, their sire,
Butcher'd to make a Roman holiday—
All this rush'd with his blood[176]—Shall he expire
And unavenged?—Arise! ye Goths, and glut your ire!

* * * * *

CLIII

But lo! the dome[177]—the vast and wondrous dome,
To which Diana's marvel[178] was a cell—   1370

---

[174] *Danube*: major river of central Europe and one of the historic frontiers of the Roman Empire.

[175] *Dacian*: The Dacians were a tribe who inhabited Dacia, which bordered the Danube (near the Carpathian Mountains and the Black Sea).

[176] *Butcher'd ... blood*: Many gladiators originated as soldiers taken prisoner in the course of Roman military campaigns; thus, Byron envisions this figure as having lost his family through Roman butchery, now reduced to serve for the entertainment of the assembled throngs.

[177] *dome*: the dome of the Basilica of Saint Peter in Rome, designed by the Italian Renaissance artist Michelangelo (1475–1564). The basilica is considered one of the world's greatest architectural achievements.

[178] *Diana's marvel*: The temple of Diana at Ephesus was one of the ancient marvels of the world. Byron thought he had seen its ruins, though he was likely mistaken as it was not excavated until 1870.

Christ's mighty shrine above his martyr's tomb!
I have beheld the Ephesian's miracle—
Its columns strew the wilderness, and dwell
The hyæna and the jackall in their shade;
I have beheld Sophia's[179] bright roofs swell   1375
Their glittering mass i' the sun, and have survey'd
Its sanctuary the while the usurping Moslem pray'd;

CLIV

But thou, of temples old, or altars new,
Standest alone—with nothing like to thee—
Worthiest of God, the holy and the true.   1380
Since Zion's[180] desolation, when that He
Forsook his former city, what could be,
Of earthly structures, in his honour piled,
Of a sublimer aspect? Majesty,
Power, Glory, Strength, and Beauty, all are aisled   1385
In this eternal ark of worship undefiled.

CLV

Enter: its grandeur overwhelms thee not;
And why? it is not lessen'd; but thy mind,
Expanded by the genius of the spot,
Has grown colossal, and can only find   1390
A fit abode wherein appear enshrined
Thy hopes of immortality; and thou
Shalt one day, if found worthy, so defined,
See thy God face to face, as thou dost now
His Holy of Holies, nor be blasted by his brow.   1395

---

[179] *Sophia's*: Hagia Sophia in Constantinople served as an Orthodox patriarchal basilica (360–1453), briefly as a Roman Catholic cathedral (1204–1261), and as an Islamic mosque (1453–1931).

[180] *Zion's*: Zion is an ancient name for Jerusalem.

CLVI

Thou movest—but increasing with the advance,
Like climbing some great Alp,[181] which still doth rise,
Deceived by its gigantic elegance;
Vastness which grows—but grows to harmonise—
All musical in its immensities;   1400
Rich marbles—richer painting—shrines where flame
The lamps of gold—and haughty dome which vies
In air with Earth's chief structures, though their frame
Sits on the firm-set ground—and this the clouds must
    claim.

CLVII

Thou seest not all; but piecemeal thou must break,   1405
To separate contemplation, the great whole;
And as the ocean many bays will make,
That ask the eye—so here condense thy soul
To more immediate objects, and control
Thy thoughts until thy mind hath got by heart   1410
Its eloquent proportions, and unroll
In mighty graduations, part by part,
The glory which at once upon thee did not dart,

CLVIII

Not by its fault—but thine: Our outward sense
Is but of gradual grasp—and as it is   1415
That what we have of feeling most intense
Outstrips our faint expression; even so this
Outshining and o'erwhelming edifice
Fools our fond gaze, and greatest of the great
Defies at first our Nature's littleness,   1420
Till, growing with its growth, we thus dilate
Our spirits to the size of that they contemplate.

---

[181] *Like . . . Alp*: In this and the subsequent stanza, Byron likens viewing the immense interior of the basilica to the experience of climbing an alp—in both cases, the enormity of the sight cannot be fully contained or captured by the human eye.

CLIX

Then pause, and be enlighten'd; there is more
In such a survey than the sating gaze
Of wonder pleased, or awe which would adore   1425
The worship of the place, or the mere praise
Of art and its great masters, who could raise
What former time, nor skill, nor thought could plan;
The fountain of sublimity displays
Its depth, and thense may draw the mind of man   1430
Its golden sands, and learn what great conceptions can.

CLX

Or, turning to the Vatican, go see
Laocoon's[182] torture dignifying pain—
A father's love and mortal's agony
With an immortal's patience blending:—Vain   1435
The struggle; vain, against the coiling strain
And gripe, and deepening of the dragon's grasp,
The old man's clench; the long envenom'd chain
Rivets the living links,—the enormous asp
Enforces pang on pang, and stifles gasp on gasp.   1440

CLXI

Or view the Lord of the unerring bow,[183]
The God of life, and poesy, and light—
The Sun in human limbs array'd, and brow
All radiant from his triumph in the fight;
The shaft hath just been shot—the arrow bright   1445
With an immortal's vengeance; in his eye
And nostril beautiful disdain, and might
And majesty, flash their full lightnings by,
Developing in that one glance the Deity.

---

[182] *Laocoon's*: Laocoön was a Trojan priest who was strangled with his two sons by two venomous sea serpents sent by the gods to stop him from exposing the Greek soldiers hidden in the Trojan Horse.

[183] *Lord of the unerring bow*: a description of the Apollo Belvedere.

CLXII

But in his delicate form—a dream of Love,   1450
Shaped by some solitary nymph, whose breast
Long'd for a deathless lover from above,
And madden'd in that vision—are exprest
All that ideal beauty ever bless'd
The mind within its most unearthly mood,   1455
When each conception was a heavenly guest—
A ray of immortality—and stood,
Starlike, around, until they gather'd to a god!

CLXIII

And if it be Prometheus stole from Heaven
The fire[184] which we endure, it was repaid   1460
By him to whom the energy was given
Which this poetic marble hath array'd
With an eternal glory—which, if made
By human hands, is not of human thought;
And Time himself hath hallow'd it, nor laid   1465
One ringlet in the dust—nor hath it caught
A tinge of years, but breathes the flame with which
'twas wrought.

CLXIV

But where is he, the Pilgrim[185] of my song,
The being who upheld it through the past?
Methinks he cometh late and tarries long.   1470
He is no more—these breathings are his last;
His wanderings done, his visions ebbing fast,
And he himself as nothing:—if he was
Aught but a phantasy, and could be class'd
With forms which live and suffer—let that pass—   1475
His shadow fades away into Destruction's mass,

[184] *Prometheus . . . fire*: see footnote 44, page 16.
[185] *Pilgrim*: i.e., Childe Harold.

CLXV

Which gathers shadow, substance, life, and all
That we inherit in its mortal shroud,
And spreads the dim and universal pall
Through which all things grow phantoms; and the
    cloud   1480
Between us sinks and all which ever glow'd,
Till Glory's self is twilight, and displays
A melancholy halo scarce allow'd
To hover on the verge of darkness; rays
Sadder than saddest night, for they distract the gaze,   1485

And send us prying into the abyss....

* * * * *

CLXXV

But I forget.—My Pilgrim's shrine is won,
And he and I must part—so let it be,—
His task and mine alike are nearly done;
Yet once more let us look upon the sea;   1570
The midland ocean[186] breaks on him and me,
And from the Alban Mount[187] we now behold
Our friend of youth, that ocean, which when we
Beheld it last by Calpe's rock[188] unfold
Those waves, we follow'd on till the dark Euxine[189]
    roll'd   1575

---

[186] *midland ocean*: i.e., the Mediterranean.
[187] *Alban Mount*: Monte Cavo, the primary peak of the Alban Hills (near Rome).
[188] *Calpe's rock*: the Rock of Gibraltar, standing at the southern end of the Iberian Peninsula, at the entrance of the Mediterranean.
[189] *dark Euxine*: the Black Sea.

CLXXVI

Upon the blue Symplegades....

* * * * *

CLXXIX

Roll on, thou deep and dark blue ocean—roll!
Ten thousand fleets sweep over thee in vain;
Man marks the earth with ruin—his control   1605
Stops with the shore;—upon the watery plain
The wrecks are all thy deed, nor doth remain
A shadow of man's ravage, save his own,
When, for a moment, like a drop of rain,
He sinks into thy depths with bubbling groan,   1610
Without a grave, unknell'd, uncoffin'd, and unknown.

CLXXX

His steps are not upon thy paths,—thy fields
Are not a spoil for him,—thou dost arise
And shake him from thee; the vile strength he wields
For earth's destruction thou dost all despise,   1615
Spurning him from thy bosom to the skies,
And send'st him, shivering in thy playful spray
And howling, to his Gods, where haply lies
His petty hope in some near port or bay,
And dashest him again to earth:—there let him lay.   1620

CLXXXI

The armaments which thunderstrike the walls
Of rock-built cities, bidding nations quake,
And monarchs tremble in their capitals,
The oak leviathans,[190] whose huge ribs make
Their clay creator the vain title take   1625

---

[190] *oak leviathans*: the warships.

Of lord of thee, and arbiter of war;
These are thy toys, and, as the snowy flake,
They melt into thy yeast of waves, which mar
Alike the Armada's pride, or spoils of Trafalgar.[191]

CLXXXII

Thy shores are empires, changed in all save thee— 1630
Assyria, Greece, Rome, Carthage,[192] what are they?
Thy waters wasted them while they were free,
And many a tyrant since; their shores obey
The stranger, slave, or savage; their decay
Has dried up realms to deserts:—not so thou, 1635
Unchangeable save to thy wild waves' play—
Time writes no wrinkle on thine azure brow—
Such as creation's dawn beheld, thou rollest now.

CLXXXIII

Thou glorious mirror, where the Almighty's form
Glasses itself in tempests; in all time, 1640
Calm or convulsed—in breeze, or gale, or storm,
Icing the pole, or in the torrid clime
Dark-heaving;—boundless, endless, and sublime—
The image of Eternity—the throne
Of the Invisible; even from out thy slime 1645
The monsters of the deep are made; each zone
Obeys thee; thou goest forth, dread, fathomless, alone.

---

[191] *Armada's . . . Trafalgar*: This is directed against smug jingoism and imperial aggression: The Armada refers to the iconic defeat by heavily outnumbered English forces of the invading Spanish fleet on August 8, 1588; Trafalgar to Nelson's crushing defeat of the Napoleonic fleet on October 21, 1805, definitively establishing Britain as the greatest naval power in the world and confirming the defense and greater expansion of her own imperial influence. The Spanish were allies of the French in 1805 and lost their fleet at Trafalgar. The Armada displayed the imperial arrogance of the Spanish, Trafalgar of the French, the aftermath and mythologizing that of the British.

[192] *Assyria . . . Carthage*: the great empires of antiquity.

CLXXXIV

And I have loved thee, Ocean! and my joy
Of youthful sports was on thy breast to be
Borne, like thy bubbles, onward: from a boy[193]   1650
I wanton'd with thy breakers—they to me
Were a delight; and if the freshening sea
Made them a terror—'twas a pleasing fear,
For I was as it were a child of thee,
And trusted to thy billows far and near,   1655
And laid my hand upon thy mane—as I do here.

CLXXXV

My task is done—my song hath ceased—my theme
Has died into an echo; it is fit
The spell should break of this protracted dream.
The torch shall be extinguish'd which hath lit   1660
My midnight lamp—and what is writ, is writ,—
Would it were worthier! but I am not now
That which I have been—and my visions flit
Less palpably before me—and the glow
Which in my spirit dwelt is fluttering, faint, and low.   1665

CLXXXVI

Farewell! a word that must be, and hath been—
A sound which makes us linger;—yet—farewell!
Ye! who have traced the Pilgrim to the scene
Which is his last, if in your memories dwell
A thought which once was his, if on ye swell   1670
A single recollection, not in vain

---

[193] *from a boy*: In his childhood, Byron often sneaked from the house and went swimming in the sea; he showed great athletic prowess in swimming, an exercise that was not impaired by his deformed right foot.

He wore his sandal-shoon,[194] and scallop-shell;[195]
Farewell! with *him* alone may rest the pain,
If such there were—with *you*, the moral of his strain![196]

The Vision of Judgment

Written September–October, 1821, in ottava rima (a stanza of eight lines with rhyme scheme of *ababab cc*), in response to the poet laureate Robert Southey's *A Vision of Judgement*. George III had died on January 29, 1820; Southey depicts the glorious entry of the late sovereign into Heaven, where he confounds his accusers and is hailed by a host of worthies including Elizabeth, Henry V, Richard the Lion Heart, and even George Washington. Southey also appears.

A radical of the 1790s turned aggressive Tory, Southey was Byron's ideal dartboard: a Romantic doctrinaire, an overrated poet puffed by the Wordsworth circle, an insulter of Byron and his friends, and (in Byron's eyes, at least), a political renegade and a toady to reactionary persecution.

Under the (apparently mistaken) belief that the laureate had been spreading inflammatory gossip about him, Byron had lampooned him in the Dedication to *Don Juan*. Southey responded in the Preface to his *Vision of Judgement* with a description of Byron and Shelley as "men of diseased hearts and depraved imaginations.... The school which they set up may properly be called the Satanic school.... The evil is political as well as moral.... Let the rulers of the state look to this, in time!"[197]

---

[194] *sandal-shoon*: sandal shoes.
[195] *scallop-shell*: Such shells were traditionally worn in the hats of pilgrims as a sign of their visiting of overseas shrines—particularly St. James of Compostela, in Spain, Harold's destination in canto 1.
[196] *Farewell . . . strain!* At the conclusion of the poem, Byron wrote: "Laus Deo! [Praise be to God!] BYRON. July 19, 1817. La Mira, near Venice".
[197] Preface to *A Vision of Judgement*, in *The Poetical Works of Robert Southey*, vol. 10 (London: Longmans, 1853), pp. 205–6.

One of Byron's greatest performances, this burlesque satire swallowed Southey's literary reputation. According to Algernon Charles Swinburne, "This poem stands alone, not in Byron's work only, but in the work of the world. Satire in earlier times had changed her rags for robes; Juvenal had clothed with fire, and Dryden with majesty, that wandering and bastard Muse. Byron gave her wings to fly with."[198]

The Vision of Judgment (1821)

I

Saint Peter[199] sat by the celestial gate:
    His keys were rusty, and the lock was dull,
So little trouble had been given of late;
    Not that the place by any means was full,
But since the Gallic era 'eighty-eight'[200]   5
    The devils had ta'en a longer, stronger pull,
And 'a pull altogether,' as they say
At sea—which drew most souls another way.

II

The angels all were singing out of tune,
    And hoarse with having little else to do,   10
Excepting to wind up the sun and moon,
    Or curb a runaway young star or two,
Or wild colt of a comet, which too soon
    Broke out of bounds o'er the ethereal blue,
Splitting some planet with its playful tail,   15
As boats are sometimes by a wanton whale.

---

[198] Algernon Charles Swinburne, *A Selection from the Works of Lord Byron* (London: Moxon, 1866), p. xxi.

[199] *Saint Peter*: Peter (c. 1 B.C.–c. A.D. 67), the Prince of the Apostles, given the keys of the kingdom by Jesus Christ (see Matthew 16:17–19).

[200] *'eighty-eight'*: In 1788, King Louis XVI of France called a meeting to address the economic crisis of his kingdom; this Congress of Estates General precipitated the bloody outbreak of the French Revolution.

III

The guardian seraphs[201] had retired on high,
    Finding their charges past all care below;
Terrestrial business fill'd nought in the sky
    Save the recording angel's black bureau;   20
Who found, indeed, the facts to multiply
    With such rapidity of vice and woe,
That he had stripp'd off both his wings in quills,
And yet was in arrear[202] of human ills.

IV

His business so augmented of late years,   25
    That he was forced, against his will, no doubt,
(Just like those cherubs,[203] earthly ministers,)
    For some resource to turn himself about
And claim the help of his celestial peers,
    To aid him ere he should be quite worn out   30
By the increased demand for his remarks;
Six angels and twelve saints were named his clerks.

V

This was a handsome board—at least for heaven;
    And yet they had even then enough to do,
So many conquerors' cars[204] were daily driven,   35
    So many kingdoms fitted up anew;
Each day too slew its thousands six or seven,
    Till at the crowning carnage, Waterloo,[205]
They threw their pens down in divine disgust—
The page was so besmear'd with blood and dust.   40

[201] *seraphs*: seraphim, one of the traditional (and the highest of) the nine choirs of angels.

[202] *in arrear*: behind in the execution of his duties (i.e., he could not write fast enough to keep up with the list of man's sins).

[203] *cherubs*: the cherubim, another class of the nine choirs of angels.

[204] *conqueror's cars*: chariots in the triumphal procession of conquering warriors.

[205] *Waterloo*: see footnote 60, page 23.

VI

This by the way; 'tis not mine to record
    What angels shrink from: even the very devil
On this occasion his own work abhorr'd,
    So surfeited with the infernal revel:
Though he himself had sharpen'd every sword,   45
    It almost quench'd his innate thirst of evil.
(Here Satan's sole good work deserves insertion—
'Tis, that he has both generals in reversion.)[206]

VII

Let's skip a few short years of hollow peace,
    Which peopled earth no better, hell as wont,   50
And heaven none—they form the tyrant's lease,
    With nothing but new names subscribed upon't;
'Twill one day finish: meantime they increase,
    'With seven heads and ten horns,'[207] and all in front,
Like Saint John's foretold beast; but ours are born   55
Less formidable in the head than horn.

VIII

In the first year of freedom's second dawn[208]
    Died George the Third; although no tyrant, one
Who shielded tyrants, till each sense withdrawn
    Left him nor mental nor external sun:[209]   60

---

[206] *reversion*: a future interest in property (i.e., Satan has a future interest or claim on the souls of Wellington and Napoleon). Napoleon was actually dead, having died on May 5, 1821, two days before Byron began writing this poem, but the news had not yet arrived in Europe.

[207] *With . . . horns*: Cf. Revelation 17:3, Saint John's description of the beast of the Apocalypse.

[208] *freedom's second dawn*: The year 1820, when George III died, also saw outbreaks of revolution through Southern Europe, particularly Italy (with which Byron was in sympathy).

[209] *Left . . . sun*: George III was blind and mad in his last illness.

A better farmer[210] ne'er brush'd dew from lawn,
 A worse king never left a realm undone!
He died—but left his subjects still behind,
One half as mad—and t'other no less blind.

IX

He died!—his death made no great stir on earth; 65
 His burial made some pomp; there was profusion
Of velvet, gilding, brass, and no great dearth
 Of aught but tears—save those shed by collusion.[211]
For these things may be bought at their true worth;
 Of elegy there was the due infusion—   70
Bought also; and the torches, cloaks, and banners,
Heralds, and relics of old Gothic manners,[212]

X

Form'd a sepulchral melodrame. Of all
 The fools who flock'd to swell or see the show,
Who cared about the corpse? The funeral   75
 Made the attraction, and the black the woe.
There throbb'd not there a thought which pierced the
   pall;[213]
 And when the gorgeous coffin was laid low,
It seem'd the mockery of hell to fold
The rottenness of eighty years in gold.   80

XI

So mix his body with the dust! It might
 Return to what it *must* far sooner, were

---

[210] *farmer*: George III passionately embraced simple virtue and values and was popularly known as "farmer George".

[211] *by collusion*: insincerely.

[212] *torches . . . manners*: Byron's description of the pomp and circumstance accompanying the laying to rest of George III tallies with popular descriptions at the time.

[213] *pall*: funereal covering for a coffin.

The natural compound left alone to fight
    Its way back into earth, and fire, and air;
But the unnatural balsams[214] merely blight   85
    What nature made him at his birth, as bare
As the mere million's base unmummied clay—
Yet all his spices but prolong decay.

XII

He's dead—and upper earth with him has done;
    He's buried; save the undertaker's bill,   90
Or lapidary scrawl,[215] the world is gone
    For him, unless he left a German will;[216]
But where's the proctor who will ask his son?
    In whom his qualities are reigning still,
Except that household virtue, most uncommon,   95
Of constancy to a bad, ugly woman.[217]

XIII

'God save the king!' It is a large economy
    In God to save the like; but if he will
Be saving, all the better; for not one am I
    Of those who think damnation better still: 100
I hardly know too if not quite alone am I
    In this small hope of bettering future ill
By circumscribing, with some slight restriction,
The eternity of hell's hot jurisdiction.

[214] *unnatural balsams*: The king's body was not embalmed as was usual, probably owing to the rapid decay brought on by the king's illness.

[215] *lapidary scrawl*: tombstone inscription.

[216] *German will*: George II hid the "German will" of his father, George I, and scandalmongers rumored that George IV did the same with George III's will.

[217] *constancy . . . woman*: The marriage of George IV to Queen Caroline was rife with adultery on both sides and ended when George IV had his wife taken up on trial for adultery in 1820.

XIV

I know this is unpopular; I know   105
　　'Tis blasphemous; I know one may be damn'd
For hoping no one else may e'er be so;
　　I know my catechism; I know we are cramm'd
With the best doctrines till we quite o'erflow;
　　I know that all save England's church have shamm'd,   110
And that the other twice two hundred churches
And synagogues have made a *damn'd* bad purchase.[218]

XV

God help us all! God help me too! I am
　　God knows, as helpless as the devil can wish,
And not a whit more difficult to damn   115
　　Than is to bring to land a late-hook'd fish,
Or to the butcher to purvey the lamb;
　　Nor that I'm fit for such a noble dish
As one day will be that immortal fry
Of almost every body born to die.   120

XVI

Saint Peter sat by the celestial gate,
　　And nodded o'er his keys; when, lo! there came
A wondrous noise he had not heard of late—
　　A rushing sound of wind, and stream, and flame;
In short, a roar of things extremely great,   125
　　Which would have made aught save a saint exclaim;
But he, with first a start and then a wink,
Said, 'There's another star gone out, I think!'

---

[218] *purchase*: bargain, exchange.

XVII

But ere he could return to his repose,
    A cherub flapp'd his right wing o'er his eyes—   130
At which Saint Peter yawn'd, and rubb'd his nose:
    'Saint porter,' said the angel, 'prithee[219] rise!'
Waving a goodly wing, which glow'd, as glows
    An earthly peacock's tail, with heavenly dyes:
To which the saint replied, 'Well, what's the matter?   135
'Is Lucifer come back with all this clatter?'

XVIII

'No,' quoth the cherub; 'George the Third is dead.'
    'And who *is* George the Third?' replied the apostle:
'*What George? what Third?*' 'The king of England,' said
    The angel. 'Well! he won't find kings to jostle   140
Him on his way; but does he wear his head?
    Because the last[220] we saw here had a tustle,
And ne'er would have got into heaven's good graces,
Had he not flung his head in all our faces.

XIX

'He was, if I remember, king of France;   145
    That head of his, which could not keep a crown
On earth, yet ventured in my face to advance
    A claim to those of martyrs—like my own:
If I had had my sword, as I had once
    When I cut ears off,[221] I had cut him down;   150
But having but my *keys*, and not my brand,
I only knock'd his head from out his hand.

---

[219] *prithee*: "I pray thee".

[220] *last*: i.e., the last king to arrive at the celestial gates, Louis XVI of France, guillotined January 21, 1793.

[221] *When . . . off*: See Matthew 26:51–52, where the Apostle Peter struck off the ear of one of the servants of the High Priest when Jesus was being arrested by Temple guards.

XX

'And then he set up such a headless howl,
    That all the saints came out and took him in;
And there he sits by St Paul,[222] cheek by jowl;[223]   155
    That fellow Paul—the parvenu![224] The skin
Of Saint Bartholomew,[225] which makes his cowl[226]
    In heaven, and upon earth redeem'd his sin
So as to make a martyr, never sped[227]
Better than did this weak and wooden head.   160

XXI

'But had it come up here upon its shoulders,
    There would have been a different tale to tell:
The fellow-feeling in the saints beholders
    Seems to have acted on them like a spell;
And so this very foolish head heaven solders   165
    Back on its trunk: it may be very well,
And seems the custom here to overthrow
Whatever has been wisely done below.'

XXII

The angel answer'd, 'Peter! do not pout:
    The king who comes has head and all entire,   170
And never knew much what it was about—
    He did as doth the puppet—by its wire,

[222] *St Paul*: Paul (c. 5–c. 67), formerly known as Saul of Tarsus, was a persecutor of the early Christians who converted and was renamed through a supernatural encounter with Jesus to become known as the Apostle Paul.

[223] *cheek by jowl*: idiomatic expression meaning close together.

[224] *parvenu*: "newly rich", referring to the fact that Saint Paul was not one of the original twelve apostles chosen by Jesus.

[225] *Saint Bartholomew*: Bartholomew (first century A.D.), also known as Nathaniel, was one of the original twelve apostles and traditionally believed to have been martyred by being flayed alive and then beheaded.

[226] *cowl*: hood (i.e., representative of his place or standing in Heaven).

[227] *sped*: succeeded.

And will be judged like all the rest, no doubt:
    My business and your own is not to enquire
Into such matters, but to mind our cue—   175
Which is to act as we are bid to do.'

XXIII

While thus they spake, the angelic caravan,
    Arriving like a rush of mighty wind,
Cleaving the fields of space, as doth the swan
    Some silver stream (say Ganges, Nile, or Inde,   180
Or Thames, or Tweed),[228] and 'midst them an old man
    With an old soul, and both extremely blind,
Halted before the gate, and in his shroud
Seated their fellow-traveller on a cloud.

XXIV

But bringing up the rear of this bright host   185
    A Spirit of a different aspect waved
His wings, like thunder-clouds above some coast
    Whose barren beach with frequent wrecks is paved;
His brow was like the deep when tempest-toss'd;
    Fierce and unfathomable thoughts engraved   190
Eternal wrath on his immortal face,
And *where* he gazed a gloom pervaded space.[229]

XXV

As he drew near, he gazed upon the gate
    Ne'er to be enter'd more by him or sin,

---

[228] *Ganges . . . Tweed*: rivers of India, northeastern Africa and Egypt, Belgium and Germany, southern England, and borderland of Scotland, respectively.

[229] *And where he . . . space*: "He" means Lucifer. "It is precisely because Byron was not his servant, that he could see the gloom. To the Devil's true servants, their Master's presence brings both cheerfulness and prosperity; with a delightful sense of their own wisdom and virtue; and of the 'progress' of things in general: in smooth sea and fair weather, and with no need either of helm touch, or oar toil: as when once one is well within the edge of Maelstrom." John Ruskin, "Fiction, Fair and Foul", in *The Ethics of the Dust: Fiction, Fair and Foul; The Elements of Drawing* (Boston: Dana Estes, 1890), p. 214.

With such a glance of supernatural hate,   195
    As made Saint Peter wish himself within;
He patter'd[230] with his keys at a great rate,
    And sweated through his apostolic skin:
Of course his perspiration was but ichor,[231]
Or some such other spiritual liquor.   200

XXVI

The very cherubs huddled all together,
    Like birds when soars the falcon; and they felt
A tingling to the tip of every feather,
    And form'd a circle like Orion's belt[232]
Around their poor old charge; who scarce knew whither   205
    His guards had led him, though they gently dealt
With royal manes (for by many stories,
And true, we learn the angels all are Tories[233]).

XXVII

As things were in this posture, the gate flew
    Asunder, and the flashing of its hinges   210
Flung over space an universal hue
    Of many-colour'd flame, until its tinges
Reach'd even our speck of earth, and made a new
    Aurora borealis[234] spread its fringes
O'er the North Pole; the same seen, when ice-bound,   215
By Captain Parry's crew, in 'Melville's Sound.'[235]

---

[230] *patter'd*: fussed or fumbled.

[231] *ichor*: in classical mythology, the blood of the gods.

[232] *Orion's belt*: the central point of one of the most conspicuous constellations of the night sky, depicting Orion, a hunter in classical mythology.

[233] *Tories*: members of the conservative, traditionalist political party in England, supportive of monarchies.

[234] *Aurora borealis*: the exquisite "northern lights", a phenomenon of natural lights visible from high latitudes.

[235] *Captain . . . Sound*: William Edward Parry (1790–1855), an English explorer, laid camp in Melville Sound (inlet in Greenland) during the winter of 1819 while exploring northern regions.

XXVIII

And from the gate thrown open issued beaming
    A beautiful and mighty Thing of Light,
Radiant with glory, like a banner streaming
    Victorious from some world-o'erthrowing fight: 220
My poor comparisons must needs be teeming
    With earthly likenesses, for here the night
Of clay[236] obscures our best conceptions, saving
Johanna Southcote,[237] or Bob Southey[238] raving.

XXIX

'Twas the archangel Michael:[239] all men know   225
    The make of angels and archangels, since
There's scarce a scribbler has not one to show,
    From the fiends' leader to the angels' prince.
There also are some altar-pieces,[240] though
    I really can't say that they much evince   230
One's inner notions of immortal spirits;
But let the connoisseurs[241] explain *their* merits.

XXX

Michael flew forth in glory and in good;
    A goodly work of him from whom all glory
And good arise; the portal past—he stood;   235
    Before him the young cherubs and saints hoary—
(I say *young*, begging to be understood
    By looks, not years; and should be very sorry
To state, they were not older than St Peter,
But merely that they seem'd a little sweeter).   240

[236] *night / Of clay*: i.e., death (of mortal flesh).

[237] *Johanna Southcote*: Johanna Southcote (1750–1814) English poet known for her *Book of Wonders* (1813–1814) and for her fanatical religious beliefs.

[238] *Bob Southey*: Robert Southey (1774–1843), English poet and the primary subject of Byron's satire here.

[239] *archangel Michael*: the greatest of the archangels, who triumphed over Satan and the other rebellious angels.

[240] *altar-pieces*: painted screens behind altars.

[241] *connoisseurs*: critics or experts in art.

XXXI

The cherubs and the saints bow'd down before
    That arch-angelic hierarch,[242] the first
Of essences angelical, who wore
    The aspect of a god; but this ne'er nursed
Pride in his heavenly bosom, in whose core   245
    No thought, save for his Maker's service, durst
Intrude, however glorified and high;
He knew him[243] but the viceroy[244] of the sky.

XXXII

He and the sombre silent Spirit met—
    They knew each other both for good and ill;   250
Such was their power, that neither could forget
    His former friend and future foe; but still
There was a high, immortal, proud regret
    In either's eye, as if 'twere less their will
Than destiny to make the eternal years   255
Their date of war, and their 'champ clos'[245] the
    spheres.[246]

XXXIII

But here they were in neutral space: we know
    From Job,[247] that Satan hath the power to pay
A heavenly visit thrice a year or so;
    And that 'the sons of God,' like those of clay,   260
Must keep him company; and we might show
    From the same book, in how polite a way
The dialogue is held between the Powers
Of Good and Evil—but 'twould take up hours.

[242] *hierarch*: one who holds high authority in a religious hierarchy.
[243] *him*: i.e., himself.
[244] *viceroy*: ruler subservient to a greater power (in this case, God).
[245] *'champ clos'*: enclosed space in which a tournament is played out.
[246] *spheres*: i.e., planets.
[247] *Job*: In the Old Testament Book of Job, the just man is tested by Satan with God's permission (established in a conversation between Satan and God, presented in the book).

XXXIV

And this is not a theologic tract,[248]   265
    To prove with Hebrew and with Arabic
If Job be allegory or a fact,
    But a true narrative; and thus I pick
From out the whole but such and such an act
    As sets aside the slightest thought of trick.   270
'Tis every tittle true, beyond suspicion,
And accurate as any other vision.

XXXV

The spirits were in neutral space, before
    The gate of heaven; like eastern thresholds[249] is
The place where Death's grand cause is argued o'er,   275
    And souls despatch'd to that world or to this;
And therefore Michael and the other wore
    A civil aspect: though they did not kiss,
Yet still between his Darkness and his Brightness
There pass'd a mutual glance of great politeness.   280

XXXVI

The Archangel bow'd, not like a modern beau,[250]
    But with a graceful oriental bend,
Pressing one radiant arm just where below
    The heart in good men is supposed to tend.
He turn'd as to an equal, not too low,   285
    But kindly; Satan met his ancient friend
With more hauteur, as might an old Castilian[251]
Poor noble meet a mushroom[252] rich civilian.

---

[248] *theologic tract*: highly popular form for religious debate in that period, represented in pamphlets published by and exchanged between religious sects.

[249] *eastern thresholds*: In Eastern nations, gates and gateways were traditionally places for public deliberation and the settling of issues of justice.

[250] *beau*: dandified court hanger-on.

[251] *old Castilian*: a man from Castile, one of the oldest and most prestigious Spanish provinces.

[252] *mushroom*: a man whose social position has newly sprung up.

XXXVII

He merely bent his diabolic brow
    An instant; and then raising it, he stood   290
In act to assert his right or wrong, and show
    Cause why King George by no means could or
        should
Make out a case to be exempt from woe
    Eternal, more than other kings, endued
With better sense and hearts, whom history mentions,   295
Who long have 'paved hell with their good
    intentions.'²⁵³

XXXVIII

Michael began: 'What wouldst thou with this man,
    Now dead, and brought before the Lord? What ill
Hath he wrought since his mortal race began,
    That thou canst claim him? Speak! and do thy will,   300
If it be just: if in this earthly span
    He hath been greatly failing to fulfil
His duties as a king and mortal, say,
And he is thine; if not, let him have way.'

XXXIX

'Michael!' replied the Prince of Air, 'even here,   305
    Before the Gate of him thou servest, must
I claim my subject: and will make appear
    That as he was my worshipper in dust,
So shall he be in spirit, although dear
    To thee and thine, because nor wine nor lust   310
Were of his weaknesses; yet on the throne
He reign'd o'er millions to serve me alone.

---

²⁵³ '*paved . . . intentions*': This established cliché was first coined by the English author Dr. Samuel Johnson (1709–1784), whom Byron much admired.

XL

'Look to *our* earth, or rather *mine*; it was,
   Once, more thy master's: but I triumph not
In this poor planet's conquest; nor, alas!   315
   Need he thou servest envy me my lot:
With all the myriads[254] of bright worlds which pass
   In worship round him, he may have forgot
Yon weak creation of such paltry things:
I think few worth damnation save their kings,—   320

XLI

'And these but as a kind of quit-rent,[255] to
   Assert my right as lord; and even had
I such an inclination, 'twere (as you
   Well know) superfluous: they are grown so bad,
That hell has nothing better left to do   325
   Than leave them to themselves: so much more mad
And evil by their own internal curse,
Heaven cannot make them better, nor I worse.

XLII

'Look to the earth, I said, and say again:
   When this old, blind, mad, helpless, weak, poor worm   330
Began in youth's first bloom and flush to reign,
   The world and he both wore a different form,
And much of earth and all the watery plain
   Of ocean call'd him king: through many a storm
His isles had floated on the abyss of time;   335
For the rough virtues chose them for their clime.[256]

---

[254] *myriads*: thousands, innumerable throngs.
[255] *quit-rent*: fee paid to a landlord to quit one's rental.
[256] *rough ... clime*: The climate of England promotes the development of "rough virtues".

XLIII

'He came to his sceptre young; he leaves it old:
    Look to the state in which he found his realm,
And left it; and his annals too behold,
    How to a minion[257] first he gave the helm;   340
How grew upon his heart a thirst for gold,
    The beggar's vice, which can but overwhelm
The meanest hearts; and for the rest, but glance
Thine eye along America and France.

XLIV

''Tis true, he was a tool from first to last   345
    (I have the workmen safe); but as a tool
So let him be consumed. From out the past
    Of ages, since mankind have known the rule
Of monarchs—from the bloody rolls amass'd
    Of sin and slaughter—from the Cæsars'[258] school,   350
Take the worst pupil; and produce a reign
More drench'd with gore, more cumber'd[259] with the slain.

XLV

'He ever warr'd with freedom and the free:
    Nations as men, home subjects, foreign foes,
So that they utter'd the word "Liberty!"   355
    Found George the Third their first opponent. Whose
History was ever stain'd as his will be
    With national and individual woes?
I grant his household abstinence; I grant
His neutral virtues, which most monarchs want;   360

---

[257] *minion*: lowly servant, here alluding to John Stuart (1713–1792), an English politician believed by some to have exercised a great deal of influence over George III after his ascension to the throne in 1760.

[258] *Cæsars'*: The Caesars were emperors of Rome.

[259] *cumber'd*: encumbered.

XLVI

'I know he was a constant consort; own
   He was a decent sire, and middling lord.
All this is much, and most upon a throne;
   As temperance, if at Apicius'[260] board,
Is more than at an anchorite's[261] supper shown.   365
   I grant him all the kindest can accord;
And this was well for him, but not for those
Millions who found him what oppression chose.

XLVII

'The New World shook him off; the Old yet groans
   Beneath what he and his prepared, if not   370
Completed: he leaves heirs on many thrones
   To all his vices, without what begot
Compassion for him—his tame virtues; drones
   Who sleep, or despots who have now forgot
A lesson which shall be re-taught them, wake   375
Upon the thrones of earth; but let them quake!

XLVIII

'Five millions of the primitive, who hold
   The faith which makes ye great on earth, implored
A *part* of that vast *all* they held of old,—
   Freedom to worship—not alone your Lord,   380
Michael, but you, and you, Saint Peter! Cold
   Must be your souls, if you have not abhorr'd
The foe to catholic participation[262]
In all the license[263] of a Christian nation.

---

[260] *Apicius'*: Marcus Gavius Apicius (c. first century A.D.), a Roman lover of luxury and good food.

[261] *anchorite's*: An anchorite is a religious hermit.

[262] *catholic participation*: George III fiercely opposed Catholic emancipation, crushing parliamentary efforts several times during his reign.

[263] *license*: i.e., liberty (e.g., voting or participation in military service).

XLIX

'True! he allow'd them to pray God; but as 385
    A consequence of prayer, refused the law
Which would have placed them upon the same base
    With those who did not hold the saints in awe.'
But here Saint Peter started from his place,
    And cried, 'You may the prisoner withdraw: 390
Ere heaven shall ope her portals to this Guelph,[264]
While I am guard, may I be damn'd myself!

L

'Sooner will I with Cerberus[265] exchange
    My office (and *his* is no sinecure[266])
Than see this royal Bedlam bigot[267] range 395
    The azure fields of heaven, of that be sure!'
'Saint!' replied Satan, 'you do well to avenge
    The wrongs he made your satellites endure
And if to this exchange you should be given,
I'll try to coax *our* Cerberus up to heaven!' 400

LI

Here Michael interposed: 'Good saint! and devil!
    Pray, not so fast; you both outrun discretion.
Saint Peter! you were wont to be more civil:
    Satan! excuse this warmth of his expression,
And condescension to the vulgar's level: 405
    Even saints sometimes forget themselves in session.
Have you got more to say?'—'No.'—'If you please,
I'll trouble you to call your witnesses.'

[264] *Guelph*: family name of the House of Hanover. Derived from the ancestors of the papal faction in medieval Italy.

[265] *Cerberus*: in classical mythology, the fierce three-headed dog that guarded the door to the underworld.

[266] *sinecure*: position requiring little real work.

[267] *Bedlam bigot*: resident of a madhouse. Bedlam was the popular name for St. Mary of Bethlehem, London hospital/asylum for lunatics.

LII

Then Satan turn'd and waved his swarthy hand,
      Which stirr'd with its electric qualities   410
Clouds farther off than we can understand,
      Although we find him sometimes in our skies;
Infernal thunder shook both sea and land
      In all the planets, and hell's batteries
Let off the artillery, which Milton[268] mentions   415
As one of Satan's most sublime inventions.[269]

LIII

This was a signal unto such damn'd souls
      As have the privilege of their damnation
Extended far beyond the mere controls
      Of worlds past, present, or to come; no station   420
Is theirs particularly in the rolls
      Of hell assign'd; but where their inclination
Or business carries them in search of game,
They may range freely—being damn'd the same.

LIV

They are proud of this—as very well they may,   425
      It being a sort of knighthood, or gilt key[270]
Stuck in their loins; or like to an 'entré'
      Up the back stairs, or such free-masonry.
I borrow my comparisons from clay,
      Being clay myself. Let not those spirits be   430
Offended with such base low likenesses;
We know their posts are nobler far than these.

---

[268] *Milton*: John Milton (1608–1674), one of the most influential poets and polemicists of the English Commonwealth and author of the blank verse epic *Paradise Lost*, which depicted the Fall of Adam and Eve and described Hell and Satan in great detail.

[269] *artillery . . . inventions*: In *Paradise Lost* (bk. 6, line 484), Milton attributes the invention of gunpowder to Satan and his fallen angels.

[270] *gilt key*: a golden key worn in the belt, part of the insignia of court officials.

LV

When the great signal ran from heaven to hell—
    About ten million times the distance reckon'd
From our sun to its earth, as we can tell   435
    How much time it takes up, even to a second,
For every ray that travels to dispel
    The fogs of London, through which, dimly beacon'd,
The weathercocks are gilt some thrice a year,
If that the *summer* is not too severe:[271]—   440

LVI

I say that I can tell—'twas half a minute:
    I know the solar beams take up more time
Ere, pack'd up for their journey, they begin it;
    But then their telegraph[272] is less sublime,
And if they ran a race, they would not win it   445
    'Gainst Satan's couriers bound for their own clime.
The sun takes up some years for every ray
To reach its goal—the devil not half a day.

LVII

Upon the verge of space, about the size
    Of half-a-crown, a little speck appear'd   450
(I've seen a something like it in the skies
    In the Ægean, ere a squall); it near'd,
And, growing bigger, took another guise;

---

[271] summer ... *severe*: This may be an oblique reference to a statement attributed to Horace Walpole (1717–1797), English man of letters.

[272] *telegraph*: Although a form of the electromagnetic telegraph would not be formally invented until the 1830s, experiments and theories worked toward forms of telegraphy in the late eighteenth and early nineteenth century (including semaphore, which was in place from London to Portsmouth at that time).

Like an aërial ship it tack'd, and steer'd,[273]
Or *was* steered (I am doubtful of the grammar   455
Of the last phrase, which makes the stanza stammer;

LVIII

But take your choice); and then it grew a cloud;
    And so it was—a cloud of witnesses.
But such a cloud! No land ere saw a crowd
    Of locusts numerous as the heavens saw these;   460
They shadow'd with their myriads space; their loud
    And varied cries were like those of wild geese
(If nations may be liken'd to a goose),
And realised the phrase of 'hell broke loose.'[274]

LIX

Here crash'd a sturdy oath of stout John Bull,[275]   465
    Who damn'd away his eyes as heretofore:
There Paddy brogued 'By Jasus!'—'What's your wull?'
    The temperate Scot exclaim'd: the French ghost
        swore
In certain terms I shan'n't translate in full,
    As the first coachman will; and 'midst the roar,   470
The voice of Jonathan[276] was heard to express,
'*Our* president is going to war, I guess.'

---

[273] *Like . . . steer'd*: This is very possibly an oblique reference to *The Rime of the Ancient Mariner* by the English Romantic poet Samuel Taylor Coleridge (1772–1834):

> A speck, a mist, a shape, I wist!
> And still it neared and neared:
> As if it dodged a water-sprite,
> It plunged and tacked and veered. (part 3, lines 153–56)

[274] '*hell . . . loose*': Cf. *Paradise Lost*: "Wherefore with thee / Came not all Hell broke loose?" John Milton, *Paradise Lost*, ed. Christopher Ricks, bk. 4, lines 917–18 (London: Penguin Classics, 1989), p. 103.

[275] *John Bull*: the personification of England.

[276] *Jonathan*: an unidentified American.

LX

Besides there were the Spaniard, Dutch, and Dane;
  In short, an universal shoal[277] of shades,
From Otaheite's isle[278] to Salisbury Plain,[279]   475
  Of all climes and professions, years and trades,
Ready to swear against the good king's reign,
  Bitter as clubs in cards are against spades:[280]
All summon'd by this grand 'subpoena,'[281] to
Try if kings mayn't be damn'd like me or you.   480

LXI

When Michael saw this host, he first grew pale,
  As angels can; next, like Italian twilight,
He turn'd all colours—as a peacock's tail,
  Or sunset streaming through a Gothic skylight
In some old abbey, or a trout not stale,   485
  Or distant lightning on the horizon *by* night,
Or a fresh rainbow, or a grand review
Of thirty regiments in red, green, and blue.

LXII

Then he address'd himself to Satan: 'Why—
  My good old friend, for such I deem you, though   490
Our different parties make us fight so shy,
  I ne'er mistake you for a *personal* foe;

---

[277] *shoal*: sandy elevation (creating a shallow place in water). The following analogy illustrates that there are so many dead souls that they create shallowness all the way from England to the Polynesian Islands, on the other side of the world.

[278] *Otaheite's isle*: the Island of Tahiti in French Polynesia.

[279] *Salisbury Plain*: an open plateau in central southern England, known particularly for housing the prehistoric monument of Stonehenge.

[280] *clubs . . . spades*: In ombre, a trick-taking card game, the ace of spades is the primary trump card and the ace of clubs is the tertiary trump card.

[281] *'subpoena'*: writ commanding someone to appear in court (the "grand 'subpoena'" is death).

Our difference is *political*, and I
    Trust that, whatever may occur below,
You know my great respect for you: and this   495
Makes me regret whate'er you do amiss—

LXIII

'Why, my dear Lucifer, would you abuse
    My call for witnesses? I did not mean
That you should half of earth and hell produce;
    'Tis even superfluous, since two honest, clean,   500
True testimonies are enough: we lose
    Our time, nay, our eternity, between
The accusation and defence: if we
Hear both, 'twill stretch our immortality.'

LXIV

Satan replied, 'To me the matter is   505
    Indifferent, in a personal point of view:
I can have fifty better souls than this
    With far less trouble than we have gone through
Already; and I merely argued his
    Late majesty of Britain's case with you   510
Upon a point of form: you may dispose
Of him; I've kings enough below, God knows!'

LXV

Thus spoke the Demon (late call'd 'multifaced'[282]
    By multo-scribbling Southey). 'Then we'll call
One or two persons of the myriads placed   515
    Around our congress, and dispense with all
The rest,' quoth Michael: 'Who may be so graced
    As to speak first? there's choice enough—who shall

---

[282] '*multifaced*': Cf. Robert Southey's *Vision of Judgement* (V., "The Accusers"): "'Caitiffs, are ye dumb?' cried the multifaced Demon in anger."

It be?' Then Satan answer'd, 'There are many;
But you may choose Jack Wilkes[283] as well as any.'   520

LXVI

A merry, cock-eyed, curious-looking sprite
    Upon the instant started from the throng,
Dress'd in a fashion now forgotten quite;
    For all the fashions of the flesh stick long
By people in the next world; where unite   525
    All the costumes since Adam's, right or wrong,
From Eve's fig-leaf down to the petticoat,
Almost as scanty, of days less remote.

LXVII

The spirit look'd around upon the crowds
    Assembled, and exclaim'd, 'My friends of all   530
The spheres, we shall catch cold amongst these clouds;
    So let's to business: why this general call?
If those are freeholders I see in shrouds,
    And 'tis for an election that they bawl,
Behold a candidate with unturn'd coat!   535
Saint Peter, may I count upon your vote?'

LXVIII

'Sir,' replied Michael, 'you mistake; these things
    Are of a former life, and what we do
Above is more august; to judge of kings
    Is the tribunal met: so now you know.'   540
'Then I presume those gentlemen with wings,'
    Said Wilkes, 'are cherubs; and that soul below
Looks much like George the Third, but to my mind
A good deal older—Bless me! is he blind?'

---

[283] *Jack Wilkes*: Jack Wilkes (1725–1797), radical English Whig politician.

LXIX

'He is what you behold him, and his doom   545
    Depends upon his deeds,' the Angel said.
'If you have aught to arraign in him, the tomb
    Gives license to the humblest beggar's head
To lift itself against the loftiest.'—'Some,'
    Said Wilkes, 'don't wait to see them laid in lead,   550
For such a liberty—and I, for one,
Have told them what I thought beneath the sun.'

LXX

'*Above* the sun repeat, then, what thou hast
    To urge against him,' said the Archangel. 'Why,'
Replied the spirit, 'since old scores are past,   555
    Must I turn evidence? In faith, not I.
Besides, I beat him hollow at the last,[284]
    With all his Lords and Commons: in the sky
I don't like ripping up old stories, since
His conduct was but natural in a prince.   560

LXXI

'Foolish, no doubt, and wicked, to oppress
    A poor unlucky devil without a shilling;
But then I blame the man himself much less
    Than Bute and Grafton,[285] and shall be unwilling
To see him punish'd here for their excess,   565
    Since they were both damn'd long ago, and still in
Their place below: for me, I have forgiven,
And vote his "habeas corpus" into heaven.'

[284] *beat . . . last*: Wilkes was unopposed when he worked toward his third return to Parliament, a term in which he was to enjoy great personal and political success.

[285] *Bute and Grafton*: John Stuart (1713–1792), the Earl of Bute, was a close friend of George III (and thus an opponent to the influence of Wilkes), and Augustus Henry FitzRoy (1735–1811), the Duke of Grafton, was only half-hearted and occasional in his support of Wilkes.

LXXII

'Wilkes,' said the Devil, 'I understand all this;
    You turn'd to half a courtier[286] ere you died,   570
And seem to think it would not be amiss
    To grow a whole one on the other side
Of Charon's ferry; you forget that *his*
    Reign is concluded; whatsoe'er betide,
He won't be sovereign more: you've lost your labour,   575
For at the best he will but be your neighbour.

LXXIII

'However, I knew what to think of it,
    When I beheld you in your jesting way
Flitting and whispering round about the spit
    Where Belial,[287] upon duty for the day,   580
With Fox's lard was basting William Pitt,
    His pupil;[288] I knew what to think, I say:
That fellow even in hell breeds farther ills;
I'll have him *gagg'd*—'twas one of his own bills.[289]

LXXIV

'Call Junius!'[290] From the crowd a shadow stalk'd,   585
    And at the name there was a general squeeze,
So that the very ghosts no longer walk'd
    In comfort, at their own aërial ease,

[286] *half a courtier*: Later in life, when he served as Lord Mayor, Jack Wilkes adopted a more civil and moderate tone toward George III.

[287] *Belial*: one of the primary devils, often considered to be Satan himself, but differentiated by John Milton in *Paradise Lost*.

[288] *Fox's . . . pupil*: Charles James Fox (1749–1806) was a radical Whig politician of great influence; William Pitt the Younger (1759–1806) was a conservative prime minister. The two men began as allies but later became archenemies. Byron disliked them both.

[289] *one . . . bills*: In November of 1795, Parliament introduced the Pitt and Grenville Acts as an attempt to limit the work and speech of Jack Wilkes.

[290] *Junius*: the pseudonym of the writer of a series of letters published in the *Public Advertiser* from 1769 to1772 and for whom Grafton was a particular target.

But were all ramm'd, and jamm'd (but to be balk'd,
    As we shall see), and jostled hands and knees,   590
Like wind compress'd and pent within a bladder,
Or like a human colic, which is sadder.

LXXV

The shadow came—a tall, thin, grey-hair'd figure,
    That look'd as it had been a shade on earth;
Quick in its motions, with an air of vigour,   595
    But nought to mark its breeding or its birth:
Now it wax'd little, then again grew bigger,
    With now an air of gloom, or savage mirth;
But as you gazed upon its features, they
Changed every instant—to *what*, none could say.   600

LXXVI

The more intently the ghosts gazed, the less
    Could they distinguish whose the features were;
The Devil himself seem'd puzzled even to guess;
    They varied like a dream—now here, now there;
And several people swore from out the press,   605
    They knew him perfectly; and one could swear
He was his father: upon which another
Was sure he was his mother's cousin's brother:

LXXVII

Another, that he was a duke, or knight,
    An orator, a lawyer, or a priest,   610
A nabob,[291] a man-midwife;[292] but the wight[293]
    Mysterious changed his countenance at least
As oft as they their minds: though in full sight

---

[291] *nabob*: person of great wealth or prominence (originally in India).

[292] *man-midwife*: men trained to assist in childbirth, a controversial profession
for men; until the seventeenth century, it was primarily restricted to women.

[293] *wight*: creature, living being.

He stood, the puzzle only was increased;
The man was a phantasmagoria[294] in   615
Himself—he was so volatile and thin.

LXXVIII

The moment that you had pronounced him *one*,
    Presto! his face changed, and he was another,
And when that change was hardly well put on,
    It varied, till I don't think his own mother   620
(If that he had a mother) would her son
    Have known, he shifted so from one to t'other;
Till guessing from a pleasure grew a task,
At this epistolary 'Iron Mask.'[295]

LXXIX

For sometimes he like Cerberus would seem—   625
    'Three gentlemen at once' (as sagely says
Good Mrs Malaprop);[296] then you might deem
    That he was not even *one*; now many rays
Were flashing round him; and now a thick steam
    Hid him from sight—like fogs on London days: 630
Now Burke,[297] now Tooke,[298] he grew to people's fancies,
And certes[299] often like Sir Philip Francis.[300]

---

[294] *phantasmagoria*: a shifting, dreamlike scene of illusory images.

[295] *'Iron Mask'*: This figure has been associated with Count Ercole Antonio Mattioli (1640–1694), a highly placed personage in the court of the Duke of Mantua; he fell from favor, was kidnapped by King Louis XIV of France, and died in prison.

[296] *Three . . . Malaprop*: Cf. *The Rivals* (Act 4, scene 2), a play by the prestigious Irish playwright and poet Richard Brisley Sheridan (1751–1816), in which the character of Mrs. Malaprop frequently makes an absurd or humorous statement by misusing words (the origin of the word "malaprop").

[297] *Burke*: Edmund Burke (1729–1797), influential conservative Irish politician and philosopher.

[298] *Tooke*: John Horne Tooke (1736–1812), English politician and philologist and an opponent of the American Revolutionary War.

[299] *certes*: truly.

[300] *Sir Philip Francis*: Sir Philip Francis (1740–1818), Irish politician.

LXXX

I've an hypothesis—'tis quite my own;
    I never let it out till now, for fear
Of doing people harm about the throne,   635
    And injuring some minister or peer,
On whom the stigma might perhaps be blown:
    It is—my gentle public, lend thine ear!
'Tis, that what Junius we are wont to call
Was *really*, *truly*, nobody at all.   640

LXXXI

I don't see wherefore letters should not be
    Written without hands, since we daily view
Them written without heads; and books, we see,
    Are fill'd as well without the latter too:
And really till we fix on somebody   645
    For certain sure to claim them as his due,
Their author, like the Niger's mouth,[301] will bother
The world to say if *there* be mouth or author.

LXXXII

'And who and what art thou?' the Archangel said.
    'For *that* you may consult my title-page,'[302]   650
Replied this mighty shadow of a shade:
    'If I have kept my secret half an age,
I scarce shall tell it now.'—'Canst thou upbraid,'
    Continued Michael, 'George Rex, or allege
Aught further?' Junius answer'd, 'You had better   655
First ask him for *his* answer to my letter:

LXXXIII

'My charges upon record will outlast
    The brass of both his epitaph and tomb.'

[301] *Niger's mouth*: the delta of the Niger River.
[302] *my title-page*: The title page of Junius' works actually says nothing beyond "*Letters of Junius, Stat Nominis Umbra*".

'Repent'st thou not,' said Michael, 'of some past
    Exaggeration? something which may doom   660
Thyself if false, as him if true? Thou wast
    Too bitter—is it not so?—in thy gloom
Of passion?'—'Passion!' cried the phantom dim,
'I loved my country, and I hated him.'

LXXXIV

'What I have written, I have written: let   665
    The rest be on his head or mine!' So spoke
Old 'Nominis Umbra;'[303] and while speaking yet,
    Away he melted in celestial smoke.
Then Satan said to Michael, 'Don't forget
    To call George Washington,[304] and John Horne
      Tooke,   670
And Franklin;'[305]—but at this time there was heard
A cry for room, though not a phantom stirr'd.

LXXXV

At length with jostling, elbowing, and the aid
    Of cherubim appointed to that post,
The devil Asmodeus[306] to the circle made   675
    His way, and look'd as if his journey cost
Some trouble. When his burden down he laid,
    'What's this?' cried Michael; 'why, 'tis not a ghost?'
'I know it,' quoth the incubus;[307] 'but he
Shall be one, if you leave the affair to me.   680

---

[303] *'Nominis Umbra'*: the shadow of a name.
[304] *George Washington*: George Washington (1732–1799), the first president of the United States of America.
[305] *Franklin*: Benjamin Franklin (1706–1790), one of the founding fathers of the United States (thus the polar opposite of John Horne Tooke, who opposed the American Revolutionary War).
[306] *Asmodeus*: king of demons, named in the Old Testament Book of Tobit (3:8).
[307] *incubus*: a demon who assaults or lies upon his female victims.

LXXXVI

'Confound the renegado![308] I have sprain'd
   My left wing, he's so heavy; one would think
Some of his works about his neck were chain'd.
   But to the point; while hovering o'er the brink
Of Skiddaw[309] (where as usual it still rain'd),   685
   I saw a taper, far below me, wink,
And stooping, caught this fellow at a libel[310]—
No less on history than the Holy Bible.

LXXXVII

'The former is the devil's scripture, and
   The latter yours, good Michael; so the affair   690
Belongs to all of us, you understand.
   I snatch'd him up just as you see him there,
And brought him off for sentence out of hand:
   I've scarcely been ten minutes in the air—
At least a quarter it can hardly be: 695
I dare say that his wife is still at tea.'

LXXXVIII

Here Satan said, 'I know this man of old,
   And have expected him for some time here;
A sillier fellow you will scarce behold,
   Or more conceited in his petty sphere: 700
But surely it was not worth while to fold
   Such trash below your wing, Asmodeus dear:
We had the poor wretch safe (without being bored
With carriage) coming of his own accord.

LXXXIX

'But since he's here, let's see what he has done.'   705
   'Done!' cried Asmodeus, 'he anticipates

---

[308] *renegado*: renegade.
[309] *Skiddaw*: mountain in the Lake District of England.
[310] *libel*: written or printed defamation.

The very business you're now upon,
    And scribbles as if head clerk to the Fates.
Who knows to what his ribaldry may run,
    When such an ass as this, like Balaam's,[311] prates?'   710
'Let's hear,' quoth Michael, 'what he has to say;
You know we're bound to that in every way.'

XC

Now the bard, glad to get an audience, which
    By no means often was his case below,
Began to cough, and hawk, and hem, and pitch   715
    His voice into that awful note of woe
To all unhappy hearers within reach
    Of poets when the tide of rhyme's in flow;
But stuck fast with his first hexameter,[312]
Not one of all whose gouty[313] feet would stir.   720

XCI

But ere the spavin'd[314] dactyls[315] could be spurr'd
    Into recitative, in great dismay
Both cherubim and seraphim were heard
    To murmur loudly through their long array;
And Michael rose ere he could get a word   725
    Of all his founder'd verses under way,
And cried, 'For God's sake stop, my friend! 'twere best—
Non Di, non homines—you know the rest.'[316]

---

[311] *ass . . . Balaam's*: Balaam, a disobedient prophet of the Old Testament, beat his donkey when the animal resisted his master's urgings to go against the will of God and reproached him for it.

[312] *hexameter*: metrical line of verse with six feet.

[313] *gouty*: Gout is a disease causing arthritis, especially in the smaller bones of feet, associated with rich foods and rich living.

[314] *spavin'd*: deteriorated, worn out.

[315] *dactyls*: a metrical poetic foot containing a long syllable followed by two short syllables.

[316] Non . . . *rest*: Cf. Horace, *Ars Poetica* (lines 372–73): "Mediocribus esse poetis/Non homines, non dî, non concessere columnæ" ("Neither men, nor gods, nor booksellers have ever tolerated or will tolerate mediocrity in poetry").

XCII

A general bustle spread throughout the throng,
    Which seem'd to hold all verse in detestation;   730
The angels had of course enough of song
    When upon service;[317] and the generation
Of ghosts had heard too much in life, not long
    Before, to profit by a new occasion;
The monarch, mute till then, exclaim'd, 'What! what![318] 735
Pye[319] come again? No more—no more of that!'

XCIII

The tumult grew; an universal cough
    Convulsed the skies, as during a debate,
When Castlereagh[320] has been up long enough
    (Before he was first minister of state,   740
I mean—the *slaves hear now*); some cried 'Off, off!'
    As at a farce; till, grown quite desperate,
The bard Saint Peter pray'd to interpose
(Himself an author) only for his prose.

XCIV

The varlet[321] was not an ill-favour'd knave;[322]   745
    A good deal like a vulture in the face,
With a hook nose and a hawk's eye, which gave
    A smart and sharper-looking sort of grace
To his whole aspect, which, though rather grave,
    Was by no means so ugly as his case;   750

[317] *When upon service*: (1) during sacramental liturgy; (2) in the course of their labors.

[318] *What! what!* The king's habit of repeating himself was sometimes popularly satirized.

[319] Pye: Henry James Pye (1745–1813), notoriously bad English poet (and one-time poet laureate).

[320] *Castlereagh*: Robert Stewart (1769–1822), Marquess of Londonderry (known as Lord Castlereagh), conservative Irish statesman. Castlereagh was a poor public speaker.

[321] *varlet*: (1) male servant or page; (2) rascal.

[322] *knave*: dishonorable, unscrupulous man.

But that indeed was hopeless as can be,
Quite a poetic felony '*de se*.'[323]

XCV

Then Michael blew his trump,[324] and still'd the noise
    With one still greater, as is yet the mode
On earth besides; except some grumbling voice,   755
    Which now and then will make a slight inroad
Upon decorous silence, few will twice
    Lift up their lungs when fairly overcrow'd;
And now the bard could plead his own bad cause,
With all the attitudes of self-applause.   760

XCVI

He said—(I only give the heads)—he said,
    He meant no harm in scribbling; 'twas his way
Upon all topics; 'twas, besides, his bread,
    Of which he butter'd both sides; 'twould delay
Too long the assembly (he was pleased to dread),   765
    And take up rather more time than a day,
To name his works—he would but cite a few—
'Wat Tyler'—'Rhymes on Blenheim'—'Waterloo.'[325]

XCVII

He had written praises of a regicide;[326]
    He had written praises of all kings whatever;   770

---

[323] 'de se:' (Latin) "of oneself". A *felo de se* was the legal term for suicide. Following a nervous breakdown, Castlereagh committed suicide, but an inquest found that he had not been of sound mind—not a *felo de se*, which made it possible (among other things) for him to be buried in Westminster Abbey.

[324] *trump*: trumpet.

[325] 'Wat Tyler' ... 'Waterloo': These are all poems by the poet Southey.

[326] *praises ... regicide*: Southey composed a series of poetic inscriptions, including a poem "For the Apartment in CHEPSTOW-CASTLE where HENRY MARTEN the Regicide was imprisoned Thirty Years", on the subject of Sir Henry Marten (1602–1680), an English politician who actively pursued the execution of King Charles I (1600–1649).

He had written for republics far and wide,
    And then against them bitterer than ever:
For pantisocracy[327] he once had cried
    Aloud, a scheme less moral than 'twas clever;
Then grew a hearty anti-jacobin[328]—   775
Had turn'd his coat—and would have turn'd his skin.

XCVIII

He had sung against all battles, and again
    In their high praise and glory; he had call'd
Reviewing 'the ungentle craft,'[329] and then
    Become as base a critic as e'er crawl'd—   780
Fed, paid, and pamper'd by the very men
    By whom his muse and morals had been maul'd:
He had written much blank verse, and blanker prose,
And more of both than any body knows.

XCIX

He had written Wesley's life:[330]—here turning round   785
    To Satan, 'Sir, I'm ready to write yours,
In two octavo volumes, nicely bound,
    With notes and preface, all that most allures
The pious purchaser; and there's no ground
    For fear, for I can choose my own reviewers: 790
So let me have the proper documents,
That I may add you to my other saints.'

C

Satan bow'd, and was silent. 'Well, if you,
    With amiable modesty, decline

---

[327] *pantisocracy*: a utopian form of community by which all have equal rule and are equal, sharing all things in common (the word "pantisocracy" was coined by Southey).

[328] *anti-jacobin*: opposer of radical leftist politics, which, it is argued, he had previously personally espoused.

[329] *'the ungentle craft'*: Cf. Southey's *Remains of Henry Kirke White* (1808).

[330] *Wesley's life*: Southey's *Life of Wesley, and Rise and Progress of Methodism* (1820), published in two volumes.

My offer, what says Michael? There are few 795
    Whose memoirs could be render'd more divine.
Mine is a pen of all work;[331] not so new
    As it was once, but I would make you shine
Like your own trumpet. By the way, my own
Has more of brass in it, and is as well blown. 800

CI

'But talking about trumpets, here's my Vision!
    Now you shall judge, all people; yes, you shall
Judge with my judgment, and by my decision
    Be guided who shall enter heaven or fall.
I settle all these things by intuition, 805
    Times present, past, to come, heaven, hell, and all,
Like King Alfonso.[332] When I thus see double,
I save the Deity some worlds of trouble.'

CII

He ceased, and drew forth an MS.; and no
    Persuasion on the part of devils, or saints, 810
Or angels, now could stop the torrent; so
    He read the first three lines of the contents;
But at the fourth, the whole spiritual show
    Had vanish'd, with variety of scents,
Ambrosial and sulphureous, as they sprang, 815
Like lightning, off from his 'melodious twang.'[333]

[331] *pen of all work*: Byron previously denounced Southey as "this arrogant scribbler of all works". *The Two Fascari*, appendix, in Lord Byron, *The Poetical Words*, vol. 6, eds. Jerome J. McGann and Barry Weller (Oxford: Clarendon Press, 1991), p. 225.

[332] *King Alfonso*: King Alfonso (1221–1284), "the Wise", astronomer king of Castile, was credited for his scholarship and purportedly stated that, had God consulted him, Alfonso would have saved God from some of the absurdities in creation.

[333] *'melodious twang'*: The origin of this phrase is unknown, but it was used repeatedly after Byron's usage here.

CIII

Those grand heroics acted as a spell;
    The angels stopp'd their ears and plied their pinions;
The devils ran howling, deafen'd, down to hell;
    The ghosts fled, gibbering, for their own dominions— 820
(For 'tis not yet decided where they dwell,
    And I leave every man to his opinions);
Michael took refuge in his trump—but, lo!
His teeth were set on edge, he could not blow!

CIV

Saint Peter, who has hitherto been known   825
    For an impetuous saint, upraised his keys,
And at the fifth line knock'd the poet down;
    Who fell like Phaeton,[334] but more at ease,
Into his lake, for there he did not drown;
    A different web being by the Destinies 830
Woven for the Laureate's final wreath, whene'er
Reform shall happen either here or there.

CV

He first sank to the bottom—like his works,
    But soon rose to the surface—like himself;
For all corrupted things are buoy'd like corks,[335] 835
    By their own rottenness, light as an elf,
Or wisp that flits o'er a morass: he lurks,
    It may be, still, like dull books on a shelf,
In his own den, to scrawl some 'Life' or 'Vision,'
As Welborn says—'the devil turn'd precisian.'[336] 840

[334] *Phaeton*: in classical mythology, the son of the sun god, who died when he tried to drive his father's chariot of the sun for a day.

[335] *all . . . corks*: Many dead things (like human corpses) lie at the bottom of the water until fully rotten, then float.

[336] *Welborn . . . 'precisian'*: In *A New Way to Pay Old Debts* (c. 1625) by the playwright Philip Massinger (1583–1640), Welborn rebukes an uncharitable Puritan: "Verily, you brache! / The devil turned precisian" (1.1).

CVI

As for the rest, to come to the conclusion
　　Of this true dream, the telescope is gone
Which kept my optics free from all delusion,
　　And show'd me what I in my turn have shown;
All I saw farther, in the last confusion,　　　　　　　845
　　Was, that King George slipp'd into heaven for one;
And when the tumult dwindled to a calm,
I left him practising the hundredth psalm.[337]

On This Day I Complete My Thirty-Sixth Year (1824)

I

'Tis time this heart should be unmoved,
　　Since others it hath ceased to move:
Yet, though I cannot be beloved,
　　Still let me love!

II

My days are in the yellow leaf;　　　　　　　　　　5
　　The flowers and fruits of love are gone;
The worm, the canker, and the grief
　　Are mine alone!

III

The fire that on my bosom preys
　　Is lone as some volcanic isle;　　　　　　　　　10
No torch is kindled at its blaze—
　　A funeral pile!

---

[337] *hundredth psalm*: The psalm begins: "Make a joyful noise unto the LORD, all ye lands." (KJV).

IV

The hope, the fear, the jealous care,
   The exalted portion of the pain
And power of love, I cannot share,   15
   But wear the chain.

V

But 'tis not *thus*—and 'tis not *here*—
   Such thoughts should shake my soul, nor *now*,
Where glory decks the hero's bier,
   Or binds his brow.   20

VI

The sword, the banner, and the field,
   Glory and Greece, around me see!
The Spartan, borne upon his shield,[338]
   Was not more free.

VII

Awake! (not Greece—she *is* awake!)   25
   Awake, my spirit! Think through *whom*
Thy life-blood tracks its parent lake,
   And then strike home!

VIII

Tread those reviving passions down,
   Unworthy manhood!—unto thee   30
Indifferent should the smile or frown
   Of beauty be.

IX

If thou regret'st thy youth, *why live?*
   The land of honourable death

---

[338] *borne ... shield*: In classical tradition, slain warriors were carried home in honor on their shields.

Is here:—up to the field, and give   35
     Away thy breath!

X

Seek out—less often sought than found—
     A soldier's grave, for thee the best;
Then look around, and choose thy ground,
     And take thy rest.   40

Don Juan

Don Juan was written between 1818 and 1823 in ottava rima and left unfinished in canto 17 at the author's death. The hero's name should be pronounced to rhyme with Marshall McLuhan or Patrick McGoohan. It is generally considered Byron's masterpiece and one of the greatest long poems in English since *Paradise Lost*. Along with Wordsworth's *Prelude* at the other end of the spectrum of experience and sensibility, it was the poem of the age, "the real epic of modern life, as the *Iliad* is the epic of ancient life".[339] We have no more idea of how Byron intended to develop and complete it than he probably did himself.

Byron has chosen for his protagonist a literary archetype, like Faust, Hamlet, or his own Manfred. However, Byron's Juan is not the Don Juan of legend—he's not even a typical Byronic hero. *This* Juan (surprisingly, given the author's reputation) is more sinned against than sinning—his amorous career begins as a teenager seduced by an attractive married woman, and in the course of the poem, he has affairs with a mere five women, seducing none of them.[340] According to W. H. Auden, "Far from being a defiant rebel against the laws of God and man, his most conspicuous traits are his good temper and his social adaptability.... Though by birth a Spaniard and a Catholic,

---

[339] Charles Whibley, *Poems of Lord Byron* (London: Caxton, 1907), p. xli.
[340] He is the victim of two more seductions; the other two relationships are consensual.

and therefore an outsider from an Englishman's point of view, he is the perfect embodiment of that very British notion that a gentleman should succeed at everything he does without appearing to make an effort."[341]

Just as Juan is no Lothario, so this "epic satire"[342] is hardly a satire in the conventional sense at all—the air the poem breathes is too tolerant and good-humored. According to Charles Whibley, "As his poetry was the fruit of experience, so with added experience it touched perfection. It was Byron's happy lot to mellow with the years. For him there was never any looking back."[343] Juan is not a cynic; he is not hostile to traditional human values and ideals. From anti-Romantics like Auden to idealistic visionaries like Percy Bysshe Shelley and John Ruskin,[344] sophisticated readers have understood Byron's "cynicism" for what it is: an attack on the hypocrisy of those—not excluding the Baudelairian reader/author doppelgänger—who damn in others what they deny in themselves.

The critical consensus remains that in *Don Juan* Byron at last found the ideal form and subject for his genius. From the very first, its qualities were recognized: the exhilarating technical virtuosity[345] combined with a unique improvisational flavor,

---

[341] W. H. Auden, "Introduction", in *The Selected Poetry and Prose of Bryon* (New York: Signet, 1966), p. vii.

[342] Byron's words, *Don Juan*, canto 14, stanza 99.

[343] Whibley, *Poems of Lord Byron*, p. xl.

[344] John Ruskin states, "Here at last I had found a man who spoke only of what he had seen, and known; and spoke without exaggeration, without mystery, without enmity, and without mercy. 'That *is* so;—make what you will of it!'" John Ruskin, *Praeterita*, vol. 1 (London: George Allen, 1907), pp. 223–24.

[345] According to Algernon Charles Swinburne, "The scheme of metre is Byron's alone; no weaker hand than his could ever bend that bow, or ever will. Even the Italian poets, working in a language more flexible and ductile than ours, could never turn their native metre to such uses, could never handle their national weapon with such grace and strength." Swinburne, *A Selection from the Works of Lord Byron*, p. xx. Johann Wolfgang von Goethe refers to the idiom of *Don Juan* as "a cultivated comic language which we Germans wholly lack." Johann Wolfgang von Goethe, "Byron's *Don Juan*", in *Goethe's Literary Essays* (New York: Harcourt, Brace, 1921), p. 205.

the humor, the mordancy, the genuine epic sweep. Byron—no great admirer of his own work—was delighted with it: "As to 'Don Juan,' confess, confess—you dog and be candid—that it is the sublime of *that there* sort of writing—it may be bawdy but is it not good English? It may be profligate, but is it not *life*, is it not *the thing*?"[346]

Its originality was arresting: epic comical, satirical, and pica-resque, it is one of the most difficult poems to classify in the canon. Shelley referred to it as "a poem totally of its own spe-cies.... Nothing has ever been written like it in English."[347] Perhaps, among poems of length and stature, it might most fruitfully—if obliquely—be compared to Lewis Carroll's *Hunting of the Snark* or G. K. Chesterton's *Ballad of the White Horse*. But it remains *sui generis*; in the words of W. H. Auden:

> In the history of English poetry before the so-called Romantic Age, comic poetry is comparatively rare.... But, from 1800 onwards comic poetry has flourished. Byron, Moore (especially in his political poems), Praed, Hood, Barham, Lear and Carroll (slightly to one side), W. S. Gilbert, J. K. Stephen, Calverley, and in this century the best of Chesterton and Belloc, not to mention the anonymous host of limerick writers, represent a tradition without which English poetry would be very much the poorer, and of them all, Byron is by far the greatest. Whatever its faults, *Don Juan* is the most original poem in English; noth-ing like it had ever been written before. Speaking for myself, I don't feel like reading it very often, but when I do, it is the only poem I want to read: no other will do.[348]

---

[346] Letter to Douglas Kinnaird, October 26, 1819. *Lord Byron: Selected Letters and Journals*, ed. Leslie A. Marchand (Cambridge, Mass.: Belknap Press of Harvard University Press, 1982), p. 328. Emphasis in original.

[347] Letter to Lord Byron, October 21, 1821. *The Letters of Percy Bysshe Shelley*, vol. 2, ed. Roger Ingbel (London: George Bell, 1915), p. 1001.

[348] W. H. Auden, "Introduction", in *The Dyer's Hand and Other Essays* (New York: Vintage, 1990), p. xxiv.

I would to Heaven that I were so much Clay—[349]
    As I am blood—bone—marrow, passion—feeling—
Because at least the past were past away—
    And for the future—(but I write this reeling
Having got drunk exceedingly to day
    So that I seem to stand upon the ceiling)
I say—the future is a serious matter—
And so—for Godsake—Hock[350] and Soda water.

From *Don Juan*: Canto the Second (1819)[351]

1

Oh ye who teach the ingenuous youth of nations,
    Holland, France, England, Germany, or Spain,
I pray ye flog them upon all occasions;
    It mends their morals, never mind the pain.
The best of mothers and of educations   5
    In Juan's case were but employed in vain,
Since in a way that's rather of the oddest, he
Became divested of his native modesty.

2

Had he but been placed at a public school,
    In the third form or even in the fourth,   10
His daily task had kept his fancy cool—
    At least had he been nurtured in the north.
Spain may prove an exception to the rule,
    But then exceptions always prove its worth.
A lad of sixteen causing a divorce   15
Puzzled his tutors very much, of course.

---

[349] *I would . . . Clay*: This fragment was written by Byron on the back of the manuscript of "Canto the First" of the poem.

[350] *Hock*: dry white wine (this mixture is a cure for a hangover, known as "hair of the dog").

[351] *Canto the Second*: In the preceding canto of the poem, Don Juan is seduced by Donna Julia, the wife of Don Alfonso (who is nearly thirty years her senior); the furor at the discovered affair prompts Juan's exile from Seville, Spain.

3

I can't say that it puzzles me at all,
　　If all things be considered: first, there was
His lady mother, mathematical,
　　A—never mind; his tutor, an old ass;　　　　　　20
A pretty woman (that's quite natural,
　　Or else the thing had hardly come to pass);
A husband rather old, not much in unity
With his young wife; a time and opportunity.

4

Well—well, the world must turn upon its axis,　　25
　　And all mankind turn with it, heads or tails,
And live and die, make love and pay our taxes,
　　And as the veering wind shifts, shift our sails.
The king commands us, and the doctor quacks us,
　　The priest instructs, and so our life exhales,　　30
A little breath, love, wine, ambition, fame,
Fighting, devotion, dust—perhaps a name.

5

I said that Juan had been sent to Cadiz,[352]
　　A pretty town, I recollect it well.
'Tis there the mart of the colonial trade is　　　　35
　　(Or was, before Peru learned to rebel),[353]
And such sweet girls—I mean, such graceful ladies.
　　Their very walk would make your bosom swell;
I can't describe it, though so much it strike,
Nor liken it—I never saw the like.　　　　　　　40

---

[352] *Cadiz*: city in southwestern Spain.
　[353] *Peru . . . rebel*: Peru, a country in western South America, was a staunch stronghold of the Spanish Empire in the early nineteenth century, while many other regions of South America sought independence (Peru would achieve independence in 1821).

6

An Arab horse, a stately stag, a barb[354]
    New broke, a cameleopard,[355] a gazelle—
No, none of these will do. And then their garb,
    Their veil and petticoat! Alas, to dwell
Upon such things would very near absorb   45
    A canto. Then their feet and ankles—well,
Thank heaven I've got no metaphor quite ready
(And so, my sober Muse, come, let's be steady,

7

Chaste Muse—well, if you must, you must)—the veil
    Thrown back a moment with the glancing hand,   50
While the o'erpowering eye that turns you pale
    Flashes into the heart. All sunny land
Of love, when I forget you, may I fail
    To—say my prayers; but never was there planned
A dress through which the eyes give such a volley,[356]   55
Accepting the Venetian *fazzioli*.[357]

8

But to our tale. The Donna Inez sent
    Her son to Cadiz only to embark;
To stay there had not answered her intent.
    But why? We leave the reader in the dark.   60
'Twas for a voyage that the young man was meant,
    As if a Spanish ship were Noah's ark,
To wean him from the wickedness of earth
And send him like a dove of promise forth.

---

[354] *barb*: Barbary stallion.
[355] *cameleopard*: giraffe.
[356] *volley*: simultaneous discharge, as from an armory.
[357] *fazzioli*: white handkerchiefs, which Byron reported as being worn by the Venetian lower orders.

9

Don Juan bade his valet pack his things   65
    According to direction, then received
A lecture with some money. For four springs
    He was to travel, and though Inez grieved
(As every kind of parting has its stings),
    She hoped he would improve, perhaps believed.   70
A letter too she gave (he never read it)
Of good advice—and two or three of credit.

10

In the meantime, to pass her hours away,
    Brave Inez now set up a Sunday school
For naughty children, who would rather play   75
    (Like truant rogues) the devil or the fool.
Infants of three years old were taught that day,
    Dunces were whipt or set upon a stool.
The great success of Juan's education
Spurred her to teach another generation.   80

11

Juan embarked, the ship got under way,
    The wind was fair, the water passing rough.
A devil of a sea rolls in that bay,
    As I, who've crossed it oft, know well enough.
And standing upon deck, the dashing spray   85
    Flies in one's face and makes it weather-tough.
And there he stood to take and take again
His first, perhaps his last, farewell of Spain.

12

I can't but say it is an awkward sight
    To see one's native land receding through   90
The growing waters; it unmans one quite,
    Especially when life is rather new.

I recollect Great Britain's coast looks white,
    But almost every other country's blue,
When gazing on them, mystified by distance,   95
We enter on our nautical existence.

13

So Juan stood bewildered on the deck.
    The wind sung, cordage strained, and sailors swore,
And the ship creaked, the town became a speck,
    From which away so fair and fast they bore.   100
The best of remedies is a beefsteak
    Against seasickness; try it, sir, before
You sneer, and I assure you this is true,
For I have found it answer—so may you.

14

Don Juan stood and gazing from the stern,   105
    Beheld his native Spain receding far.
First partings form a lesson hard to learn;
    Even nations feel this when they go to war.
There is a sort of unexprest concern,
    A kind of shock that sets one's heart ajar.   110
At leaving even the most unpleasant people
And places, one keeps looking at the steeple.

15

But Juan had got many things to leave,
    His mother and a mistress and no wife,
So that he had much better cause to grieve   115
    Than many persons more advanced in life.
And if we now and then a sigh must heave
    At quitting even those we quit in strife,
No doubt we weep for those the heart endears,
That is, till deeper griefs congeal our tears.   120

16

So Juan wept, as wept the captive Jews
    By Babel's waters, still remembering Sion.
I'd weep, but mine is not a weeping Muse,
    And such light griefs are not a thing to die on.
Young men should travel, if but to amuse   125
    Themselves; and the next time their servants tie on
Behind their carriages their new portmanteau,
Perhaps it may be lined with this my canto.

17

And Juan wept and much he sighed and thought,
    While his salt tears dropped into the salt sea.   130
'Sweets to the sweet' (I like so much to quote,
    You must excuse this extract; 'tis where she,
The Queen of Denmark, for Ophelia brought
    Flowers to the grave).[358] And sobbing often, he
Reflected on his present situation   135
And seriously resolved on reformation.

18

'Farewell, my Spain, a long farewell!' he cried,
    'Perhaps I may revisit thee no more,
But die, as many an exiled heart hath died,
    Of its own thirst to see again thy shore.   140
Farewell, where Guadalquivir's[359] waters glide.
    Farewell, my mother, and, since all is o'er,
Farewell too, dearest Julia!' Here he drew
Her letter out again and read it through.

---

[358] *Sweets . . . grave*: In William Shakespeare's *Hamlet* (Act 5, scene 1, lines 242–46), Queen Gertude, the mother of Hamlet, scatters flowers at the grave of Ophelia, with whom Hamlet had at one time been purportedly in love.
[359] *Guadalquivir's*: The Guadalquivir is one of the primary rivers of Spain.

19

'And oh, if e're I should forget, I swear—   145
    But that's impossible and cannot be.
Sooner shall this blue ocean melt to air,
    Sooner shall earth resolve itself to sea
Than I resign thine image, oh my fair!
    Or think of anything excepting thee.   150
A mind diseased no remedy can physic.'
(Here the ship gave a lurch, and he grew seasick.)

20

'Sooner shall heaven kiss earth' (here he fell sicker)—
    'Oh Julia, what is every other woe?
(For God's sake let me have a glass of liquor,   155
    Pedro, Battista, help me down below.)
Julia, my love (you rascal, Pedro, quicker),
    Oh Julia (this curst vessel pitches so),
Belovèd Julia, hear me still beseeching!'
(Here he grew inarticulate with retching.)   160

21

He felt that chilling heaviness of heart,
    Or rather stomach, which alas, attends,
Beyond the best apothecary's[360] art,
    The loss of love, the treachery of friends,
Or death of those we dote on, when a part   165
    Of us dies with them as each fond hope ends.
No doubt he would have been much more pathetic,
But the sea acted as a strong emetic.[361]

22

Love's a capricious power. I've known it hold
    Out through a fever caused by its own heat,   170

---

[360] *apothecary's*: An apothecary is a druggist, the lowest social rank of medical men.

[361] *emetic*: medicine inducing vomiting.

But be much puzzled by a cough and cold
   And find a quinsy[362] very hard to treat.
Against all noble maladies he's bold,
   But vulgar illnesses don't like to meet,
Nor that a sneeze should interrupt his sigh,   175
Nor inflammations redden his blind eye.

23

But worst of all is nausea or a pain
   About the lower region of the bowels.
Love, who heroically breathes a vein,[363]
   Shrinks from the application of hot towels,   180
And purgatives[364] are dangerous to his reign,
   Seasickness death. His love was perfect; how else
Could Juan's passion, while the billows roar,
Resist his stomach, ne'er at sea before?

24

The ship,[365] called the most holy *Trinidada*,[366]   185
   Was steering duly for the port Leghorn,[367]
For there the Spanish family Moncada[368]
   Were settled long ere Juan's sire was born.
They were relations, and for them he had a
   Letter of introduction, which the morn   190
Of his departure had been sent him by
His Spanish friends for those in Italy.

---

[362] *quinsy*: inflammation or abscess of the tonsils (i.e., a sore throat).

[363] *breathes a vein*: lances a vein, letting blood.

[364] *purgatives*: laxatives.

[365] *ship*: Byron based his description of the subsequent shipwreck on reports of actual shipwrecks of the time, drawn in particular from Sir G. Dalzell's *Shipwrecks and Disasters at Sea* (published in 1812 in eight volumes).

[366] *most holy* Trinidada: named after the most holy Trinity (in Spanish).

[367] *port Leghorn*: the English name for the port city of Livorno in western Tuscany, Italy.

[368] *Moncada*: a respected, but not royal, family.

25

His suite consisted of three servants and
    A tutor, the licentiate[369] Pedrillo,
Who several languages did understand,   195
    But now lay sick and speechless on his pillow,
And rocking in his hammock, longed for land,
    His headache being increased by every billow.
And the waves oozing through the porthole made
His berth a little damp, and him afraid.   200

26

'Twas not without some reason, for the wind
    Increased at night until it blew a gale;
And though 'twas not much to a naval mind,
    Some landsmen would have looked a little pale,
For sailors are in fact a different kind.   205
    At sunset they began to take in sail,
For the sky showed it would come on to blow
And carry away perhaps a mast or so.

27

At one o'clock the wind with sudden shift
    Threw the ship right into the trough of the sea,   210
Which struck her aft and made an awkward rift,
    Started the sternpost, also shattered the
Whole of her stern-frame, and ere she could lift
    Herself from out her present jeopardy
The rudder tore away. 'Twas time to sound   215
The pumps, and there were four feet water found.

28

One gang of people instantly was put
    Upon the pumps and the remainder set

[369] *licentiate*: one who holds an academic degree, a scholar.

To get up part of the cargo and what not,
    But they could not come at the leak as yet.   220
At last they did get at it really, but
    Still their salvation was an even bet.
The water rushed through in a way quite puzzling,
While they thrust sheets, shirts, jackets, bales of muslin

29

Into the opening, but all such ingredients   225
    Would have been vain, and they must have gone down,
Despite of all their efforts and expedients,
    But for the pumps. I'm glad to make them known
To all the brother tars who may have need hence,
    For fifty tons of water were upthrown   230
By them per hour, and they had all been undone
But for the maker, Mr Mann, of London.[370]

30

As day advanced the weather seemed to abate,
    And then the leak they reckoned to reduce
And keep the ship afloat, though three feet yet   235
    Kept two hand and one chain pump still in use.
The wind blew fresh again; as it grew late
    A squall came on, and while some guns broke loose,
A gust, which all descriptive power transcends,
Laid with one blast the ship on her beam ends.   240

31

There she lay, motionless, and seemed upset.
    The water left the hold and washed the decks
And made a scene men do not soon forget,
    For they remember battles, fires, and wrecks,

---

[370] *Mr . . . London*: This detail is cribbed from *Shipwrecks and Disasters at Sea*, referring to an actual English shipbuilder.

Or any other thing that brings regret   245
   Or breaks their hopes or hearts or heads or necks.
Thus drownings are much talked of by the divers
And swimmers who may chance to be survivors.

32

Immediately the masts were cut away,
   Both main and mizen. First the mizen went,   250
The mainmast followed, but the ship still lay
   Like a mere log and baffled our intent.
Foremast and bowsprit were cut down, and they
   Eased her at last (although we never meant
To part with all till every hope was blighted),   255
And then with violence the old ship righted.[371]

33

It may be easily supposed, while this
   Was going on, some people were unquiet,
That passengers would find it much amiss
   To lose their lives as well as spoil their diet,   260
That even the able seaman, deeming his
   Days nearly o'er, might be disposed to riot,
As upon such occasions tars will ask
For grog and sometimes drink rum from the cask.

34

There's nought no doubt so much the spirit calms   265
   As rum and true religion; thus is was,
Some plundered, some drank spirits, some sung psalms.
   The high wind made the treble, and as bass
The hoarse harsh waves kept time. Fright cured the qualms
   Of all the luckless landsmen's seasick maws.   270
Strange sounds of wailing, blasphemy, devotion
Clamoured in chorus to the roaring ocean.

---

[371] *righted*: straightened itself.

35

Perhaps more mischief had been done,[372] but for
    Our Juan, who with sense beyond his years,
Got to the spirit-room and stood before   275
    It with a pair of pistols. And their fears,
As if Death were more dreadful by his door
    Of fire than water, spite of oaths and tears,
Kept still aloof the crew, who ere they sunk,
Thought it would be becoming to die drunk.   280

36

'Give us more grog,' they cried, 'for it will be
    All one an hour hence.' Juan answered, 'No!
'Tis true that death awaits both you and me,
    But let us die like men, not sink below
Like brutes.' And thus his dangerous post kept he,   285
    And none liked to anticipate the blow,
And even Pedrillo, his most reverend tutor,
Was for some rum a disappointed suitor.

37

The good old gentleman was quite aghast
    And made a loud and pious lamentation,   290
Repented all his sins, and made a last
    Irrevocable vow of reformation:
Nothing should tempt him more (this peril past)
    To quit his academic occupation
In cloisters of the classic Salamanca,[373]   295
To follow Juan's wake like Sancho Panca.[374]

---

[372] *more mischief . . . done*: i.e., the men would all have gotten drunk.

[373] *Salamanca*: city in western Spain and home to the most prestigious university (founded in 1218) in that country.

[374] *Sancho Panca*: in *Don Quixote* (1605) by Don Miguel de Cervantes (1548–1616), the servant and boon companion of the titular hero.

38

But now there came a flash of hope once more;
    Day broke, and the wind lulled. The masts were gone,
The leak increased, shoals round her, but no shore;
    The vessel swam, yet still she held her own.   300
They tried the pumps again, and though before
    Their desperate efforts seemed all useless grown,
A glimpse of sunshine set some hands to bale;
The stronger pumped, the weaker thrummed a sail.

39

Under the vessel's keel[375] the sail was past,   305
    And for the moment it had some effect;
But with a leak and not a stick of mast
    Nor rag of canvas, what could they expect?
But still 'tis best to struggle to the last,
    'Tis never too late to be wholly wrecked.   310
And though 'tis true that man can only die once,
'Tis not so pleasant in the Gulf of Lyons.[376]

40

There winds and waves had hurled them, and from thence
    Without their will they carried them away,
For they were forced with steering to dispense,   315
    And never had as yet a quiet day
On which they might repose, or even commence
    A jury mast[377] or rudder, or could say
The ship would swim an hour, which, by good luck
Still swam—though not exactly like a duck.   320

---

[375] *keel*: a central structural element of the hull of a ship.
[376] *Gulf of Lyons*: the Gulf of Lion, on the southeastern Mediterranean coast of France.
[377] *jury mast*: a "jury-rigged", or temporary replacement, mast.

41

The wind in fact perhaps was rather less,
    But the ship laboured so, they scarce could hope
To weather out much longer. The distress
    Was also great with which they had to cope
For want of water, and their solid mess   325
    Was scant enough. In vain the telescope
Was used; nor sail nor shore appeared in sight,
Nought but the heavy sea and coming night.

42

Again the weather threatened, again blew
    A gale, and in the fore and after hold[378]   330
Water appeared; yet, though the people knew
    All this, the most were patient, and some bold,
Until the chains and leathers were worn through
    Of all our pumps. A wreck complete she rolled
At mercy of the waves, whose mercies are   335
Like human beings during civil war.

43

Then came the carpenter, at last, with tears
    In his rough eyes and told the captain he
Could do no more. He was a man in years
    And long had voyaged through many a stormy sea,   340
And if he wept at length, they were not fears
    That made his eyelids as a woman's be,
But he, poor fellow, had a wife and children,
Two things for dying people quite bewildering.

44

The ship was evidently settling now   345
    Fast by the head; and all distinction gone,

[378] fore . . . hold: the fore (front) and after (back) spaces for cargo storage.

Some went to prayers again and made a vow
    Of candles to their saints,[379] but there were none
To pay them with; and some looked o'er the bow;
    Some hoisted out the boats; and there was one   350
That begged Pedrillo for an absolution,[380]
Who told him to be damned—in his confusion.

45

Some lashed them in their hammocks; some put on
    Their best clothes, as if going to a fair;
Some cursed the day on which they saw the sun   355
    And gnashed their teeth and howling tore their hair;
And others went on as they had begun,
    Getting the boats out, being well aware
That a tight boat will live in a rough sea,
Unless with breakers close beneath her lee.[381]   360

46

The worst of all was that in their condition,
    Having been several days in great distress,
'Twas difficult to get out such provision
    As now might render their long suffering less.
Men, even when dying, dislike an inanition.[382]   365
    Their stock was damaged by the weather's stress;
Two casks of biscuit and a keg of butter
Were all that could be thrown into the cutter.[383]

---

[379] *vow ... saints*: In their desperation, sailors are driven to attempt negotiating with divine intercessors.

[380] *absolution*: sacramental cleansing from his sins (i.e., in the Sacrament of Confession).

[381] *lee*: the leeward (downwind) side.

[382] *inanition*: lack of nourishment.

[383] *cutter*: a single-masted sailing vessel.

47

But in the longboat[384] they contrived to stow
    Some pounds of bread, though injured by the wet;   370
Water, a twenty gallon cask or so;
    Six flasks of wine. And they contrived to get
A portion of their beef up from below,
    And with a piece of pork moreover met,
But scarce enough to serve them for a luncheon;   375
Then there was rum, eight gallons in a puncheon.

48

The other boats, the yawl and pinnace,[385] had
    Been stove in the beginning of the gale;
And the longboat's condition was but bad,
    As there were but two blankets for a sail   380
And one oar for a mast, which a young lad
    Threw in by good luck over the ship's rail.
And two boats could not hold, far less be stored,
To save one half the people then on board.

49

'Twas twilight and the sunless day went down   385
    Over the waste of waters. Like a veil,
Which if withdrawn would but disclose the frown
    Of one whose hate is masked but to assail,
Thus to their hopeless eyes the night was shown
    And grimly darkled o'er their faces pale   390
And the dim desolate deep. Twelve days had Fear
Been their familiar,[386] and now Death was here.

---

[384] *longboat*: large boat that can be launched from a sailing ship.

[385] *yawl and pinnace*: smaller boats attached to serve the larger (as tenders).

[386] *familiar*: familiar to them or, more specifically, an attendant spirit or close friend.

50

Some trial had been making at a raft
    With little hope in such a rolling sea,
A sort of thing at which one would have laughed,   395
    If any laughter at such times could be,
Unless with people who too much have quaffed[387]
    And have a kind of wild and horrid glee,
Half epileptical[388] and half hysterical.
Their preservation would have been a miracle.   400

51

At half past eight o'clock, booms,[389] hencoops, spars[390]
    And all things for a chance had been cast loose,
That still could keep afloat the struggling tars,[391]
    For yet they strove, although of no great use.
There was no light in heaven but a few stars,   405
    The boats put off o'ercrowded with their crews.
She gave a heel[392] and then a lurch to port,[393]
And going down head foremost—sunk, in short.

52

Then rose from sea to sky the wild farewell,
    Then shrieked the timid, and stood still the brave,   410
Then some leaped overboard with dreadful yell,
    As eager to anticipate their grave.

[387] *quaffed*: drunk.

[388] *epileptical*: stunned and motionless (epilepsy is a neurological disorder characterized by seizures or fits).

[389] *booms*: poles used for a variety of purposes on the ship (e.g., for extending the feet of sails, handling cargo, suspending mooring lines alongside a vessel, pushing a vessel away from wharves).

[390] *spars*: any pole-like structural component on the ship (e.g., the ship's mast, boom, yard, or gaff).

[391] *tars*: "Jack Tar" was a slang term for a sailor used since the seventeenth century, referring to the tarpaulin fabric (containing actual tar) used to make the hats of early sailors.

[392] *gave a heel*: tilted to one side.

[393] *port*: when facing to the forward end of the ship, the left-hand side of the ship.

And the sea yawned around her like a hell,
    And down she sucked with her the whirling wave,
Like one who grapples with his enemy   415
And strives to strangle him before he die.

53

And first one universal shriek there rushed,
    Louder than the loud ocean, like a crash
Of echoing thunder, and then all was hushed,
    Save the wild wind and the remorseless dash   420
Of billows; but at intervals there gushed,
    Accompanied with a convulsive splash,
A solitary shriek, the bubbling cry
Of some strong swimmer in his agony.

54

The boats, as stated, had got off before,   425
    And in them crowded several of the crew.
And yet their present hope was hardly more
    Than what it had been, for so strong it blew
There was slight chance of reaching any shore.
    And then they were too many, though so few,   430
Nine in the cutter, thirty in the boat
Were counted in them when they got afloat.

55

All the rest perished; near two hundred souls
    Had left their bodies. And what's worse, alas,
When over Catholics the ocean rolls,   435
    They must wait several weeks before a mass
Takes off one peck of purgatorial coals,
    Because, till people know what's come to pass,
They won't lay out their money on the dead.
It cost three francs for every mass that's said.[394]   440

[394] *When over Catholics . . . said*: This refers to the practice of pious Catholics to offer up Masses with the prayerful hope of alleviating the process of purification in Purgatory for the dead.

56

Juan got into the longboat and there
   Contrived to help Pedrillo to a place.
It seemed as if they had exchanged their care,
   For Juan wore the magisterial face
Which courage gives, while poor Pedrillo's pair   445
   Of eyes were crying for their owner's case.
Battista, though (a name called shortly Tita),
Was lost by getting at some aqua vita.[395]

57

Pedro, his valet, too he tried to save,
   But the same cause, conducive to his loss,   450
Left him so drunk he jumped into the wave
   As o'er the cutter's edge he tried to cross,
And so he found a wine-and-watery grave.
   They could not rescue him although so close,
Because the sea ran higher every minute,   455
And for the boat—the crew kept crowding in it.

58

A small old spaniel, which had been Don Jóse's,
   His father's, whom he loved as ye may think
(For on such things the memory reposes
   With tenderness), stood howling on the brink,   460
Knowing (dogs have such intellectual noses),
   No doubt the vessel was about to sink.
And Juan caught him up and ere he stepped
Off threw him in, then after him he leaped.

---

[395] *aqua vita:* (translated literally, the "water of life"); strong distilled alcohol such as whiskey or brandy.

59

He also stuffed his money where he could 465
    About his person and Pedrillo's too,
Who let him do in fact whate'er he would,
    Not knowing what himself to say or do,
As every rising wave his dread renewed.
    But Juan, trusting they might still get through 470
And deeming there were remedies for any ill,
Thus re-embarked his tutor and his spaniel.

60

'Twas a rough night and blew so stiffly yet
    That the sail was becalmed between the seas,
Though on the wave's high top too much to set, 475
    They dared not take it in for all the breeze.
Each sea curled o'er the stern and kept them wet
    And made them bail without a moment's ease,
So that themselves as well as hopes were damped,
And the poor little cutter quickly swamped. 480

61

Nine souls more went in her. The longboat still
    Kept above water, with an oar for mast.
Two blankets stitched together, answering ill
    Instead of sail, were to the oar made fast.
Though every wave rolled menacing to fill, 485
    And present peril all before surpassed,
They grieved for those who perished with the cutter,
And also for the biscuit casks and butter.

62

The sun rose red and fiery, a sure sign
    Of the continuance of the gale. To run 490
Before the sea until it should grow fine
    Was all that for the present could be done.

A few teaspoonfuls of their rum and wine
    Were served out to the people, who begun
To faint, and damaged bread wet through the bags.   495
And most of them had little clothes but rags.

63

They counted thirty, crowded in a space
    Which left scarce room for motion or exertion.
They did their best to modify their case;
    One half sate up, though numbed with the immersion   500
While t'other half were laid down in their place,
    At watch and watch. Thus, shivering like the tertian
Ague[396] in its cold fit, they filled their boat,
With nothing but the sky for a greatcoat.

64

'Tis very certain the desire of life   505
    Prolongs it; this is obvious to physicians,
When patients, neither plagued with friends nor wife,
    Survive through very desperate conditions,
Because they still can hope, nor shines the knife
    Nor shears of Atropos[397] before their visions.   510
Despair of all recovery spoils longevity,
And makes men's miseries of alarming brevity.

65

'Tis said that persons living on annuities[398]
    Are longer lived than others, God knows why,

---

[396] *tertian / Ague*: a form of malaria (characterized by feverous shivering). See footnote 14, page 4 (on ague).

[397] *Atropos*: in classical mythology, one of the three Fates, who cuts the thread of a man's destiny with her shears.

[398] *annuities*: An annuity is a fixed sum of money paid to someone each year, typically for the rest of his life.

Unless to plague the grantors;[399] yet so true it is,   515
   That some, I really think, do never die.
Of any creditors the worst a Jew it is,
   And that's their mode of furnishing supply.
In my young days they lent me cash that way,
Which I found very troublesome to pay.   520

66

'Tis thus with people in an open boat;
   They live upon the love of life and bear
More than can be believed or even thought,
   And stand like rocks the tempest's wear and tear.
And hardship still has been the sailor's lot,   525
   Since Noah's ark[400] went cruising here and there.
She had a curious crew as well as cargo,
Like the first old Greek privateer, the *Argo*.[401]

67

But man is a carnivorous production
   And must have meals, at least one meal a day.   530
He cannot live like woodcocks upon suction,
   But like the shark and tiger must have prey.
Although his anatomical construction
   Bears vegetables in a grumbling way,
Your labouring people think beyond all question,   535
Beef, veal, and mutton better for digestion.

[399] *grantors*: people or institution making the grant or conveyance.

[400] *Noah's ark*: As the Bible memorably retells, Noah, the last righteous man, was spared by God from the cleansing power of the Flood and sailed forty days and forty nights in an ark with his family and a male and female of every living creature (see Gen 6–8).

[401] Argo: in classical mythology, the boat (built by Argus) of the hero Jason and his Argonauts (sailors and fellow adventurers) in their quest for the Golden Fleece.

68

And thus it was with this our hapless crew,
    For on the third day there came on a calm,
And though at first their strength it might renew,
    And lying on their weariness like balm,   540
Lulled them like turtles sleeping on the blue[402]
    Of ocean, when they woke they felt a qualm
And fell all ravenously on their provision,[403]
Instead of hoarding it with due precision.

69

The consequence was easily foreseen: 545
    They ate up all they had and drank their wine
In spite of all remonstrances, and then
    On what in fact next day were they to dine?
They hoped the wind would rise, these foolish men,
    And carry them to shore. These hopes were fine,   550
But as they had but one oar, and that brittle,
It would have been more wise to save their victual.[404]

70

The fourth day came, but not a breath of air,
    And ocean slumbered like an unweaned child.
The fifth day, and their boat lay floating there,   555
    The sea and sky were blue and clear and mild.
With their one oar (I wish they had had a pair)
    What could they do? And hunger's rage grew wild,
So Juan's spaniel, spite of his entreating,
Was killed and portioned out for present eating.   560

---

[402] *turtles . . . blue*: Sea turtles can indeed sleep on the surface of the water or down at the bottom of the ocean.

[403] *provision*: i.e., food.

[404] *victual*: i.e., food.

71

On the sixth day they fed upon his hide,
    And Juan, who had still refused, because
The creature was his father's dog that died,
    Now feeling all the vulture in his jaws,[405]
With some remorse received (though first denied)   565
    As a great favour one of the forepaws,
Which he divided with Pedrillo, who
Devoured it, longing for the other too.

72

The seventh day and no wind. The burning sun
    Blistered and scorched, and, stagnant on the sea   570
They lay like carcasses, and hope was none,
    Save in the breeze that came not. Savagely
They glared upon each other. All was done,
    Water and wine and food, and you might see
The longings of the cannibal arise   575
(Although they spoke not) in their wolfish eyes.

73

At length one whispered his companion, who
    Whispered another, and thus it went around,
And then into a hoarser murmur grew,
    An ominous and wild and desperate sound,   580
And when his comrade's thought each sufferer knew,
    'Twas but his own, suppressed till now, he found.
And out they spoke of lots for flesh and blood,
And who should die to be his fellow's food.

---

[405] *vulture . . . jaws*: He is so hungry he is turned vulturous and is willing to feast on the dead.

74

But ere they came to this, they that day shared   585
    Some leathern caps and what remained of shoes;
And when they looked around them and despaired,
    And none to be the sacrifice would choose.
At length the lots were torn up and prepared,
    But of materials that much shock the Muse.[406]   590
Having no paper, for the want of better,
They took by force from Juan Julia's letter.

75

The lots were made and marked and mixed and handed
    In silent horror, and their distribution
Lulled even the savage hunger which demanded,   595
    Like the Promethean vulture,[407] this pollution.
None in particular had sought or planned it;
    'Twas nature gnawed them to this resolution,
By which none were permitted to be neuter,
And the lot fell on Juan's luckless tutor.   600

76

He but requested to be bled to death.
    The surgeon had his instruments and bled
Pedrillo, and so gently ebbed his breath
    You hardly could perceive when he was dead.
He died as born, a Catholic in faith,   605
    Like most in the belief in which they're bred,
And first a little crucifix he kissed,
And then held out his jugular and wrist.

---

[406] *Muse*: i.e., the muse that inspired his romantic correspondence with Julia.
[407] *Promethean vulture*: in classical mythology, the beast that fed daily on the liver of Prometheus. See footnote 44, page 16 (on Prometheus).

77

The surgeon, as there was no other fee,
    Had his first choice of morsels for his pains,   610
But being thirstiest at the moment, he
    Preferred a draught from the fast-flowing veins.
Part was divided, part thrown in the sea,
    And such things as the entrails and the brains
Regaled two sharks who followed o'er the billow.   615
The sailors ate the rest of poor Pedrillo.

78

The sailors ate him, all save three or four,
    Who were not quite so fond of animal food.
To these was added Juan, who, before
    Refusing his own spaniel, hardly could   620
Feel now his appetite increased much more.
    'Twas not to be expected that he should,
Even in extremity of their disaster,
Dine with them on his pastor and his master.

79

'Twas better that he did not, for in fact   625
    The consequence was awful in the extreme.
For they who were most ravenous in the act
    Went raging mad. Lord! how they did blaspheme
And foam and roll, with strange convulsions racked,
    Drinking salt water like a mountain stream,   630
Tearing and grinning, howling, screeching, swearing,
And with hyena laughter died despairing.

80

Their numbers were much thinned by this infliction,
    And all the rest were thin enough, heaven knows,
And some of them had lost their recollection,   635
    Happier than they who still perceived their woes,
But others pondered on a new dissection,
    As if not warned sufficiently by those
Who had already perished, suffering madly,
For having used their appetites so sadly.   640

81

And next they thought upon the master's mate
    As fattest, but he saved himself, because,
Besides being much averse from such a fate,
    There were some other reasons: the first was
He had been rather indisposed of late,   645
    And that which chiefly proved his saving clause
Was a small present made to him at Cadiz,
By general subscription of the ladies.[408]

82

Of poor Pedrillo something still remained,
    But was used sparingly. Some were afraid,   650
And others still their appetites constrained,
    Or but at times a little supper made;
All except Juan, who throughout abstained,
    Chewing a piece of bamboo and some lead,
At length they caught two boobies and a noddy,[409]   655
And then they left off eating the dead body.

---

[408] *small present . . . ladies*: i.e., a "pox", a sexually transmitted disease (probably syphilis), popularly believed to cause madness.
[409] *boobies . . . noddy*: seabirds.

83

And if Pedrillo's fate should shocking be,
  Remember Ugolino[410] condescends
To eat the head of his archenemy,
  The moment after he politely ends   660
His tale. If foes be food in hell, at sea
  'Tis surely fair to dine upon our friends
When shipwreck's short allowance grows too scanty,
Without being much more horrible than Dante.

84

And the same night there fell a shower of rain,   665
  For which their mouths gaped like the cracks of earth
When dried to summer dust. Till taught by pain,
  Men really know not what good water's worth.
If you had been in Turkey or in Spain,[411]
  Or with a famished boat's crew had your berth,   670
Or in the desert heard the camel's bell,
You'd wish yourself where truth is—in a well.[412]

---

[410] *Ugolino*: Count Ugolino della Gherardesca (c. 1220–1289), frequently accused of treason, was betrayed by Archbishop Ruggieri degli Ubaldini and condemned to starve to death with his two sons and two grandsons. Both Ugolino and Ruggieri are described by Dante Alighieri (1265–1321), Italian poet and author of *The Divine Comedy*, as suffering in a circle of Hell where Ugolino constantly gnaws at his betrayer's skull:

> I saw two shades frozen in a single hole
> packed so close, one head hooded the other one;
> the way the starving devour their bread, the soul
> above had clenched the other with his teeth
> where the brain meets the nape. (Cantos 32–33)

[411] *Turkey . . . Spain*: i.e., hot, dry regions around the Mediterranean.
[412] *truth . . . well*: This expression, placing truth in a well, has classical origins.

85

It poured down torrents, but they were no richer
    Until they found a ragged piece of sheet,
Which served them as a sort of spongy pitcher,   675
    And when they deemed its moisture was complete,
They wrung it out, and though a thirsty ditcher
    Might not have thought the scanty draught so sweet
As a full pot of porter, to their thinking
They ne'er till now had known the joys of drinking.   680

86

And their baked lips, with many a bloody crack,
    Sucked in the moisture, which like nectar streamed.
Their throats were ovens, their swoll'n tongues were black,
    As the rich man's in hell, who vainly screamed
To beg the beggar, who could not rain back   685
    A drop of dew, when every drop had seemed
To taste of heaven.[413] If this be true, indeed
Some Christians have a comfortable creed.

87

There were two fathers in this ghastly crew
    And with them their two sons, of whom the one   690
Was more robust and hardy to the view,
    But he died early, and when he was gone,
He nearest messmate told his sire, who threw
    One glance at him and said, 'Heaven's will be done!
I can do nothing,' and he saw him thrown   695
Into the deep without a tear or groan.

88

The other father had a weaklier child,
    Of a soft cheek and aspect delicate,

---

[413] *the rich man's . . . heaven*: See the parable of the rich man and the beggar Lazarus (Luke 16:19–31), where the rich man begs Father Abraham to send Lazarus with cooling water but is refused.

But the boy bore up long and with a mild
   And patient spirit held aloof his fate.   700
Little he said and now and then he smiled,
   As if to win a part from off the weight
He saw increasing on his father's heart,
With the deep deadly thought that they must part.

89

And o'er him bent his sire and never raised   705
   His eyes from off his face, but wiped the foam
From his pale lips, and ever on him gazed,
   And when the wished-for shower at length was come,
And the boy's eyes, which the dull film half glazed,
   Brightened and for a moment seemed to roam,   710
He squeezed from out a rag some drops of rain
Into his dying child's mouth—but in vain.

90

The boy expired. The father held the clay
   And looked upon it long, and when at last
Death left no doubt, and the dead burden lay   715
   Stiff on his heart, and pulse and hope were past,
He watched it wistfully, until away
   'Twas borne by the rude wave wherein 'twas cast.
Then he himself sunk down all dumb and shivering,
And gave no sign of life, save his limbs quivering.   720

91

Now overhead a rainbow, bursting through
   The scattering clouds, shone, spanning the dark sea,
Resting its bright base on the quivering blue,
   And all with its arch appeared to be
Clearer than that without, and its wide hue   725
   Waxed broad and waving, like a banner free,
Then changed like to a bow that's bent, and then
Forsook the dim eyes of these shipwrecked men.

92

It changed of course—a heavenly chameleon,
     The airy child of vapour and the sun,   730
Brought forth in purple, cradled in vermilion,[414]
     Baptized in molten gold and swathed in dun,[415]
Glittering like crescents o'er a Turk's pavilion
     And blending every colour into one,
Just like a black eye in a recent scuffle   735
(For sometimes we must box without the muffle).[416]

93

Our shipwrecked seamen thought it a good omen;
     It is as well to think so now and then.
'Twas an old custom of the Greek and Roman,
     And may become of great advantage when   740
Folks are discouraged; and most surely no men
     Had greater need to nerve themselves again
Than these, and so this rainbow looked like hope,
Quite a celestial kaleidoscope.

94

About this time a beautiful white bird,   745
     Webfooted, not unlike a dove in size[417]
And plumage (probably it might have erred
     Upon its course), passed oft before their eyes

---

[414] *vermilion*: orange-red.

[415] *dun*: drab, dull gray-yellow.

[416] *box ... muffle*: Mufflers or leather gloves were introduced into the sport of boxing during the mid-eighteenth century.

[417] *beautiful white bird ... size*: This bird combines two particular images: the albatross (believed to be a good omen for sailors) that comes into Samuel Taylor Coleridge's *Rime of the Ancient Mariner* (a highly influential shipwreck poem with profound influence on Byron in this canto), and the dove that brought Noah the olive branch signifying the end of the great Flood (see Gen 8:11).

And tried to perch, although it saw and heard
   The men within the boat, and in this guise   750
It came and went and fluttered round them till
Night fell. This seemed a better omen still.

95

But in this case I also must remark,
   'Twas well this bird of promise did not perch,
Because the tackle of our shattered bark   755
   Was not so safe for roosting as a church,
And had it been the dove from Noah's ark,
   Returning there from her successful search,
Which in their way that moment chanced to fall,
They would have eat her, olive branch and all.   760

96

With twilight it again came on to blow,
   But not with violence. The stars shown out,
The boat made way; yet now they were so low
   They knew not where nor what they were about.
Some fancied they saw land, and some said 'No!'   765
   The frequent fog banks gave them cause to doubt.
Some swore that they heard breakers, others guns,   .
And all mistook about the latter once.

97

As morning broke the light wind died away,
   When he who had the watch sung out and swore,   770
If 'twas not land that rose with the sun's ray,
   He wished that land he never might see more.
And the rest rubbed their eyes and say a bay
   Or thought they saw, and shaped their course for shore,
For shore it was and gradually grew   775
Distinct and high and palpable to view.

98

And then of these some part burst into tears,
    And others, looking with a stupid stare,
Could not yet separate their hopes from fears
    And seemed as if they had no further care,   780
While a few prayed (the first time for some years).
    And at the bottom of the boat three were
Asleep; they shook them by the hand and head
And tried to awaken them, but found them dead.

99

The day before, fast sleeping on the water,   785
    They found a turtle of the hawksbill kind,[418]
And by good fortune gliding softly, caught her,
    Which yielded a day's life and to their mind
Proved even still a more nutritious matter,
    Because it left encouragement behind.   790
They thought that in such perils more than chance
Had sent them this for their deliverance.

100

The land appeared a high and rocky coast,
    And higher grew the mountains as they drew,
Set by a current, toward it. They were lost   795
    In various conjectures, for none knew
To what part of the earth they had been tost,
    So changeable had been the winds that blew.
Some thought it was Mount Etna,[419] some the highlands
Of Candia, Cyprus, Rhodes, or other islands.[420]   800

---

[418] *turtle . . . kind*: The hawksbill sea turtle primarily lives in shallow lagoons and coral reefs but can sometimes be seen in the open ocean.

[419] *Mount Etna*: the largest active volcano in Europe, located on the east coast of Sicily.

[420] *Candia . . . islands*: Greek islands in the eastern Mediterranean and Aegean Seas (Candia is another name for Crete, the largest of the Greek islands).

101

Meantime the current, with a rising gale,
    Still set them onwards to the welcome shore,
Like Charon's bark of spectres,[421] dull and pale.
    Their living freight was now reduced to four,
And three dead, whom their strength could not avail   805
    To heave into the deep with those before,
Though the two sharks still followed them and dashed
The spray into their faces as they splashed.

102

Famine, despair, cold, thirst, and heat had done
    Their work on them by turns, and thinned them to   810
Such things a mother had not known her son
    Amidst the skeletons of that gaunt crew.
By night chilled, by day scorched, thus one by one
    They perished, until withered to these few,
But chiefly by a species of self-slaughter,   815
In washing down Pedrillo with salt water.

103

As they drew nigh the land, which now was seen
    Unequal in its aspect here and there,
They felt the freshness of its growing green,
    That waved in forest-tops and smoothed the air,   820
And fell upon their glazed eyes like a screen
    From glistening waves and skies so hot and bare.
Lovely seemed any object that should sweep
Away the vast, salt, dread, eternal deep.

---

[421]*Charon's . . . spectres*: In classical mythology, Charon is the boatman of the underworld, bearing dead souls across the River Styx.

104

The shore lookd wild without a trace of man   825
 And girt by formidable waves; but they
Were mad for land, and thus their course they ran,
 Though right ahead the roaring breakers[422] lay.
A reef[423] between them also now began
 To show its boiling surf and bounding spray,   830
But finding no place for their landing better,
They ran the boat for shore and overset[424] her.

105

But in his native stream, the Guadalquivir,
 Juan to lave[425] his youthful limbs was wont;
And having learnt to swim in that sweet river,   835
 Had often turned the art to some account.
A better swimmer you could scarce see ever,
 He could perhaps have passed the Hellespont,
As once (a feat on which ourselves we prided)
Leander, Mr Ekenhead, and I did.[426]   840

106

So here, though faint, emaciated, and stark,
 He buoyed his boyish limbs and strove to ply
With the quick wave and gain, ere it was dark,
 The beach which lay before him, high and dry.

---

[422] *breakers*: heavy sea waves breaking into white foam on the shore or any submerged ridges on the shallow ocean floor.

[423] *reef*: ridge of jagged rock, coral, or sand just above or below the surface of the sea.

[424] *overset*: flipped.

[425] *lave*: bathe.

[426] *passed . . . I did*: On May 3, 1810, Byron and Lieutenant Ekenhead (a marine of the HMS *Salsette*) swam the Hellespont. Cf. "Written after Swimming from Sestos to Abydos", page 4.

The greatest danger here was from a shark,   845
    That carried off his neighbour by the thigh.
As for the other two they could not swim,
So nobody arrived on shore but him.

107

Nor yet had he arrived but for the oar,
    Which providentially for him was washed   850
Just as his feeble arms could strike no more,
    And the hard wave o'erwhelmed him as 'twas dashed
Within his grasp. He clung to it, and sore
    The waters beat while he thereto was lashed.
At last with swimming, wading, scrambling, he   855
Rolled on the beach, half senseless, from the sea.

108

There breathless, with his digging nails he clung
    Fast to the sand, lest the returning wave,
From whose reluctant roar his life he wrung,
    Should suck him back to her insatiate grave.   860
And there he lay full length, where he was flung,
    Before the entrance of a cliff-worn cave,
With just enough of life to feel its pain
And deem that it was saved, perhaps in vain.

109

With slow and staggering effort he arose,   865
    But sunk again upon his bleeding knee
And quivering hand; and then he looked for those
    Who long had been his mates upon the sea,
But none of them appeared to share his woes,
    Save one, a corpse from out the famished three,   870
Who died two days before and now had found
An unknown barren beach for burial ground.

110

And as he gazed, his dizzy brain spun fast
 And down he sunk, and as he sunk, the sand
Swam round and round, and all his senses passed. 875
 He fell upon his side, and his stretched hand
Drooped dripping on the oar (their jury mast),
 And, like a withered lily, on the land
His slender frame and pallid aspect lay,
As fair a thing as e'er was formed of clay. 880

111

How long in his damp trance young Juan lay
 He knew not, for the earth was gone for him,
And time had nothing more of night nor day
 For his congealing blood and senses dim.
And how this heavy faintness passed away 885
 He knew not, till each painful pulse and limb
And tingling vein seemed throbbing back to life,
For Death, though vanquished, still retired with strife.

112

His eyes he opened, shut, again unclosed,
 For all was doubt and dizziness. He thought 890
He still was in the boat and had but dozed,
 And felt again with his despair o'erwrought,
And wished it death in which he had reposed,
 And then once more his feelings back were brought,
And slowly by his swimming eyes was seen 895
A lovely female face of seventeen.

113

'Twas bending close o'er his, and the small mouth
 Seemed almost prying into his for breath.
And chafing him, the soft warm hand of youth
 Recalled his answering spirits back from death, 900

And, bathing his chill temples tried to soothe
    Each pulse to animation, till beneath
Its gentle touch and trembling care, a sigh
To these kind efforts made a low reply.

114

Then was the cordial poured, and mantle flung   905
    Around his scarce-clad limbs; and the fair arm
Raised higher the faint head which o'er it hung.
    And her transparent cheek, all pure and warm,
Pillowed his death-like forehead. Then she wrung
    His dewy curls, long drenched by every storm,   910
And watched with eagerness each throb that drew
A sigh from his heaved bosom—and hers too.

115

And lifting him with care into the cave,
    The gentle girl and her attendant—one
Young, yet her elder, and of brow less grave,   915
    And more robust of figure—then begun
To kindle fire, and as the new flames gave
    Light to the rocks that roofed them, which the sun
Had never seen, the maid or whatso'er
She was appeared distinct and tall and fair.   920

116

Her brow was overhung with coins of gold,
    That sparkled o'er the auburn of her hair,
Her clustering hair, whose longer locks were rolled
    In braids behind, and though her stature were
Even of the highest for a female mould,   925
    They nearly reached her heel. And in her air
There was a something which bespoke command,
As one who was a lady in the land.

117

Her hair, I said, was auburn, but her eyes
    Were black as death, their lashes the same hue,   930
Of downcast length, in whose silk shadow lies
    Deepest attraction, for when to the view
Forth from its raven fringe the full glance flies,
    Ne'er with such force the swiftest arrow flew.
'Tis as the snake late coiled, who pours his length   935
And hurls at once his venom and his strength.

118

Her brow was white and low, her cheek's pure dye
    Like twilight rosy still with the set sun.
Short upper lip—sweet lips! that make us sigh
    Ever to have seen such; for she was one   940
Fit for the model of a statuary
    (A race of mere imposters, when all's done;
I've seen much finer women, ripe and real,
Than all the nonsense of their stone ideal).

119

I'll tell you why I say so, for 'tis just   945
    One should not rail without a decent cause.
There was an Irish lady, to whose bust
    I ne'er saw justice done, and yet she was
A frequent model; and if e'er she must
    Yeild to stern Time and Nature's wrinkling laws,   950
They will destroy a face which mortal thought
Ne'er compassed, nor less mortal chisel wrought.

120

And such was she, the lady of the cave.
    Her dress was very different from the Spanish,
Simpler and yet of colours not so grave,   955
    For as you know, the Spanish women banish

Bright hues when out of doors, and yet, while wave
    Around them (what I hope will never vanish)
The *basquina* and the mantilla,[427] they
Seem at the same time mystical and gay.   960

121

But with our damsel this was not the case;
    Her dress was many-coloured, finely spun.
Her locks curled negligently round her face,
    But through them gold and gems profusely shone.
Her girdle sparkled, and the richest lace   965
    Flowed in her veil, and many a precious stone
Flashed on her little hand, but what was shocking,
Her small snow feet had slippers, but no stocking.[428]

122

The other female's dress was not unlike,
    But of inferior materials. She   970
Had not so many ornaments to strike,
    Her hair had silver only, bound to be
Her dowry, and her veil, in form alike,
    Was coarser, and her air, though firm, less free.
Her hair was thicker, but less long, her eyes   975
As black, but quicker and of smaller size.

123

And these two tended him and cheered him both
    With food and raiment and those soft attentions,
Which are (as I must own) of female growth,
    And have ten thousand delicate inventions.   980

---

[427] *basquina ... mantilla*: A basquiña is a kind of skirt, and a mantilla is a lace or silk veil or shawl worn over the head and the shoulders (often over a tall comb)—each indicative of a fashionable Spanish style of dress.

[428] *slippers ... stocking*: Spanish ladies would certainly not have been seen barelegged in public.

They made a most superior mess of broth,
    A thing which poesy but seldom mentions,
But the best dish that e'er was cooked since Homer's
Achilles ordered dinner for newcomers.[429]

124

I'll tell you who they were, this female pair,   985
    Lest they should seem princesses in disguise.
Besides I hate all mystery and that air
    Of claptrap, which your recent poets prize.
And so in short the girls they really were
    They shall appear before your curious eyes,   990
Mistress and maid; the first was only daughter
Of an old man, who lived upon the water.

125

A fisherman he had been in his youth,
    And still a sort of fisherman was he.
But other speculations were, in sooth,   995
    Added to his connexion to the sea,
Perhaps not so respectable, in truth.
    A little smuggling and some piracy
Left him at last the sole of many masters
Of an ill-gotten million of piastres.[430]   1000

---

[429] *Homer's . . . newcomers*: In book 9 of the epic poem *The Iliad* by Homer (the greatest classical Greek poet, living circa eighth century B.C.), the Achaean hero Achilles presents a splendid feast before the men who have come to plead with him to return to battle against the Trojans.

[430] *piastres*: "pieces of eight" or "pesos", units of currency used throughout the Mediterranean (particularly associated with Spain, Latin America, and Turkey).

126

A fisher therefore was he, though of men,
  Like Peter the Apostle,[431] and he fished
For wandering merchant vessels now and then
  And sometimes caught as many as he wished.
The cargoes he confiscated, and gain   1005
  He sought in the slave market too and dished
Full many a morsel for that Turkish trade,
By which no doubt a good deal may be made.

127

He was a Greek, and on his isle had built
  (One of the wild and smaller Cyclades)[432]   1010
A very handsome house from out his guilt,
  And there he lived exceedingly at ease.
Heaven knows what cash he got or blood he spilt;
  A sad old fellow was he, if you please.
But this I know, it was a spacious building,   1015
Full of barbaric carving, paint, and gilding.

128

He had an only daughter, called Haidée,
  The greatest heiress of the Eastern Isles;
Besides, so very beautiful was she
  Her dowry was as nothing to her smiles.   1020
Still in her teens, and like a lovely tree
  She grew to womanhood, and between whiles
Rejected several suitors, just to learn
How to accept a better in his turn.

---

[431] *Peter the Apostle*: When Jesus called the fisherman Peter and his fellows to be his apostles, he bade him: "Follow me, and I will make you fishers of men" (Matthew 4:19).
[432] *Cyclades*: group of Greek islands in the Aegean Sea, southeast of mainland Greece.

129

And walking out upon the beach below   1025
    The cliff, towards sunset, on that day she found,
Insensible, not dead, but nearly so,
    Don Juan, almost famished, and half drowned.
But being naked, she was shocked, you know,
    Yet deemed herself in common pity bound,   1030
As far as in her lay, 'to take him in,
A stranger'[433] dying, with so white a skin.

130

But taking him into her father's house
    Was not exactly the best way to save,
But like conveying to the cat the mouse,   1035
    Or people in a trance into their grave,
Because the good old man had so much νους.[434]
    Unlike the honest Arab thieves so brave,
He would have hospitably cured the stranger
And sold him instantly when out of danger.   1040

131

And therefore with her maid she thought it best
    (A virgin always on her maid relies)
To place him in the cave for present rest.
    And when at last he opened his black eyes,
Their charity increased about their guest,   1045
    And their compassion grew to such a size
It opened half the turnpike gates to heaven
(St Paul says 'tis the toll which must be given).

---

[433] *'to take . . . stranger'*: See Matthew 25:35: "I was a stranger, and ye took me in" (KJV).
[434] νους: Greek, meaning "mind or spirit", "native intuition or intelligence" (common sense).

132

They made a fire, but such a fire as they
  Upon the moment could contrive with such   1050
Materials as were cast up round the bay,
  Some broken planks and oars, that to the touch
Were nearly tinder, since so long they lay;
  A mast was almost crumbled to a crutch,
But by God's grace, here wrecks were in such plenty   1055
That there was fuel to have furnished twenty.

133

He had a bed of furs and a pelisse,[435]
  For Haidée stripped her sables off to make
His couch, and that he might be more at ease
  And warm, in case by chance he should awake,   1060
They also gave a petticoat apiece,
  She and her maid, and promised by daybreak
To pay him a fresh visit with a dish
For breakfast of eggs, coffee, bread, and fish.

134

And thus they left him to his lone repose.   1065
  Juan slept like a top or like the dead,
Who sleep at last perhaps (God only knows),
  Juan for the present. And in his lulled head
Not even a vision of his former woes
  Throbbed in accursèd dreams, which sometimes
      spread   1070
Unwelcome visions of our former years,
Till the eye, cheated, opens thick with tears.

[435] *pelisse*: long fur coat.

135

Young Juan slept all dreamless, but the maid,[436]
 Who smoothed his pillow as she left the den,
Looked back upon him and a moment stayed   1075
 And turned, believing that he called again.
He slumbered, yet she thought, at least she said
 (The heart will slip even as the tongue and pen),
He had pronounced her name, but she forgot
That at this moment Juan knew it not.   1080

136

And pensive to her father's house she went,
 Enjoining silence strict to Zoe, who
Better than her knew what in fact she meant,
 She being wiser by a year or two.
A year or two's an age when rightly spent,   1085
 And Zoe spent hers, as most women do,
In gaining all that useful sort of knowledge
Which is acquired in Nature's good old college.

137

The morn broke, and found Juan slumbering still
 Fast in his cave, and nothing clashed upon   1090
His rest. The rushing of the neighbouring rill[437]
 And the young beams of the excluded sun
Troubled him not, and he might sleep his fill.
 And need he had of slumber yet, for none
Had suffered more; his hardships were comparative   1095
To those related in my grand-dad's narrative.[438]

---

[436] *maid*: i.e., Haidée.

[437] *rill*: very small brook.

[438] *my . . . narrative*: Admiral John "Foulweather Jack" Byron (1723–1786), Byron's grandfather, was shipwrecked as a midshipman off the coast of Chile in 1740, returning to England in 1746, and wrote a popular account of his sufferings and adventures (published in 1768).

138

Not so Haidée; she sadly tossed and tumbled
    And started from her sleep, and turning o'er,
Dreamed of a thousand wrecks, o'er which she stumbled,
    And handsome corpses strewed upon the shore,   1100
And woke her maid so early that she grumbled,
    And called her father's old slaves up, who swore
In several oaths—Armenian, Turk, and Greek—
They knew not what to think of such a freak.[439]

139

But up she got and up she made them get,   1105
    With some pretence about the sun, that makes
Sweet skies just when he rises or is set.
    And 'tis no doubt a sight to see when breaks
Bright Phoebus[440] while the mountains still are wet
    With mist, and every bird with him awakes,   1110
And night is flung off like a mourning suit
Worn for a husband, or some other brute.

140

I say, the sun is a most glorious sight,
    I've seen him rise full oft; indeed of late
I have sate up on purpose all the night,   1115
    Which hastens, as physicians say, one's fate.
And so all ye who would be in the right
    In health and purse, begin your day to date
From daybreak, and when coffined at fourscore,[441]
Engrave upon the plate, you rose at four.   1120

---

[439] *freak*: odd behavior, sudden whim.
[440] *Bright Phoebus*: i.e., the sun. In classical mythology, Phoebus Apollo is the god of music, poetry, and the sun.
[441] *fourscore*: eighty years old.

141

And Haidée met the morning face to face.
 Her own was freshest, though a feverish flush
Had dyed it with the headlong blood, whose race
 From heart to cheek is curbed into a blush,
Like to a torrent which a mountain's base,   1125
 That overpowers some alpine river's rush,
Checks to a lake, whose waves in circles spread;
Or the Red Sea[442]—but the sea is not red.

142

And down the cliff the island virgin came,
 And near the cave her quick light footsteps drew, 1130
While the sun smiled on her with his first flame,
 And young Aurora[443] kissed her lips with dew,
Taking her for a sister. Just the same
 Mistake you would have made on seeing the two,
Although the mortal, quite as fresh and fair,   1135
Had all the advantage too of not being air.

143

And when into the cavern Haidée stepped
 All timidly, yet rapidly, she saw
That like an infant Juan sweetly slept.
 And then she stopped, and stood as if in awe   1140
(For sleep is awful) and on tiptoe crept
 And wrapt him closer, lest the air, too raw,
Should reach his blood, then o'er him still as death
Bent, with hushed lips, that drank his scarce drawn breath.

---

[442] *Red Sea*: seawater inlet of the Indian Ocean, located between Africa and Asia and now known as the Arabian Gulf.

[443] *Aurora*: i.e., dawn. In classical mythology, Aurora is the goddess of the dawn.

144

And thus like to an angel o'er the dying   1145
    Who die in righteousness she leaned; and there
All tranquilly the shipwrecked boy was lying,
    As o'er him lay the calm and stirless air.
But Zoe the meantime some eggs was frying,
    Since, after all, no doubt the youthful pair   1150
Must breakfast; and betimes, lest they should ask it,
She drew out her provision from the basket.

145

She knew that the best feelings must have victual,
    And that a shipwrecked youth would hungry be.
Besides, being less in love, she yawned a little   1155
    And felt her veins chilled by the neighbouring sea.
And so she cooked their breakfast to a tittle;[444]
    I can't say that she gave them any tea,
But there were eggs, fruit, coffee, bread, fish, honey,
With Scio[445] wine, and all for love, not money.   1160

146

And Zoe, when the eggs were ready and
    The coffee made, would fain have wakened Juan,
But Haidée stopped her with her quick small hand,
    And without word, a sign her finger drew on
Her lip, which Zoe needs must understand,   1165
    And the first breakfast spoilt, prepared a new one,
Because her mistress would not let her break
That sleep which seemed as it would ne'er awake.

---

[444] *to a tittle*: to the tiniest bit (precisely or perfectly).
[445] *Scio*: Chios, a Greek island.

147

For still he lay, and on his thin worn cheek
　　A purple hectic[446] played like dying day　　　　　1170
On the snow-tops of distant hills. The streak
　　Of sufferance yet upon his forehead lay,
Where the blue veins looked shadowy, shrunk, and weak;
　　And his black curls were dewy with the spray,
Which weighed upon them yet, all damp and salt,　　1175
Mixed with the stony vapours of the vault.

148

And she bent o'er him, and he lay beneath,
　　Hushed as the babe upon its mother's breast,
Drooped as the willow when no winds can breathe,
　　Lulled like the depth of ocean when at rest,　　　1180
Fair as the crowning rose of the whole wreath,
　　Soft as the callow[447] cygnet[448] in its nest.
In short he was a very pretty fellow,
Although his woes had turned him rather yellow.

149

He woke and gazed and would have slept again,　　1185
　　But the fair face which met his eyes forbade
Those eyes to close, though weariness and pain
　　Had further sleep a further pleasure made;
For woman's face was never formed in vain
　　For Juan, so that even when he prayed　　　　　1190
He turned from grisly saints and martyrs hairy
To the sweet portraits of the Virgin Mary.

---

[446] *hectic*: fever, flush.
[447] *callow*: inexperienced, green.
[448] *cygnet*: young swan.

150

And thus upon his elbow he arose
    And looked upon the lady, in whose cheek
The pale contended with the purple rose,   1195
    As with an effort she began to speak.
Her eyes were eloquent, her words would pose,
    Although she told him in good modern Greek
With an Ionian accent,[449] low and sweet,
That he was faint and must not talk, but eat.   1200

151

Now Juan could not understand a word,
    Being no Grecian, but he had an ear,
And her voice was the warble of a bird,
    So soft, so sweet, so delicately clear
That finer, simpler music ne'er was heard,   1205
    The sort of sound we echo with a tear,
Without knowing why, an overpowering tone,
Wence melody descends as from a throne.

152

And Juan gazed as one who is awoke
    By a distant organ, doubting if he be   1210
Not yet a dreamer, till the spell is broke
    By the watchman or some such reality,
Or by one's early valet's cursèd knock.
    At least it is a heavy sound to me,
Who like a morning slumber; for the night   1215
Shows stars and women in a better light.

[449] *Ionian accent*: Ionia was the ancient region (now in Turkey) to the east across the Aegean Sea from Greece, where Eastern Greek was spoken.

153

And Juan too was helped out from his dream
    Or sleep, or whatso'er it was, by feeling
A most prodigious appetite. The steam
    Of Zoe's cookery no doubt was stealing   1220
Upon his senses, and the kindling beam
    Of the new fire, which Zoe kept up, kneeling
To stir her viands, made him quite awake
And long for food, but chiefly a beefsteak.

154

But beef is rare within these oxless isles;   1225
    Goat's flesh there is, no doubt, the kid and mutton.
And when a holiday upon them smiles,
    A joint upon their barbarous spits they put on.
But this occurs but seldom, between whiles,
    For some of these are rocks with scarce a hut on;   1230
Others are fair and fertile, among which
This, though not large, was one of the most rich.

155

I say that beef is rare, and can't help thinking
    That the old fable of the Minotaur[450]—
From which our modern morals, rightly shrinking,   1235
    Condemn the royal lady's taste who wore
A cow's shape for a mask—was only (sinking
    The allegory) a mere type, no more,
That Pasiphae promoted breeding cattle,
To make the Cretans bloodier in battle.   1240

---

[450] *Minotaur*: in classical mythology, creature that was part man (in its body) and part bull (in its head), born of Pasiphaë, the daughter of the Sun, who was cursed by the sea god Poseidon with lust for a white bull.

156

For we all know that English people are
    Fed upon beef. I won't say much of beer,
Because 'tis liquor only, and being far
    From this my subject, it has no business here.
We know too they are very fond of war,   1245
    A pleasure, like all pleasures, rather dear;
So were the Cretans, from which I infer
That beef and battles both were owing to her.

157

But to resume. The languid Juan raised
    His hand upon his elbow and he saw   1250
A sight on which he had not lately gazed,
    As all his latter meals had been quite raw,
Three or four things, for which the Lord he praised,
    And feeling still the famished vulture gnaw,
He fell upon whate'er was offered, like   1255
A priest, a shark, an alderman, or pike.[451]

158

He ate, and he was well supplied, and she,
    Who watched him like a mother, would have fed
Him past all bounds, because she smiled to see
    Such appetite in one she had deemed dead.   1260
But Zoe, being older than Haidée,
    Knew (by tradition, for she ne'er had read)
That famished people must be slowly nurst
And fed by spoonfuls, else they always burst.

[451] *like / A . . . pike*: i.e., all satirically derided as vicious predators here.

159

And so she took the liberty to state,　　　　　　　1265
　　Rather by deeds than words, because the case
Was urgent, that the gentleman whose fate
　　Had made her mistress quit her bed to trace
The seashore at this hour must leave his plate,
　　Unless he wished to die upon the place.　　　　1270
She snatched it and refused another morsel,
Saying, he had gorged enough to make a horse ill.

160

Next they—he being naked, save a tattered
　　Pair of scarce decent trousers—went to work
And in the fire his recent rags they scattered,　　1275
　　And dressed him, for the present, like a Turk
Or Greek; that is, although it not much mattered,
　　Omitting turban, slippers, pistols, dirk,
They furnished him, entire except some stitches,
With a clean shirt and very spacious breeches.　　1280

161

And then fair Haidée tried her tongue at speaking,
　　But not a word could Juan comprehend,
Although he listened so that the young Greek in
　　Her earnestness would ne'er have made an end,
And as he interrupted not, went eking　　　　　　1285
　　Her speech out to her protégé and friend,
Till pausing at the last her breath to take,
She saw he did not understand Romaic.[452]

---

[452] *Romaic:* Greek.

162

And then she had recourse to nods and signs
    And smiles and sparkles of the speaking eye,   1290
And read (the only book she could) the lines
    Of his fair face and found, by sympathy,
The answer eloquent, where the soul shines
    And darts in one quick glance a long reply;
And thus in every look she saw exprest   1295
A world of words, and things at which she guessed.

163

And now by dint of fingers and of eyes
    And words repeated after her, he took
A lesson in her tongue, but by surmise
    No doubt less of her language than her look.   1300
As he who studies fervently the skies
    Turns oftener to the stars than to his book,
Thus Juan learned his alpha beta[453] better
From Haidée's glance than any graven letter.

164

'Tis pleasing to be schooled in a strange tongue   1305
    By female lips and eyes, that is, I mean,
When both the teacher and the taught are young,
    As was the case at least where I have been.
They smile so when one's right, and when one's wrong
    They smile still more, and then there intervene   1310
Pressure of hands, perhaps even a chaste kiss.
I learned the little that I know by this;

---

[453] *alpha beta*: alphabet.

165

That is, some words of Spanish, Turk, and Greek,
   Italian not at all, having no teachers.
Much English I cannot pretend to speak,   1315
   Learning that language chiefly from its preachers,
Barrow, South, Tillotson,[454] whom every week
   I study, also Blair,[455] the highest reachers
Of eloquence in piety and prose.
I hate your poets, so read none of those.   1320

166

As for the ladies, I have nought to say,
   A wanderer from the British world of fashion,
Where I, like other 'dogs, have had my day',[456]
   Like other men too, may have had my passion,
But that, like other things, has passed away,   1325
   And all her fools whom I *could* lay the lash on,
Foes, friends, men, women, now are nought to me
But dreams of what has been, no more to be.

167

Return we to Don Juan. He begun
   To hear new words and to repeat them; but   1330
Some feelings, universal as the sun,
   Were such as could not in his breast be shut
More than within the bosom of a nun.
   He was in love, as you would be no doubt,
With a young benefactress; so was she,   1335
Just in the way we very often see.

---

[454] *Barrow . . . Tillotson*: Isaac Barrow (1630–1677), an English theologian and mathematician; Robert South (1634–1716), an English clergyman; and John Tillotson (1630–1694), archbishop of Canterbury.

[455] *Blair*: Hugh Blair (1718–1800), a Scottish minister and professor of rhetoric at Edinburgh University.

[456] '*dogs . . . day*': See Shakespeare's *Hamlet* (Act 5, scene 1, line 286): "The cat will mew, and dog will have his day."

168

And every day by daybreak, rather early
    For Juan, who was somewhat fond of rest,
She came into the cave, but it was merely
    To see her bird reposing in his nest.   1340
And she would softly stir his locks so curly,
    Without disturbing her yet slumbering guest,
Breathing all the gently o'er his cheek and mouth,
As o'er a bed of roses the sweet south.

169

And every morn his colour freshlier came,   1345
    And every day helped on his convalescence.
'Twas well, because health in the human frame
    Is pleasant, besides being true love's essence,
For health and idleness to passion's flame
    Are oil and gunpowder; and some good lessons   1350
Are also learnt from Ceres[457] and from Bacchus,[458]
Without whom Venus will not long attack us.

170

While Venus fills the heart (without heart really
    Love, though good always, is not quite so good),
Ceres presents a plate of vermicelli   1355
    (For love must be sustained like flesh and blood),
While Bacchus pours out wine or hands a jelly.
    Eggs, oysters too, are amatory food,
But who is their purveyor from above
Heaven knows; it may be Neptune, Pan or Jove.[459]   1360

[457] *Ceres*: in classical mythology, goddess of the harvest.

[458] *Bacchus*: in classical mythology, god of wine.

[459] *Neptune . . . Jove*: in classical mythology, gods of the sea, shepherds and flocks, and the sky and thunder (king of the gods), respectively.

171

When Juan woke he found some good things ready,
    A bath, a breakfast, and the finest eyes
That ever made a youthful heart less steady,
    Besides her maid's, as pretty for their size;
But I have spoken of all this already,   1365
    And repetition's tiresome and unwise.
Well, Juan, after bathing in the sea,
Came always back to coffee and Haidée.

172

Both were so young and one so innocent
    That bathing passed for nothing. Juan seemed   1370
To her, as 'twere, the kind of being sent,
    Of whom these two years she had nightly dreamed,
A something to be loved, a creature meant
    To be her happiness, and whom she deemed
To render happy. All who joy would win   1375
Must share it; Happiness was born a twin.

173

It was such pleasure, to behold him, such
    Enlargement of existence to partake
Nature with him, to thrill beneath his touch,
    To watch him slumbering and to see him wake.   1380
To live with him forever were too much,
    But then the thought of parting made her quake.
He was her own, her ocean-treasure, cast
Like a rich wreck, her first love and her last.

174

And thus a moon rolled on, and fair Haidée   1385
    Paid daily visits to her boy and took
Such plentiful precautions that still he
    Remained unknown within his craggy nook.

At last her father's prows[460] put out to sea,
    For certain merchantmen upon the look,   1390
Not as of yore to carry off an Io,[461]
But three Ragusan vessels[462] bound for Scio.

175

Then came her freedom, for she had no mother,
    So that, her father being at sea, she was
Free as a married woman, or such other   1395
    Female, as where she likes may freely pass,
Without even the incumbrance of a brother,
    The freest she that ever gazed on glass.
I speak of Christian lands in this comparison,
Where wives, at least, are seldom kept in garrison.   1400

176

Now she prolonged her visits and her talk
    (For they must talk), and he had learnt to say
So much as to propose to take a walk,
    For little had he wandered since the day
On which, like a young flower snapped from the stalk,   1405
    Drooping and dewy on the beach he lay,
And thus they walked out in the afternoon
And saw the sun set opposite the moon.

177

It was a wild and breaker-beaten coast,
    With cliffs above and a broad sandy shore,   1410
Guarded by shoals and rocks as by an host,
    With here and there a creek, whose aspect wore

---

[460] *prows*: i.e., ships. The prow is the forward part of the ship.
[461] *Io*: in classical mythology, a priestess of Hera seduced by Jupiter and transformed into a cow, fleeing the fury of Hera to Egypt.
[462] *Ragusan vessels*: ships from Ragusa, a maritime commercial center on the Adriatic Sea coast (centered on the city of Dubrovnik, "the Pearl of the Adriatic", in modern-day Croatia).

A better welcome to the tempest-tost.
   And rarely ceased the haughty billow's roar,
Save on the dead long summer days, which make   1415
The outstretched ocean glitter like a lake.

178

And the small ripple spilt upon the beach
   Scarcely o'erpassed the cream of your champagne,
When o'er the brim the sparkling bumpers reach,
   That spring-dew of the spirit, the heart's rain!   1420
Few things surpass old wine; and they may preach
   Who please—the more because they preach in vain.
Let us have wine and woman, mirth and laughter,
Sermons and soda water the day after.

179

Man being reasonable must get drunk;   1425
   The best of life is but intoxication.
Glory, the grape, love, gold, in these are sunk
   The hopes of all men and of every nation;
Without their sap, how branchless were the trunk
   Of life's strange tree, so fruitful on occasion.   1430
But to return. Get very drunk, and when
You wake with headache, you shall see what then.

180

Ring for your valet, bid him quickly bring
   Some hock and soda-water.[463] Then you'll know
A pleasure worthy Xerxes, the great king;[464]   1435
   For not the blest sherbet, sublimed with snow,
Nor the first sparkle of the desert spring,
   Nor Burgundy in all its sunset glow,

---

[463] *hock and soda-water*: i.e., a cure for a hangover. See footnote 350, page 120.
[464] *Xerxes . . . king*: Xerxes I of Persia (519–465 B.C.), also known as "Xerxes the Great".

After long travel, ennui,[465] love, or slaughter,
Vie with that draught of hock and soda water.   1440

181

The coast—I think it was the coast that I
    Was just describing—yes, it was the coast—
Lay at this period quiet as the sky,
    The sands untumbled, the blue waves untost,
And all was stillness, save the sea bird's cry   1445
    And dolphin's leap and little billow crost
By some low rock or shelve, that made it fret
Against the boundary it scarcely wet.

182

And forth they wandered, her sire being gone,
    As I have said, upon an expedition.   1450
And mother, brother, guardian, she had none,
    Save Zoe, who although with due precision
She waited on her lady with the sun,
    Thought daily service was her only mission,
Bringing warm water, wreathing her long tresses,   1455
And asking now and then for cast-off dresses.[466]

183

It was the cooling hour, just when the rounded
    Red sun sinks down behind the azure hill,
Which then seems as if the whole earth it bounded,
    Circling all nature, hushed and dim and still,   1460
With the far mountain-crescent half surrounded
    On one side, and the deep sea calm and chill
Upon the other, and the rosy sky
With one star sparkling through it like an eye.

[465] *ennui*: a depression or gripping melancholia caused by boredom.
[466] *cast-off dresses*: i.e., from her mistress. It was common for ladies to give their old, discarded dresses to their maids.

184

And thus they wandered forth, and hand in hand,   1465
    Over the shining pebbles and the shells
Glided along the smooth and hardened sand,
    And in the worn and wild receptacles
Worked by the storms, yet worked as it were planned,
    In hollow halls with sparry roofs and cells,   1470
They turned to rest, and, each clasped by an arm,
Yielded to the deep twilight's purple charm.

185

They looked up to the sky, whose floating glow
    Spread like a rosy ocean, vast and bright.
They gazed upon the glittering sea below,   1475
    Whence the broad moon rose circling into sight.
They heard the wave's splash and the wind so low,
    And saw each other's dark eyes darting light
Into each other, and beholding this,
Their lips drew near and clung into a kiss,   1480

186

A long, long kiss, a kiss of youth and love
    And beauty, all concentrating like rays
Into one focus, kindled from above;
    Such kisses as belong to early days,
Where heart and soul and sense in concert move,   1485
    And the blood's lava, and the pulse a blaze,
Each kiss a heart-quake, for a kiss's strength,
I think, it must be reckoned by its length.

187

By length I mean duration; theirs endured
    Heaven knows how long; no doubt they never
        reckoned,   1490
And if they had, they could not have secured
    The sum of their sensations to a second.

They had not spoken, but they felt allured,
    As if their souls and lips each other beckoned,
Which, being joined, like swarming bees they clung,   1495
Their hearts the flowers from whence the honey sprung.

188

They were alone, but not alone as they
    Who shut in chambers think it loneliness.
The silent ocean and the starlight bay,
    The twilight glow, which momently grew less,   1500
The voiceless sands and dropping caves, that lay
    Around them, made them to each other press,
As if there were no life beneath the sky
Save theirs, and that their life could never die.

189

They feared no eyes nor ears on that lone beach,   1505
    They felt no terrors from the night, they were
All in all to each other. Though their speech
    Was broken words, they thought a language there,
And all the burning tongues the passions teach
    Found in one sigh the best interpreter   1510
Of nature's oracle, first love, that all
Which Eve has left her daughters since her fall.

190

Haidée spoke not of scruples, asked no vows
    Nor offered any; she had never heard
Of plight and promises to be a spouse,   1515
    Or perils by a loving maid incurred.
She was all which pure ignorance allows
    And flew to her young mate like a young bird,
And never having dreamt of falsehood, she
Had not one word to say of constancy.   1520

191

She loved and was belovèd, she adored
    And she was worshipped after nature's fashion.
Their intense souls, into each other poured,
    If souls could die, had perished in that passion,
But by degrees their senses were restored,   1525
    Again to be o'ercome, again to dash on.
And beating 'gainst *his* bosom, Haidée's heart
Felt as if never more to beat apart.

192

Alas, they were so young, so beautiful,
    So lonely, loving, helpless, and the hour   1530
Was that in which the heart is always full,
    And having o'er itself no further power,
Prompts deeds eternity cannot annul,
    But pays off moments in an endless shower
Of hell-fire, all prepared for people giving   1535
Pleasure or pain to one another living.

193

Alas for Juan and Haidée! They were
    So loving and so lovely; till then never,
Excepting our first parents, such a pair
    Had run the risk of being damned for ever.   1540
And Haidée, being devout as well as fair,
    Had doubtless heard about the Stygian river[467]
And hell and purgatory, but forgot
Just in the very crisis she should not.

194

They look upon each other, and their eyes   1545
    Gleam in the moonlight, and her white arm clasps
Round Juan's head, and his around hers lies
    Half buried in the tresses which it grasps.

[467] *Stygian river*: i.e., the River Styx.

She sits upon his knee and drinks his sighs,
    He hers, until they end in broken gasps;   1550
And thus they form a group that's quite antique,
Half naked, loving, natural, and Greek.

195

And when those deep and burning moments passed,
    And Juan sunk to sleep within her arms,
She slept not, but all tenderly, though fast,   1555
    Sustained his head upon her bosom's charms.
And now and then her eye to heaven is cast,
    And then on the pale cheek her breast now warms,
Pillowed on her o'erflowing heart, which pants
With all it granted and with all it grants.   1560

196

An infant when it gazes on a light,
    A child the moment when it drains the breast,
A devotee when soars the Host[468] in sight,
    An Arab with a stranger for a guest,
A sailor when the prize has struck in fight,   1565
    A miser filling his most hoarded chest
Feel rapture, but not such true joy are reaping
As they who watch o'er what they love while sleeping.

197

For there it lies so tranquil, so beloved;
    All that it hath of life with us is living,   1570
So gentle, stirless, helpless, and unmoved,
    And all unconscious of the joy 'tis giving.
All it hath felt, inflicted, passed, and proved,
    Hushed into depths beyond the watcher's diving,
There lies the thing we love with all its errors   1575
And all its charms, like death without its terrors.

---

[468] *devotee . . . Host:* a Catholic before the consecrated Host.

198

The lady watched her lover; and that hour
   Of love's and night's and ocean's solitude.
O'erflowed her soul with their united power.
   Amidst the barren sand and rocks so rude   1580
She and her wave-worn love had made their bower,
   Where nought upon their passion could intrude,
And all the stars that crowded the blue space
Saw nothing happier than her glowing face.

199

Alas, the love of women! It is known   1585
   To be a lovely and a fearful thing,
For all of theirs upon that die is thrown,
   And if 'tis lost, life hath no more to bring
To them but mockeries of the past alone,
   And their revenge is as the tiger's spring,   1590
Deadly and quick and crushing; yet as real
Torture is theirs, what they inflict they feel.

200

They are right, for man, to man so oft unjust,
   Is always so to women. One sole bond
Awaits them, treachery is all their trust.   1595
   Taught to conceal, their bursting hearts despond
Over their idol, till some wealthier lust
   Buys them in marriage—and what rests beyond?
A thankless husband, next a faithless lover,
Then dressing, nursing, praying, and all's over.   1600

201

Some take a lover, some take drams or prayers,
   Some mind their household, others dissipation,

Some run away and but exchange their cares,
    Losing the advantage of a virtuous station.
Few changes e'er can better their affairs,   1605
    Theirs being an unnatural situation,
From the dull palace to the dirty hovel.
Some play the devil, and then write a novel.[469]

202

Haidée was Nature's bride and knew not this;
    Haidée was Passion's child, born where the sun   1610
Showers triple light and scorches even the kiss
    Of his gazelle-eyed daughters. She was one
Made but to love, to feel that she was his
    Who was her chosen. What was said or done
Elsewhere was nothing. She had nought to fear,   1615
Hope, care, nor love beyond; her heart beat here.

203

And oh, that quickening of the heart, that beat!
    How much it costs us! Yet each rising throb
Is in its cause as its effect so sweet
    That Wisdom, ever on the watch to rob   1620
Joy of its alchymy[470] and to repeat
    Fine truths—even Conscience too—has a tough job
To make us understand each good old maxim,
So good I wonder Castlereagh[471] don't tax 'em.

---

[469] *Some play . . . novel*: Lady Caroline Lamb, Byron's discarded married lover, included a great deal of poorly disguised details from her notorious affair with the poet in the scandalous novel *Glenarvon* (1816).

[470] *alchymy*: Alchemy, a form of chemistry and speculative philosophy popular in the Middle Ages and the Renaissance, sought for methods to transform various metals into gold and to discover an "elixir of life".

[471] *Castlereagh*: see footnote 320, page 110.

204

And now 'twas done; on the lone shore were plighted   1625
   Their hearts. The stars, their nuptial torches, shed
Beauty upon the beautiful they lighted.
   Ocean their witness, and the cave their bed,
By their own feelings hallowed and united;
   Their priest was Solitude, and they were wed.   1630
And they were happy, for to their young eyes
Each was an angel, and earth Paradise.

205

Oh Love, of whom great Caesar was the suitor,[472]
   Titus the master,[473] Antony the slave,[474]
Horace, Catullus, scholars,[475] Ovid tutor,[476]   1635
   Sappho the sage bluestocking, in whose grave
All those may leap who rather would be neuter
   (Leucadia's rock still overlooks the wave)[477]—
Oh Love, thou art the very god of evil,
For after all, we cannot call thee devil.   1640

206

Thou mak'st the chaste connubial state precarious
   And jestest with the brows of mightiest men.

[472] *Caesar . . . suitor*: Gaius Julius Caesar (100–44 B.C.), the Roman general and dictator in whose line the Roman Empire followed.

[473] *Titus the master*: Titus Flavius Caesar (39–81), Roman emperor, was purportedly a skilled poet and, in addition, was considered a "master" of passion because he decided not to marry a foreign wife because of popular national prejudice against "alien" intermarriage.

[474] *Antony the slave*: Marcus Antonius (83–30 B.C.), Roman politician and general, known as the lover of Cleopatra (69–30 B.C.), the last Egyptian pharaoh.

[475] *Horace, Catullus, scholars*: Quintus Horatius Flaccus (65–27 B.C.) and Gaius Valerius Catullus (c. 84–c. 54 B.C.), influential Roman lyric poets.

[476] *Ovid tutor*: Publius Ovidius Naso (43 B.C.–A.D. 18), a Roman poet known as the author of the *Metamorphoses* as well as three collections of erotic poetry: *Amores*, *Ars Amatoria*, and *Heroides*.

[477] *Sappho . . . wave*: Sappho (c. 630–c. 570 B.C.) was a female Greek lyric poet who, according to legend, committed suicide by throwing herself from the cliffs of Leucadia because of her unrequited love for Phaon.

Caesar and Pompey,[478] Mahomet,[479] Belisarius[480]
    Have much employed the Muse of history's pen.
Their lives and fortunes were extremely various; 1645
    Such worthies Time will never see again.
Yet to these four in three things the same luck holds;
They all were heroes, conquerors, and cuckolds.

207

Thou mak'st philosophers; there's Epicurus[481]
    And Aristippus,[482] a material crew, 1650
Who to immoral courses would allure us
    By theories quite practicable too.
If only from the devil they would insure us,
    How pleasant were the maxim (not quite new),
'Eat, drink, and love, what can the rest avail us?' 1655
So said the royal sage Sardanapalus.[483]

208

But Juan, had he quite forgotten Julia?
    And should he have forgotten her so soon?
I can't but say it seems to me most truly a
    Perplexing question, but no doubt the moon 1660

---

[478] *Caesar and Pompey*: Caesar's third wife was suspected of infidelity, and Caesar himself was believed to have carried on an affair with the wife of his enemy and onetime friend Gnaeus Pompeius Magnus, "Pompey the Great" (106–48 B.C.).

[479] *Mahomet*: Aisha bint Abu Bakr (612–678), the "most beloved wife" of Muhammad (c. 570–632), the founder of Islam, was at one time accused of adultery.

[480] *Belisarius*: Antonina, the wife of Flavius Belisarius (c. 500–565), a general of the Byzantine Empire, was purportedly debauched.

[481] *Epicurus*: Epicurus (341–270 B.C.), Greek philosopher and founder of Epicureanism, an ancient form of materialism that promoted happiness through freedom from pain and fear.

[482] *Aristippus*: Aristippus (c. 435–356 B.C.), Greek philosopher and founder of Cyrenaic philosophy, an early form of hedonism and early materialism.

[483] *Sardanapalus*: legendary last king of Assyria (date of life unknown, roughly associated with the seventh century B.C., and perhaps a corruption of the name of a historic king), notorious for his decadence and supposed to have died in an orgy of self-destruction along with his household.

Does these things for us,[484] and whenever newly a
   Strong palpitation rises, 'tis her boon,
Else how the devil is it that fresh features
Have such a charm for us poor human creatures?

209

I hate inconstancy; I loathe, detest,   1665
   Abhor, condemn, abjure the mortal made
Of such quicksilver clay that in his breast
   No permanent foundation can be laid.
Love, constant love, has been my constant guest,
   And yet last night, being at a masquerade,   1670
I saw the prettiest creature, fresh from Milan,
Which gave me some sensations like a villain.

210

But soon Philosophy came to my aid
   And whispered, 'Think of every sacred tie!'
'I will, my dear Philosophy,' I said,   1675
   'But then her teeth, and then oh heaven, her eye!
I'll just inquire if she be wife or maid
   Or neither—out of curiosity.'
'Stop!' cried Philosophy with air so Grecian
(Though she was masked then as a fair Venetian).   1680

211

'Stop!' So I stopped. But to return. That which
   Men call inconstancy is nothing more
Than admiration due where Nature's rich
   Profusion with young beauty covers o'er
Some favoured object; and as in the niche   1685
   A lovely statue we almost adore,

---

[484] *the moon . . . for us*: There is a long-standing association of madness, romance, and the influence of the moon on human passions.

This sort of adoration of the real
Is but a heightening of the beau ideal.[485]

212

'Tis the perception of the beautiful,
    A fine extension of the faculties,   1690
Platonic,[486] universal, wonderful,
    Drawn from the stars and filtered through the skies,
Without which life would be extremely dull.
    In short it is the use of our own eyes,
With one or two small senses added, just   1695
To hint that flesh is formed of fiery dust.

213

Yet 'tis a painful feeling, and unwilling,
    For surely if we always could perceive
In the same object graces quite as killing
    As when she rose upon us like an Eve,   1700
'Twould save us many a heartache, many a shilling
    (For we must get them anyhow or grieve),
Whereas if one sole lady pleased forever,
How pleasant for the heart, as well as liver!

214

The heart is like the sky, a part of heaven,   1705
    But changes night and day too, like the sky.
Now o'er it clouds and thunder must be driven,
    And darkness and destruction as on high,
But when it hath been scorched and pierced and riven,
    Its storms expire in water drops. The eye   1710
Pours forth at last the heart's blood turned to tears,
Which make the English climate of our years.

---

[485] *beau ideal*: concept of perfect beauty.
[486] *Platonic*: nonsexual.

215

The liver is the lazaret[487] of bile,
    But very rarely executes its function,
For the first passion stays there such a while   1715
    That all the rest creep in and form a junction,
Life knots of vipers on a dunghill's soil—
    Rage, fear, hate, jealousy, revenge, compunction—
So that all mischiefs spring up from this entrail,
Like earthquakes from the hidden fire called 'central'.   1720

216

In the meantime, without proceeding more
    In this anatomy, I've finished now
Two hundred and odd stanzas as before,
    That being about the number I'll allow
Each canto of the twelve or twenty-four;   1725
    And laying down my pen, I make my bow,
Leaving Don Juan and Haidée to plead
For them and theirs with all who deign to read.

[487] *lazaret*: hospital treating contagious diseases. The function of bile explored analogically here is based on the classical theory that human temperaments were derived from four bodily humors: yellow bile (choleric temperament), black bile (melancholic), phlegm (phlegmatic), and blood (sanguine).

PERCY BYSSHE SHELLEY
(1792–1822)

Mutability[1] (1816)

We are as clouds that veil the midnight moon;
　　How restlessly they speed, and gleam, and quiver,
Streaking the darkness radiantly!—yet soon
　　Night closes round, and they are lost for ever:
Or like forgotten lyres,[2] whose dissonant strings　　　　5
　　Give various response to each varying blast,
To whose frail frame no second motion brings
　　One mood or modulation like the last.

We rest.—A dream has power to poison sleep;
　　We rise.—One wandering thought pollutes the day;　　10
We feel, conceive or reason, laugh or weep;
　　Embrace fond woe, or cast our cares away:

It is the same!—For, be it joy or sorrow,
　　The path of its departure still is free:
Man's yesterday may ne'er be like his morrow;　　　　15
　　Nought may endure but Mutability.

Sonnets:

Ozymandias[3] (late 1817)

I met a traveller from an antique land,
Who said—"Two vast and trunkless legs of stone
Stand in the desart.[4] … Near them, on the sand,
Half sunk a shattered visage lies, whose frown,

---

[1] *Mutability*: changeability.
[2] *lyres*: Greek stringed instruments (harps or wind lyres).
[3] *Ozymandias*: Ramesses II (c. 1303–1213 B.C.), one of the most powerful Egyptian pharaohs, often identified as Moses' antagonist in the Book of Exodus.
[4] *desart*: deserted, desolate.

And wrinkled lip, and sneer of cold command,   5
Tell that its sculptor well those passions read
Which yet survive, stamped on these lifeless things,
The hand that mocked[5] them, and the heart that fed:[6]
And on the pedestal, these words appear:
My name is Ozymandias, King of Kings,   10
Look on my Works, ye Mighty, and despair!
Nothing beside remains. Round the decay
Of that colossal Wreck, boundless and bare
The lone and level sands stretch far away."

"Lift Not the Painted Veil" (1819)

Lift not the painted veil which those who live
Call Life; though unreal shapes be pictured there
And it but mimic all we would believe
With colours idly spread,—behind, lurk Fear
And Hope, twin Destinies, who ever weave   5
Their shadows o'er the chasm, sightless and drear.
I knew one who had lifted it—he sought,
For his lost heart was tender, things to love
But found them not, alas; nor was there aught
The world contains, the which he could approve.   10
Through the unheeding many he did move,
A splendour[7] among shadows—a bright blot
Upon this gloomy scene—a Spirit that strove
For truth, and like the Preacher, found it not.—

[5] *mocked*: imitated and derided.
[6] *Tell that . . . fed*: i.e., the sculpted face shows that the sculptor read the passions of Ozymandias—passions that, shown (perhaps mockingly) by the hand of the sculptor, outlive both the hand (of the sculptor) and the heart (of Ozymandias).
[7] *splendour*: angel.

England in 1819 (late 1819)

An old, mad, blind, despised, and dying King;[8]
Princes,[9] the dregs of their dull race, who flow
Through public scorn,—mud from a muddy spring;
Rulers who neither see nor feel nor know,
But leechlike to their fainting country cling   5
Till they drop, blind in blood, without a blow.
A people starved and stabbed in th'untilled field;[10]
An army, which liberticide[11] and prey
Makes as a two-edged sword to all who wield;
Golden and sanguine[12] laws which tempt and slay;   10
Religion Christless, Godless—a book sealed;
A senate,[13] Time's worst statute, unrepealed—
Are graves from which a glorious Phantom may
Burst, to illumine our tempestous day.

Prometheus[14] *Unbound*

Prometheus Unbound was written between 1818 and 1819. The influence of Plato and Neoplatonism is pervasive—as elsewhere in Shelley—but above all, there is felt the presence of Aeschylus,[15] writer of *Prometheus Bound*, of which Shelley's poem is the ostensible sequel.

---

[8] *old . . . King*: i.e., King George III. (Cf. introduction to Byron's *The Vision of Judgment*.)

[9] *Princes*: The sons of George III (described in the following lines) were notorious libertines, fathers to numerous illegitimate children.

[10] *people . . . field*: On August 16, 1819, the "Peterloo Massacre" took place at St. Peter's Field in Manchester, England, when English cavalry clashed with protesters demanding parliamentary reform.

[11] *liberticide*: murder of liberty.

[12] *sanguine*: i.e., bloody (gold and blood being traditionally considered foundations for tyranny).

[13] *senate*: i.e., the British Parliament.

[14] *Prometheus*: In classical mythology, Prometheus, a Titan, stole the fire of the gods and gave it to mankind. He was punished by Jupiter (or Zeus) by being chained to a rock, where his liver was daily consumed by a mighty eagle.

[15] Assuming that Aeschylus (525–455 B.C.) wrote the play—a position now much disputed.

In Aeschylus' play (the first in a trilogy of which the sequels are lost), the Titan Prometheus—Zeus' ally in the latter's war against the Titans—has frustrated Zeus' intention to destroy the human race and gifted man with fire as well as the arts and sciences. As a punishment, Zeus has fettered him to a high rock and sent an eagle daily to devour his immortal liver. The play concludes with Prometheus cast into an abyss upon refusing to divulge his foreknowledge of the circumstances of Zeus' contingent downfall.

Shelley was happy to take this as a mythic blueprint for his own (rather divergent[16]) visions of human destiny.

A good deal of ink has been wasted upon *Prometheus* in the past century. This editor is content to invite one of Shelley's ablest modern champions to raise the curtain:

> The main theme—the myth of a universal rebirth, a restoration of all things—is one which may occur in any age and which falls naturally into place beside Isaiah or the Fourth Eclogue.[17] … Like all great myths its primary appeal to the will and understanding can therefore be diversely interpreted according as the reader is a Christian, a politician, a psycho-analyst, or what not. Myth is thus like manna; it is to each man a different dish and to each the dish he needs. …
>
> We are to start with the soul chained, aged, suffering; and we are to end with the soul free, rejuvenated, and blessed. The selection of the Prometheus story (a selection which seems obvious only because we did not have to make it) is the first step to the solution. But nearly everything has still to be done. By what steps are we to pass from Prometheus in his chains to Prometheus free? …
>
> The whole of the next act, in story, is occupied with the difficult efforts of Asia to apprehend and follow a dream dreamed in the shadow of Prometheus: the difficult journey which it leads her; her difficult descent to the depths of the earth; and her final re-ascension, transformed, to the light. Difficulty is, so to speak, the subject of this act. …

---

[16] From the surviving fragments and classical commentary, it seems clear that Zeus and Prometheus were reconciled in the original trilogy.

[17] The *Fourth Eclogue* is a poem by Virgil.

The third act is the least successful.... Yet ... we are certainly not ready for the fourth act at once. Between the end of torment and the beginning of ecstasy there must be a pause: peace comes before beatitude. It would be ridiculous, in point of achievement, to compare this weak act in Shelley's play with the triumphant conclusion of the *Purgatorio*; but structurally it corresponds to the position of the earthly paradise between purgatory and heaven.

The fourth act I shall not attempt to analyse. It is an intoxication, a riot, a complicated and uncontrollable splendour, long, and yet not too long, sustained on the note of ecstasy such as no other English poet, perhaps no other poet has given us. It can be achieved by more than one artist in music: to do it in words has been, I think, beyond the reach of nearly all. It has not, and cannot have, the solemnity and overwhelming realism of the *Paradiso*, but it has all its fire and light.[18]

From *Prometheus Unbound* (1819)

ACT I

Scene: A Ravine of Icy Rocks in the Indian Caucasus.[19] *Prometheus is discovered bound to the Precipice.* Panthea *and* Ione[20] *are seated at his feet. Time, Night. During the Scene, Morning slowly breaks.*

SCENE I

PROMETHEUS

Monarch of Gods and Dæmons,[21] and all Spirits
But One,[22] who throng those bright and rolling Worlds

---

[18] C. S. Lewis, "Shelley, Dryden, and Mr Eliot", in *Selected Literary Essays*, ed. Walter Hooper (Cambridge: Cambridge University Press, 1979), pp. 195, 205–8.

[19] Indian Caucasus: perhaps the Himalayas, a mountain range immediately north of the Indian subcontinent. Prometheus was traditionally believed to have been chained in the European Caucasus, between the Black and Caspian Seas; though Shelley's reason for relocating the myth is unknown, it is hypothesized that he was simultaneously universalizing the Greek myth and working within contemporary scientific theories that human life originated in central Asia.

[20] *Ione*: in classical mythology, one of the Nereids or sea nymphs.

[21] *Dæmons*: subordinate deities.

[22] *But One*: i.e., Prometheus himself—defiant even when chained in punishment, since he has the power of foreknowing the cause of Jupiter's eventual overthrow.

Which Thou and I alone of living things
Behold with sleepless eyes! regard this Earth
Made multitudinous with thy slaves, whom thou   5
Requitest for knee-worship, prayer and praise,
And toil, and hecatombs[23] of broken hearts,
With fear and self contempt and barren hope;
Whilst me, who am thy foe, eyeless[24] in hate,
Hast thou made reign and triumph, to thy scorn,   10
O'er mine own misery and thy vain revenge.—
Three thousand years[25] of sleep-unsheltered hours
And moments—aye[26] divided by keen pangs
Till they seemed years, torture and solitude,
Scorn and despair,—these are mine empire:—   15
More glorious far than that which thou surveyest
From thine unenvied throne, O Mighty God!
Almighty, had I deigned to share the shame
Of thine ill tyranny, and hung not here
Nailed to this wall of eagle-baffling mountain,   20
Black, wintry, dead, unmeasured; without herb,
Insect, or beast, or shape or sound of life.
Ah me, alas, pain, pain ever, forever!

No change, no pause, no hope!—Yet I endure.
I ask the Earth, have not the mountains felt?   25
I ask yon Heaven—the all-beholding Sun,
Has it not seen? The Sea, in storm or calm,
Heaven's ever-changing Shadow, spread below—
Have its deaf waves not heard my agony?
Ah me, alas, pain, pain ever, forever!   30

---

[23] *hecatombs*: religious sacrifices, technically consisting of one hundred oxen or cattle.

[24] *eyeless*: blind.

[25] *Three thousand years*: It was believed in the nineteenth century that three thousand years was precisely the distance from antiquity to their contemporary modern age.

[26] *aye*: continually.

The crawling glaciers pierce me with the spears
Of their moon-freezing chrystals; the bright chains
Eat with their burning cold into my bones.
Heaven's winged hound,[27] polluting from thy lips
His beak in poison not his own, tears up   35
My heart; and shapeless sights come wandering by,
The ghastly people of the realm of dream,
Mocking me: and the Earthquake-fiends are charged
To wrench the rivets from my quivering wounds
When the rocks split and close again behind;   40
While from their loud abysses howling throng
The genii[28] of the storm, urging the rage
Of whirlwind, and afflict me with keen hail.
And yet to me welcome is Day and Night,
Whether one breaks the hoar frost of the morn,   45
Or starry, dim, and slow, the other climbs
The leaden-coloured East; for then they lead
Their wingless, crawling Hours,[29] one among whom
—As some dark Priest hales[30] the reluctant victim—
Shall drag thee, cruel King, to kiss the blood   50
From these pale feet, which then might trample thee
If they disdained not such a prostrate slave.
Disdain? Ah no! I pity thee.—What Ruin
Will hunt thee undefended through wide Heaven!
How will thy soul, cloven to its depth with terror,   55
Gape like a Hell within! I speak in grief,
Not exultation, for I hate no more,
As then, ere misery made me wise.—The Curse
Once breathed on thee I would recall.[31] Ye Mountains,
Whose many-voiced Echoes, through the mist   60

---

[27] *Heaven's ... hound*: i.e., the eagle that visits Prometheus daily to tear out his liver.

[28] *genii*: animating spirit.

[29] *wingless ... Hours*: the Horae, in classical mythology, winged, anthropomorphized creatures, representing the hours and seasons.

[30] *hales*: drags in.

[31] *recall*: (1) remember; (2) call down once more.

Of cataracts,[32] flung the thunder of that spell!
Ye icy Springs, stagnant with wrinkling frost,
Which vibrated to hear me, and then crept
Shuddering through India! Thou serenest Air,
Through which the Sun walks burning without beams!   65
And ye swift Whirlwinds, who on poised wings
Hung mute and moveless o'er yon hushed abyss,
As thunder louder than your own made rock
The orbed world! If then my words had power
—Though I am changed so that aught evil wish   70
Is dead within, although no memory be
Of what is hate—let them not lose it now!
What was that curse? for ye all heard me speak.

* * * * *

PROMETHEUS

Venerable mother!
All else who live and suffer take from thee
Some comfort; flowers and fruits and happy sounds
And love, though fleeting; these may not be mine.
But mine own words, I pray, deny me not.   190

THE EARTH

They shall be told.—Ere Babylon[33] was dust,
The Magus Zoroaster,[34] my dead child,
Met his own image walking in the garden.
That apparition, sole of men, he saw.
For know, there are two worlds of life and death: 195
One that which thou beholdest, but the other

---

[32] *cataracts*: waterfalls.

[33] *Babylon*: alongside Assyria, one of the primary civilizations of antiquity.

[34] *Magus Zoroaster*: the possibly mythological figure of an ancient prophet and king, credited with the invention of magic, the followers of whom were called Magi.

Is underneath the grave, where do inhabit
The shadows of all forms that think and live
Till death unite them, and they part no more;
Dreams and the light imaginings of men   200
And all that faith creates, or love desires,
Terrible, strange, sublime and beauteous shapes.
There thou art, and dost hang, a writhing shade
'Mid whirlwind-peopled mountains; all the Gods
Are there, and all the Powers of nameless worlds,   205
Vast, sceptred phantoms; heroes, men, and beasts;
And Demogorgon,[35] a tremendous Gloom;
And he, the supreme Tyrant,[36] on his throne
Of burning Gold. Son,[37] one of these shall utter
The curse which all remember. Call at will   210
Thine own ghost, or the ghost of Jupiter,
Hades[38] or Typhon,[39] or what mightier Gods
From all-prolific Evil, since thy ruin
Have sprung, and trampled on my prostrate sons.—
Ask and they must reply—so the revenge   215
Of the Supreme may sweep through vacant shades
As rainy wind through the abandoned gate
Of a fallen palace.

PROMETHEUS

Mother, let not aught
Of that which may be evil, pass again
My lips, or those of aught resembling me.—   220
Phantasm of Jupiter, arise, appear!

---

[35] *Demogorgon*: a phantom demon, believed to be father of sky, earth, underworld, and the Fates.

[36] *supreme Tyrant*: i.e., Jupiter.

[37] *Son*: i.e., Prometheus, to whom the earth speaks.

[38] *Hades*: in classical mythology, god of the underworld.

[39] *Typhon*: in classical mythology, the hundred-headed giant who waged war against Jupiter but, upon his defeat, was imprisoned by Jupiter in the volcanic Mount Aetna.

IONE

My wings are folded o'er mine ears,
My wings are crossed over mine eyes,
Yet through their silver shade appears
And through their lulling plumes arise   225
   A Shape, a throng of sounds:
     May it be, no ill to thee
    O thou of many wounds!
Near whom, for our sweet sister's sake
Ever thus we watch and wake.   230

PANTHEA

The sound is of whirlwind underground,
Earthquake and fire, and mountains cloven;
The Shape is awful like the sound,
Clothed in dark purple, star-inwoven.
   A sceptre of pale gold   235
    To stay steps proud, o'er the slow cloud
    His veined hand doth hold.
Cruel he looks but calm and strong
Like one who does, not suffers wrong.

PHANTASM OF JUPITER

Why have the secret powers of this strange world   240
Driven me, a frail and empty phantom, hither
On direst storms? What unaccustomed sounds
Are hovering on my lips, unlike the voice
With which our pallid race hold ghastly talk
In darkness? And, proud Sufferer, who art thou?   245

PROMETHEUS

Tremendous Image! as thou art must be
He whom thou shadowest forth. I am his foe
The Titan. Speak the words which I would hear,
Although no thought inform thine empty voice.

THE EARTH

Listen! and though your echoes must be mute, 250
Gray mountains and old woods and haunted springs,
Prophetic caves and isle-surrounding streams
Rejoice to hear what yet ye cannot speak.

PHANTASM

A spirit seizes me, and speaks within:
It tears me as fire tears a thunder-cloud! 255

PANTHEA

See how he lifts his mighty looks, the Heaven
Darkens above.

IONE

He speaks! O shelter me—

PROMETHEUS

I see the curse on gestures proud and cold,
And looks of firm defiance, and calm hate,
And such despair as mocks itself with smiles, 260
Written as on a scroll ... yet speak—O speak!

PHANTASM

Fiend, I defy thee! with a calm, fixed mind,
   All that thou canst inflict I bid thee do;
Foul Tyrant both of Gods and Humankind,
   One only being shalt thou not subdue. 265
      Rain then thy plagues upon me here,
      Ghastly disease and frenzying fear;
      And let alternate frost and fire
      Eat into me, and be thine ire
Lightning and cutting hail and legioned[40] forms 270
Of furies, driving by upon the wounding storms.

[40] *legioned*: appearing as if organized in legions (in armies).

Aye, do thy worst. Thou art Omnipotent.
    O'er all things but thyself I gave thee power,
And my own will. Be thy swift mischiefs sent
    To blast mankind, from yon etherial tower.   275
        Let thy malignant spirit move
        Its darkness over those I love:
        On me and mine I imprecate[41]
        The utmost torture of thy hate
And thus devote to sleepless agony   280
This undeclining head while thou must reign on
    high.

But thou who art the God and Lord—O thou
    Who fillest with thy soul this world of woe,
To whom all things of Earth and Heaven do bow
    In fear and worship—all-prevailing foe!   285
        I curse thee! let a sufferer's curse
        Clasp thee, his torturer, like remorse,
        Till thine Infinity shall be
        A robe of envenomed agony;
And thine Omnipotence a crown of pain[42]   290
To cling like burning gold round thy dissolving
    brain.

Heap on thy soul by virtue of this Curse
    Ill deeds, then be thou damned, beholding good,
Both infinite as is the Universe,
    And thou, and thy self-torturing solitude.   295
        An awful Image of calm power
        Though now thou sittest, let the hour
        Come, when thou must appear to be
        That which thou art internally.

[41] *imprecate*: curse.
[42] *robe . . . pain*: This may allude both to the death of the Greek hero Hercules
and to the figure of Jesus Christ, mocked by the Romans before being crucified,
robed in a purple robe and with a crown of thorns upon his head (see Matthew
27:28–29; Mark 15:17; Luke 23:11).

And after many a false and fruitless crime   300
Scorn track thy lagging fall through boundless space
    and time.

                  [*The Phantasm vanishes.*]

PROMETHEUS

Were these my words, O Parent?

THE EARTH

          They were thine.

PROMETHEUS

  It doth repent me: words are quick and vain;
Grief for awhile is blind, and so was mine.
  I wish no living thing to suffer pain.   305

         * * * * *

IONE

Behold'st thou not two shapes from the East and West
Come, as two doves to one beloved nest,
Twin nurslings of the all-sustaining air,
On swift still wings glide down the atmosphere?   755
And hark! their sweet, sad voices! 'tis despair
Mingled with love, and then dissolved in sound.—

PANTHEA

Canst thou speak, sister? all my words are drowned.

IONE

Their beauty gives me voice. See how they float
On their sustaining wings of skiey grain,   760
Orange and azure, deepening into gold:
Their soft smiles light the air like a star's fire.

CHORUS OF SPIRITS

Hast thou beheld the form of Love?

FIFTH SPIRIT

As over wide dominions
  I sped, like some swift cloud that wings the wide air's
      wildernesses,
That planet-crested Shape swept by on lightning-braided
      pinions,[43]   765
  Scattering the liquid joy of life from his ambrosial[44]
      tresses:
His footsteps paved the world with light—but as I past
      'twas fading
  And hollow Ruin yawned behind. Great Sages bound in
      madness
And headless patriots and pale youths who perished
      unupbraiding,
  Gleamed in the Night I wandered o'er—till thou,
      O King of sadness,   770
Turned by thy smile the worst I saw to recollected
      gladness.

SIXTH SPIRIT

Ah, sister! Desolation is a delicate thing:
It walks not on the Earth, it floats not on the air,
But treads with silent footstep, and fans with silent wing
The tender hopes which in their hearts the best and
    gentlest bear,   775
Who soothed to false repose by the fanning plumes
    above
And the music-stirring motion of its soft and busy feet,
Dream visions of aerial joy, and call the monster, Love,
And wake, and find the shadow Pain, as he whom now
      we greet.

[43] *pinions*: wings.
[44] *ambrosial*: the food or drink of the gods.

CHORUS

Though Ruin now Love's shadow[45] be,   780
Following him destroyingly
On Death's white and winged steed,
Which the fleetest cannot flee—
Trampling down both flower and weed,
Man and beast and foul and fair,   785
Like a tempest through the air;
Thou shalt quell this Horseman grim,
Woundless though in heart or limb.—

PROMETHEUS

Spirits! how know ye this shall be?

CHORUS

In the atmosphere we breathe—   790
As buds grow red when the snow-storms flee
From spring gathering up beneath,
Whose mild winds shake, the elder brake[46]
And the wandering herdsmen know
That the white-thorn soon will blow—   795
Wisdom, Justice, Love and Peace,
When they struggle to increase,
Are to us as soft winds be
To shepherd-boys—the prophecy
Which begins and ends in thee.   800

* * * * *

SCENE IV

The Cave of Demogorgon. Asia *and* Panthea.

PANTHEA

What veiled form sits on that ebon[47] throne?

---

[45] *Ruin . . . shadow*: In classical mythology, Love is one of the children of night.
[46] *elder brake*: thicket of elderberry (Sambucus) trees.
[47] *ebon*: ebony.

ASIA

The veil has fallen!…

PANTHEA

                    I see a mighty Darkness
Filling the seat of power; and rays of gloom
Dart round, as light from the meridian Sun,
Ungazed upon and shapeless—neither limb   5
Nor form—nor outline;[48] yet we feel it is
A living Spirit.

DEMOGORGON

          Ask what thou wouldst know.

ASIA

What canst thou tell?

DEMOGORGON

               All things thou dar'st demand.

ASIA

Who made the living world?

DEMOGORGON

          God.

ASIA

                         Who made all
That it contains—thought, passion, reason, will,   10
Imagination?

---

[48] *shapeless … outline*: Cf. Milton's description of Death in *Paradise Lost*
(bk. 2, lines 666–73): "The other shape,/If shape it might be call'd that shape
had none/Distinguishable in member, joynt, or limb".

DEMOGORGON

God, Almighty God.

ASIA

Who made that sense which, when the winds of
    Spring
In rarest visitation, or the voice
Of one beloved heard in youth alone,
Fills the faint eyes with falling tears, which dim   15
The radiant looks of unbewailing flowers,
And leaves this peopled earth a solitude
When it returns no more?

DEMOGORGON

Merciful God.

ASIA

And who made terror, madness, crime, remorse,
Which from the links of the great chain of things   20
To every thought within the mind of man
Sway and drag heavily—and each one reels
Under the load towards the pit of death;
Abandoned hope, and love that turns to hate;
And self-contempt, bitterer to drink than blood;   25
Pain whose unheeded and familiar speech
Is howling and keen shrieks, day after day;
And Hell, or the sharp fear of Hell?

DEMOGORGON

He reigns.

ASIA

Utter his name—a world pining in pain
Asks but his name; curses shall drag him down.   30

DEMOGORGON

He reigns.

ASIA

I feel, I know it—who?

DEMOGORGON

He reigns.

ASIA

Who reigns? There was the Heaven and Earth at first
And Light and Love;—then Saturn,[49] from whose throne
Time fell, an envious shadow; such the state
Of the earth's primal spirits beneath his sway   35
As the calm joy of flowers and living leaves
Before the wind or sun has withered them
And semivital worms; but he refused
The birthright of their being, knowledge, power,
The skill which wields the elements, the thought   40
Which pierces this dim Universe like light,
Self-empire and the majesty of love,
For thirst of which they fainted. Then Prometheus
Gave wisdom, which is strength, to Jupiter
And with this law alone: "Let man be free,"   45
Clothed him with the dominion of wide Heaven.
To know nor faith nor love nor law, to be
Omnipotent but friendless, is to reign;
And Jove[50] now reigned; for on the race of man
First famine and then toil and then disease,   50
Strife, wounds, and ghastly death unseen before,
Fell; and the unseasonable seasons drove,

[49] *Saturn*: in classical mythology, the ancient god of the harvest, father of Jupiter or Jove, and closely associated with the Greek god Chronos (meaning "time").
[50] *Jove*: i.e., Jupiter.

With alternating shafts of frost and fire,
Their shelterless, pale tribes to mountain caves;
And in their desart[51] hearts fierce wants he sent   55
And mad disquietudes, and shadows idle
Of unreal good, which levied mutual war,
So ruining the lair wherein they raged.
Prometheus saw, and waked the legioned hopes
Which sleep within folded Elysian[52] flowers,   60
Nepenthe,[53] Moly,[54] Amaranth,[55] fadeless blooms;
That they might hide with thin and rainbow wings
The shape of Death; and Love he sent to bind
The disunited tendrils[56] of that vine
Which bears the wine of life, the human heart;   65
And he tamed fire, which like some beast of prey
Most terrible, but lovely, played beneath
The frown of man, and tortured to his will
Iron and gold, the slaves and signs of power,
And gems and poisons, and all subtlest forms   70
Hidden beneath the mountains and the waves.
He gave man speech, and speech created thought,
Which is the measure of the Universe;
And Science struck the thrones of Earth and Heaven
Which shook but fell not; and the harmonious mind   75
Poured itself forth in all-prophetic song,
And music lifted up the listening spirit
Until it walked, exempt from mortal care,
Godlike, o'er the clear billows of sweet sound;
And human hands first mimicked[57] and then mocked   80

---

[51] *desart*: see footnote 4, page 191.

[52] *Elysian*: Elysium is an ancient conception of the afterlife.

[53] *Nepenthe*: magical herb, believed to have the power of banishing grief. Cf. Homer's *Odyssey*, bk. 4, lines 220ff.

[54] *Moly*: magical herb, believed to have the property of a charm against sorcery, given by the gods to the hero Odysseus when he visited the island of the sorceress Circe (see *Odyssey*, bk. 10, lines 302ff.).

[55] *Amaranth*: magical herb, believed to have incorruptible properties. Cf. *Paradise Lost*, bk. 3, lines 352–60.

[56] *tendrils*: branches.

[57] *mimicked*: imitated and copied.

With moulded limbs more lovely than its own
The human form, till marble grew divine,[58]
And mothers, gazing, drank the love men see
Reflected in their race, behold, and perish.
He told the hidden power of herbs and springs,   85
And Disease drank and slept—Death grew like sleep.—
He taught the implicated orbits woven
Of the wide-wandering stars, and how the Sun
Changes his lair, and by what secret spell
The pale moon is transformed, when her broad eye   90
Gazes not on the interlunar sea;[59]
He taught to rule, as life directs the limbs,
The tempest-winged chariots of the Ocean,[60]
And the Celt[61] knew the Indian.[62] Cities then
Were built, and through their snow-like columns flowed   95
The warm winds, and the azure æther shone,
And the blue sea and shadowy hills were seen ...
Such the alleviations of his state
Prometheus gave to man—for which he hangs
Withering in destined pain—but who rains down   100
Evil, the immedicable plague, which while
Man looks on his creation like a God
And sees that it is glorious, drives him on,
The wreck of his own will, the scorn of Earth,
The outcast, the abandoned, the alone?—   105
Not Jove: while yet his frown shook Heaven, aye when
His adversary from adamantine[63] chains
Cursed him, he trembled like a slave. Declare
Who is his master? Is he too a slave?

---

[58] *moulded ... divine*: This example of men falling in love with the idealized
beauty of a statue demonstrates the devilment and sorcery of love.

[59] *interlunar sea*: the space between the moon and the earth.

[60] *tempest-winged ... Ocean*: i.e., boats.

[61] *Celt*: Northern European barbarians.

[62] *Indian*: man from India, like the Celt, differentiated from the Greco-Roman
civilizations.

[63] *adamantine*: made of unbreakable metal.

DEMOGORGON

All spirits are enslaved who serve things evil: 110
Thou knowest if Jupiter be such or no.

ASIA

Whom calledst thou God?

DEMOGORGON

               I spoke but as ye speak—
For Jove is the supreme of living things.

ASIA

Who is the master of the slave?

DEMOGORGON

               —If the Abysm
Could vomit forth its secrets;—but a voice   115
Is wanting, the deep truth is imageless;
For what would it avail to bid thee gaze
On the revolving world? what to bid speak
Fate, Time, Occasion, Chance and Change? To these
All things are subject but eternal Love.   120

ASIA

So much I asked before, and my heart gave
The response thou hast given; and of such truths
Each to itself must be the oracle.—
One more demand … and do thou answer me
As my own soul would answer, did it know   125
That which I ask.—Prometheus shall arise
Henceforth the Sun of this rejoicing world:
When shall the destined hour arrive?

DEMOGORGON

Behold!

ASIA

The rocks are cloven, and through the purple night
I see Cars drawn by rainbow-winged steeds   130
Which trample the dim winds—in each there stands
A wild-eyed charioteer, urging their flight.
Some look behind, as fiends pursued them there
And yet I see no shapes but the keen stars:
Others with burning eyes lean forth, and drink   135
With eager lips the wind of their own speed
As if the thing they loved fled on before,
And now—even now they clasped it; their bright
    locks
Stream like a comet's flashing hair: they all
Sweep onward.—

DEMOGORGON

These are the immortal Hours   140
Of whom thou didst demand.—One waits for thee.

ASIA

A Spirit with a dreadful countenance
Checks its dark chariot by the craggy gulph.
Unlike thy brethren, ghastly charioteer,
Who art thou? whither wouldst thou bear me? Speak!   145

SPIRIT

I am the shadow of a destiny
More dread than is mine aspect—ere yon planet
Has set, the Darkness which ascends with me
Shall wrap in lasting night Heaven's kingless throne.

ASIA

What meanest thou?

PANTHEA

   That terrible shadow floats   150
Up from its throne, as may the lurid[64] smoke
Of earthquake-ruined cities o'er the sea.—
Lo! it ascends the Car ... the coursers fly
Terrified; watch its path among the stars
Blackening the night!

ASIA

   Thus I am answered—strange!   155

PANTHEA

See, near the verge[65] another chariot stays;
An ivory shell inlaid with crimson fire
Which comes and goes within its sculptured rim
Of delicate strange tracery—the young Spirit
That guides it, has the dovelike eyes of hope.   160
How its soft smiles attract the soul!—as light
Lures winged insects through the lampless air.

SPIRIT

My coursers are fed with the lightning,
 They drink of the whirlwind's stream
And when the red morning is brightning   165
 They bathe in the fresh sunbeam;
  They have strength for their swiftness, I deem:
   Then ascend with me, daughter of Ocean.

---

[64] *lurid*: vividly colored, glowing amid the darkness.
[65] *verge*: horizon.

I desire—and their speed makes night kindle;
   I fear—they outstrip the Typhoon;   170
Ere the cloud piled on Atlas[66] can dwindle
   We encircle the earth and the moon:
   We shall rest from long labours at noon:
      Then ascend with me, daughter of Ocean.

SCENE V

The Car[67] *pauses within a Cloud on the Top of a snowy Mountain.*
Asia, Panthea *and the* Spirit *of the Hour.*

SPIRIT

On the brink of the night and the morning
   My coursers[68] are wont[69] to respire,[70]
But the Earth has just whispered a warning
   That their flight must be swifter than fire:
   They shall drink the hot speed of desire!   5

ASIA

Thou breathest on their nostrils—but my breath
Would give them swifter speed.

SPIRIT

               Alas, it could not.

PANTHEA

O Spirit! pause and tell whence is the light
Which fills the cloud? the sun is yet unrisen.

[66] *Atlas*: in classical mythology, the Titan brother of Prometheus, transformed into a mountain (located in Morocco and Algeria) by the Greek hero Perseus, who carried with him the head of the Gorgon Medusa, so hideous that it turned any who gazed upon it to stone.
[67] *Car*: chariot.
[68] *coursers*: horses.
[69] *are wont*: tend.
[70] *respire*: (1) breathe; (2) slow their pace.

SPIRIT

The sun will rise not until noon.—Apollo 10
Is held in Heaven by wonder—and the light
Which fills this vapour, as the aerial hue
Of fountain-gazing roses fills the water,
Flows from thy mighty sister.

PANTHEA

Yes, I feel . . .

ASIA

What is it with thee, sister? Thou art pale. 15

PANTHEA

How thou art changed! I dare not look on thee;
I feel, but see thee not. I scarce endure
The radiance of thy beauty. Some good change
Is working in the elements, which suffer
Thy presence thus unveiled.—The Nereids[71] tell 20
That on the day when the clear hyaline[72]
Was cloven at thy uprise, and thou didst stand
Within a veined shell, which floated on
Over the calm floor of the chrystal sea,
Among the Ægean isles,[73] and by the shores 25
Which bear thy name,[74] love, like the atmosphere
Of the sun's fire filling the living world,
Burst from thee, and illumined Earth and Heaven
And the deep ocean and the sunless caves,
And all that dwells within them; till grief cast 30

[71] *Nereids*: water nymphs.

[72] *hyaline*: glassy, transparent appearance (of the sea).

[73] *Ægean isles*: islands within the Aegean Sea, a lengthy arm of the Mediterranean Sea, as well as mainland Greece.

[74] *on the day . . . name*: In some tales of classical mythology, Venus, the goddess of love, was said to have risen from a shell in the midst of the sea.

Eclipse upon the soul from which it came:
Such art thou now, nor is it I alone,
Thy sister, thy companion, thine own chosen one,
But the whole world which seeks thy sympathy.
Hearest thou not sounds i' the air which speak the love   35
Of all articulate beings? Feelest thou not
The inanimate winds enamoured of thee?—List!⁷⁵

                                                    [*Music*.]

* * * * *

VOICE (*in the air, singing*)

Life of Life! thy lips enkindle
    With their love the breath between them
And thy smiles before they dwindle   50
    Make the cold air fire; then screen them
In those looks where whoso gazes
Faints, entangled in their mazes.

Child of Light! thy limbs are burning
    Through the vest which seems to hide them   55
As the radiant lines of morning
    Through the clouds ere they divide them,
And this atmosphere divinest
Shrouds thee wheresoe'er thou shinest.

Fair are others;—none beholds thee   60
    But thy voice sounds low and tender
Like the fairest—for it folds thee
    From the sight, that liquid splendour,
And all feel, yet see thee never
As I feel now, lost forever!   65

Lamp of Earth! where'er thou movest
    Its dim shapes are clad with brightness

---

⁷⁵ *List!* Listen! (an imperative).

And the souls of whom thou lovest
    Walk upon the winds with lightness
Till they fail, as I am failing,   70
Dizzy, lost … yet unbewailing!

ASIA

    My soul is an enchanted Boat
    Which, like a sleeping swan, doth float
Upon the silver waves of thy sweet singing,
    And thine doth like an Angel sit   75
    Beside a helm conducting it
Whilst all the winds with melody are ringing.
    It seems to float ever—forever—
    Upon that many winding River
    Between mountains, woods, abysses,   80
    A Paradise of wildernesses,
Till like one in slumber bound
Borne to the Ocean, I float down, around,
Into a Sea profound, of ever-spreading sound.

    Meanwhile thy Spirit lifts its pinions   85
    In Music's most serene dominions,
Catching the winds that fan that happy Heaven.
    And we sail on, away, afar,
    Without a course—without a star—
But by the instinct of sweet Music driven   90
    Till, through Elysian garden islets
    By thee, most beautiful of pilots,
    Where never mortal pinnace[76] glided,
    The boat of my desire is guided—
Realms where the air we breathe is Love   95
Which in the winds and on the waves doth move,
Harmonizing this Earth with what we feel above.

[76] *pinnace*: small boat.

We have passed Age's icy caves,
And Manhood's dark and tossing waves
And Youth's smooth ocean, smiling to betray;   100
Beyond the glassy gulphs we flee
Of shadow-peopled Infancy,
Through Death and Birth to a diviner day,
A Paradise of vaulted bowers
Lit by downward-gazing flowers   105
And watery paths that wind between
Wildernesses calm and green,
Peopled by shapes too bright to see,
And rest, having beheld—somewhat like thee,
Which walk upon the sea, and chaunt melodiously!   110

END OF THE SECOND ACT.

ACT III

SCENE I

Scene: Heaven. Jupiter *on his Throne;* Thetis *and the other Deities assembled.*

JUPITER

Ye congregated Powers of Heaven who share
The glory and the strength of him ye serve,
Rejoice! henceforth I am omnipotent.
All else had been subdued to me—alone
The soul of man, like unextinguished fire,   5
Yet burns towards Heaven with fierce reproach and doubt
And lamentation and reluctant prayer,
Hurling up insurrection, which might make
Our antique empire insecure, though built
On eldest faith, and Hell's coeval,[77] fear.   10

[77] *coeval:* (1) equal; (2) originating at the same time.

And though my curses through the pendulous[78] air
Like snow on herbless peaks, fall flake by flake
And cling to it—though under my wrath's night
It climb the crags of life, step after step,
Which wound it, as ice wounds unsandalled feet,   15
It yet remains supreme o'er misery,
Aspiring ... unrepressed; yet soon to fall:
Even now have I begotten a strange wonder,
That fatal Child,[79] the terror of the Earth,
Who waits but till the destined Hour arrive,   20
Bearing from Demogorgon's vacant throne
The dreadful might of ever living limbs
Which clothed that awful spirit unbeheld—
To redescend and trample out the spark ...
Pour forth Heaven's wine, Idæan Ganymede,[80]   25
And let it fill the dædal[81] cups like fire
And from the flower-inwoven soil divine
Ye all triumphant harmonies arise
As dew from Earth under the twilight stars;
Drink! be the nectar circling through your veins   30
The soul of joy, ye everliving Gods,
Till exultation burst in one wide voice
Like music from Elysian winds.—
                              And thou
Ascend beside me, veiled in the light
Of the desire which makes thee one with me,   35
Thetis,[82] bright Image of Eternity!—
When thou didst cry, "Insufferable might!
God! spare me! I sustain not the quick flames,

---

[78] *pendulous*: (1) vacillating; (2) floating in space.

[79] *fatal Child*: i.e., the offspring of Jupiter fated to overthrow his father.

[80] *Idæan Ganymede*: In classical mythology, Jupiter carried off the young shepherd Ganymede from Mount Ida to serve as cupbearer to the gods on Mount Olympus.

[81] *dædal*: cunningly, skillfully wrought.

[82] *Thetis*': In classical mythology, Thetis is a sea nymph and mother of the Greek warrior Achilles.

The penetrating presence;[83] all my being,
Like him whom the Numidian seps[84] did thaw   40
Into a dew with poison, is dissolved,
Sinking through its foundations"—even then
Two mighty spirits, mingling, made a third
Mightier than either—which unbodied now
Between us, floats, felt although unbeheld,   45
Waiting the incarnation, which ascends—
Hear ye the thunder of the fiery wheels
Griding[85] the winds?—from Demogorgon's throne.—
Victory! victory! Feel'st thou not, O World,
The Earthquake of his chariot thundering up   50
Olympus?[86]
[*The Car of the* Hour *arrives.* Demogorgon *descends and moves
towards the Throne of* Jupiter.]
          Awful Shape, what art thou? Speak!

DEMOGORGON

Eternity—demand no direr name.
Descend, and follow me down the abyss;
I am thy child, as thou wert Saturn's child,
Mightier than thee;[87] and we must dwell together   55
Henceforth in darkness.—Lift thy lightnings not.
The tyranny of Heaven none may retain,
Or reassume, or hold succeeding thee …
Yet if thou wilt—as 'tis the destiny
Of trodden worms to writhe till they are dead—   60
Put forth thy might.

---

[83] *I sustain … presence*: In classical mythology, Semele, the lover of Jupiter, forced him (in fulfillment of a promise and at the prompting of his jealous wife, Hera) to reveal himself in his glory and was burnt to a crisp at the sight.

[84] *Numidian seps*: legendary snakes carrying poison that causes their victims to dissolve when bitten.

[85] *Griding*: grating against.

[86] *Olympus*: mountain home of the gods.

[87] *I am … thee*: In classical mythology, it was predicted that Jupiter would be overthrown by his own son, just as he overthrew his father, Saturn.

JUPITER

Detested prodigy!
Even thus beneath the deep Titanian prisons[88]
I trample thee! ... Thou lingerest?
                              Mercy! mercy!
No pity—no release, no respite! ... Oh,
That thou wouldst make mine enemy my judge.   65
Even where he hangs, seared by my long revenge
On Caucasus—he would not doom me thus.—
Gentle and just and dreadless, is he not
The monarch of the world?—what then art thou? ...
No refuge! no appeal— ...
                              Sink with me then—   70
We two will sink in the wide waves of ruin
Even as a vulture and a snake outspent
Drop, twisted in inextricable fight,
Into a shoreless sea.—Let Hell unlock
Its mounded Oceans of tempestuous fire,   75
And whelm on them into the bottomless void
This desolated world and thee and me,
The conqueror and the conquered, and the wreck
Of that for which they combated.
                              Ai! Ai!
The elements obey me not ... I sink ...   80
Dizzily down—ever, forever, down—
And, like a cloud, mine enemy above
Darkens my fall with victory!—Ai! Ai!

SCENE II

The Mouth of a great River in the Island Atlantis. Ocean *is discov-
ered reclining near the Shore;* Apollo *stands beside him.*

OCEAN

He fell, thou sayest, beneath his conqueror's frown?

---

[88] *deep Titanian prisons:* According to mythology, the Titans were buried deep
below the earth, imprisoned in Tartarus.

APOLLO

Aye, when the strife was ended which made dim
The orb[89] I rule, and shook the solid stars.[90]
The terrors of his eye illumined Heaven
With sanguine[91] light, through the thick ragged skirts   5
Of the victorious Darkness, as he fell;
Like the last glare of day's red agony
Which from a rent among the fiery clouds
Burns far along the tempest-wrinkled Deep.

OCEAN

He sunk to the abyss? to the dark void?   10

APOLLO

An eagle so, caught in some bursting cloud
On Caucasus, his thunder-baffled wings
Entangled in the whirlwind, and his eyes
Which gazed on the undazzling sun, now blinded
By the white lightning, while the ponderous hail   15
Beats on his struggling form which sinks at length
Prone, and the aerial ice clings over it.

OCEAN

Henceforth the fields of Heaven-reflecting sea
Which are my realm, will heave, unstain'd with blood
Beneath the uplifting winds—like plains of corn   20
Swayed by the summer air; my streams will flow
Round many-peopled continents and round
Fortunate isles; and from their glassy thrones
Blue Proteus and his humid Nymphs shall mark
The shadow of fair ships, as mortals see   25
The floating bark of the light-laden moon

[89] *orb*: i.e., sun.
[90] *solid stars*: Most of the stars were believed to be fixed and immovable, differentiated from the omen-relevant comets and other shooting stars.
[91] *sanguine*: blood red.

With that white star,[92] its sightless pilot's crest,
Borne down the rapid sunset's ebbing sea;
Tracking their path no more by blood and groans;
And desolation, and the mingled voice   30
Of slavery and command—but by the light
Of wave-reflected flowers, and floating odours,
And music soft, and mild, free, gentle voices,
That sweetest music, such as spirits love.

APOLLO

And I shall gaze not on the deeds which make   35
My mind obscure with sorrow, as Eclipse
Darkens the sphere I guide—but list, I hear
The small, clear, silver lute of the young spirit
That sits i' the Morning star.[93]

OCEAN

Thou must away?
Thy steeds will pause at even—till when, farewell.   40
The loud Deep calls me home even now, to feed it
With azure calm out of the emerald urns
Which stand forever full beside my throne.
Behold the Nereids under the green sea,
Their wavering limbs borne on the windlike stream,   45
Their white arms lifted o'er their streaming hair
With garlands pied[94] and starry sea-flower crowns,
Hastening to grace their mighty Sister's joy.
                              [*A sound of waves is heard.*]
It is the unpastured Sea hung'ring for Calm.
Peace, Monster—I come now! Farewell.

APOLLO

Farewell!   50

* * * * *

---

[92] *white star*: Venus, the "morning star".
[93] *Morning star*: i.e., Venus.
[94] *pied*: multicolored.

SCENE IV

A Forest. In the Background a Cave. Prometheus, Asia, Panthea, Ione, *and the* Spirit of the Earth.

IONE

Sister, it is not Earthly ... how it glides
Under the leaves! how on its head there burns
A light like a green star, whose emerald beams
Are twined with its fair hair! how, as it moves
The splendour drops in flakes upon the grass!   5
Knowest thou it?

PANTHEA

             It is the delicate spirit
That guides the earth through Heaven. From afar
The populous constellations call that light
The loveliest of the planets, and sometimes
It floats along the spray of the salt sea   10
Or makes its chariot of a foggy cloud
Or walks through fields or cities while men sleep
Or o'er the mountain tops, or down the rivers,
Or through the green waste wilderness, as now,
Wondering at all it sees. Before Jove reigned   15
It loved our sister Asia, and it came
Each leisure hour to drink the liquid light
Out of her eyes, for which it said it thirsted
As one bit by a dipsas;[95] and with her
It made its childish confidence, and told her   20
All it had known or seen, for it saw much,
Yet idly reasoned what it saw; and called her—
For whence it sprung it knew not nor do I—
"Mother, dear Mother."

[95] *dipsas*: a snake, closely associated with the story of Prometheus, that (according to myth) infected those it bit with an intense thirst.

SPIRIT OF THE EARTH [*running to* Asia]

                    Mother, dearest Mother;
May I then talk with thee as I was wont?   25
May I then hide mine eyes in thy soft arms
After thy looks have made them tired of joy?
May I then play beside thee the long noons
When work is none in the bright silent air?

ASIA

I love thee, gentlest being, and henceforth   30
Can cherish thee unenvied.—Speak, I pray:
Thy simple talk once solaced, now delights.

SPIRIT OF THE EARTH

Mother, I am grown wiser, though a child
Cannot be wise like thee, within this day
And happier too, happier and wiser both.   35
Thou knowest that toads and snakes and loathly worms
And venomous and malicious beasts, and boughs
That bore ill berries in the woods, were ever
An hindrance to my walks o'er the green world,
And that, among the haunts of humankind   40
Hard-featured men, or with proud, angry looks
Or cold, staid gait, or false and hollow smiles
Or the dull sneer of self-loved ignorance
Or other such foul masks with which ill thoughts
Hide that fair being whom we spirits call man;   45
And women too, ugliest of all things evil,
Though fair, even in a world where thou art fair
When good and kind, free and sincere like thee,
When false or frowning made me sick at heart
To pass them, though they slept, and I unseen.   50
Well—my path lately lay through a great City
Into the woody hills surrounding it.
A sentinel was sleeping at the gate:
When there was heard a sound, so loud, it shook

The towers amid the moonlight, yet more sweet 55
Than any voice but thine, sweetest of all,
A long long sound, as it would never end:
And all the inhabitants leapt suddenly
Out of their rest, and gathered in the streets,
Looking in wonder up to Heaven, while yet 60
The music pealed along. I hid myself
Within a fountain in the public square
Where I lay like the reflex[96] of the moon
Seen in a wave under green leaves—and soon
Those ugly human shapes and visages 65
Of which I spoke as having wrought me pain,
Past floating through the air, and fading still
Into the winds that scattered them; and those
From whom they past seemed mild and lovely forms
After some foul disguise had fallen—and all 70
Were somewhat changed, and after brief surprise
And greetings of delighted wonder, all
Went to their sleep again: and when the dawn
Came—wouldst thou think that toads and snakes and
        efts[97]
Could e'er be beautiful?—yet so they were 75
And that with little change of shape or hue:
All things had put their evil nature off.
I cannot tell my joy, when o'er a lake,
Upon a drooping bough with nightshade[98] twined,
I saw two azure halcyons[99] clinging downward 80
And thinning one bright bunch of amber berries
With quick, long beaks, and in the deep there lay
Those lovely forms imaged as in a sky.—
So with my thoughts full of these happy changes
We meet again, the happiest change of all. 85

[96] *reflex*: reflection.
[97] *efts*: newts or other lizard-like creatures.
[98] *nightshade*: a genus of herbs, shrubs, and trees that bears flowers and sometimes poisonous red or black berries.
[99] *halcyons*: mythical birds, associated with kingfishers, thought to exert a calming influence.

ASIA

And never will we part, till thy chaste Sister
Who guides the frozen and inconstant moon
Will look on thy more warm and equal light
Till her heart thaw like flakes of April snow
And love thee.

SPIRIT OF THE EARTH

What, as Asia loves Prometheus?　　　　　　90

ASIA

Peace, Wanton[100]—thou art yet not old enough.
Think ye, by gazing on each other's eyes
To multiply your lovely selves, and fill
With sphered fires the interlunar[101] air?

SPIRIT OF THE EARTH

Nay, Mother, while my sister trims[102] her lamp　　　95
'Tis hard I should go darkling[103]—

ASIA

　　　　　　　　—Listen! look!
　　　　　　　[*The* Spirit of the Hour *enters*.]

PROMETHEUS

We feel what thou hast heard and seen—yet speak.

SPIRIT OF THE HOUR

Soon as the sound had ceased whose thunder filled
The abysses of the sky, and the wide earth,

---

[100] *Wanton*: spoiled child.
[101] *interlunar*: i.e., dark, between the old and new moon, when the night sky is in need of "sphered fires" to brighten it.
[102] *trims*: attends to (e.g., trimming the wick to prolong the life of the candle).
[103] *darkling*: in the dark.

There was a change ... the impalpable thin air   100
And the all-circling sunlight were transformed
As if the sense of love dissolved in them
Had folded itself round the sphered world.
My vision then grew clear and I could see
Into the mysteries of the Universe.   105
Dizzy as with delight I floated down,
Winnowing[104] the lightsome air with languid plumes,
My coursers sought their birthplace in the sun
Where they henceforth will live exempt from toil,
Pasturing flowers of vegetable fire—   110
And where my moonlike car will stand within
A temple, gazed upon by Phidian forms,[105]
Of thee, and Asia and the Earth, and me
And you fair nymphs, looking the love we feel,
In memory of the tidings it has borne,   115
Beneath a dome fretted with graven flowers,
Poised on twelve columns of resplendent stone[106]
And open to the bright and liquid sky.
Yoked to it by an amphisbænic snake[107]
The likeness of those winged steeds will mock   120
The flight from which they find repose.[108]—Alas,
Whither has wandered now my partial[109] tongue
When all remains untold which ye would hear!—
As I have said, I floated to the Earth:
It was, as it is still, the pain of bliss   125

---

[104] *Winnowing*: flapping, beating.

[105] *Phidian forms*: Phidias (c. 480–430 B.C.) was one of the greatest sculptors of classical Greece, and his "forms" were considered representative of exquisite perfection.

[106] *dome ... stone*: Shelley may be referencing here the Parthenon in Rome, a temple to all the gods.

[107] *amphisbænic snake*: a mythical serpent having heads at both ends of its body and able to move forward or backward.

[108] *likeness ... repose*: Shelley may have in mind an ancient statue of the biga (chariot), a statue of the victorious charioteer housed in the Sala della Biga (the Vatican Museum), which also houses a statue of the amphisbaena.

[109] *partial*: favorably biased, prejudiced.

To move, to breathe, to be; I wandering went
Among the haunts and dwellings of mankind
And first was disappointed not to see
Such mighty change as I had felt within
Expressed in outward things; but soon I looked,   130
And behold! thrones were kingless, and men walked
One with the other even as spirits do,
None fawned, none trampled; hate, disdain or fear,
Self-love or self-contempt on human brows
No more inscribed, as o'er the gate of hell,   135
"All hope abandon, ye who enter here";[110]
None frowned, none trembled, none with eager fear
Gazed on another's eye of cold command
Until the subject of a tyrant's will
Became, worse fate, the abject[111] of his own   140
Which spurred him, like an outspent horse, to death.
None wrought his lips in truth-entangling lines
Which smiled the lie his tongue disdained to speak;
None with firm sneer trod out in his own heart
The sparks of love and hope, till there remained   145
Those bitter ashes, a soul self-consumed,
And the wretch crept, a vampire among men,
Infecting all with his own hideous ill.
None talked that common, false, cold, hollow talk
Which makes the heart deny the *yes* it breathes   150
Yet question that unmeant hypocrisy
With such a self-mistrust as has no name.
And women too, frank, beautiful and kind
As the free Heaven which rains fresh light and dew
On the wide earth, past: gentle, radiant forms,   155
From custom's evil taint exempt and pure;
Speaking the wisdom once they could not think,
Looking emotions once they feared to feel
And changed to all which once they dared not be,

---

[110] "*All . . . here*": see Dante's *Inferno* in *The Divine Comedy* (canto 3, line 9).
[111] *abject*: exile, outcast.

Yet being now, made Earth like Heaven—nor pride   160
Nor jealousy nor envy nor ill shame,
The bitterest of those drops of treasured gall,
Spoilt the sweet taste of the nepenthe,[112] love.

Thrones, altars, judgement-seats and prisons; wherein
And beside which, by wretched men were borne   165
Sceptres, tiaras, swords and chains, and tomes
Of reasoned wrong glozed[113] on by ignorance,
Were like those monstrous and barbaric shapes,
The ghosts of a no more remembered fame,
Which from their unworn obelisks[114] look forth   170
In triumph o'er the palaces and tombs
Of those who were their conquerors, mouldering round.
Those imaged to the pride of Kings and Priests
A dark yet mighty faith, a power as wide
As is the world it wasted, and are now   175
But an astonishment; even so the tools
And emblems of its last captivity
Amid the dwellings of the peopled Earth,
Stand, not o'erthrown, but unregarded now.
And those foul shapes, abhorred by God and man—   180
Which under many a name and many a form
Strange, savage, ghastly, dark and execrable
Were Jupiter, the tyrant of the world;
And which the nations panic-stricken served
With blood, and hearts broken by long hope, and love   185
Dragged to his altars soiled and garlandless
And slain amid men's unreclaiming tears,
Flattering the thing they feared, which fear was hate—

---

[112] *nepenthe*: see footnote 53, page 209.

[113] *glozed*: glossed, explained.

[114] *obelisks*: These mighty four-sided, thin monuments of antiquity, inscribed with hieroglyphics that were not then decipherable, were carried throughout the world and installed in places of honor in the lands of those who conquered their ancient homes (such as Rome).

Frown, mouldering fast, o'er their abandoned shrines.
The painted veil, by those who were, called life,   190
Which mimicked,[115] as with colours idly spread,
All men believed and hoped, is torn aside—
The loathsome mask has fallen, the man remains
Sceptreless, free, uncircumscribed—but man:
Equal, unclassed, tribeless and nationless,   195
Exempt from awe, worship, degree,—the King
Over himself; just, gentle, wise—but man:
Passionless? no—yet free from guilt or pain
Which were, for his will made, or suffered them,
Nor yet exempt, though ruling them like slaves,   200
From chance and death and mutability,
The clogs[116] of that which else might oversoar
The loftiest star of unascended Heaven
Pinnacled dim in the intense inane.[117]

END OF THE THIRD ACT.

ACT IV

Scene: A Part of the Forest near the Cave of Prometheus.

* * * * *

IONE

What is that awful sound?   185

PANTHEA

'Tis the deep music of the rolling world,
Kindling within the strings of the waved air
Æolian modulations.

---

[115] *mimicked*: imitated (with a negative connotation).
[116] *clogs*: impediments, blocks.
[117] *intense inane*: the formless void, space, infinity.

IONE

> Listen too,
> How every pause is filled with under-notes,
> Clear, silver, icy, keen awakening tones   190
> Which pierce the sense and live within the soul
> As the sharp stars pierce Winter's chrystal air
> And gaze upon themselves within the sea.

PANTHEA

> But see, where through two openings in the forest
> Which hanging branches overcanopy,   195
> And where two runnels[118] of a rivulet
> Between the close moss violet-inwoven
> Have made their path of melody, like sisters
> Who part with sighs that they may meet in smiles,
> Turning their dear disunion to an isle   200
> Of lovely grief, a wood of sweet sad thoughts;
> Two visions of strange radiance float upon
> The Ocean-like inchantment of strong sound
> Which flows intenser, keener, deeper yet
> Under the ground and through the windless air.   205

IONE

> I see a chariot like that thinnest boat
> In which the Mother of the Months[119] is borne
> By ebbing light into her western cave
> When she upsprings from interlunar dreams,
> O'er which is curved an orb-like canopy   210
> Of gentle darkness, and the hills and woods
> Distinctly seen through that dusk aery veil
> Regard[120] like shapes in an enchanter's glass;
> Its wheels are solid clouds, azure and gold,
> Such as the genii[121] of the thunderstorm   215

[118] *runnels*: brooks or small streams.
[119] *Mother of the Months*: i.e., the moon.
[120] *Regard*: appear.
[121] *genii*: see footnote 28, page 197.

Pile on the floor of the illumined sea
When the Sun rushes under it; they roll
And move and grow as with an inward wind.
Within it sits a winged Infant,[122] white
Its countenance, like the whiteness of bright snow,   220
Its plumes are as feathers of sunny frost,
Its limbs gleam white, through the wind-flowing folds
Of its white robe, woof of ætherial pearl.
Its hair is white,—the brightness of white light
Scattered in strings, yet its two eyes are Heavens   225
Of liquid darkness, which the Deity
Within, seems pouring, as a storm is poured
From jagged clouds, out of their arrowy lashes,
Tempering the cold and radiant air around
With fire that is not brightness;[123] in its hand   230
It sways a quivering moonbeam, from whose point
A guiding power directs the chariot's prow
Over its wheeled clouds, which as they roll
Over the grass and flowers and waves, wake sounds
Sweet as a singing rain of silver dew.   235

PANTHEA

And from the other opening in the wood
Rushes with loud and whirlwind harmony
A sphere, which is as many thousand spheres,
Solid as chrystal, yet through all its mass
Flow, as through empty space, music and light: 240
Ten thousand orbs involving and involved,[124]
Purple and azure, white and green and golden,
Sphere within sphere, and every space between
Peopled with unimaginable shapes
Such as ghosts dream dwell in the lampless deep   245
Yet each intertranspicuous,[125] and they whirl

[122] *winged Infant*: the new moon.
[123] *fire . . . brightness*: i.e., dark infrared emanations, discovered by the astronomer Sir Frederick William Herschel (1738–1822).
[124] *involving and involved*: entwining and intertwined (i.e., in their orbits).
[125] *intertranspicuous*: transparent within or between.

Over each other with a thousand motions
Upon a thousand sightless[126] axles spinning
And with the force of self-destroying swiftness,
Intensely, slowly, solemnly roll on[127]—   250
Kindling with mingled sounds, and many tones,
Intelligible words and music wild.—
With mighty whirl the multidinous Orb
Grinds the bright brook into an azure mist
Of elemental subtlety, like light,   255
And the wild odour of the forest flowers,
The music of the living grass and air,
The emerald light of leaf-entangled beams
Round its intense, yet self-conflicting speed,[128]
Seem kneaded into one aerial mass   260
Which drowns the sense. Within the Orb itself,
Pillowed upon its alabaster arms
Like to a child o'erwearied with sweet toil,
On its own folded wings and wavy hair
The Spirit of the Earth is laid asleep,   265
And you can see its little lips are moving
Amid the changing light of their own smiles
Like one who talks of what he loves in dream—

IONE

'Tis only mocking the Orb's harmony . . .

PANTHEA

And from a star upon its forehead, shoot,   270
Like swords of azure fire, or golden spears
With tyrant-quelling myrtle[129] overtwined,

---

[126] *sightless*: invisible.

[127] *A sphere . . . roll on*: This description takes much from Milton's *Paradise Lost* (bk. 5, lines 620–24; bk. 6, lines 749ff.) as well as Dante's *Purgatorio* in *The Divine Comedy* (canto 29).

[128] *self-conflicting speed*: i.e., because the concentric and intertwined spheres are orbiting and spinning in different directions.

[129] *myrtle*: flowering plants associated with Venus, the goddess of love.

Embleming Heaven and Earth united now,
Vast beams like spokes of some invisible wheel
Which whirl as the Orb whirls, swifter than thought,   275
Filling the abyss with sunlike lightenings,
And perpendicular now, and now transverse,
Pierce the dark soil, and as they pierce and pass
Make bare the secrets of the Earth's deep heart,
Infinite mine of adamant[130] and gold,   280
Valueless[131] stones and unimagined gems,
And caverns on chrystalline columns poised
With vegetable silver[132] overspread,
Wells of unfathomed fire, and watersprings
Whence the great Sea, even as a child, is fed   285
Whose vapours clothe Earth's monarch mountain-tops
With kingly, ermine snow; the beams flash on
And make appear the melancholy ruins
Of cancelled cycles; anchors, beaks of ships,
Planks turned to marble, quivers, helms[133] and spears   290
And gorgon-headed targes,[134] and the wheels
Of scythed chariots,[135] and the emblazonry
Of trophies, standards and armorial beasts
Round which Death laughed, sepulchred emblems
Of dead Destruction, ruin within ruin!   295
The wrecks beside of many a city vast,
Whose population which the Earth grew over
Was mortal but not human; see, they lie,
Their monstrous works and uncouth skeletons,
Their statues, homes, and fanes;[136] prodigious shapes   300

---

[130] *adamant*: see footnote 63, page 210.

[131] *Valueless*: immeasurably valuable.

[132] *vegetable silver*: Cf. Milton's *Paradise Lost* (bk. 4, lines 218–20): the Tree of Life bears "Ambrosial Fruit/Of vegetable Gold".

[133] *helms*: helmets.

[134] *gorgon-headed targes*: archers' shields, emblazoned with gorgon's heads (in classical mythology, the heads of women so hideous that the sight of them turned those who looked upon them to stone).

[135] *scythed chariots*: chariots armed with scythes.

[136] *fanes*: temples.

Huddled in grey annihilation, split,
Jammed in the hard black deep; and over these
The anatomies[137] of unknown winged things,
And fishes which were isles of living scale,
And serpents, bony chains, twisted around   305
The iron crags, or within heaps of dust
To which the tortuous strength of their last pangs
Had crushed the iron crags;—and over these
The jagged alligator and the might
Of earth-convulsing behemoth,[138] which once   310
Were monarch beasts, and on the slimy shores
And weed-overgrown continents of Earth
Increased and multiplied like summer worms
On an abandoned corpse, till the blue globe
Wrapt Deluge round it like a cloak, and they   315
Yelled, gaspt and were abolished; or some God
Whose throne was in a Comet, past, and cried—
"Be not!"—and like my words they were no more.

* * * * *

DEMOGORGON

Thou Earth, calm empire of a happy Soul,
    Sphere of divinest shapes and harmonies,   520
Beautiful orb! gathering as thou dost roll
    The Love which paves thy path along the skies:

THE EARTH

I hear,—I am as a drop of dew that dies!

DEMOGORGON

Thou Moon, which gazest on the nightly Earth
    With wonder, as it gazes upon thee,   525

---

[137] *anatomies*: skeletons.
[138] *behemoth*: monstrous, powerful creature with a special place in myth and mentioned in the biblical Book of Job (see 40:15–24).

Whilst each to men and beasts and the swift birth
   Of birds, is beauty, love, calm, harmony:

THE MOON

I hear—I am a leaf shaken by thee!

DEMOGORGON

Ye Kings of suns and stars, Dæmons and Gods,
   Æthereal Dominations,[139] who possess   530
Elysian, windless, fortunate abodes
   Beyond Heaven's constellated wilderness:

A VOICE: *from above*

Our great Republic hears … we are blest, and bless.

DEMOGORGON

Ye happy dead, whom beams of brightest verse
   Are clouds to hide, not colours to portray,   535
Whether your nature is that Universe
   Which once ye saw and suffered—

A VOICE: *from beneath*

                         Or as they
Whom we have left, we change and pass away.—

DEMOGORGON

Ye elemental Genii,[140] who have homes
   From man's high mind even to the central stone   540
Of sullen lead, from Heaven's star-fretted domes
   To the dull weed some sea-worm battens[141] on—

---

[139] *Ye … Dominations*: In Shelley's described heavenly hierarchy—which imitates that of Dante's *Paradiso* in *The Divine Comedy* (canto 28, lines 121–26) and Milton's *Paradise Lost* (bk. 2, lines 310–11; bk. 5, line 772)—there are only three levels: dæmons (which rule over the tangible world), gods (which rule likewise), and dominations (which are at rest outside the tangible universe).

[140] *Genii*: see footnote 28, page 197.

[141] *battens*: feeds gluttonously.

A *confused* VOICE

We hear: thy words waken Oblivion.

DEMOGORGON

Spirits whose homes are flesh—ye beasts and birds—
  Ye worms and fish—ye living leaves and buds—   545
Lightning and Wind—and ye untameable herds,
  Meteors and mists, which throng Air's solitudes:

A VOICE

Thy voice to us is wind among still woods.

DEMOGORGON

Man, who wert once a despot and a slave,—
  A dupe and a deceiver,—a Decay,   550
A Traveller from the cradle to the grave
  Through the dim night of this immortal Day:

ALL

Speak—thy strong words may never pass away.

DEMOGORGON

This is the Day which down the void Abysm
At the Earth-born's spell yawns for Heaven's Despotism,   555
  And Conquest is dragged Captive through the Deep;
Love from its awful throne of patient power
In the wise heart, from the last giddy hour
  Of dread endurance, from the slippery, steep,
And narrow verge of crag-like Agony, springs   560
And folds over the world its healing wings.

Gentleness, Virtue, Wisdom and Endurance,—
These are the seals of that most firm assurance
  Which bars the pit over Destruction's strength;

And if, with infirm hand, Eternity, 565
Mother of many acts and hours, should free
    The serpent that would clasp her with his length—
These are the spells by which to reassume
An empire o'er the disentangled Doom.

To suffer woes which Hope thinks infinite; 570
To forgive wrongs darker than Death or Night;
    To defy Power which seems Omnipotent;
To love, and bear; to hope, till Hope creates
From its own wreck the thing it contemplates;
    Neither to change nor falter nor repent:[142] 575
    This, like thy glory, Titan! is to be
    Good, great and joyous, beautiful and free;
    This is alone Life, Joy, Empire and Victory.

Ode to the West Wind (late 1819)

I

O wild West Wind, thou breath of Autumn's being,
Thou, from whose unseen presence the leaves dead
Are driven, like ghosts from an enchanter fleeing,

Yellow, and black, and pale, and hectic[143] red,
Pestilence-stricken multitudes; O Thou, 5
Who chariotest to their dark wintry bed

The winged seeds, where they lie cold and low,
Each like a corpse within its grave, until
Thine azure sister of the Spring shall blow

---

[142] *Neither ... repent*: Cf. *Paradise Lost* (bk. 1, lines 94–96): "[Y]et not for those/Nor what the Potent Victor in his rage/Can else inflict, do I repent or change."

[143] *hectic*: wasting, as in the effects of tuberculosis, which prompted a "hectic flush" in its sufferers.

Her clarion[144] o'er the dreaming earth, and fill   10
(Driving sweet buds like flocks to feed in air)
With living hues and odours plain and hill:
Wild Spirit, which art moving everywhere;
Destroyer and Preserver;[145] hear, O hear!

II

Thou on whose stream, 'mid the steep sky's commotion,   15
Loose clouds like Earth's decaying leaves are shed,
Shook from the tangled boughs of Heaven and Ocean,

Angels[146] of rain and lightning: they are spread
On the blue surface of thine aery surge,
Like the bright hair uplifted from the head   20

Of some fierce Mænad,[147] even from the dim verge
Of the horizon to the zenith's height,
The locks of the approaching storm. Thou Dirge[148]

Of the dying year, to which this closing night
Will be the dome of a vast sepulchre,   25
Vaulted with all thy congregated might

Of vapours,[149] from whose solid atmosphere
Black rain and fire and hail will burst: O hear!

III

Thou who didst waken from his summer dreams
The blue Mediterranean, where he lay,   30
Lulled by the coil of his chrystalline streams,

[144] *clarion*: loud, clear call of a war trumpet.
[145] *Destroyer and Preserver*: the titles of the Hindu gods Siva and Vishnu.
[146] *Angels*: messengers.
[147] *Mænad*: in classical mythology, a frenzied nymph and follower of the god Dionysius.
[148] *Dirge*: funeral song.
[149] *vapours*: clouds.

Beside a pumice isle in Baiæ's bay,[150]
And saw in sleep old palaces and towers
Quivering within the wave's intenser day,

All overgrown with azure moss and flowers 35
So sweet, the sense faints picturing them! Thou
For whose path the Atlantic's level powers

Cleave themselves into chasms, while far below
The sea-blooms and the oozy woods which wear
The sapless foliage of the ocean,[151] know 40

Thy voice, and suddenly grow grey with fear,
And tremble and despoil themselves: O hear!

IV

If I were a dead leaf thou mightest bear;
If I were a swift cloud to fly with thee;
A wave to pant beneath thy power, and share 45

The impulse of thy strength, only less free
Than thou, O Uncontrollable! If even
I were as in my boyhood, and could be

The comrade of thy wanderings over Heaven,
As then, when to outstrip thy skiey speed 50
Scarce seemed a vision; I would ne'er have striven

As thus with thee in prayer in my sore need.
Oh! lift me as a wave, a leaf, a cloud!
I fall upon the thorns of life! I bleed!

[150] *Baiæ's bay*: a seaside resort in Naples, visited by Shelley in 1818.
[151] *while . . . ocean*: As Shelley himself wrote: "The phenomenon alluded to at
the conclusion of the third stanza is well known to naturalists. The vegetation
at the bottom of the sea, of rivers, and of lakes, sympathizes with that of the land
in the change of seasons, and is consequently influenced by the winds which
announce it." *The Complete Poetical Works of Percy Bysshe Shelley*, ed. Thoman
Hutchinson (London: Oxford University Press, 1914), p. 573.

A heavy weight of hours has chained and bowed 55
One too like thee: tameless, and swift, and proud.

V

Make me thy lyre, even as the forest is:
What if my leaves are falling like its own!
The tumult of thy mighty harmonies

Will take from both a deep, autumnal tone, 60
Sweet though in sadness. Be thou, Spirit fierce,
My spirit! Be thou me, impetuous one!

Drive my dead thoughts over the universe
Like withered leaves to quicken a new birth!
And, by the incantation of this verse, 65

Scatter, as from an unextinguished hearth
Ashes and sparks, my words among mankind!
Be through my lips to unawakened Earth

The trumpet of a prophecy! O Wind,
If Winter comes, can Spring be far behind? 70

The Indian Girl's Song (1820?)

I arise from dreams of thee
In the first sleep of night—
The winds are breathing low
And the stars are burning bright.
I arise from dreams of thee— 5
And a spirit in my feet
Has borne me—Who knows how?
To thy chamber window, sweet!—

The wandering airs they faint
On the dark silent stream— 10

The champak[152] odours fail
Like sweet thoughts in a dream;
The nightingale's complaint—
It dies upon her heart—
As I must die on thine   15
O beloved as thou art!

O lift me from the grass!
I die, I faint, I fail!
Let thy love in kisses rain
On my lips and eyelids pale.   20
My cheek is cold and white, alas!
My heart beats loud and fast.
Oh press it close to thine again
Where it will break at last.

The Sensitive-Plant[153]

"The Sensitive-Plant" was written in 1820. The leaves of the plant—the *mimosa pudica*—shrink away and fold when touched.

This is a symbolist poem. According to the editor of Shelley's *Alastor and Other Poems*, "On one level we can read the poem simply as a description of a beautiful garden, of the lady who tended it, of her death and its decay in winter. But it is not just an ordinary garden. It is an 'undefilèd Paradise'", yet "it is not abstracted from the normal world of change. It images a certain psychological state, a fragile one, rather like that suggested in Blake's *Songs of Innocence*."[154]

Interpretations of the identity of the plant have included Shelley himself, the poet, the unusually sensitive person, and mankind in general.

---

[152] *champak*: an evergreen timber tree (a species of magnolia) native to India and bearing fragrant blooms.

[153] *Sensitive-Plant*: a form of mimosa (also known as the "touch-me-not") that curls up when touched.

[154] In Percy Bysshe Shelley, *Alastor and Other Poems; Prometheus Unbound with Other Poems; Adonais*, ed. P. H. Butter (Plymouth, U.K.: Macdonald and Evans, 1981), pp. 316–17.

The poet's widow wrote that some of its stanzas

> express, in some degree, the almost inexpressible idea, not that
> we die into another state, when this state is no longer ... but
> that those who rise above the ordinary nature of man, fade from
> before our imperfect organs; they remain in their "love, beauty,
> and delight," in a world congenial to them—we, clogged by
> "error, ignorance, and strife," see them not, till we are fitted by
> purification and improvement for their higher state.[155]

The Sensitive-Plant (1820)

PART FIRST

A Sensitive-plant in a garden grew,
And the young winds fed it with silver dew,
And it opened its fan-like leaves to the light.
And closed them beneath the kisses of night.

And the Spring arose on the garden fair   5
Like the Spirit of love felt every where;
And each flower and herb on Earth's dark breast
Rose from the dreams of its wintry rest.

But none ever trembled and panted with bliss
In the garden, the field or the wilderness,   10
Like a doe in the noontide with love's sweet want
As the companionless Sensitive-plant.[156]

The snow-drop and then the violet
Arose from the ground with warm rain wet
And their breath was mixed with fresh odour, sent   15
From the turf, like the voice and the instrument.

[155] In Percy Bysshe Shelley, *Essays, Letters from Abroad, Translations and Fragments*, vol. 1, ed. Mary Shelley (Philadelphia: Lea & Blanchard, 1840), pp. 11–12.

[156] *companionless Sensitive-plant*: i.e., annual (while the other plants mentioned in part 1 are all perennials).

Then the pied[157] wind-flowers and the tulip tall,
And narcissi, the fairest among them all
Who gaze on their eyes in the stream's recess
Till they die of their own dear loveliness;[158]   20

And the Naiad-like[159] lily of the vale
Whom youth makes so fair and passion so pale,
That the light of its tremulous bells is seen
Through their pavilions of tender green;

And the hyacinth[160] purple, and white, and blue,   25
Which flung from its bells a sweet peal anew
Of music so delicate, soft and intense,
It was felt like an odour within the sense;

And the rose like a nymph to the bath addresst,
Which unveiled the depth of her glowing breast,   30
Till, fold after fold, to the fainting air
The soul of her beauty and love lay bare:

And the wand-like lily, which lifted up,
As a Mænad,[161] its moonlight-coloured cup
Till the fiery star, which is its eye,   35
Gazed through clear dew on the tender sky;

And the jessamine faint, and the sweet tuberose,
The sweetest flower for scent that blows;[162]
And all rare blossoms from every clime
Grew in that garden in perfect prime.   40

---

[157] *pied*: multicolored.

[158] *narcissi . . . loveliness*: In classical mythology, the beautiful hunter Narcissus fell in love with his own reflection in a pool and died because he could not bear to leave that spot. After death, he underwent metamorphosis, becoming a flower.

[159] *Naiad-like*: In classical mythology, a naiad is a water nymph.

[160] *hyacinth*: in classical mythology, a young man beloved by both Apollo and Zephyrus (god of the West Wind), killed in their rivalry and transformed by Apollo into a flower.

[161] *Mænad*: see footnote 147, page 240.

[162] *blows*: blooms.

And on the stream whose inconstant bosom
Was prankt[163] under boughs of embowering blossom
With golden and green light, slanting through
Their heaven of many a tangled hue,

Broad water-lilies lay tremulously,   45
And starry river-buds glimmered by,
And around them the soft stream did glide and dance
With a motion of sweet sound and radiance.

And the sinuous paths of lawn and of moss,
Which led through the garden along and across—   50
Some open at once to the sun and the breeze,
Some lost among bowers of blossoming trees—

Were all paved with daisies and delicate bells
As fair as the fabulous asphodels[164]
And flowrets which drooping as day drooped too   55
Fell into pavilions, white, purple and blue,
To roof the glow-worm from the evening dew.

And from this undefiled Paradise
The flowers, as an infant's awakening eyes
Smile on its mother, whose singing sweet   60
Can first lull, and at last must awaken it,

When Heaven's blithe winds had unfolded them,
As mine-lamps enkindle a hidden gem,
Shone smiling to Heaven; and every one
Shared joy in the light of the gentle sun,   65

---

[163] *prankt*: ostentatiously decorated.
[164] *asphodels*: common Mediterranean flowering plants, associated in classical mythology with the afterlife, being the flowers of Hades and the dead, sacred to Prosperine (also known as Persephone), the wife of the god of the dead, and also believed to be prevalent in Elysium.

For each one was interpenetrated
With the light and the odour its neighbour shed
Like young lovers, whom youth and love makes dear
Wrapt and filled by their mutual atmosphere.

But the Sensitive-plant which could give small fruit   70
Of the love which it felt from the leaf to the root,
Received more than all—it loved more than ever,
Where none wanted but it, could belong to the giver.

For the Sensitive-Plant has no bright flower;
Radiance and odour are not its dower—   75
It loves—even like Love—its deep heart is full—
It desires what it has not—the beautiful!

The light winds which from unsustaining wings
Shed the music of many murmurings;
The beams which dart from many a star   80
Of the flowers whose hues they bear afar;

The plumed[165] insects swift and free
Like golden boats on a sunny sea,
Laden with light and odour which pass
Over the gleam of the living grass;   85

The unseen clouds of the dew which lie
Like fire in the flowers till the Sun rides high,
Then wander like spirits among the spheres,
Each cloud faint with the fragrance it bears;

The quivering vapours of dim noontide,   90
Which like a sea o'er the warm earth glide
In which every sound, and odour, and beam
Move, as reeds in a single stream;

[165] *plumed*: feathered.

Each, and all, like ministering angels were
For the Sensitive-plant sweet joy to bear   95
Whilst the lagging hours of the day went by
Like windless clouds o'er a tender sky.

And when evening descended from Heaven above,
And the Earth was all rest, and the Air was all love;
And delight, though less bright, was far more deep,   100
And the day's veil fell from the world of sleep,

And the beasts, and the birds, and the insects were
    drowned
In an ocean of dreams without a sound
Whose waves never mark, though they ever impress
The light sand which paves it—Consciousness.   105

(Only over head the sweet nightingale
Ever sang more sweet as the day might fail
And snatches of its Elysian chant
Were mixed with the dreams of the Sensitive-plant).

The Sensitive-plant was the earliest   110
Upgathered into the bosom of rest;
A sweet child weary of its delight,
The feeblest and yet the favourite,
Cradled within the embrace of night.

PART SECOND

There was a Power in this sweet place,
An Eve in this Eden; a ruling grace
Which to the flowers did they waken or dream
Was as God is to the starry scheme:

A Lady[166]—the wonder of her kind,   5
Whose form was upborne by a lovely mind

---

[166] *Lady*: Shelley identified two ladies with this poem: Lady Margaret Cashell
(1773–1835), a notorious divorcee who had been kind to Shelley and his second
wife, Mary; and Jane Williams (1798–1884), another close friend of the poet.

Which, dilating, had moulded her mien and motion,
Like a sea-flower unfolded beneath the Ocean—

Tended the garden from morn to even:
And the meteors[167] of that sublunar[168] Heaven   10
Like the lamps of the air when night walks forth,
Laughed round her footsteps up from the Earth.

She had no companion of mortal race,
But her tremulous breath and her flushing face
Told, whilst the morn kissed the sleep from her eyes   15
That her dreams were less slumber than Paradise:

As if some bright Spirit for her sweet sake
Had deserted heaven while the stars were awake
As if yet around her he lingering were,
Though the veil of daylight concealed him from her.   20

Her step seemed to pity the grass it prest;
You might hear by the heaving of her breast,
That the coming and going of the wind
Brought pleasure there and left passion behind,

And wherever her aery footstep trod,   25
Her trailing hair from the grassy sod
Erased its light vestige, with shadowy sweep
Like a sunny storm o'er the dark green deep.

I doubt not the flowers of that garden sweet
Rejoiced in the sound of her gentle feet;   30
I doubt not they felt the spirit that came
From her glowing fingers through all their frame.

She sprinkled bright water from the stream
On those that were faint with the sunny beam;
And out of the cups of the heavy flowers   35
She emptied the rain of the thunder showers.

---

[167] *meteors*: in this case, the winds.
[168] *sublunar*: under the moon (i.e., on the earth).

She lifted their heads with her tender hands
And sustained them with rods and ozier bands;[169]
If the flowers had been her own infants she
Could never have nursed them more tenderly.   40

And all killing insects and gnawing worms
And things of obscene and unlovely forms
She bore, in a basket of Indian woof,[170]
Into the rough woods far aloof,

In a basket of grasses and wild flowers full,   45
The freshest her gentle hands could pull
For the poor banished insects, whose intent,
Although they did ill, was innocent.

But the bee and the beam-like ephemeris[171]
Whose path is the lightning's, and soft moths that kiss   50
The sweet lips of the flowers, and harm not, did she
Make her attendant angels be.

And many an antenatal tomb
Where butterflies dream of the life to come
She left clinging round the smooth and dark   55
Edge of the odorous cedar bark.

This fairest creature from earliest spring
Thus moved through the garden ministering
All the sweet season of summertide,
And ere the first leaf looked brown—she died!   60

PART THIRD

Three days the flowers of the garden fair,
Like stars when the moon is awakened, were;

---

[169] *ozier bands*: straps used to tie up and support the plants.
[170] *woof*: woven pattern.
[171] *ephemeris*: the dayfly or ephemerid, a small insect that lives for only one day.

Or the waves of Baiæ, ere luminous
She floats up through the smoke of Vesuvius.[172]

And on the fourth, the Sensitive-plant   5
Felt the sound of the funeral chaunt
And the steps of the bearers heavy and slow,
And the sobs of the mourners deep and low,

The weary sound and the heavy breath
And the silent motions of passing death   10
And the smell, cold, oppressive and dank,
Sent through the pores of the coffin plank.

The dark grass and the flowers among the grass
Were bright with tears as the crowd did pass;
From their sighs the wind caught a mournful tone,   15
And sate in the pines and gave groan for groan.

The garden once fair became cold and foul
Like the corpse of her who had been its soul
Which at first was lovely as if in sleep,
Then slowly changed, till it grew a heap   20
To make men tremble who never weep.

Swift summer into the autumn flowed,
And frost in the mist of the morning rode,
Though the noonday sun looked clear and bright,
Mocking the spoil of the secret night.   25

The rose leaves like flakes of crimson snow
Paved the turf and the moss below:
The lilies were drooping, and white, and wan,
Like the head and the skin of a dying man.

[172] *waves . . . Vesuvius*: The volcanic Mount Vesuvius is visible from Baiae bay.

And Indian plants, of scent and hue   30
The sweetest that ever were fed on dew;
Leaf by leaf, day after day,
Were massed into the common clay.

And the leaves, brown, yellow, and grey, and red,
And white, with the whiteness of what is dead,   35
Like troops of ghosts on the dry wind past—
Their whistling noise made the birds aghast.

And the gusty winds waked the winged seeds
Out of their birthplace of ugly weeds,
Till they clung round many a sweet flower's stem   40
Which rotted into the earth with them.

The water blooms under the rivulet
Fell from the stalks on which they were set;
And the eddies drove them here and there
As the winds did those of the upper air.   45

Then the rain came down, and the broken stalks
Were bent and tangled across the walks;
And the leafless network of parasite bowers
Massed into ruin; and all sweet flowers.

Between the time of the wind and the snow   50
All loathliest weeds began to grow,
Whose coarse leaves were splashed with many a speck
Like the water-snake's belly and the toad's back.

And thistles, and nettles, and darnels[173] rank,
And the dock,[174] and henbane, and hemlock[175] dank,   55
Stretched out its long and hollow shank
And stifled the air, till the dead wind stank.

[173] *darnels*: weedy grasses.
[174] *dock*: a thick-rooted, coarse plant.
[175] *henbane . . . hemlock*: poisonous plants.

And plants, at whose names the verse feels loath,
Filled the place with a monstrous undergrowth,
Prickly, and pulpous,[176] and blistering, and blue,   60
Livid, and starred with a lurid dew.

And agarics[177] and fungi with mildew and mould
Started like mist from the wet ground cold;
Pale, fleshy,—as if the decaying dead
With a spirit of growth had been animated!   65

Their moss rotted off them, flake by flake,
Till the thick stalk stuck like a murderer's stake,
Where rags of loose flesh yet tremble on high,
Infecting the winds that wander by.

Spawn,[178] weeds, and filth, a leprous scum,
Made the running rivulet thick and dumb   70
And at its outlet flags[179] huge as stakes
Dammed it up with roots knotted like water snakes.

And hour by hour when the air was still
The vapours arose which have strength to kill:
At morn they were seen, at noon they were felt,   75
At night they were darkness no star could melt.

And unctuous meteors[180] from spray[181] to spray
Crept and flitted in broad noonday
Unseen; every branch on which they alit
By a venomous blight was burned and bit.   80

---

[176] *pulpous*: fleshy, moist.
[177] *agarics*: mushrooms.
[178] *Spawn*: egg deposits or other murky growth.
[179] *flags*: cattails or other reed-like water plants.
[180] *unctuous meteors*: oily winds.
[181] *spray*: stems or branches.

The Sensitive-plant like one forbid
Wept, and the tears, within each lid
Of its folded leaves which together grew,
Were changed to a blight of frozen glue.

For the leaves soon fell, and the branches soon   85
By the heavy axe of the blast were hewn;
The sap shrank to the root through every pore
As blood to a heart that will beat no more.

For Winter came—the wind was his whip—
One choppy finger was on his lip: 90
He had torn the cataracts[182] from the hills
And they clanked at his girdle like manacles;

His breath was a chain which without a sound
The earth and the air and the water bound;
He came, fiercely driven, in his Chariot-throne   95
By the tenfold blasts of the arctic zone.

Then the weeds which were forms of living death
Fled from the frost to the Earth beneath.
Their decay and sudden flight from frost
Was but like the vanishing of a ghost!   100

And under the roots of the Sensitive-plant
The moles and the dormice died for want.
The birds dropped stiff from the frozen air
And were caught in the branches naked and bare.

First there came down a thawing rain   105
And its dull drops froze on the boughs again;
Then there steamed up a freezing dew
Which to the drops of the thaw-rain grew;

[182] *cataracts*: see footnote 32, page 198.

And a northern whirlwind, wandering about
Like a wolf that had smelt a dead child out,   110
Shook the boughs thus laden and heavy and stiff
And snapped them off with his rigid griff.[183]

When winter had gone and spring came back
The Sensitive-plant was a leafless wreck;
But the mandrakes and toadstools and docks and
        darnels   115
Rose like the dead from their ruined charnels.

CONCLUSION

Whether the Sensitive-plant, or that
Which within its boughs like a spirit sat
Ere its outward form had known decay,
Now felt this change,—I cannot say.

Whether that Lady's gentle mind,   5
No longer with the form combined
Which scattered love—as stars do light,
Found sadness, where it left delight,

I dare not guess; but in this life
Of error, ignorance and strife—   10
Where nothing is—but all things seem,
And we the shadows of the dream,

It is a modest creed, and yet
Pleasant if one considers it,
To own that death itself must be,   15
Like all the rest,—a mockery.

---

[183] *griff*: claw.

That garden sweet, that lady fair
And all sweet shapes and odours there
In truth have never past away—
'Tis we, 'tis ours, are changed—not they.   20

For love, and beauty, and delight
There is no death nor change: their might
Exceeds our organs—which endure
No light—being themselves obscure.

To a Sky-Lark (1820)

Hail to thee, blithe Spirit!
　　Bird thou never wert—
That from Heaven or near it,
　　Pourest thy full heart
In profuse strains of unpremeditated art.   5
　　Higher still and higher
　　　From the earth thou springest
　　Like a cloud of fire;
　　　The blue deep thou wingest,
And singing still dost soar, and soaring ever singest.   10

In the golden lightning
　　Of the sunken Sun—
O'er which clouds are brightning,
　　Thou dost float and run;
Like an unbodied joy whose race is just begun.   15
　　The pale purple even
　　　Melts around thy flight,
　　Like a star of Heaven[184]
　　　In the broad day-light
Thou art unseen,—but yet I hear thy shrill delight,   20

---

[184] *star of Heaven*: probably Venus or Mercury (planets that are seen both as morning and evening "stars").

Keen as are the arrows
    Of that silver sphere,
Whose intense lamp narrows
    In the white dawn clear
Until we hardly see—we feel that it is there.[185]   25

All the earth and air
    With thy voice is loud,
As when Night is bare
    From one lonely cloud
The moon rains out her beams—and Heaven is
    overflowed.   30

What thou art we know not;
    What is most like thee?
From rainbow clouds there flow not
    Drops so bright to see,
As from thy presence showers a rain of melody.   35

Like a Poet hidden
    In the light of thought,
Singing hymns unbidden,
    Till the world is wrought
To sympathy with hopes and fears it heeded not: 40

Like a high-born maiden
    In a palace-tower,
Soothing her love-laden
    Soul in secret hour,
With music sweet as love—which overflows her
    bower: 45

---

[185] *Keen ... there*: "Quintilian says that you will never understand the poets unless you learn astronomy.... The silver sphere is the Morning Star, the planet Venus; and Shelley is giving a true description of her disappearance and using an apt comparison." A. E. Housman, *Collected Poems and Selected Prose* (London: Penguin, 1989), p. 467.

Like a glow-worm golden
   In a dell of dew,
Scattering unbeholden
   Its aerial hue
Among the flowers and grass which screen it from the
   view: 50

Like a rose embowered
   In its own green leaves—
By warm winds deflowered—
   Till the scent it gives
Makes faint with too much sweet these heavy-winged
   thieves: 55

Sound of vernal showers
   On the twinkling grass,
Rain-awakened flowers,
   All that ever was
Joyous, and clear and fresh, thy music doth surpass.   60

Teach us, Sprite or Bird,
   What sweet thoughts are thine;
I have never heard
   Praise of love or wine[186]
That panted forth a flood of rapture so divine: 65

Chorus Hymeneal
   Or triumphal chaunt
Matched with thine would be all
   But an empty vaunt,
A thing wherein we feel there is some hidden want.   70

---

[186] *Praise . . . wine*: Following the example of the poet Anacreon (c. 563–478 B.C.), short poems in praise of love or wine have endured through the classical tradition.

What objects are the fountains
    Of thy happy strain?
What fields or waves or mountains?
    What shapes of sky or plain?
What love of thine own kind? what ignorance of pain?   75

With thy clear keen joyance
    Languor cannot be—
Shadow of annoyance
    Never came near thee;
Thou lovest—but ne'er knew love's sad satiety.   80

Waking or asleep,
    Thou of death must deem
Things more true and deep
    Than we mortals dream,
Or how could thy notes flow in such a chrystal stream?   85

We look before and after,
    And pine for what is not—
Our sincerest laughter
    With some pain is fraught—
Our sweetest songs are those that tell of saddest
    thought.   90

Yet if we could scorn
    Hate and pride and fear;
If we were things born
    Not to shed a tear,
I know not how thy joy we ever should come near.   95

Better than all measures
    Of delightful sound—
Better than all treasures
    That in books are found—
Thy skill to poet were, thou Scorner of the ground!   100

Teach me half the gladness
　That thy brain must know,
Such harmonious madness
　From my lips would flow
The world should listen then—as I am listening now.　　105

The Witch of Atlas

The Witch of Atlas was written August 14–16, 1820. Though Byron was the only major Romantic to write intentionally funny verse,[187] Shelley was able to achieve a lightness of touch, a gracefulness, in *The Witch of Atlas* that reminds one of Byron's *Beppo*. For C. S. Lewis, the poem is utterly unique: "We must go to another art, namely to music, to find anything at all similar; and there we shall hardly find it outside Mozart."[188] It is one of the masterworks of fantasy; Arthur Symons describes it as "a glittering cobweb, hung on the horns of the moon's crescent, and left to swing in the wind there. What Fletcher would have shown and withdrawn in a single glimpse of magic, Shelley calls up in a vast wizard landscape which he sets steadily before us."[189]

Characteristic of Shelley, the Witch, for all her perfections, is incapable of true sympathy for human beings.

---

[187] With the exception of a few *jeux d'esprit* by Coleridge.

[188] C. S. Lewis, "Shelley, Dryden, and Mr Eliot", in *Selected Literary Essays* (Cambridge: Cambridge University Press, 1979), p. 200.

[189] Arthur Symons, *The Romantic Movement in English Literature* (New York: Dutton, 1909), p. 275.

From *The Witch of Atlas* (1820)

To Mary

(ON HER OBJECTING TO THE FOLLOWING POEM,
UPON THE SCORE OF ITS CONTAINING NO HUMAN INTEREST)

I

How, my dear Mary, are you critic-bitten
    (For vipers kill, though dead)[190] by some review,
That you condemn these verses I have written
    Because they tell no story, false or true?
What, though no mice are caught by a young kitten,   5
    May it not leap and play as grown cats do,
Till its claws come? Prithee, for this one time,
Content thee with a visionary rhyme.

II

What hand would crush the silken-winged fly,[191]
    The youngest of inconstant April's minions,   10
Because it cannot climb the purest sky
    Where the swan sings, amid the sun's dominions?[192]
Not thine. Thou knowest tis its doom to die
    When Day shall hide within her twilight pinions[193]
The lucent[194] eyes, and the eternal smile,   15
Serene as thine, which lent it life awhile.

---

[190] *vipers . . . dead*: A snake head, severed from its body, can remain alive for some time and is capable of attacking an unsuspecting victim.

[191] *silken-winged fly*: i.e., an ephemerid (the dayfly, a small insect that lives for only one day).

[192] *swan . . . dominions*: In classical mythology, the swan would sing most sweetly just before its death. Additionally, the bird was sacred to Apollo (god of the sun) and was commemorated in the constellation Cygnus, part of the northern panoply of stars.

[193] *pinions*: see footnote 43, page 204.

[194] *lucent*: luminous, bright.

III

To thy fair feet a winged Vision came
    Whose date should have been longer than a day,
And o'er thy head did beat its wings for fame
    And in thy sight its fading plumes display;   20
The watery bow burned in the evening flame,
    But the shower fell,—the swift Sun went his way.
And that is dead: O, let me not believe
That anything of mine is fit to live![195]

IV

Wordsworth[196] informs us he was nineteen years   25
    Considering and retouching Peter Bell;[197]
Watering his laurels[198] with the killing tears
    Of slow, dull care, so that their roots to hell
Might pierce, and their wide branches blot the spheres
    Of Heaven, with dewy leaves and flowers; this well   30
May be, for Heaven and Earth conspire to foil
The over busy gardener's blundering toil.

V

My Witch indeed is not so sweet a creature
    As Ruth or Lucy,[199] whom his graceful praise
Clothes for our grandsons—but she matches Peter   35
    Though he took nineteen years, and she three days

---

[195] *To thy . . . live!* In this stanza, Shelley refers to his long poem *Laon and Cythna* (*The Revolt of Islam*), which did not sell well.

[196] *Wordsworth*: William Wordsworth (1770–1850), poet laureate and (with Coleridge) one of the first Romantic poets.

[197] *Peter Bell*: Wordsworth's long poem, first published in 1819, commemorating a simple rustic lad.

[198] *laurels*: in classical tradition, the poet's crown, here specifically referring to Wordsworth's laureateship.

[199] *Ruth or Lucy*: women mentioned in Wordsworth's *Lyrical Ballads*.

In dressing. Light the vest of flowing metre
    She wears: he, proud as dandy with his stays,
Has hung upon his wiry limbs a dress
Like King Lear's "looped and windowed raggedness."[200]   40

VI

If you strip Peter, you will see a fellow
    Scorched by Hell's hyperequatorial climate[201]
Into a kind of a sulphureous yellow,
    A lean mark hardly fit to fling a rhyme at;
In shape a Scaramouch,[202] in hue Othello.[203]   45
    If you unveil my Witch, no Priest nor Primate
Can shrive[204] you of that sin, if sin there be
In love, when it becomes idolatry.

The Witch of Atlas

I

Before those cruel Twins, whom at one birth
    Incestuous Change bore to her father Time,   50
Error and Truth, had hunted from the earth
    All those bright natures which adorned its prime,
And left us nothing to believe in, worth
    The pains of putting into learned rhyme,
A lady-witch there lived on Atlas' mountain[205]   55
Within a cavern, by a secret fountain.

---

[200] "*King . . . raggedness*": Cf. Shakespeare's *King Lear*, Act 3, scene 44, line 31.

[201] *hyperequatorial climate*: i.e., insufferable heat.

[202] *Scaramouch*: a stock character of the Italian *commedia dell'arte*, depicted satirically as a roguish, boastful coward.

[203] *Othello*: i.e., dark-skinned, like the titular Moor of Shakespeare's *Othello*.

[204] *shrive*: absolve.

[205] *Atlas' mountain*: see footnote 66, page 214.

II

Her mother was one of the Atlantides[206]—
    The all-beholding Sun[207] had ne'er beholden
In his wide voyage o'er continents and seas
    So fair a creature, as she lay enfolden   60
In the warm shadow of her loveliness …
    He kissed her with his beams, and made all golden
The chamber of grey rock in which she lay—
She, in that dream of joy, dissolved away.

III

'Tis said, she first was changed into a vapour,   65
    And then into a cloud, such clouds as flit,
Like splendour-winged moths about a taper,
    Round the red West when the sun dies in it:
And then into a meteor, such as caper
    On hill-tops when the moon is in a fit:[208]   70
Then, into one of those mysterious stars
Which hide themselves between the Earth and Mars.

IV

Ten times the Mother of the Months[209] had bent
    Her bow beside the folding-star,[210] and bidden
With that bright sign the billows[211] to indent   75
    The sea-deserted sand—like children chidden
At her command they ever came and went—
    Since in that cave a dewy splendour hidden
Took shape and motion: with the living form
Of this embodied Power, the cave grew warm.   80

---

[206] *Atlantides*: in classical mythology, the Pleiades, daughters of Atlas, nymphs transformed after death into seven stars.

[207] *Sun*: i.e., god Apollo.

[208] *when … fit*: i.e., when the moon is not visible.

[209] *Mother … Months*: i.e., the moon.

[210] *folding-star*: i.e., Venus (sometime morning star and sometime evening star, here associated with the bringing of sheep to folds in the evening).

[211] *billows*: i.e., waves (referring to the moon's influence over the tides).

V

A lovely lady garmented in light
    From her own beauty—deep her eyes, as are
Two openings of unfathomable night
    Seen through a Temple's cloven roof—her hair
Dark—the dim brain whirls dizzy with delight   85
    Picturing her form—her soft smiles shone afar,
And her low voice was heard like love, and drew
All living things towards this wonder new.

VI

And first the spotted cameleopard[212] came,
    And then the wise and fearless elephant;   90
Then the sly serpent, in the golden flame
    Of his own volumes intervolved;[213]—all gaunt
And sanguine beasts[214] her gentle looks made tame—
    They drank before her at her sacred fount—
And every beast of beating heart grew bold,   95
Such gentleness and power even to behold.

VII

The brinded[215] lioness led forth her young
    That she might teach them how they should forego
Their inborn thirst of death—the pard[216] unstrung
    His sinews at her feet, and sought to know   100
With looks whose motions spoke without a tongue
    How he might be as gentle as the doe.
The magic circle of her voice and eyes
All savage natures did imparadise.

---

[212] *cameleopard*: giraffe.
[213] *in the golden . . . intervolved*: coiled up.
[214] *sanguine beasts*: i.e., predators.
[215] *brinded*: gray or tawny-colored.
[216] *pard*: leopard.

VIII

And old Silenus,[217] shaking a green stick   105
　　Of lilies, and the wood-gods[218] in a crew
Came, blithe, as in the olive copses thick
　　Cicadæ[219] are, drunk with the noonday dew:
And Dryope[220] and Faunus[221] followed quick,
　　Teasing the God to sing them something new   110
Till in this cave they found the lady lone,
Sitting upon a seat of emerald stone.

IX

And Universal Pan,[222] 'tis said, was there,
　　And though none saw him,—through the adamant
Of the deep mountains, through the trackless air,   115
　　And through those living spirits, like a want[223]
He past out of his everlasting lair
　　Where the quick heart of the great world doth pant—
And felt that wondrous lady all alone—
And she felt him upon her emerald throne.   120

X

And every Nymph of stream and spreading tree
　　And every shepherdess of Ocean's flocks[224]
Who drives her white waves over the green Sea;
　　And Ocean with the brine on his grey locks,

---

[217] *Silenus*: in classical mythology, companion and tutor of the god Dionysus.

[218] *wood-gods*: fawns, wood sprites, and satyrs (mythological forest creatures).

[219] *Cicadæ*: locusts, noisy woodland insects.

[220] *Dryope*: in classical mythology, a nymph (either a lover of Apollo or the beloved of Faunus and mother, by him, of Tarquitus, a legendary ruler of Italy).

[221] *Faunus*: in classical mythology, the god of the woods.

[222] *Pan*: in classical mythology, the satyr god of shepherds, huntsmen, the wilderness, and rustic music (sometimes conflated with Faunus).

[223] *want*: mole.

[224] *shepherdess . . . flocks*: in classical mythology, the Oceanides, the three thousand nymphs who watched over all waters and (in the oceans) guarded over sailors.

And quaint Priapus[225] with his company   125
    All came, much wondering how the enwombed
        rocks
Could have brought forth so beautiful a birth;—
Her love subdued their wonder and their mirth.

XI

The herdsmen and the mountain maidens came
    And the rude kings of Pastoral Garamant[226]—   130
Their spirits shook within them, as a flame
    Stirred by the air under a cavern gaunt:
Pigmies,[227] and Polyphemes,[228] by many a name,
    Centaurs[229] and Satyrs,[230] and such shapes as haunt
Wet clefts,—and lumps neither alive nor dead,   135
Dog-headed, bosom-eyed[231] and bird-footed.

XII

For she was beautiful—her beauty made
    The bright world dim, and every thing beside
Seemed like the fleeting image of a shade:
    No thought of living spirit could abide—   140
Which to her looks had ever been betrayed,
    On any object in the world so wide,
On any hope within the circling skies,
But on her form, and in her inmost eyes.

---

[225] *Priapus*: in classical mythology, rustic god of fertility and rich harvest.

[226] *Garamant*: an African tribe.

[227] *Pigmies*: in classical mythology, tribes of tiny people.

[228] *Polyphemes*: one-eyed giants. In classical mythology, Polyphemus was a one-eyed giant, son of the sea god Poseidon.

[229] *Centaurs*: in classical mythology, creatures with the head and torso of a man and the body of a horse.

[230] *Satyrs*: in classical mythology, lascivious, playful creatures with the head and torso of a man and the feet and legs of a goat.

[231] *bosom-eyed*: i.e., with bulging eyes.

XIII

Which when the lady knew she took her spindle   145
    And twined three threads of fleecy mist, and three
Long lines of light such as the Dawn may kindle
    The clouds and waves and mountains with, and she
As many star-beams, ere their lamps could dwindle
    In the belated moon, wound skilfully;   150
And with these threads a subtle veil she wove—
A shadow for the splendour of her love.

XIV

The deep recesses of her odorous dwelling
    Were stored with magic treasures—Sounds of air,
Which had the power all spirits of compelling,   155
    Folded in cells[232] of chrystal silence there;
Such as we hear in youth, and think the feeling
    Will never die—yet ere we are aware,
The feeling and the sound are fled and gone,
And the regret they leave remains alone.   160

XV

And there lay Visions swift and sweet and quaint,
    Each in its thin sheath like a chrysalis,[233]
Some eager to burst forth, some weak and faint
    With the soft burthen of intensest bliss;
It was its work to bear to many a saint   165
    Whose heart adores the shrine which holiest is,
Even Love's—and others white, green, grey and black,
And of all shapes—and each was at her beck.

[232] *cells*: rooms in a monastery (not a prison) where a vow of silence might be observed.
[233] *chrysalis*: cocoon.

XVI

And odours in a kind of aviary
    Of ever-blooming Eden-trees she kept,   170
Clipt[234] in a floating net a love-sick Fairy
    Had woven from dew beams while the moon yet slept—
As bats at the wired window of a dairy
    They beat their vans;[235] and each was an adept,
When loosed and missioned, making wings of winds,   175
To stir sweet thoughts or sad, in destined minds.

XVII

And liquors clear and sweet, whose healthful might
    Could medicine the sick soul to happy sleep
And change eternal death into a night
    Of glorious dreams—or if eyes needs must weep,   180
Could make their tears all wonder and delight,
    She in her chrystal vials did closely keep—
If men could drink of those clear vials, 'tis said
The living were not envied of[236] the dead.

XVIII

Her cave was stored with scrolls of strange device,   185
    The works of some Saturnian Archimage,[237]
Which taught the expiations at whose price
    Men from the Gods might win that happy age
Too lightly lost, redeeming native vice[238]—
    And which might quench the earth-consuming rage   190
Of gold and blood—till men should live and move
Harmonious as the sacred stars above.

---

[234] *Clipt*: caught, held.
[235] *vans*: wings.
[236] *of*: by.
[237] *Saturnian Archimage*: great magician, schooled in the rites of the ancient god Saturn.
[238] *native vice*: the pagan equivalent of original sin.

XIX

And how all things that seem untameable,
    Not to be checked and not to be confined,
Obey the spells of wisdom's wizard skill;   195
    Time, Earth, and Fire—the Ocean and the Wind
And all their shapes—and man's imperial Will—
    And other scrolls whose writings did unbind
The inmost lore of Love—let the prophane[239]
Tremble to ask what secrets they contain.   200

XX

And wondrous works of substances unknown,
    To which the enchantment of her father's power
Had changed those ragged blocks of savage stone,
    Were heaped in the recesses of her bower;
Carved lamps and chalices and phials which shone   205
    In their own golden beams—each like a flower
Out of whose depth a fire fly shakes his light
Under a cypress in a starless night.

* * * * *

XXXI

She had a Boat which some say Vulcan[240] wrought
    For Venus, as the chariot of her star;   290
But it was found too feeble to be fraught
    With all the ardours in that Sphere which are,
And so she sold it, and Apollo bought
    And gave it to this daughter: from a car[241]
Changed to the fairest and the lightest boat   295
Which ever upon mortal stream did float.

---

[239] *prophane*: uninitiated.
[240] *Vulcan*: in classical mythology, the deformed, blacksmith god, husband of Venus, goddess of love.
[241] *car*: i.e., chariot.

XXXII

And others say, that when but three hours old
    The first-born Love out of his cradle leapt,[242]
And clove[243] dun Chaos with his wings of gold,
    And like an horticultural adept,   300
Stole a strange seed, and wrapt it up in mould
    And sowed it in his mother's star,[244] and kept
Watering it all the summer with sweet dew,
And with his wings fanning it as it grew.

XXXIII

The plant grew strong and green—the snowy flower   305
    Fell, and the long and gourd-like fruit began
To turn the light and dew by inward power
    To its own substance; woven tracery ran
Of light firm texture, ribbed and branching, o'er
    The solid rind, like a leaf's veined fan—   310
Of which Love scooped this boat—and with soft motion
Piloted it round the circumfluous[245] Ocean.

XXXIV

This boat she moored upon her fount, and lit
    A living spirit within all its frame,
Breathing the soul of swiftness into it—   315
    Couched on the fountain, like a panther tame,
One of the twain at Evan's[246] feet that sit—
    Or as on Vesta's sceptre[247] a swift flame—

---

[242] *others . . . leapt:* Shelley takes this image from Plato's *Symposium* (which he himself translated): "Hesiod says … that after Chaos these two were produced, the Earth and Love." *The Symposium of Plat: The Shelley Translation* (South Bend, Ind.: St. Augustine's Press, 2002), p. 11.

[243] *clove:* cut through or split.

[244] *mother's star:* i.e., the planet Venus, whose son, Cupid, is figured here.

[245] *circumfluous:* surrounding.

[246] *Evan's:* Evan (or Euan) is another name for Bacchus or Dionysus, god of wine.

[247] *Vesta's sceptre:* in classical mythology, the virgin goddess of the hearth.

Or on blind Homer's heart a winged thought—
In joyous expectation lay the Boat. 320

XXXV

Then by strange art she kneaded fire and snow
 Together, tempering the repugnant mass
With liquid love—all things together grow
 Through which the harmony of love can pass;
And a fair Shape out of her hands did flow— 325
 A living Image, which did far surpass
In beauty that bright shape of vital stone
Which drew the heart out of Pygmalion.[248]

XXXVI

A sexless thing it was,[249] and in its growth
 It seemed to have developed no defect 330
Of either sex, yet all the grace of both—
 In gentleness and strength its limbs were decked;
The bosom swelled lightly with its full youth—
 The countenance was such as might select
Some artist that his skill should never die, 335
Imaging forth such perfect purity.

XXXVII

From its smooth shoulders hung two rapid wings,
 Fit to have borne it to the seventh sphere,[250]
Tipt with the speed of liquid lightenings—
 Dyed in the ardours of the atmosphere— 340

[248] *Pygmalion*: in classical mythology, a sculptor who created a beautiful woman and then fell in love with his own creation, which the merciful Venus transformed into a living woman.

[249] *A sexless . . . was*: The Witch crafts a hermaphrodite. In classical mythology, Hermaphroditus was the child of Hermes and Aphrodite whose body was united with that of a nymph.

[250] *seventh sphere*: in classical astronomy, the sphere in which Saturn revolved, the closest sphere to the fixed stars.

She led her creature to the boiling springs
   Where the light boat was moored, and said: "Sit
      here!"
And pointed to the prow, and took her seat
Beside the rudder, with opposing feet.

XXXVIII

And down the streams which clove those mountains
     vast   345
   Around their inland islets, and amid
The panther-peopled forests, whose shade cast
   Darkness and odours and a pleasure hid
In melancholy gloom, the pinnace[251] past
   By many a star-surrounded pyramid   350
Of icy crag cleaving the purple sky
And caverns yawning round unfathomably.

XXXIX

The silver noon into that winding dell
   With slanted gleam athwart the forest tops
Tempered like golden evening, feebly fell;   355
   A green and glowing light like that which drops
From folded lilies in which glow worms dwell
   When Earth over her face night's mantle wraps;
Between the severed mountains lay on high
Over the stream, a narrow rift[252] of sky.   360

XL

And ever as she went, the Image lay
   With folded wings and unawakened eyes;
And o'er its gentle countenance did play
   The busy dreams, as thick as summer flies,

---

[251] *pinnace*: see footnote 76, page 217.
[252] *rift*: split (i.e., a gap of sky appearing between two clouds).

Chasing the rapid smiles that would not stay,   365
    And drinking the warm tears, and the sweet sighs
Inhaling, which, with busy murmur vain,
They had aroused from that full heart and brain.

XLI

And ever down the prone[253] vale, like a cloud
    Upon a stream of wind, the pinnace went;   370
Now lingering on the pools, in which abode
    The calm and darkness of the deep content
In which they paused, now o'er the shallow road
    Of white and dancing waters all besprent[254]
With sand and polished pebbles ... mortal Boat   375
In such a shallow rapid could not float.

XLII

And down the earthquaking cataracts which shiver
    Their snowlike waters into golden air,
Or under chasms unfathomable ever
    Sepulchre[255] them, till in their rage they tear   380
A subterranean portal for the river,
    It fled ... the circling sunbows[256] did upbear
Its fall down the hoar[257] precipice of spray,
Lighting it far upon its lampless way.

XLIII

And when the wizard lady would ascend   385
    The labyrinths of some many winding vale
Which to the inmost mountain upward tend—
    She called "Hermaphroditus!"—and the pale
And heavy hue which slumber could extend
    Over its lips and eyes, as on the gale   390

---

[253] *prone*: descending sloped or low.
[254] *besprent*: sprinkled.
[255] *Sepulchre*: entomb.
[256] *sunbows*: rainbow-like refraction of sunlight.
[257] *hoar*: hoary (i.e., white or gray).

A rapid shadow from a slope of grass,
Into the darkness of the stream did pass.

XLIV

And it unfurled its heaven-coloured pinions
 With stars of fire spotting the stream below;
And from above into the Sun's dominions   395
 Flinging a glory, like the golden glow
In which Spring clothes her emerald-winged minions,
 All interwoven with fine feathery snow
And moonlight splendour of intensest rime[258]
With which Frost paints the pines in winter time. 400

XLV

And then it winnowed the Elysian air
 Which ever hung about that lady bright,
With its ætherial vans—and speeding there
 Like a star up the torrent of the night
Or a swift eagle in the morning glare   405
 Breasting the whirlwind with impetuous flight,
The pinnace, oared by those enchanted wings,
Clove the fierce streams towards their upper springs.

Epipsychidion[259]

Epipsychidion was written and published in 1821. The first 189 lines tell of the poet's relationship to "Emily" (Teresa Viviani, the nineteen-year-old daughter of the governor of Pisa, confined in a convent awaiting an arranged marriage). This is subdivided into three parts: lines 1–71 address Emily as a captive, kindred soul and dedicate the poem to her; lines 72–129, a brief description of the poet's encounter with her, expatiate

[258] *rime:* frost.
[259] *Epipsychidion:* Greek, meaning "concerning a [little] soul", or "soul out of my soul".

on her exalted identity in symbolic terms; in lines 130–189, Shelley expounds to her his doctrine of love (including a condemnation of marriage and possession).

The second section of the poem is a sort of spiritual autobiography. From line 216, the poet recounts his youthful awakening to the presence of a beautiful spirit, "the harmony of truth", who draws his soul into an impassioned pursuit, continually frustrated, until "a voice" (line 232) informs him that this "soul out of [his] soul" (line 238) is close to him, and he begins to seek her in a woman. Just as he despairs, Mary Shelley, represented as the moon (lines 276–307), shines upon him and holds him spellbound in a beautiful but fruitless, cold relationship. This ends in storms and sorrow, quelled at last by the arrival of the sun (line 335), who is Emily, and the embodiment of the spirit he has sought: she brings to him a fuller, more joyous life, in which the moon (and even the occasional comet) still has a place.

From line 383, Shelley addresses Emily, his "Lady", directly, inviting her to fly with him, under the auspices of the all-conquering power of love. He describes for her the prelapsarian existence they might lead, on an idyllic (yet real) island paradise. At line 573 comes an attempt to describe the ecstatic union of these two souls, culminating in an almost apocalyptic disintegration of the poet's articulacy. The poem ends with a twelve-line envoi.

According to Harold Bloom, "The myth of *Epipsychidion* drives toward relationship and life, but is countered by an incestuous antimyth of despair, moving toward death. The poem alternates between two quests: for an emanation and for a female counterpart of the spectral self.... The poem's myth seeks defeat, and finds it, for the understanding of human limitations has now conflicted openly with the theme of transcendent desire."[260]

---

[260] Harold Bloom, *The Visionary Company: A Reading of English Romantic Poetry* (Ithaca, N.Y.: Cornell University Press, 1971), pp. 337, 340.

Epipsychidion (1820–1821)

VERSES ADDRESSED TO THE NOBLE AND UNFORTUNATE LADY, EMILIA
V———,[261] NOW IMPRISONED IN THE CONVENT OF———

L'anima amante si slancia fuori del creato, e si crea nel infinito
un Mondo tutto per essa, diverso assai da questo oscuro e
pauroso baratro.[262]

HER OWN WORDS.

ADVERTISEMENT

The Writer of the following Lines died at Florence, as he was
preparing for a voyage to one of the wildest of the Sporades,
which he had bought, and where he had fitted up the ruins of
an old building, and where it was his hope to have realised a
scheme of life, suited perhaps to that happier and better world
of which he is now an inhabitant, but hardly practicable in this.
His life was singular; less on account of the romantic vicissitudes
which diversified it, than the ideal tinge which it received from
his own character and feelings. The present Poem, like the *Vita
Nuova*[263] of Dante, is sufficiently intelligible to a certain class
of readers without a matter-of-fact history of the circumstances
to which it relates; and to a certain other class it must ever
remain incomprehensible, from a defect of a common organ of
perception for the ideas of which it treats. Not but that, *gran
vergogna sarebbe a colui, che rimasse cosa sotto veste di figura, o di
colore rettorico: e domandato non sapesse denudare le sue parole da
cotal veste, in guisa che avessero verace intendimento.*[264]

---

[261] LADY, EMILIA V———: Teresa Viviani, the nineteen-year-old daughter of the
governor of Pisa, was confined in the Convent of St. Anna in Pisa while her
father dealt with the complex business of her arranged marriage.

[262] *L'anima ... baratro*: "The loving soul launches beyond creation, and
creates for itself in the infinite a world all its own, far different from this dark and
terrifying gulf."

[263] Vita Nuova: Dante's *La Vita Nuova* (1295), exemplifying the medieval
ideals of courtly love, developing toward divine love.

[264] *gran ... intendimento*: "Great would be his shame who should rhyme
anything under the garb of metaphor or rhetorical figure; and, being requested,
could not strip his words of this dress so that they might have a true meaning."

The present poem appears to have been intended by the Writer as the dedication to some longer one. The stanza on the opposite page is almost a literal translation from Dante's famous *Canzone*

Voi, ch'intendendo, il terzo ciel movete, etc.[265]

The presumptuous application of the concluding lines to his own composition will raise a smile at the expense of my unfortunate friend: be it a smile not of contempt, but pity.   S.

> My Song, I fear that thou wilt find but few
> Who fitly shall conceive thy reasoning,
> Of such hard matter dost thou entertain;
> Whence, if by misadventure, chance should bring
> Thee to base company (as chance may do),
> Quite unaware of what thou dost contain,
> I prithee, comfort thy sweet self again,
> My last delight! tell them that they are dull,
> And bid them own that thou art beautiful.

EPIPSYCHIDION

Sweet Spirit! Sister of that orphan one,
Whose empire is the name thou weepest on,[266]
In my heart's temple I suspend to thee
These votive[267] wreaths of withered memory.

Poor captive bird! who, from thy narrow cage,   5
Pourest such music, that it might assuage
The rugged hearts of those who prisoned thee,
Were they not deaf to all sweet melody;

---

[265] Voi ... etc.: "Ye who intelligent, the third sphere move ..." (the final lines of Dante's *Il Convito*, "The Banquet", Trattato 2).

[266] *Sister ... on*: The "Sister", Teresa Vivani, referred in correspondence to Shelley and his wife, Mary, as her "Brother" and "Sister". The "orphan one" refers either to Shelley or to Mary.

[267] *votive*: dedicated, offered in accordance with a vow.

This song shall be thy rose: its petals pale
Are dead, indeed, my adored Nightingale!   10
But soft and fragrant is the faded blossom,
And it has no thorn left to wound thy bosom.

  High, spirit-winged Heart! who dost for ever
Beat thine unfeeling bars with vain endeavour,
'Till those bright plumes of thought, in which arrayed   15
It over-soared this low and worldly shade,
Lie shattered; and thy panting, wounded breast
Stains with dear blood its unmaternal nest!
I weep vain tears: blood would less bitter be,
Yet poured forth gladlier, could it profit thee.   20

  Seraph[268] of Heaven! too gentle to be human,
Veiling beneath that radiant form of Woman
All that is insupportable in thee
Of light, and love, and immortality!
Sweet Benediction in the eternal Curse!   25
Veiled Glory of this lampless Universe!
Thou Moon beyond the clouds! Thou living Form
Among the Dead! Thou Star above the Storm!
Thou Wonder, and thou Beauty, and thou Terror!
Thou Harmony of Nature's art! Thou Mirror   30
In whom, as in the splendour of the Sun,
All shapes look glorious which thou gazest on!
Ay, even the dim words which obscure thee now
Flash, lightning-like, with unaccustomed glow;
I pray thee that thou blot from this sad song   35
All of its much mortality and wrong,
With those clear drops, which start like sacred dew
From the twin lights thy sweet soul darkens through,
Weeping, till sorrow becomes ecstasy:
Then smile on it, so that it may not die.   40

---

[268] *Seraph*: seraphim, one of the traditional (and the highest of) the nine choirs of angels.

I never thought before my death to see
Youth's vision thus made perfect. Emily,[269]
I love thee; though the world by no thin name
Will hide that love from its unvalued[270] shame.[271]
Would we two had been twins of the same mother![272]   45
Or, that the name of my heart[273] lent to another
Could be a sister's bond for her and thee,
Blending two beams of one eternity!
Yet were one lawful and the other true,
These names, though dear, could paint not, as is due,   50
How beyond refuge I am thine. Ah me!
I am not thine: I am part of *thee*.

    Sweet Lamp! my moth-like Muse has burnt its
        wings;
Or, like a dying swan[274] who soars and sings,
Young Love should teach Time, in his own grey style,   55
All that thou art. Art thou not void of guile,
A lovely soul formed to be blest and bless?
A well of sealed and secret happiness,
Whose waters like blithe light and music are,
Vanquishing dissonance and gloom? A Star   60
Which moves not in the moving Heavens,[275] alone?
A smile amid dark frowns? a gentle tone
Amid rude voices? a beloved light?
A Solitude, a Refuge, a Delight?

[269] *Emily*: see footnote 261, page 277.

[270] *unvalued*: beyond value.

[271] *shame*: the shame of being shut up in the monastery as if she has done something wrong.

[272] *Would . . . mother!* Cf. the biblical Song of Solomon (8:1): "O that you were like a brother to me, that nursed at my mother's breast! . . . I would kiss you, and none would despise me."

[273] *name of my heart*: i.e., Mary Shelley, but also simply his own heart (personified here as a sister).

[274] *dying swan*: In classical mythology, the swan would sing most sweetly just before its death.

[275] *Star . . . Heavens*: i.e., Polestar, which, because of the rotation of the earth, appears to remain fixed while the rest of the stars appear to move.

A lute, which those whom love has taught to play 65
Make music on, to soothe the roughest day
And lull fond[276] grief asleep? a buried treasure?
A cradle of young thoughts of wingless pleasure?
A violet-shrouded grave of Woe?[277]—I measure
The world of fancies, seeking one like thee, 70
And find—alas! mine own infirmity.

    She met me, Stranger,[278] upon life's rough way,
And lured me towards sweet Death; as Night by Day,
Winter by Spring, or Sorrow by swift Hope,
Led into light, life, peace. An antelope, 75
In the suspended impulse of its lightness,
Were less ethereally light: the brightness
Of her divinest presence trembles through
Her limbs, as underneath a cloud of dew
Embodied in the windless Heaven of June 80
Amid the splendour-winged stars, the Moon
Burns, inextinguishably beautiful:
And from her lips, as from a hyacinth full
Of honey-dew,[279] a liquid murmur drops,
Killing the sense with passion; sweet as stops 85
Of planetary music heard in trance.[280]
In her mild lights the starry spirits dance,
The sun-beams of those wells which ever leap
Under the lightnings of the soul—too deep
For the brief fathom-line[281] of thought or sense. 90
The glory of her being, issuing thence,
Stains the dead, blank, cold air with a warm shade

---

[276] *fond*: silly, trivial.

[277] *violet-shrouded . . . Woe*: The violet is poetically considered a symbol of hope and rebirth because it is a perennial that blooms in early spring.

[278] *Stranger*: i.e., the reader of this poem.

[279] *honey-dew*: sweet, sticky substance excreted by insects onto plant leaves.

[280] *stops . . . trance*: It was traditionally believed that the music of the planets was inaudible except to the ears of the innocent or those in an ecstasy.

[281] *fathom-line*: line on a nautical chart indicating the depth and contour of the ocean floor.

Of unentangled intermixture, made
By Love, of light and motion: one intense
Diffusion, one serene Omnipresence,   95
Whose flowing outlines mingle in their flowing,
Around her cheeks and utmost fingers glowing
With the unintermitted[282] blood, which there
Quivers (as in a fleece of snow-like air
The crimson pulse of living morning quiver),   100
Continuously prolonged, and ending never,
Till they are lost, and in that Beauty furled
Which penetrates and clasps and fills the world;
Scarce visible from extreme loveliness.
Warm fragrance seems to fall from her light dress,   105
And her loose hair; and where some heavy tress
The air of her own speed has disentwined,
The sweetness seems to satiate the faint wind;
And in the soul a wild odour is felt,
Beyond the sense, like fiery dews that melt   110
Into the bosom of a frozen bud.—
See where she stands! a mortal shape indued[283]
With love and life and light and deity,
And motion which may change but cannot die;
An image of some bright Eternity;   115
A shadow of some golden dream; a Splendour[284]
Leaving the third sphere[285] pilotless; a tender
Reflection of the eternal Moon of Love
Under whose motions life's dull billows move;
A Metaphor of Spring and Youth and Morning;   120
A Vision like incarnate April, warning,
With smiles and tears, Frost the Anatomy[286]
Into his summer grave.

[282] *unintermitted*: uninterrupted, ceaseless.

[283] *indued*: endued (i.e., endowed, given).

[284] *Splendour*: angel.

[285] *third sphere*: according to Dante's imaginative cosmology, Venus, the realm of lovers.

[286] *Anatomy*: skeleton.

Ah, woe is me!
What have I dared? where am I lifted? how
Shall I descend, and perish not? I know   125
That Love makes all things equal: I have heard
By mine own heart this joyous truth averred:
The spirit of the worm beneath the sod
In love and worship, blends itself with God.

Spouse! Sister! Angel! Pilot of the Fate   130
Whose course has been so starless! O too late
Beloved! O too soon adored, by me!
For in the fields of immortality[287]
My spirit should at first have worshipped thine,
A divine presence in a place divine;   135
Or should have moved beside it on this earth,
A shadow of that substance, from its birth;
But not as now:—I love thee; yes, I feel
That on the fountain of my heart a seal
Is set, to keep its waters pure and bright   140
For thee, since in those *tears* thou hast delight.
We—are we not formed, as notes of music are,
For one another, though dissimilar;
Such difference without discord, as can make
Those sweetest sounds, in which all spirits shake 145
As trembling leaves in a continuous air?

Thy wisdom speaks in me, and bids me dare
Beacon the rocks on which high hearts are wreckt.
I never was attached to that great sect,
Whose doctrine is, that each one should select   150
Out of the crowd a mistress or a friend,
And all the rest, though fair and wise, commend
To cold oblivion, though it is in the code
Of modern morals, and the beaten road

[287] *fields of immortality*: i.e., the Elysian fields. Elysium is an ancient conception of the afterlife.

Which those poor slaves with weary footsteps tread,   155
Who travel to their home among the dead
By the broad highway of the world, and so
With one chained friend, perhaps a jealous foe,
The dreariest and the longest journey go.

    True Love in this differs from gold and clay,   160
That to divide is not to take away.
Love is like understanding, that grows bright,
Gazing on many truths; 'tis like thy light,
Imagination! which from earth and sky,
And from the depths of human phantasy,   165
As from a thousand prisms and mirrors, fills
The Universe with glorious beams, and kills
Error, the worm, with many a sun-like arrow
Of its reverberated lightning.[288] Narrow
The heart that loves, the brain that contemplates,   170
The life that wears, the spirit that creates
One object, and one form, and builds thereby
A sepulchre for its eternity.

    Mind from its object differs most in this:
Evil from good; misery from happiness;   175
The baser from the nobler; the impure
And frail, from what is clear and must endure.
If you divide suffering and dross,[289] you may
Diminish till it is consumed away;
If you divide pleasure and love and thought,   180
Each part exceeds the whole; and we know not
How much, while any yet remains unshared,
Of pleasure may be gained, of sorrow spared:
This truth is that deep well, whence sages draw
The unenvied light of hope; the eternal law   185

---

[288] *Imagination . . . lightning*: In classical mythology, the archer god Apollo killed the serpent Python.
[289] *dross*: waste, scum (valueless matter).

By which those live, to whom this world of life
Is as a garden ravaged, and whose strife
Tills for the promise of a later birth
The wilderness of this Elysian earth.

There was a Being whom my spirit oft   190
Met on its visioned wanderings, far aloft,
In the clear golden prime of my youth's dawn,
Upon the fairy isles of sunny lawn,
Amid the enchanted mountains, and the caves
Of divine sleep, and on the air-like waves   195
Of wonder-level dream, whose tremulous floor
Paved her light steps;—on an imagined shore,
Under the grey beak of some promontory
She met me, robed in such exceeding glory,
That I beheld her not. In solitudes   200
Her voice came to me through the whispering woods,
And from the fountains, and the odours deep
Of flowers, which, like lips murmuring in their sleep
Of the sweet kisses which had lulled them there,
Breathed but of *her* to the enamoured air;   205
And from the breezes whether low or loud,
And from the rain of every passing cloud,
And from the singing of the summer-birds,
And from all sounds, all silence. In the words
Of antique verse and high romance,—in form,   210
Sound, colour—in whatever checks that Storm
Which with the shattered present chokes the past;
And in that best philosophy,[290] whose taste
Makes this cold common hell, our life, a doom[291]
As glorious as a fiery martyrdom;   215
Her Spirit was the harmony of truth.—

---

[290] *best philosophy*: Shelley is not referring to a particular philosophical school; rather, he is setting the stage for the articulation of his own ideals regarding imagination, love, and human existence.

[291] *doom*: destiny, fate.

Then, from the caverns of my dreamy youth
I sprang, as one sandalled with plumes of fire,
And towards the loadstar[292] of my one desire,
I flitted, like a dizzy moth, whose flight   220
Is as a dead leaf's in the owlet light,[293]
When it would seek in Hesper's setting sphere[294]
A radiant death, a fiery sepulchre,
As if it were a lamp of earthly flame.—
But She, whom prayers or tears then could not tame,   225
Past, like a God throned on a winged planet,
Whose burning plumes to tenfold swiftness fan it,
Into the dreary cone of our life's shade;[295]
And as a man with mighty loss dismayed,
I would have followed, though the grave between   230
Yawned like a gulph whose spectres are unseen:
When a voice said:—"O thou of hearts the weakest,
The phantom is beside thee whom thou seekest."
Then I—"where?"—the world's echo answered "where!"
And in that silence, and in my despair,   235
I questioned every tongueless wind that flew
Over my tower of mourning, if it knew
Whither 'twas fled, this soul out of my soul;
And murmured names and spells which have controul
Over the sightless tyrants of our fate;   240
But neither prayer nor verse could dissipate
The night which closed on her; nor uncreate
That world within this Chaos, mine and me,
Of which she was the veiled Divinity,
The world I say of thoughts that worshipped her: 245

---

[292] *loadstar*: literally, a star used as the central point of a ship's navigation; figuratively, a person or thing serving as guide.

[293] *owlet light*: i.e., the light in which the owl (and the moth) fly.

[294] *Hesper's ... sphere*: the name of Venus as evening star (as opposed to Phosphor, Venus as morning star).

[295] *cone ... shade*: "cone" of darkness or of night. Literally, the shadow the earth casts upon itself when the sun is on the other side of the earth and the earth faces the moon.

And therefore I went forth, with hope and fear
And every gentle passion sick to death,
Feeding my course with expectation's breath,
Into the wintry forest of our life;
And struggling through its error with vain strife,   250
And stumbling in my weakness and my haste,
And half bewildered by new forms, I past,
Seeking among those untaught foresters[296]
If I could find one form resembling hers,
In which she might have masked herself from me.   255
There,—One,[297] whose voice was venomed melody
Sate by a well, under blue night-shade[298] bowers;
The breath of her false mouth was like faint flowers,
Her touch was as electric poison,—flame
Out of her looks into my vitals came,   260
And from her living cheeks and bosom flew
A killing air, which pierced like honey-dew
Into the core of my green heart, and lay
Upon its leaves; until, as hair grown grey
O'er a young brow, they hid its unblown[299] prime   265
With ruins of unseasonable time.

    In many mortal forms I rashly sought[300]
The shadow of that idol of my thought.
And some were fair—but beauty dies away:
Others were wise—but honeyed words betray: 270
And One was true—oh! why not true to me?
Then, as a hunted deer that could not flee,

---

[296] *untaught foresters*: unshaped or uninitiated youths.

[297] *One*: No particular woman has been identified in association with Shelley here, but the imagery simply suggests a woman of ill intent and probably loose morals.

[298] *night-shade*: a genus of herbs, shrubs, and trees that bears flowers and (sometimes) poisonous red or black berries.

[299] *unblown*: not yet blossomed.

[300] *In many . . . sought*: Many critics have sought to find particular biographical details in the following description, but to be appreciated most fruitfully, it should simply be read in artistic terms.

I turned upon my thoughts, and stood at bay,
Wounded and weak and panting; the cold day
Trembled, for pity of my strife and pain.   275
When, like a noon-day dawn, there shone again
Deliverance. One stood on my path who seemed
As like the glorious shape which I had dreamed,
As is the Moon, whose changes ever run
Into themselves, to the eternal Sun;   280
The cold chaste Moon,[301] the Queen of Heaven's bright
     isles,
Who makes all beautiful on which she smiles,
That wandering shrine of soft yet icy flame
Which ever is transformed, yet still the same,
And warms not but illumines. Young and fair   285
As the descended Spirit of that sphere,
She hid me, as the Moon may hide the night
From its own darkness, until all was bright
Between the Heaven and Earth of my calm mind,
And, as a cloud charioted by the wind,   290
She led me to a cave in that wild place,
And sate beside me, with her downward face
Illumining my slumbers, like the Moon
Waxing and waning o'er Endymion.[302]
And I was laid asleep, spirit and limb,   295
And all my being became bright or dim
As the Moon's image in a summer sea,
According as she smiled or frowned on me;
And there I lay, within a chaste cold bed:
Alas, I then was nor alive nor dead:—   300
For at her silver voice came Death and Life,
Unmindful each of their accustomed strife,
Masked like twin babes, a sister and a brother,

---

[301] *cold chaste Moon*: In classical mythology, the moon was partly associated with the virgin goddess of the hunt, Diana, though it bore other less-chaste mythological associations. Cf. the following footnote.

[302] *Endymion*: in classical mythology, a youth beloved of the Titan moon goddess and granted by Zeus to remain ageless and deathless forever in sleep.

The wandering hopes of one abandoned mother,
And through the cavern without wings they flew,   305
And cried "Away, he is not of our crew."
I wept, and though it be a dream, I weep.

What storms then shook the ocean of my sleep,
Blotting that Moon, whose pale and waning lips
Then shrank as in the sickness of eclipse;—   310
And how my soul was as a lampless sea,
And who was then its Tempest; and when She,
The Planet of that hour,[303] was quenched, what frost
Crept o'er those waters, 'till from coast to coast
The moving billows of my being fell   315
Into a death of ice, immoveable;—
And then—what earthquakes made it gape and split,
The white Moon smiling all the while on it,
These words conceal:—If not, each word would be
The key of staunchless tears. Weep not for me!   320

At length, into the obscure Forest[304] came
The Vision I had sought through grief and shame.
Athwart that wintry wilderness of thorns
Flashed from her motion splendour like the Morn's,
And from her presence life was radiated   325
Through the grey earth and branches bare and dead;
So that her way was paved, and roofed above
With flowers as soft as thoughts of budding love;
And music from her respiration spread
Like light,—all other sounds were penetrated   330
By the small, still, sweet spirit of that sound,
So that the savage winds hung mute around;
And odours warm and fresh fell from her hair
Dissolving the dull cold in the froze air:

---

[303] *She . . . hour*: i.e., Venus.
[304] *obscure Forest*: Cf. the opening lines of Dante's *Inferno*, which famously begins in the "selva oscura" (canto 1, line 2).

Soft as an Incarnation of the Sun,   335
When light is changed to love, this glorious One
Floated into the cavern where I lay,
And called my Spirit, and the dreaming clay
Was lifted by the thing that dreamed below
As smoke by fire, and in her beauty's glow   340
I stood, and felt the dawn of my long night
Was penetrating me with living light:
I knew it was the Vision veiled from me
So many years—that it was Emily.

   Twin Spheres of light[305] who rule this passive Earth,   345
This world of love, this *me*; and into birth
Awaken all its fruits and flowers, and dart
Magnetic might into its central heart;
And lift its billows and its mists, and guide
By everlasting laws, each wind and tide   350
To its fit cloud, and its appointed cave;
And lull its storms, each in the craggy grave
Which was its cradle, luring to faint bowers
The armies of the rainbow-winged showers;
And, as those married lights, which from the towers   355
Of Heaven look forth and fold the wandering globe
In liquid sleep and splendour, as a robe;
And all their many-mingled influence blend,
If equal, yet unlike, to one sweet end;—
So ye, bright regents, with alternate sway   360
Govern my sphere of being, night and day!
Thou, not disdaining even a borrowed might;
Thou, not eclipsing a remoter light;
And, through the shadow of the seasons three,
From Spring to Autumn's sere maturity,   365
Light it into the Winter of the tomb,
Where it may ripen to a brighter bloom.
Thou too, O Comet beautiful and fierce,

[305] *Twin . . . light*: sun and moon.

Who drew the heart of this frail Universe
Towards thine own; till, wreckt in that convulsion,   370
Alternating attraction and repulsion,
Thine went astray and that was rent in twain;
Oh, float into our azure heaven again!
Be there love's folding-star[306] at thy return;
The living Sun will feed thee from its urn   375
Of golden fire; the Moon will veil her horn
In thy last smiles; adoring Even and Morn
Will worship thee with incense of calm breath
And lights and shadows; as the star of Death
And Birth[307] is worshipped by those sisters wild   380
Called Hope and Fear—upon the heart are piled
Their offerings,—of this sacrifice divine
A World shall be the altar.

                                        Lady mine,
Scorn not these flowers of thought, the fading birth
Which from its heart of hearts that plant puts forth   385
Whose fruit, made perfect by thy sunny eyes,
Will be as of the trees of Paradise.

    The day is come, and thou wilt fly with me.
To whatsoe'er of dull mortality
Is mine, remain a vestal sister still;   390
To the intense, the deep, the imperishable,
Not mine but me, henceforth be thou united
Even as a bride, delighting and delighted.
The hour is come:—the destined Star has risen
Which shall descend upon a vacant prison.   395
The walls are high, the gates are strong, thick set
The sentinels—but true love never yet
Was thus constrained: it overleaps all fence:

---

[306] *folding-star*: i.e., Venus (sometime morning star and sometime evening star, here associated with the bringing of sheep to folds in the evening).

[307] *star . . . Birth*: i.e., Venus (morning and evening star).

Like lightning, with invisible violence
Piercing its continents; like Heaven's free breath, 400
Which he who grasps can hold not; liker Death,
Who rides upon a thought, and makes his way
Through temple, tower, and palace, and the array
Of arms: more strength has Love than he or they;
For it can burst his charnel, and make free 405
The limbs in chains, the heart in agony,
The soul in dust and chaos.

　　　　　　　　　Emily,
A ship is floating in the harbour now,
A wind is hovering o'er the mountain's brow;
There is a path on the sea's azure floor, 410
No keel has ever ploughed that path before;
The halcyons[308] brood around the foamless isles;
The treacherous Ocean has forsworn its wiles;
The merry mariners are bold and free:
Say, my heart's sister, wilt thou sail with me? 415
Our bark[309] is as an albatross,[310] whose nest
Is a far Eden of the purple East;
And we between her wings will sit, while Night
And Day, and Storm, and Calm, pursue their flight,
Our ministers, along the boundless Sea, 420
Treading each other's heels, unheededly.
It is an isle under Ionian skies,[311]
Beautiful as a wreck of Paradise,
And, for[312] the harbours are not safe and good,

---

[308] *halcyons*: identified with kingfishers. In classical mythology, Alcyone (the daughter of the wind, Aeolus) and Ceyx (son of the morning star) were transformed into halcyon birds. From their mythological love story comes the idea of the "halcyon days": the seven days in winter when there are no storms and Alcyone lays her eggs and tends her nest in peace.

[309] *bark*: sailing ship.

[310] *albatross*: believed to be a good omen for sailors.

[311] *Ionian skies*: Ionia was the ancient region (now in Turkey) to the east across the Aegean Sea from Greece.

[312] *for*: because.

This land would have remained a solitude 425
But for some pastoral people native there,
Who from the Elysian, clear, and golden air
Draw the last spirit of the age of gold,
Simple and spirited; innocent and bold.
The blue Ægean[313] girds[314] this chosen home, 430
With ever-changing sound and light and foam,
Kissing the sifted sands, and caverns hoar;
And all the winds wandering along the shore
Undulate with the undulating tide:
There are thick woods where sylvan forms abide; 435
And many a fountain, rivulet, and pond,
As clear as elemental diamond,
Or serene morning air; and far beyond,
The mossy tracks made by the goats and deer
(Which the rough shepherd treads but once a year,) 440
Pierce into glades, caverns, and bowers, and halls
Built round with ivy, which the waterfalls
Illumining, with sound that never fails
Accompany the noon-day nightingales;[315]
And all the place is peopled with sweet airs; 445
The light clear element which the isle wears
Is heavy with the scent of lemon-flowers,
Which floats like mist laden with unseen showers,
And falls upon the eye-lids like faint sleep;
And from the moss violets and jonquils peep, 450
And dart their arrowy odour through the brain
'Till you might faint with that delicious pain.
And every motion, odour, beam, and tone,
With that deep music is in unison:
Which is a soul within the soul—they seem 455
Like echoes of an antenatal dream.—
It is an isle 'twixt Heaven, Air, Earth, and Sea,

---

[313] *Ægean*: the Aegean Sea, a rich embayed arm of the Mediterranean Sea.
[314] *girds*: encircles, secures.
[315] *noon-day nightingales*: Usually, nightingales sing only at night.

Cradled, and hung in clear tranquillity;
Bright as that wandering Eden Lucifer,[316]
Washed by the soft blue Oceans of young air.   460
It is a favoured place. Famine or Blight,
Pestilence, War and Earthquake, never light
Upon its mountain-peaks; blind vultures, they
Sail onward far upon their fatal way:
The winged storms, chaunting their thunder-psalm   465
To other lands, leave azure chasms of calm
Over this isle, or weep themselves in dew,
From which its fields and woods ever renew
Their green and golden immortality.[317]
And from the sea there rise, and from the sky   470
There fall, clear exhalations, soft and bright,
Veil after veil, each hiding some delight,
Which Sun or Moon or zephyr[318] draw aside,
Till the isle's beauty, like a naked bride
Glowing at once with love and loveliness,   475
Blushes and trembles at its own excess:
Yet, like a buried lamp, a Soul no less
Burns in the heart of this delicious isle,
An atom[319] of th' Eternal, whose own smile
Unfolds itself, and may be felt not seen   480
O'er the grey rocks, blue waves, and forests green,
Filling their bare and void interstices.—
But the chief marvel of the wilderness
Is a lone dwelling, built by whom or how
None of the rustic island-people know: 485
'Tis not a tower of strength, though with its height
It overtops the woods; but, for delight,

---

[316] *wandering Eden Lucifer*: Lucifer means "light-bearer" and here refers to Venus as the morning star.

[317] *green . . . immortality*: The passage of the seasons and the "rebirth" of the trees were taken as symbolic of immortality.

[318] *zephyr*: mild breeze.

[319] *atom*: tiny particle. Atoms were theoretically believed by the Greeks to be the smallest indivisible particle and were identified through scientific experimentation and empirical observation by scientists of the seventeenth and eighteenth centuries.

Some wise and tender Ocean-King,[320] ere crime
Had been invented, in the world's young prime,
Reared it, a wonder of that simple time,   490
An envy of the isles, a pleasure-house
Made sacred to his sister and his spouse.
It scarce seems now a wreck of human art,
But, as it were Titanic;[321] in the heart
Of Earth having assumed its form, then grown   495
Out of the mountains, from the living stone,
Lifting itself in caverns light and high:
For all the antique and learned imagery
Has been erased, and in the place of it
The ivy and the wild-vine interknit   500
The volumes[322] of their many twining stems;
Parasite flowers illume with dewy gems
The lampless halls, and when they fade, the sky
Peeps through their winter-woof of tracery
With Moon-light patches, or star atoms keen,   505
Or fragments of the day's intense serene;—
Working mosaic on their Parian floors.[323]
And, day and night, aloof, from the high towers
And terraces, the Earth and Ocean seem
To sleep in one another's arms, and dream   510
Of waves, flowers, clouds, woods, rocks, and all that we
Read in their smiles, and call reality.

This isle and house are mine, and I have vowed
Thee to be lady of the solitude.—
And I have fitted up some chambers there   515
Looking towards the golden Eastern air,

---

[320] *Ocean-King*: Shelley may be referencing Oceanus or his son Nereus, sea gods of classical mythology, but it is more likely that his treatment of myth here is conflated and indistinct.

[321] *Titanic*: i.e., from the age of the Titans, buried in the earth (like the Titans imprisoned by Zeus).

[322] *volumes*: coils.

[323] *mosaic . . . floors*: Parian marble, from the Greek island Paros, was highly valued and used in sculpture.

And level with the living winds, which flow
Like waves above the living waves below.—
I have sent books and music there, and all
Those instruments with which high spirits call   520
The future from its cradle, and the past
Out of its grave, and make the present last
In thoughts and joys which sleep, but cannot die,
Folded within their own eternity.
Our simple life wants little, and true taste   525
Hires not the pale drudge Luxury, to waste
The scene it would adorn, and therefore still,
Nature, with all her children, haunts the hill.
The ring-dove,[324] in the embowering ivy, yet
Keeps up her love-lament, and the owls flit   530
Round the evening tower, and the young stars glance
Between the quick bats in their twilight dance;
The spotted deer bask in the fresh moon-light
Before our gate, and the slow, silent night
Is measured by the pants of their calm sleep.   535
Be this our home in life, and when years heap
Their withered hours, like leaves, on our decay,
Let us become the over-hanging day,
The living soul of this Elysian isle,
Conscious, inseparable, one. Meanwhile   540
We two will rise, and sit, and walk together,
Under the roof of blue Ionian weather,
And wander in the meadows, or ascend
The mossy mountains, where the blue heavens bend
With lightest winds, to touch their paramour;[325]   545
Or linger, where the pebble-paven shore,
Under the quick, faint kisses of the sea
Trembles and sparkles as with ecstacy,—
Possessing and possest by all that is
Within that calm circumference of bliss,   550

[324] *ring-dove*: the ringneck dove or Barbary dove.
[325] *paramour*: lover (i.e., the island).

And by each other, till to love and live
Be one:—or, at the noontide hour, arrive
Where some old cavern hoar seems yet to keep
The moonlight of the expired night asleep,
Through which the awakened day can never peep;   555
A veil for our seclusion, close as Night's,
Where secure sleep may kill thine innocent lights;
Sleep, the fresh dew of languid love, the rain
Whose drops quench kisses till they burn again.
And we will talk, until thought's melody   560
Become too sweet for utterance, and it die
In words, to live again in looks, which dart
With thrilling tone into the voiceless heart,
Harmonizing silence without a sound.
Our breath shall intermix, our bosoms bound,   565
And our veins beat together; and our lips
With other eloquence than words, eclipse
The soul that burns between them, and the wells
Which boil under our being's inmost cells,
The fountains of our deepest life, shall be   570
Confused in passion's golden purity,
As mountain-springs under the morning Sun.[326]
We shall become the same, we shall be one
Spirit within two frames, oh! wherefore two?
One passion in twin-hearts, which grows and grew,   575
'Till like two meteors of expanding flame,
Those spheres instinct with[327] it become the same,
Touch, mingle, are transfigured; ever still
Burning, yet ever inconsumable:
In one another's substance finding food,   580

---

[326] *wells . . . Sun*: This may be a subtle allusion to the Alpheus and Arethusa story in classical mythology: Alpheus, a river-god, was in love with Arethusa, one of Diana's nymphs. When she was transformed into a well, with an underground spring running into the ocean off the coast of Sicily, he followed her there and mingled with his beloved.

[327] *instinct with*: animated by.

Like flames too pure and light and unimbued[328]
To nourish their bright lives with baser prey,
Which point to Heaven and cannot pass away:
One hope within two wills, one will beneath
Two overshadowing minds, one life, one death,   585
One Heaven, one Hell, one immortality,
And one annihilation. Woe is me!
The winged words on which my soul would pierce
Into the height of love's rare Universe,
Are chains of lead around its flight of fire.—   590
I pant, I sink, I tremble, I expire!

    Weak Verses, go, kneel at your Sovereign's[329] feet,
And say:—"We are the masters of thy slave;[330]
What wouldest thou with us and ours and thine?"
Then call your sisters from Oblivion's cave,   595
All singing loud: "Love's very pain is sweet,
But its reward is in the world divine
Which, if not here, it builds beyond the grave."
So shall ye live when I am there. Then haste
Over the hearts of men, until ye meet   600
Marina,[331] Vanna,[332] Primus,[333] and the rest,
And bid them love each other and be blest:
And leave the troop which errs, and which reproves,
And come and be my guest,—for I am Love's.

---

[328] *unimbued*: unsustained, lacking what is necessary.

[329] *Sovereign's*: i.e., "Emily's" (i.e., Teresa's).

[330] *thy slave*: i.e., Shelley (the poet).

[331] *Marina*: Mary ("Marina") Shelley (1797–1851), English novelist and second wife of Percy Shelley.

[332] *Vanna*: Jane ("Giovanna") Williams (1798–1884), companion and common-law wife of Edward Williams, a close friend of Shelley.

[333] *Primus*: Edward Williams (1793–1822), retired army officer and close or "primary" ("Primus") friend of Shelley, who died in the same boating accident as the poet.

A Lament (1821)

I

O World! O Life! O Time!
On whose last steps I climb,
Trembling at that where I had stood before;
When will return the glory of your prime?
No more—Oh, never more!   5

II

Out of the day and night
A joy has taken flight;
Fresh spring, and summer, and winter hoar,
Move my faint heart with grief, but with delight
No more—Oh, never more!   10

Adonais: An Elegy on the Death of John Keats, Author of Endymion, Hyperion, Etc.

Adonais: An Elegy on the Death of John Keats, Author of Endymion, Hyperion, Etc. was written April–July 1821 as an elegy for John Keats, who had died on February 23, 1821. Shelley here uses the Spenserian stanza employed by his friend Byron in *Childe Harold* and Keats himself in *The Eve of St. Agnes*. The title bears a similarity to the Hebrew term *Adonai* ("Lord"), used in Jewish tradition in place of the sacred name of God—but also evokes the name of "Adonis", the slain Greek youth beloved of Aphrodite.

In form, it is a pastoral elegy, complete with dirge, processional allegory, and a resolving consolation—while echoes of Bion's *Lament of Venus for Adonis* and Moschus' *Lament for Bion* (Greek elegies from the second century B.C.) befit the tribute to a poet so Hellenistic in his sympathies. Yet, in the last eighteen stanzas, the bucolic gives way to a Neoplatonic philosophizing.

According to Lionel Trilling and Harold Bloom, "Shelley, in the last third of his poem, is not mourning at all. He struggles to attain a luminous self-recognition that will prepare him for his own death, which he accurately senses is coming shortly (only a year away), and he strives to secure also some vision of the state of being of poetry itself, in its border relations both to life and death."[334]

Shelley was justly proud of *Adonais*, which is generally ranked with Milton's "Lycidas" as the greatest elegy in the English language.

> *Thou wert the morning star among the living,*
> *Ere thy fair light had fled—*
> *Now, having died, thou are as Hesperus, giving*
> *New splendour to the dead.*—Plato[335]

Adonais: An Elegy on the Death of John Keats, Author of Endymion, Hyperion, Etc. (1821)

I

I weep for Adonais—he is dead!
O, weep for Adonais! though our tears
Thaw not the frost which binds so dear a head!
And thou, sad Hour, selected from all years
To mourn our loss, rouse thy obscure compeers,   5
And teach them thine own sorrow, say: with me
Died Adonais; till the Future dares
Forget the Past, his fate and fame shall be
An echo and a light unto eternity!

---

[334] Lionel Trilling and Harold Bloom, *The Oxford Anthology of English Literature*, vol. 4, *Romantic Poetry and Prose* (Oxford: Oxford University Press, 1973), p. 458.

[335] Epigraph, ascribed to Plato, provided by Shelley in the original Greek. It is given here in Shelley's translation (To Stella). *The Complete Poetical Works of Percy Bysshe Shelley*, ed. Thoman Hutchinson (London: Oxford University Press, 1914), p. 712.

II

Where wert thou mighty Mother,[336] when he lay,   10
When thy Son lay, pierced by the shaft which flies
In darkness?[337] where was lorn[338] Urania
When Adonais died? With veiled eyes,
'Mid listening Echoes, in her Paradise
She sate, while one,[339] with soft enamoured breath,   15
Rekindled all the fading melodies,
With which, like flowers that mock the corse[340]
    beneath,
He had adorned and hid the coming bulk of death.

III

O, weep for Adonais—he is dead!
Wake, melancholy Mother, wake and weep!   20
Yet wherefore? Quench within their burning bed
Thy fiery tears, and let thy loud heart keep
Like his, a mute and uncomplaining sleep;
For he is gone, where all things wise and fair
Descend;—oh, dream not that the amorous Deep   25
Will yet restore him to the vital air;
Death feeds on his mute voice, and laughs at our
    despair.

---

[336] *Mother*: i.e., Urania, in classical mythology, goddess of astronomy but more likely Aphrodite Urania (title of Venus), "heavenly Venus", distinguished from the more worldly Venus (Aphrodite Pandemos, for all the people), Uranian Venus—ideal love.

[337] *the shaft . . . darkness*: Cf. Psalm 91:5: "You will not fear the terror of the night, nor the arrow that flies by day." This "shaft" probably refers to the anonymous attack on Keats' *Endymion*, published in the *Quarterly Review* 19 (April 1818).

[338] *lorn*: desolate, forlorn.

[339] *one*: i.e., one echo.

[340] *corse*: corpse.

IV

Most musical of mourners, weep again!
Lament anew, Urania!—He died,
Who was the Sire of an immortal strain,[341]   30
Blind, old, and lonely, when his country's pride,
The priest, the slave, and the liberticide,
Trampled and mocked with many a loathed rite
Of lust and blood; he went, unterrified,
Into the gulph of death;[342] but his clear Sprite[343]   35
Yet reigns o'er earth; the third among the sons of
      light.[344]

V

Most musical of mourners, weep anew!
Not all to that bright station dared to climb;
And happier they their happiness who knew,
Whose tapers yet burn through that night of time   40
In which suns perished;[345] others more sublime,
Struck by the envious wrath of man or God,
Have sunk, extinct in their refulgent prime;
And some[346] yet live, treading the thorny road,
Which leads, through toil and hate, to Fame's serene
      abode.   45

[341] *He . . . strain*: i.e., John Milton.

[342] *when his country's . . . death*: Here Shelley references the history surrounding the English Civil Wars, the regicide of 1649, and the Restoration in 1660. After a period of intense conflict between Royalists (and members of the Church of England's hierarchy) and Puritan Parliamentary supporters, King Charles I (1600–1649) was executed and the Commonwealth of England was established. In 1660, the monarchy was restored and King Charles II (1630–1685) took control of the English government. Throughout, John Milton remained a loyal civil servant of the Commonwealth.

[343] *Sprite*: spirit.

[344] *the third . . . light*: In his *Defence of Poetry*, Shelley names Homer, Dante, and Milton as the three great epic poets.

[345] *they . . . perished*: i.e., minor poets, not widely known.

[346] *some*: i.e., great poets, of lasting fame.

VI

But now, thy youngest, dearest one, has perished
The nursling of thy widowhood,[347] who grew,
Like a pale flower by some sad maiden cherished,
And fed with true love tears, instead of dew;[348]
Most musical of mourners, weep anew!   50
Thy extreme hope, the loveliest and the last,
The bloom, whose petals nipt before they blew[349]
Died on the promise of the fruit, is waste;
The broken lily lies—the storm is overpast.

VII

To that high Capital,[350] where kingly Death   55
Keeps his pale court in beauty and decay,
He came; and bought, with price of purest breath,
A grave among the eternal.—Come away!
Haste, while the vault of blue Italian day
Is yet his fitting charnel-roof![351] while still   60
He lies, as if in dewy sleep he lay;
Awake him not! surely he takes his fill
Of deep and liquid rest, forgetful of all ill.

VIII

He will awake no more, oh, never more!—
Within the twilight chamber spreads apace,   65
The shadow of white Death, and at the door
Invisible Corruption waits to trace
His extreme way to her dim dwelling-place;

---

[347] *nursling . . . widowhood*: i.e., Keats, seen here as Milton's poetic offspring.
[348] *Like . . . dew*: This is probably an oblique reference to Keats' "Isabella, or the Pot of Basil" (1818), a narrative poem concerning a young woman who cherishes the head of her murdered lover in a pot of basil.
[349] *blew*: bloomed.
[350] *Capital*: i.e., Rome, where Keats died.
[351] *charnel-roof*: the roof of the place where his bones repose.

The eternal Hunger sits, but pity and awe
Soothe her pale rage, nor dares she to deface   70
So fair a prey, till darkness, and the law
Of change, shall o'er his sleep the mortal curtain draw.

IX

O, weep for Adonais!—The quick Dreams,
The passion-winged Ministers of thought,
Who were his flocks, whom near the living streams   75
Of his young spirit he fed, and whom he taught
The love which was its music, wander not,—
Wander no more, from kindling brain to brain,
But droop there, whence they sprung; and mourn
          their lot
Round the cold heart, where, after their sweet pain,   80
They ne'er will gather strength, or find a home again.

X

And one[352] with trembling hands clasps his cold head,
And fans him with her moonlight wings, and cries;
"Our love, our hope, our sorrow, is not dead;
See, on the silken fringe of his faint eyes,   85
Like dew upon a sleeping flower, there lies
A tear some Dream has loosened from his brain."
Lost Angel of a ruined Paradise!
She knew not 'twas her own; as with no stain
She faded, like a cloud which had outwept its rain.   90

XI

One from a lucid[353] urn of starry dew
Washed his light limbs as if embalming them;
Another clipt her profuse locks, and threw

[352] *one*: i.e., one dream.
[353] *lucid*: clear, luminous, suffused with light.

The wreath upon him, like an anadem,[354]
Which frozen tears instead of pearls begem;   95
Another in her wilful grief would break
Her bow and winged reeds,[355] as if to stem
A greater loss with one which was more weak;
And dull the barbed fire against his frozen cheek.

XII

Another Splendour[356] on his mouth alit,   100
That mouth, whence it was wont to draw the breath
Which gave it strength to pierce the guarded wit,
And pass into the panting heart beneath
With lightning and with music: the damp death
Quenched its caress upon his icy lips;   105
And, as a dying meteor stains a wreath
Of moonlight vapour, which the cold night clips,[357]
It flushed through his pale limbs, and past to its eclipse.

XIII

And others came … Desires and Adorations,
Winged Persuasions and veiled Destinies,   110
Splendours, and Glooms, and glimmering
        Incarnations
Of hopes and fears, and twilight Phantasies;
And Sorrow, with her family of Sighs,
And Pleasure, blind with tears, led by the gleam
Of her own dying smile instead of eyes,   115
Came in slow pomp;—the moving pomp might seem
Like pageantry of mist on an autumnal stream.[358]

[354] *anadem*: garland worn upon the head.

[355] *winged reeds*: arrows.

[356] *Splendour*: angel.

[357] *clips*: embraces.

[358] *autumnal stream*: Cf. Keats' "To Autumn".

XIV

All he had loved, and moulded into thought,
From shape, and hue, and odour, and sweet sound,
Lamented Adonais. Morning sought   120
Her eastern watchtower, and her hair unbound,
Wet with the tears which should adorn the ground,
Dimmed the aerial eyes that kindle day;
Afar the melancholy thunder moaned,
Pale Ocean in unquiet slumber lay,   125
And the wild winds flew round, sobbing in their dismay.

XV

Lost Echo sits amid the voiceless mountains,
And feeds her grief with his remembered lay,
And will no more reply to winds or fountains,
Or amorous birds perched on the young green spray,   130
Or herdsman's horn, or bell at closing day;
Since she can mimic not his lips, more dear
Than those for whose disdain she pined away
Into a shadow of all sounds:[359]—a drear
Murmur, between their songs, is all the woodmen hear.   135

XVI

Grief made the young Spring wild, and she threw down
Her kindling buds, as if she Autumn were,
Or they dead leaves; since her delight is flown
For whom should she have waked the sullen year?
To Phœbus was not Hyacinth so dear[360]   140

---

[359] *Lost . . . sounds*: In classical mythology, the nymph Echo was cursed so that she could repeat only the words of others. When she fell in love with the beautiful youth Narcissus (who ignored her and fell in love with himself), she wasted away into an echo.

[360] *Phœbus . . . dear*: In classical mythology, Hyacinth was a young man beloved by both Phoebus Apollo and Zephyrus (god of the west wind), killed in their rivalry and transformed by Apollo into a flower.

Nor to himself Narcissus,[361] as to both
Thou Adonais: wan they stand and sere[362]
Amid the faint companions of their youth,
With dew all turned to tears; odour, to sighing ruth.[363]

XVII

Thy spirit's sister, the lorn nightingale[364]   145
Mourns not her mate with such melodious pain;
Not so the eagle, who like thee could scale
Heaven, and could nourish in the sun's domain
Her mighty youth with morning,[365] doth complain,
Soaring and screaming round her empty nest,   150
As Albion[366] wails for thee: the curse of Cain[367]
Light on his head who pierced thy innocent breast,
And scared the angel soul that was its earthly guest!

XVIII

Ah woe is me! Winter is come and gone,
But grief returns with the revolving year;   155
The airs and streams renew their joyous tone;
The ants, the bees, the swallows reappear;
Fresh leaves and flowers deck the dead Seasons'
        bier;
The amorous birds now pair in every brake,[368]

---

[361] *Narcissus*: In classical mythology, the beautiful hunter Narcissus fell in love with his own reflection in a pool and died because he could not bear to leave that spot. After death, he underwent metamorphosis, becoming a flower.

[362] *sere*: withered, dry.

[363] *ruth*: pity.

[364] *nightingale*: Cf. Keats' "Ode to a Nightingale".

[365] *eagle . . . morning*: According to popular legend, the eagle could renew his youth by flying toward the sun and then diving into a fountain.

[366] *Albion*: England.

[367] *curse of Cain*: In the biblical Book of Genesis, Cain is cursed to wander the earth as punishment for killing his brother Abel and is marked by God so that he will not himself be slain (see 4:10–15).

[368] *brake*: thicket, area overgrown densely with briars.

And build their mossy homes in field and brere;[369]   160
And the green lizard, and the golden snake,
Like unimprisoned flames, out of their trance awake.

XIX

Through wood and stream and field and hill and
          Ocean
A quickening life from the Earth's heart has burst
As it has ever done, with change and motion,   165
From the great morning of the world when first
God dawned on Chaos; in its steam immersed
The lamps of Heaven flash with a softer light;
All baser things pant with life's sacred thirst;
Diffuse themselves; and spend in love's delight,   170
The beauty and the joy of their renewed might.

XX

The leprous corpse, touched by this spirit tender
Exhales itself in flowers of gentle breath;[370]
Like incarnations of the stars, when splendour
Is changed to fragrance, they illumine death   175
And mock the merry worm that wakes beneath;
Nought we know, dies. Shall that alone which
          knows[371]
Be as a sword consumed before the sheath
By sightless[372] lightning?—th'intense atom glows
A moment, then is quenched in a most cold repose.   180

---

[369] *brere*: brier.

[370] *flowers . . . breath*: i.e., windflowers or anemones, the Greek name of which is derived from the word for "wind", which are supposed to open only when the wind blows on it. In classical mythology, these were formed from the blood of Adonis, the slain lover of Venus.

[371] *that . . . knows*: i.e., the mind of man.

[372] *sightless*: blind, invisible, lacking in reason (contrasting the mind of man).

XXI

Alas! that all we loved of him should be,
But for our grief, as if it had not been,
And grief itself be mortal! Woe is me!
Whence are we, and why are we? of what scene
The actors or spectators? Great and mean　　　185
Meet massed in death, who lends what life must borrow.
As long as skies are blue, and fields are green,
Evening must usher night, night urge the morrow,
Month follow month with woe, and year wake year to
　　　sorrow.

XXII

He will awake no more, oh, never more!　　　190
"Wake thou," cried Misery, "childless Mother, rise
Out of thy sleep, and slake,[373] in thy heart's core,
A wound more fierce than his with tears and sighs."
And all the Dreams that watched Urania's eyes,
And all the Echoes whom their sister's song[374]　　　195
Had held in holy silence, cried: "Arise!"
Swift as a Thought by the snake Memory stung,
From her ambrosial rest the fading Splendour sprung.

XXIII

She rose like an autumnal Night, that springs
Out of the East, and follows wild and drear　　　200
The golden Day, which, on eternal wings,
Even as a ghost abandoning a bier,
Had left the Earth a corpse. Sorrow and fear
So struck, so roused, so rapt Urania;
So saddened round her like an atmosphere　　　205
Of stormy mist; so swept her on her way
Even to the mournful place where Adonais lay.

---

[373] *slake*: lessen, moderate.
[374] *sister's song*: i.e., the echoes respond like sister voices.

XXIV

Out of her secret Paradise she sped,
Through camps and cities rough with stone, and
    steel,
And human hearts, which to her aery tread   210
Yielding not, wounded the invisible
Palms[375] of her tender feet where'er they fell:
And barbed tongues, and thoughts more sharp than
    they
Rent the soft Form they never could repel,
Whose sacred blood, like the young tears of May,   215
Paved with eternal flowers that undeserving way.

XXV

In the death chamber for a moment Death
Shamed by the presence of that living Might
Blushed to annihilation, and the breath
Revisited those lips, and life's pale light   220
Flashed through those limbs, so late her dear
    delight.
"Leave me not wild and drear and comfortless,
As silent lightning leaves the starless night!
Leave me not!" cried Urania: her distress
Roused Death: Death rose and smiled, and met her
    vain caress.   225

XXVI

"Stay yet awhile! speak to me once again;
Kiss me, so long but as a kiss may live;
And in my heartless breast and burning brain
That word, that kiss shall all thoughts else survive
With food of saddest memory kept alive,   230
Now thou art dead, as if it were a part

---

[375] *Palms:* i.e., soles.

Of thee, my Adonais! I would give
All that I am to be as thou now art!
But I am chained to Time, and cannot thence depart!

XXVII

"O gentle child, beautiful as thou wert, 235
Why didst thou leave the trodden paths of men
Too soon, and with weak hands though mighty
     heart
Dare the unpastured dragon[376] in his den?
Defenceless as thou wert, oh, where was then
Wisdom the mirrored shield,[377] or scorn the spear? 240
Or hadst thou waited the full cycle, when
Thy spirit should have filled its crescent[378] sphere,
The monsters of life's waste had fled from thee like
     deer.

XXVIII

"The herded wolves, bold only to pursue;
The obscene ravens, clamorous o'er the dead; 245
The vultures to the conqueror's banner true
Who feed where Desolation first has fed,
And whose wings rain contagion;—how they fled,
When like Apollo, from his golden bow,
The Pythian of the age[379] one arrow[380] sped 250
And smiled!—The spoilers tempt no second blow,
They fawn on the proud feet that spurn them lying low.

[376] *unpastured dragon*: i.e., poetry critic(s).

[377] *mirrored shield*: The mirrored shield has a place in classical mythology: the hero Perseus used a mirrored shield to battle against Medusa, the hideous Gorgon, for he knew that those who looked at her directly were turned to stone at the sight.

[378] *crescent*: waxing.

[379] *Pythian . . . age*: i.e., Byron.

[380] *one arrow*: Byron's satirical poem "English Bards and Scotch Reviewers", originally published (anonymously) in early 1809, effectively lampooned poetic critics.

XXIX

"The sun comes forth, and many reptiles spawn;
He sets, and each ephemeral insect[381] then
Is gathered into death without a dawn,   255
And the immortal stars awake again;
So is it in the world of living men:
A godlike mind soars forth, in its delight
Making earth bare and veiling heaven, and when
It sinks, the swarms that dimmed or shared its light   260
Leave to its kindred lamps[382] the spirit's awful night."

XXX

Thus ceased she: and the mountain shepherds[383]
    came
Their garlands sere, their magic mantles rent;
The Pilgrim of Eternity,[384] whose fame
Over his living head like Heaven is bent,   265
An early but enduring monument,
Came, veiling all the lightnings of his song
In sorrow; from her wilds Ierne[385] sent
The sweetest lyrist[386] of her saddest wrong,
And love taught grief to fall like music from his
    tongue.   270

---

[381] *ephemeral insect*: the dayfly or ephemerid, a small insect that lives for only one day.

[382] *kindred lamps*: i.e., the stars, figuratively representing other artists.

[383] *mountain shepherds*: i.e., other artists, both drawing on the pastoral poetic tradition that linked poetic inspiration with the figure of the shepherd and gesturing toward Romantic associations with the mountain as a place of primitive artistic inspiration as well as the expression of idealized rustic independence.

[384] *Pilgrim of Eternity*: i.e., Byron. Cf. his *Childe Harold's Pilgrimage*, pp. 20, 48.

[385] *Ierne*: Ireland.

[386] *sweetest lyrist*: i.e., Thomas Moore (1779–1852), Irish poet and songwriter, a close friend of Byron.

XXXI

Midst others of less note, came one frail Form,[387]
A phantom among men; companionless
As the last cloud of an expiring storm
Whose thunder is its knell; he, as I guess,
Had gazed on Nature's naked loveliness,   275
Actæon-like, and now he fled astray
With feeble steps o'er the world's wilderness,
And his own thoughts, along that rugged way,
Pursued, like raging hounds, their father and their
    prey.[388]

XXXII

A pardlike[389] Spirit beautiful and swift—   280
A Love in desolation masked:—a Power
Girt round with weakness;—it can scarce uplift
The weight of the superincumbent hour;
It is a dying lamp, a falling shower,
A breaking billow;—even whilst we speak   285
Is it not broken? On the withering flower
The killing sun smiles brightly: on a cheek
The life can burn in blood, even while the heart may
    break.

XXXIII

His head was bound with pansies overblown,
And faded violets, white, and pied, and blue;   290
And a light spear topped with a cypress cone,
Round whose rude shaft dark ivy tresses grew[390]

---

[387] *one . . . Form*: i.e., Shelley.

[388] *he, as I guess, . . . prey*: In classical mythology, the huntsman Actaeon witnessed the goddess Diana bathing. In her fury, she transformed the hunter into a hart and he was pursued and torn to pieces by his own hunting hounds.

[389] *pardlike*: A pard is an archaic term for a leopard or other large wildcat.

[390] *spear . . . grew*: i.e., the thyrsus, a staff associated with the revels and festivals of the god Dionysus, the classical god of the grape harvest.

Yet dripping with the forest's noonday dew,
Vibrated, as the ever-beating heart
Shook the weak hand that grasped it; of that crew   295
He came the last, neglected and apart;
A herd-abandoned deer struck by the hunter's dart.

XXXIV

All stood aloof, and at his partial[391] moan
Smiled through their tears; well knew that gentle band
Who in another's fate now wept his own;   300
As in the accents of an unknown land,
He sung new sorrow; sad Urania scanned
The Stranger's mien, and murmured: "who art thou?"
He answered not, but with a sudden hand
Made bare his branded and ensanguined brow,   305
Which was like Cain's or Christ's[392]—Oh! that it should
be so!

XXXV

What softer voice is hushed over the dead?
Athwart what brow is that dark mantle thrown?
What form leans sadly o'er the white death-bed,
In mockery[393] of monumental stone,   310
The heavy heart heaving without a moan?
If it be He,[394] who, gentlest of the wise,
Taught, soothed, loved, honoured the departed one;
Let me not vex, with inharmonious sighs
The silence of that heart's accepted sacrifice.   315

---

[391] *partial*: prejudiced, affectionate.

[392] *branded . . . Christ's*: Cf. the mark of Cain (see Genesis 4:15) and the crown of thorns placed upon the head of Christ (see Matthew 27:29; Mark 15:17; John 19:2, 5).

[393] *mockery*: imitation, also literally "mockery" because he is living and not stone.

[394] *He*: i.e., James Henry Leigh Hunt (1784–1859), a poet and close friend of Keats.

XXXVI

Our Adonais has drunk poison—oh!
What deaf and viperous murderer[395] could crown
Life's early cup with such a draught of woe?
The nameless worm[396] would now itself disown:
It felt, yet could escape the magic tone   320
Whose prelude held all envy, hate, and wrong,
But what was howling in one breast alone,
Silent with expectation of the song,
Whose master's hand is cold, whose silver lyre unstrung.

XXXVII

Live thou, whose infamy is not thy fame!   325
Live! fear no heavier chastisement from me,
Thou noteless blot on a remembered name!
But be thyself, and know thyself to be!
And ever at thy season be thou free
To spill the venom when thy fangs o'erflow: 330
Remorse and Self-contempt shall cling to thee;
Hot Shame shall burn upon thy secret brow,
And like a beaten hound tremble thou shalt—as now.

XXXVIII

Nor let us weep that our delight is fled
Far from these carrion kites[397] that scream below;   335
He wakes or sleeps with the enduring dead;
Thou canst not soar where he is sitting now.[398]—

---

[395] *murderer*: i.e., Keats' anonymous reviewer in the *Quarterly Review*, believed by Shelley to be the poet Robert Southey (1774–1843), whom he suspected of criticizing his own work; in fact, Keats' anonymous critic was the Irish author and statesman John Wilson Croker (1780–1857), while Shelley's was Sir John Taylor Coleridge (1790–1876), the nephew of the early Romantic poet Samuel Taylor Coleridge (1772–1834).

[396] *worm*: snake.

[397] *kites*: hawks or other predatory birds.

[398] *Thou . . . now*: Cf. Milton's *Paradise Lost* (bk. 4, lines 828–29), where Satan, who once soared, is not recognized by the angels sitting low in Hell.

Dust to the dust! but the pure spirit shall flow
Back to the burning fountain whence it came,
A portion of the Eternal, which must glow   340
Through time and change, unquenchably the same,
Whilst thy cold embers choke the sordid hearth of
    shame.

XXXIX

Peace, peace! he is not dead, he doth not sleep—
He hath awakened from the dream of life—
'Tis we, who lost in stormy visions, keep   345
With phantoms an unprofitable strife,
And in mad trance, strike with our spirit's knife
Invulnerable nothings.—*We* decay
Like corpses in a charnel; fear and grief
Convulse us and consume us day by day,   350
And cold hopes swarm like worms within our living clay.

XL

He has outsoared the shadow of our night;
Envy and calumny and hate and pain,
And that unrest which men miscall delight,
Can touch him not and torture not again;   355
From the contagion of the world's slow stain
He is secure, and now can never mourn
A heart grown cold, a head grown grey in vain;[399]
Nor, when the spirit's self has ceased to burn,
With sparkless ashes load an unlamented urn.   360

XLI

He lives, he wakes—'tis Death is dead, not he;
Mourn not for Adonais.—Thou young Dawn
Turn all thy dew to splendour, for from thee

[399] *He . . . vain*: i.e., Southey, whom Shelley attacks here.

The spirit thou lamentest is not gone;
Ye caverns and ye forests, cease to moan!   365
Cease ye faint flowers and fountains, and thou Air
Which like a mourning veil thy scarf hadst thrown
O'er the abandoned Earth, now leave it bare
Even to the joyous stars which smile on its despair![400]

XLII

He is made one with Nature: there is heard   370
His voice in all her music, from the moan
Of thunder, to the song of night's sweet bird;[401]
He is a presence to be felt and known
In darkness and in light, from herb and stone,
Spreading itself where'er that Power may move   375
Which has withdrawn his being to its own;
Which wields the world with never wearied love,
Sustains it from beneath, and kindles it above.

XLIII

He is a portion of the loveliness
Which once he made more lovely: he doth bear   380
His part, while the one Spirit's plastic[402] stress
Sweeps through the dull dense world, compelling
       there,
All new successions to the forms they wear;
Torturing th' unwilling dross that checks its flight
To its own likeness, as each mass may bear;   385
And bursting in its beauty and its might
From trees and beasts and men into the Heaven's
       light.

[400] *Air . . . despair*: The stars are rendered invisible by the moisture in the air, which reflects and diffuses the rays of sunlight.

[401] *night's sweet bird*: i.e., nightingale.

[402] *plastic*: having the power of shaping matter.

XLIV

The splendours of the firmament of time
May be eclipsed, but are extinguished not;
Like stars to their appointed height they climb   390
And death is a low mist which cannot blot
The brightness it may veil. When lofty thought
Lifts a young heart above its mortal lair,
And love and life contend in it, for what
Shall be its earthly doom,[403] the dead live there   395
And move like winds of light on dark and stormy air.

XLV

The inheritors of unfulfilled renown[404]
Rose from their thrones, built beyond mortal thought,
Far in the Unapparent. Chatterton[405]
Rose pale, his solemn agony had not   400
Yet faded from him; Sidney,[406] as he fought
And as he fell and as he lived and loved
Sublimely mild, a Spirit without spot,
Arose; and Lucan,[407] by his death approved:
Oblivion as they rose shrank like a thing reproved.   405

XLVI

And many more, whose names on Earth are dark
But whose transmitted effluence[408] cannot die
So long as fire outlives the parent spark,
Rose, robed in dazzling immortality.

---

[403] *doom*: destiny, fate.

[404] *inheritors . . . renown*: poets not recognized in life.

[405] *Chatterton*: The poet Thomas Chatterton (1752–1770), to whom Keats dedicated *Endymion*, died after taking arsenic (possibly suicidal).

[406] *Sidney*: The poet Sir Philip Sidney (1554–1586) died of wounds sustained in battle.

[407] *Lucan*: The Roman poet and revolutionary Marcus Annaeus Lucanus (39–65) was forced by Nero to commit suicide and chose to bleed to death while reading his poetry aloud.

[408] *effluence*: emanation, thing flowing forth.

"Thou art become as one of us," they cry,   410
"It was for thee yon kingless sphere[409] has long
Swung blind in unascended majesty,
Silent alone amid an Heaven of song.
Assume thy winged throne, thou Vesper[410] of our throng!"

XLVII

Who mourns for Adonais? oh come forth   415
Fond[411] wretch! and know thyself and him aright.
Clasp with thy panting soul the pendulous[412] Earth;
As from a centre, dart thy spirit's light
Beyond all worlds, until its spacious might
Satiate the void circumference:[413] then shrink   420
Even to a point within our day and night;
And keep thy heart light lest it make thee sink
When hope has kindled hope, and lured thee to the
    brink.[414]

XLVIII

Or go to Rome, which is the sepulchre
O, not of him, but of our joy: 'tis nought   425
That ages, empires, and religions there
Lie buried in the ravage they[415] have wrought;
For such as he can lend,—they[416] borrow not
Glory from those who made the world their prey;
And he is gathered to the kings of thought   430
Who waged contention with their time's decay,
And of the past are all that cannot pass away.

---

[409] *kingless sphere*: In classical mythology, the spheres were associated with the gods.

[410] *Vesper*: i.e., the planet Venus as the evening star.

[411] *Fond*: foolish, affectionate.

[412] *pendulous*: i.e., moving like a pendulum as it rotates on its axis.

[413] *void circumference*: Cf. Shelley's *Defence of Poetry*, p. 328: "Poetry is indeed something divine. It is at once the centre and circumference of knowledge."

[414] *brink*: i.e., of the grave or of a precipice.

[415] *they*: i.e., the representatives of empires or religions.

[416] *they*: i.e., "such as he", meaning Keats.

XLIX

Go thou to Rome,—at once the Paradise,
The grave, the city, and the wilderness;
And where its wrecks like shattered mountains rise,   435
And flowering weeds, and fragrant copses dress
The bones of Desolation's nakedness
Pass, till the Spirit of the spot shall lead
Thy footsteps to a slope of green access
Where, like an infant's smile, over the dead,   440
A light of laughing flowers along the grass is spread.[417]

L

And grey walls moulder round,[418] on which dull Time
Feeds, like slow fire upon a hoary brand;[419]
And one keen pyramid with wedge sublime,
Pavilioning the dust of him[420] who planned   445
This refuge for his memory, doth stand
Like flame transformed to marble; and beneath,
A field is spread, on which a newer band
Have pitched in Heaven's smile their camp of
          death[421]
Welcoming him we lose with scarce extinguished breath. 450

LI

Here pause: these graves are all too young as yet
To have outgrown the sorrow which consigned

[417] *Go . . . spread*: This stanza and the stanzas that follow describe the Protestant cemetery (Cimitero Acattolico) in Rome where Keats is buried. Shelley's son William, who died in 1819 of malaria, is buried close to Keats.

[418] *gray walls . . . round*: The Aurelian walls (built in the third century) form part of the boundary of the cemetery.

[419] *hoary brand*: burning or moldering log.

[420] *one keen . . . him*: The Pyramid of Cestius, the tomb of a Roman magistrate, also borders the cemetery.

[421] *camp of death*: The Italian word for "cemetery" is *camposanto*, meaning "holy camp".

Its charge to each; and if the seal is set,
Here, on one fountain of a mourning mind,[422]
Break it not thou! too surely shalt thou find   455
Thine own well full, if thou returnest home,
Of tears and gall. From the world's bitter wind[423]
Seek shelter in the shadow of the tomb.
What Adonais is, why fear we to become?

LII

The One remains, the many change and pass;   460
Heaven's light forever shines, Earth's shadows fly;
Life, like a dome of many-coloured glass,
Stains the white radiance of Eternity,
Until Death tramples it to fragments.—Die,
If thou wouldst be with that which thou dost seek!   465
Follow where all is fled!—Rome's azure sky,
Flowers, ruins, statues, music, words, are weak
The glory they transfuse with fitting truth to speak.

LIII

Why linger, why turn back, why shrink, my Heart?
Thy hopes[424] are gone before; from all things here   470
They have departed; thou shouldst now depart!
A light is past from the revolving year,
And man, and woman; and what still is dear
Attracts to crush, repels to make thee wither.
The soft sky smiles,—the low wind whispers near: 475
'Tis Adonais calls! oh, hasten thither,
No more let Life divide what Death can join together.

---

[422] *these graves . . . mourning mind*: Shelley's grief continues at the tragic death of his son William.

[423] *bitter wind*: "Malaria" literally means a "bad wind".

[424] *hopes*: This may refer to many things lost by Shelley: his children, his first marriage (and the children from it), his political ambitions, etc.

LIV

That Light whose smile kindles the Universe,[425]
That Beauty in which all things work and move,
That Benediction which the eclipsing Curse   480
Of birth can quench not, that sustaining Love
Which through the web of being blindly wove
By man and beast and earth and air and sea,
Burns bright or dim, as each are mirrors of
The fire for which all thirst; now beams on me,   485
Consuming the last clouds of cold mortality.

LV

The breath whose might I have invoked in song
Descends on me; my spirit's bark is driven,
Far from the shore, far from the trembling throng
Whose sails were never to the tempest given;[426]   490
The massy earth and sphered skies are riven!
I am borne darkly, fearfully, afar:
Whilst burning through the inmost veil of Heaven,
The soul of Adonais, like a star,
Beacons from the abode where the Eternal are.   495

---

[425] *Light . . . Universe*: Cf. the *Paradiso* of Dante's *Divine Comedy* (canto 1, lines 1–3): "The glory of him who moves all things penetrates throughout the universe and rekindles." *The Paradiso of Dante Alighieri*, ed. and trans. Philip Henry Wicksteed and Hermann Oelsner (London: J. M. Dent, 1900), p. 15.

[426] *my spirit's . . . given*: Cf. Dante's *Paradiso*, canto 2: "O ye who in your little skiff, longing to hear, / Warning have followed on my keel that singeth on its way."

To Night (1821)

I

Swiftly walk o'er the western wave,
     Spirit of Night!
  Out of the misty eastern cave,
  Where, all the long and lone daylight,
    Thou wovest dreams of joy and fear,   5
  Which make thee terrible and dear,—
      Swift be thy flight!

II

  Wrap thy form in a mantle gray,
     Star-inwrought!
  Blind with thine hair the eyes of Day;   10
Kiss her until she be wearied out,
  Then wander o'er city, and sea, and land,
    Touching all with thine opiate wand—
      Come, long-sought!

III

  When I arose and saw the dawn,   15
     I sighed for thee;
When light rode high, and the dew was gone,
  And noon lay heavy on flower and tree,
And the weary Day turned to his rest,
Lingering like an unloved guest, I sighed for thee.   20

IV

Thy brother Death came, and cried,
     Wouldst thou me?
Thy sweet child Sleep, the filmy-eyed,
Murmured like a noontide bee,   25
Shall I nestle near thy side?
Wouldst thou me?—And I replied,
     No, not thee!

V

Death will come when thou art dead,
Soon, too soon—   30
Sleep will come when thou art fled;
Of neither would I ask the boon
I ask of thee, beloved Night—
Swift be thine approaching flight,
          Come soon, soon!   35

"Music, when soft voices die" (1821)

          To _____
Music, when soft voices die,
Vibrates in the memory.—
Odours, when sweet violets sicken,
Live within the sense they quicken.—

Rose leaves, when the rose is dead,   5
Are heaped for the beloved's bed—
And so thy thoughts, when thou art gone,
Love itself shall slumber on....

A Defence of Poetry

Dante understood the secret things of love even more than
Petrarch. His Vita Nuova is an inexhaustible fountain of purity
of sentiment and language: it is the idealized history of that
period, and those intervals of his life which were dedicated to
love. His apotheosis of Beatrice in Paradise, and the gradations
of his own love and her loveliness, by which as by steps he
feigns himself to have ascended to the throne of the Supreme
Cause, is the most glorious imagination of modern poetry.
The acutest critics have justly reversed the judgement of the
vulgar, and the order of the great acts of the "Divine Drama", in
the measure of the admiration which they accord to the Hell,

Purgatory, and Paradise. The latter[427] is a perpetual hymn of everlasting love. Love, which found a worthy poet in Plato[428] alone of all the ancients, has been celebrated by a chorus of the greatest writers of the renovated world; and the music has penetrated the caverns of society, and its echoes still drown the dissonance of arms and superstition. At successive intervals, Ariosto,[429] Tasso,[430] Shakespeare,[431] Spenser,[432] Calderon,[433] Rousseau,[434] and the great writers of our own age, have celebrated the dominion of love, planting as it were trophies in the human mind of that sublimest victory over sensuality and force. The true relation borne to each other by the sexes into which human kind is distributed has become less misunderstood; and if the error which confounded diversity with inequality of the powers of the two sexes has become partially recognized in the opinions and institutions of modern Europe, we owe this great benefit to the worship of which Chivalry[435] was the law, and poets the prophets.

---

[427] *latter*: Shelley is speaking of the *Paradiso* in *The Divine Comedy* of Dante Alighieri (1265–1321), Italian poet.

[428] *Plato*: (c. 424–347 B.C.), Greek philosopher, student of the philosopher Socrates (whose dialogues Plato recorded), and founder of the Athenian Academy, the first major institution of learning in Western history.

[429] *Ariosto*: Ludovico Ariosto (1474–1533), Italian poet and dramatist, author of the epic *Orlando Furioso*.

[430] *Tasso*: Torquato Tasso (1544–1595), Italian poet and dramatist, author of the epic *Gerusalemme Liberata*.

[431] *Shakespeare*: William Shakespeare (c. 1564–1616), the most influential English poet and playwright.

[432] *Spenser*: Edmund Spenser (c. 1552–1599), English Elizabethan poet, author of the epic poem *The Faerie Queene*.

[433] *Calderon*: Pedro Calderón de la Barca (1600–1681), poet and dramatist of the Spanish Golden Age.

[434] *Rousseau*: Jean-Jacques Rousseau (1712–1778), Genevan philosopher and writer, influential as a thinker in the rise of the French Revolution at the end of the eighteenth century.

[435] *Chivalry*: Chivalry, historically concerned with the rules and customs of medieval knighthood, became representative of the ideal qualifications for a knight, including courtesy, generosity, valor, military dexterity, and (often) romantic charm.

The poetry of Dante may be considered as the bridge thrown over the stream of time, which unites the modern and ancient world. The distorted notions of invisible things which Dante and his rival Milton[436] have idealized, are merely the mask and the mantle in which these great poets walk through eternity enveloped and disguised. It is a difficult question to determine how far they were conscious of the distinction which must have subsisted in their minds between their own creeds and that of the people. Dante at least appears to wish to mark the full extent of it by placing Riphæus,[437] whom Virgil calls *justissimus unus*, in Paradise, and observing a most heretical caprice in his distribution of rewards and punishments. And Milton's poem contains within itself a philosophical refutation of that system of which, by a strange and natural antithesis, it has been a chief popular support. Nothing can exceed the energy and magnificence of the character of Satan as expressed in *Paradise Lost*. It is a mistake to suppose that he could ever have been intended for the popular personification of evil.[438] Implacable hate, patient cunning, and a sleepless refinement of device to inflict the extremest anguish on an enemy, these things are evil; and although venial in a slave are not to be forgiven in a tyrant; although redeemed by much that ennobles his defeat in one subdued, are marked by all that dishonours his conquest

[436] *rival Milton*: John Milton (1608–1674), one of the most influential poets and polemicists of the English Commonwealth, author of the blank verse epic *Paradise Lost*, which depicted the Fall of Adam and Eve and described Hell and Satan in great detail. Here, "rival" is meant as a compliment to Milton, putting him on the same level as Dante.

[437] *Riphæus*: in classical mythology, a Trojan hero killed in the sack of Troy, and called the "*justissimus unus*" (the most just) by the Roman poet Virgil (*Aeneid*, bk. 2, lines 424–27).

[438] *Nothing . . . evil*: This interpretation of the work of the Puritan Milton, championed by the Romantics, especially Shelley, was famously introduced by the poet William Blake (1757–1827) in his *Marriage of Heaven and Hell*: "The reason Milton wrote in fetters when he wrote of Angels & God, and at liberty when of Devils & Hell, is because he was a true Poet and of the Devils party without knowing it." William Blake, *The Marriage of Heaven and Hell*, "The Voice of the Devil", Note in *The Complete Illuminated Books* (London: Thames and Hudson, 2002), p. 112.

in the victor. Milton's Devil as a moral being is as far supe-
rior to his God as one who perseveres in some purpose which
he has conceived to be excellent in spite of adversity and tor-
ture, is to one who in the cold security of undoubted triumph
inflicts the most horrible revenge upon his enemy, not from
any mistaken notion of inducing him to repent of a persever-
ance in enmity, but with the alleged design of exasperating
him to deserve new torments. Milton has so far violated the
popular creed (if this shall be judged to be a violation) as to
have alleged no superiority of moral virtue to his God over his
Devil. And this bold neglect of a direct moral purpose is the
most decisive proof of the supremacy of Milton's genius. He
mingled as it were the elements of human nature, as colours
upon a single pallet, and arranged them into the composition
of his great picture according to the laws of epic truth; that
is, according to the laws of that principle by which a series of
actions of the external universe and of intelligent and ethical
beings is calculated to excite the sympathy of succeeding gen-
erations of mankind. *The Divina Commedia* and *Paradise Lost*
have conferred upon modern mythology a systematic form; and
when change and time shall have added one more superstition
to the mass of those which have arisen and decayed upon the
earth, commentators will be learnedly employed in elucidat-
ing the religion of ancestral Europe, only not utterly forgotten
because it will have been stamped with the eternity of genius.

Homer was the first, and Dante the second epic poet: that
is, the second poet the series of whose creations bore a defined
and intelligible relation to the knowledge, and sentiment, and
religion, and political conditions of the age in which he lived,
and of the ages which followed it, developing itself in corre-
spondence with their development. For Lucretius had limed
the wings of his swift spirit in the dregs of the sensible world;
and Virgil, with a modesty that ill became his genius, had
affected the fame of an imitator. . . .

The cultivation of those sciences which have enlarged the
limits of the empire of man over the external world, has, for want
of the poetical faculty, proportionally circumscribed those of the

internal world; and man, having enslaved the elements, remains himself a slave. To what but a cultivation of the mechanical arts in a degree disproportioned to the presence of the creative faculty, which is the basis of all knowledge, is to be attributed the abuse of all invention for abridging and combining labour, to the exasperation of the inequality of mankind? From what other cause has it arisen that the discoveries which should have lightened, have added a weight to the curse imposed on Adam? Poetry, and the principle of Self, of which money is the visible incarnation, are the God and the Mammon of the world.[439]

The functions of the poetical faculty are two-fold; by one it creates new materials of knowledge, and power and pleasure; by the other it engenders in the mind a desire to reproduce and arrange them according to a certain rhythm and order which may be called the beautiful and the good. The cultivation of poetry is never more to be desired than at periods when, from an excess of the selfish and calculating principle, the accumulation of the materials of external life exceed the quantity of the power of assimilating them to the internal laws of human nature. The body has then become too unwieldly for that which animates it.

Poetry is indeed something divine. It is at once the centre and circumference of knowledge; it is that which comprehends all science, and that to which all science must be referred. It is at the same time the root and blossom of all other systems of thought: it is that from which all spring, and that which adorns all; and that which, if blighted, denies the fruit and the seed, and withholds from the barren world the nourishment and the succession of the scions of the tree of life. It is the perfect and consummate surface and bloom of things; it is as the odour and the colour of the rose to the texture of the elements which compose it, as the form and the splendour of unfaded beauty to the secrets of anatomy and corruption. What were Virtue, Love, Patriotism, Friendship &c.—what were the scenery of

[439] *God . . . world*: Cf. Matthew 6:24 and Luke 16:13: "No [man] can serve two masters; for either he will hate the one and love the other, or he will be devoted to the one and despise the other. You cannot serve God and mammon." ("Mammon" is a word for material wealth.)

this beautiful Universe which we inhabit—what were our con-
solations on this side of the grave—and what were our aspi-
rations beyond it—if Poetry did not ascend to bring light and
fire from those eternal regions where the owl-winged faculty
of calculation dare not ever soar? Poetry is not like reasoning,
a power to be exerted according to the determination of the
will. A man cannot say, "I will compose poetry." The great-
est poet even cannot say it: for the mind in creation is as a
fading coal which some invisible influence, like an inconstant
wind, awakens to transitory brightness: this power arises from
within, like the colour of a flower which fades and changes as
it is developed, and the conscious portions of our natures are
unprophetic either of its approach or its departure. Could this
influence be durable in its original purity and force, it is impos-
sible to predict the greatness of the results: but when composi-
tion begins, inspiration is already on the decline, and the most
glorious poetry that has ever been communicated to the world
is probably a feeble shadow of the original conception of the
poet. I appeal to the greatest Poets of the present day, whether
it be not an error to assert that the finest passages of poetry are
produced by labour and study. The toil and the delay recom-
mended by critics can be justly interpreted to mean no more
than a careful observation of the inspired moments, and an
artificial connexion of the spaces between their suggestions by
the intertexture of conventional expressions; a necessity only
imposed by the limitedness of the poetical faculty itself. For
Milton conceived the *Paradise Lost* as a whole before he exe-
cuted it in portions. We have his own authority also for the
Muse having "dictated" to him the "unpremeditated song,"[440]
and let this be an answer to those who would allege the fifty-
six various readings of the first line of the *Orlando Furioso*.
Compositions so produced are to poetry what mosaic is to

[440] *the Muse . . . song*: Cf. Milton's *Paradise Lost* (bk. 9, lines 21–24):

> my Celestial Patroness, who deigns
> Her nightly visitation unimplor'd,
> And dictates to me slumb'ring, or inspires
> Easie my unpremeditated Verse

painting. This instinct and intuition of the poetical faculty is still more observable in the plastic and pictorial arts: a great statue or picture grows under the power of the artist as a child in the mother's womb, and the very mind which directs the hands in formation is incapable of accounting to itself for the origin, the gradations, or the *media* of the process....

The most unfailing herald, companion, and follower of the awakening of a great people to work a beneficial change in opinion or institution, is Poetry. At such periods there is an accumulation of the power of communicating and receiving intense and impassioned conceptions respecting man and nature. The persons in whom this power resides, may often, as far as regards many portions of their nature, have little apparent correspondence with that spirit of good of which they are the ministers. But even whilst they deny and abjure, they are yet compelled to serve, the Power which is seated upon the throne of their own soul. It is impossible to read the compositions of the most celebrated writers of the present day without being startled with the electric life which burns within their words. They measure the circumference and sound the depths of human nature with a comprehensive and all-penetrating spirit, and they are themselves perhaps the most sincerely astonished at its manifestations, for it is less their spirit than the spirit of the age. Poets are the hierophants of an unapprehended inspiration, the mirrors of the gigantic shadows which futurity casts upon the present, the words which express what they understand not; the trumpets which sing to battle, and feel not what they inspire: the influence which is moved not, but moves. Poets are the unacknowledged legislators of the World.

"When the lamp is shattered" (1822)

I

When the lamp is shattered
The light in the dust lies dead—
When the cloud is scattered
The rainbow's glory is shed.

When the lute is broken,   5
Sweet tones are remembered not;
When the lips have spoken,
Loved accents are soon forgot.

II

As music and splendour
Survive not the lamp and the lute,   10
The heart's echoes render
No song when the spirit is mute:—
No song but sad dirges,
Like the wind through a ruined cell,
Or the mournful surges   15
That ring the dead seaman's knell.[441]

III

When hearts have once mingled
Love first leaves the well-built nest;
The weak one is singled
To endure what it once possessed.   20
O Love! who bewailest
The frailty of all things here,
Why choose you the frailest
For your cradle, your home, and your bier?

IV

Its passions will rock thee   25
As the storms rock the ravens on high;
Bright reason will mock thee,
Like the sun from a wintry sky.
From thy nest every rafter
Will rot, and thine eagle home   30
Leave thee naked to laughter,
When leaves fall and cold winds come.

---

[441] *knell*: funeral bell tones.

To the Moon (1822/posth.)

I

Art thou pale for weariness
Of climbing heaven and gazing on the earth,
Wandering companionless
Among the stars that have a different birth,—
And ever changing, like a joyless eye   5
That finds no object worth its constancy?

II

Thou chosen sister of the Spirit,
That grazes on thee till in thee it pities ...

The Triumph of Life

The Triumph of Life was written May–June 1822, the last of
Shelley's major poems; although he left it unfinished and unre-
vised at his death, it is generally reckoned one of his greatest
achievements.

The form is that of the *Trionfi* of Petrarch (1304–1374).
There were six of these Petrarchan Triumphs, each in the *terza
rima* of Dante: that of Love over man, of Chastity over Love, of
Death over mortality, of Fame over Death, of Time over Fame,
of Divinity over Time. The general scheme of Shelley's poem
follows the "Triumph of Love" closely. It is the influence of
Dante, however, which is most significant, as Eliot recognized:

> Shelley is the English poet, more than all others, upon whom
> the influence of Dante was remarkable. It seems to me that
> Shelley confirms also my impression that the influence of
> Dante, where it really is powerful, is a *cumulative* influence: that
> is, the older you grow, the stronger the domination becomes.
> *The Triumph of Life*, a poem which is Shelley's greatest tribute
> to Dante, was the last of his great poems. I think it was also
> the greatest. It was left unfinished; it breaks off abruptly in the

middle of a line; and one wonders whether even Shelley could have carried it to successful completion.[442]

The first forty lines of Shelley's poem introduce the narrator and his experience of a crisis (of what nature we are not told) and so lead us to a dream in which he beholds the following vision.

He sees (lines 41–175) a triumphal procession, such as celebrated the victories of Roman conquerors; but the crowd are fearful, sorry, frenzied mortals, oblivious to natural beauty; a cold glare from the chariot obscures the sun, and the figure of "Life" it bears is hunched and hooded. Winged creatures of blinding light pull it, and the driver has Janus' four faces—but all eight eyes are blindfolded and the car moves heedlessly over littered corpses of the wild, mothlike people. Those far from its pathway age and rot striving to reach its side; only a burning few flee the chariot for the sun from which they came.

At line 175 the narrator is left in the company of a wizened root, who is Rousseau. The philosopher explains his own decrepit state and the pageant witnessed, especially the slaves chained to the chariot: all the proud rulers and thinkers of this world.

From line 296 onward, Rousseau tells his own story in allegorical forms: wakening to consciousness in a pleasant glade; struck by a beautiful, brilliant vision emanating from the sun's reflection—a figure of Nepenthe, who offers him the cup of "knowledge", which erases his memory of this life; he is then caught up in Life's procession, whence (line 434) his story further interprets the vision; there he sees all people shedding and surrounded by the phantom shapes of their own feelings and desires, until many, exhausted, withdraw to finish by the wayside.

The fragment as we have it breaks off with the tantalizing beginning of Rousseau's answer to the question of "what is Life?" (line 544).

---

[442] T. S. Eliot, "What Dante Means to Me", in *To Criticize the Critic* (London: Faber, 1978), p. 130.

   The only answer we can gather from the poem as it stands is from negative inference and by contrasting the images already there. It is important to realize the significance of the sun to Shelley. The sun is, or is symbolic of, the source of all good—or God, as Shelley calls it himself—and is opposed, here, to "Life".

The Triumph of Life (1822)

Swift as a spirit hastening to his task
   Of glory and of good, the Sun sprang forth
Rejoicing in his splendour, and the mask

   Of darkness fell from the awakened Earth.
The smokeless altars of the mountain snows   5
   Flamed above crimson clouds, and at the birth

Of light, the Ocean's orison[443] arose
   To which the birds tempered their matin lay.[444]
All flowers in field or forest which unclose

   Their trembling eyelids to the kiss of day,   10
Swinging their censers[445] in the element,
   With orient incense lit by the new ray

Burned slow and inconsumably, and sent
   Their odorous sighs up to the smiling air,
And in succession due, did Continent,   15

   Isle, Ocean, and all things that in them wear
The form and character of mortal mould
   Rise as the Sun their father rose, to bear

---

[443] *orison*: prayer.
[444] *matin lay*: morning song.
[445] *censers*: vessels for burning incense, to be swung, that the perfumed smoke may spread.

Their portion of the toil which he of old
   Took as his own and then imposed on them;   20
But I, whom thoughts which must remain untold

   Had kept as wakeful as the stars that gem
The cone of night,[446] now they were laid asleep,
    Stretched my faint limbs beneath the hoary stem

Which an old chestnut flung athwart the steep   25
   Of a green Apennine:[447] before me fled
The night; behind me rose the day; the Deep

   Was at my feet, and Heaven above my head
When a strange trance over my fancy grew
    Which was not slumber, for the shade it spread   30

Was so transparent that the scene came through
   As clear as when a veil of light is drawn
O'er evening hills they[448] glimmer; and I knew

   That I had felt the freshness of that dawn,
Bathed in the same cold dew my brow and hair   35
    And sate as thus upon that slope of lawn

Under the self same bough, and heard as there
   The birds, the fountains and the Ocean hold
Sweet talk in music through the enamoured air.
    And then a Vision on my brain was rolled....   40

————

[446] *cone of night*: the shadow the earth casts upon itself when the sun is on the other side of the earth and the earth faces the moon.

[447] *a green Apennine*: i.e., a peak of one of the Apennine mountains, an Italian mountain range.

[448] *they*: i.e., the hills.

As in that trance of wondrous thought I lay
    This was the tenour of my waking dream.
Methought I sate beside a public way

    Thick strewn with summer dust, and a great stream
Of people there was hurrying to and fro   45
    Numerous as gnats upon the evening gleam,

All hastening onward, yet none seemed to know
    Whither he went, or whence he came, or why
He made one of the multitude, and so

    Was borne amid the crowd as through the sky   50
One of the million leaves of summer's bier.—
    Old age and youth, manhood and infancy,

Mixed in one mighty torrent did appear,
    Some flying from the thing they feared and some
Seeking the object of another's fear,   55

    And others as with steps towards the tomb
Pored on the trodden worms that crawled beneath,
    And others mournfully within the gloom

Of their own shadow walked, and called it death …
    And some fled from it[449] as it were a ghost,   60
Half fainting in the affliction of vain breath.

    But more with motions which each other crost
Pursued or shunned the shadows the clouds threw
    Or birds within the noonday ether lost,

Upon that path where flowers never grew;   65
    And weary with vain toil and faint for thirst
Heard not the fountains whose melodious dew

[449] *it*: i.e., the shadow.

Out of their mossy cells forever burst
Nor felt the breeze which from the forest told
    Of grassy paths, and wood lawns interspersed   70

With overarching elms and caverns cold,
    And violet banks where sweet dreams brood, but they
Pursued their serious folly as of old....

And as I gazed methought that in the way
The throng grew wilder, as the woods of June   75
    When the South wind[450] shakes the extinguished
        day.—

And a cold glare, intenser than the noon
    But icy cold, obscured with blinding[451] light
The Sun as he the stars. Like the young Moon

When on the sunlit limits of the night   80
Her white shell trembles amid crimson air
    And whilst the sleeping tempest gathers might

Doth, as a herald of its coming, bear
    The ghost of her dead Mother, whose dim form
Bends in dark ether from her infant's chair,[452]   85

So came a chariot on the silent storm
Of its own rushing splendour, and a Shape
    So sate within as one whom years deform

Beneath a dusky hood and double cape
    Crouching within the shadow of a tomb,   90
And o'er what seemed the head a cloud like crape[453]

[450] *South wind*: libeccio, western or southwestern wind associated with storms on the sea.

[451] *blinding*: The original manuscript had a blank in this place, with the adjective added by Mary Shelley.

[452] *Bends . . . chair*: i.e., like the crescent new moon.

[453] *crape*: fabric used in (black) mourning clothes.

Was bent, a dun and faint etherial gloom
Tempering the light; upon the chariot's beam
   A Janus-visaged[454] Shadow did assume

The guidance of that wonder-winged team.   95
   The Shapes which drew it in thick lightnings
Were lost: I heard alone on the air's soft stream

   The music of their ever moving wings.
All the four faces of that charioteer
   Had their eyes banded … little profit brings   100

Speed in the van and blindness in the rear,
   Nor then avail the beams that quench the Sun
Or that these banded eyes could pierce the sphere

   Of all that is, has been, or will be done.—
So ill was the car guided, but it past   105
   With solemn speed majestically on …

The crowd gave way, and I arose aghast,
   Or seemed to rise, so mighty was the trance,
And saw like clouds upon the thunder blast

   The million with fierce song and maniac dance   110
Raging around; such seemed the jubilee[455]
   As when to greet some conqueror's advance[456]

Imperial Rome poured forth her living sea
   From senatehouse and prison and theatre
When Freedom left those who upon the free   115

---

[454] *Janus-visaged*: In classical mythology, Janus was the two- or four-faced Roman god of doorways and beginnings, from whose name the month of January is derived.

[455] *jubilee*: In ancient civilizations, during the year of jubilee slaves were freed. See Deuteronomy 15.

[456] *conqueror's advance*: as in a triumphal procession celebrating a military victory.

Had bound a yoke which soon they stooped to bear.
Nor wanted here the just similitude
    Of a triumphal pageant, for where'er

The chariot rolled a captive multitude
    Was driven; all those who had grown old in power   120
Or misery,—all who have their age subdued,

    By action or by suffering, and whose hour
Was drained to its last sand in weal or woe,
    So that the trunk survived both fruit and flower;

All those whose fame or infamy must grow   125
    Till the great winter lay the form and name
Of their own earth with them forever low—

    All but the sacred few[457] who could not tame
Their spirits to the Conqueror, but as soon
    As they had touched the world with living flame   130

Fled back like eagles to their native noon,
    Or those who put aside the diadem
Of earthly thrones or gems, till the last one

    Were there; for they of Athens and Jerusalem
Were neither mid the mighty captives seen   135
    Nor mid the ribald crowd that followed them

Or fled before.... Swift, fierce and obscene
    The wild dance maddens in the van, and those
Who lead it, fleet as shadows on the green,

    Outspeed the chariot and without repose   140
Mix with each other in tempestuous measure
    To savage music.... Wilder as it grows,

---

[457] *sacred few*: e.g., any in Hellenic or Hebraic history, like the philosopher Socrates or Jesus, who did not simply fall in with the reigning philosophy or politics.

They, tortured by the agonizing pleasure,
     Convulsed and on the rapid whirlwinds[458] spun
Of that fierce spirit, whose unholy leisure   145

     Was soothed by mischief since the world begun,
Throw back their heads and loose their streaming hair,
     And in their dance round her who dims the Sun

Maidens and youths fling their wild arms in air
     As their feet twinkle; now recede and now   150
Bending within each other's atmosphere

     Kindle invisibly; and as they glow
Like moths by light attracted and repelled,
     Oft to new bright destruction come and go,

Till like two clouds into one vale impelled   155
     That shake the mountains when their lightnings
          mingle
And die in rain,—the fiery band which held

     Their natures, snaps … ere the shock cease to
          tingle
One falls and then another in the path
     Senseless, nor is the desolation single,   160

Yet ere I can say *where* the chariot hath
     Past over them; nor other trace I find
But as of foam after the Ocean's wrath

     Is spent upon the desert shore.—Behind,
Old men, and women foully disarrayed   165
     Shake their grey hair in the insulting wind,

---

[458] *tortured … whirlwinds*: In Dante's *Inferno* in canto 5 of *The Divine Comedy*, the second circle of Hell holds those whose passions drove them to sin, and they are punished by being buffeted about by fierce winds.

Limp in the dance and strain with limbs decayed
    To reach the car of light which leaves them still
Farther behind and deeper in the shade.

    But not the less with impotence of will   170
They wheel, though ghastly shadows interpose
    Round them and round each other, and fulfill

Their work and to the dust whence they arose
    Sink and corruption veils them as they lie—
And frost in these performs what fire in those.[459]   175

    Struck to the heart by this sad pageantry,
Half to myself I said, "And what is this?
    Whose shape is that within the car? & why"—

I would have added—"is all here amiss?"
    But a voice answered … "Life" … I turned and knew   180
(O Heaven have mercy on such wretchedness!)

    That what I thought was an old root which grew
To strange distortion out of the hill side
    Was indeed one of that deluded crew,

And that the grass which methought hung so wide   185
    And white, was but his thin discoloured hair,
And that the holes it vainly sought to hide

    Were or had been eyes.—"If thou canst forbear
To join the dance, which I had well forborne,"
    Said the grim Feature,[460] of my thought aware,   190

---

[459] *Their … those*: i.e., the coldness of those described here destroys them as effectively as does the fire of passion in the young.

[460] *Feature*: identified below as Jean-Jacques Rousseau (1712–1778), Genevan philosopher and writer, influential as a thinker in the rise of the French Revolution at the end of the eighteenth century.

"I will tell all that which to this deep scorn
    Led me and my companions, and relate
The progress of the pageant since the morn;

    "If thirst of knowledge doth not thus abate,
Follow it even to the night, but I   195
    Am weary" . . . Then like one who with the weight

Of his own words is staggered, wearily
    He paused, and ere he could resume, I cried,
"First who art thou?" . . . "Before thy memory

    "I feared, loved, hated, suffered, did, and died,   200
And if the spark with which Heaven lit my spirit
    Earth had with purer nutriment supplied

"Corruption would not now thus much inherit
    Of what was once Rousseau—nor this disguise
Stain that within which still disdains to wear it.[461]—   205

    "If I have been extinguished, yet there rise
A thousand beacons from the spark I bore."—
    "And who are those chained to the car?" "The
        Wise,

"The great, the unforgotten: they who wore
    Mitres and helms and crowns, or wreathes of light,[462]   210
Signs of thought's empire over thought; their lore

---

[461] "I must quote one passage which made an indelible impression upon me over forty-five years ago: [here Eliot quotes lines 176—*Struck to the heart by this sad pageantry*—to 205—*Stain that which ought to have disdained to wear it* [sic]—in their integrity]. Well, this is better than I could do. But I quote it, as one of the supreme tributes to Dante in English; for it testifies to what Dante has done, both for the style and for the soul, of a great English poet. And incidentally, a very interesting comment on Rousseau." Eliot, "What Dante Means to Me", pp. 130–32.

[462] *they . . . light*: i.e., bishops (wearing mitres), soldiers (wearing helms), kings (wearing crowns), and saints and sages (wearing wreaths of light).

"Taught them not this—to know themselves; their
    might
Could not repress the mutiny within,
    And for the morn of truth they feigned, deep night

"Caught them ere evening." "Who is he with chin   215
    Upon his breast and hands crost on his chain?"
"The Child of a fierce hour;[463] he sought to win

    "The world, and lost all it did contain
Of greatness, in its hope destroyed; and more
    Of fame and peace than Virtue's self can gain   220

"Without the opportunity which bore
    Him on its eagle's pinion to the peak
From which a thousand climbers have before

    "Fall'n as Napoleon fell."—I felt my cheek
Alter to see the great form pass away   225
    Whose grasp had left the giant world so weak

That every pigmy kicked it as it lay—
    And much I grieved to think how power and will
In opposition rule our mortal day—

    And why God made irreconcilable   230
Good and the means of good; and for despair
    I half disdained mine eye's desire to fill

With the spent vision of the times that were
    And scarce have ceased to be ... "Dost thou behold,"
Said then my guide, "those spoilers spoiled, Voltaire,[464]   235

---

[463] *The Child . . . hour*: i.e., the emperor Napoleon Bonaparte (1769–1821).
[464] *Voltaire*: François-Marie Arouet de Voltaire (1694–1778), French Enlightenment thinker and writer.

"Frederic,[465] and Kant,[466] Catherine,[467] and Leopold,[468]
Chained hoary anarchs, demagogue and sage[469]
   Whose names the fresh world thinks already
       old—

"For in the battle Life and they did wage
   She remained conqueror—I was overcome   240
By my own heart alone, which neither age

   "Nor tears nor infamy nor now the tomb
Could temper to its object."—"Let them pass"—
   I cried—"the world and its mysterious doom

"Is not so much more glorious than it was   245
   That I desire to worship those who drew
New figures on its false and fragile glass

   "As the old faded."—"Figures ever new
Rise on the bubble, paint them how you may;
   We have but thrown, as those before us threw,   250

"Our shadows on it as it past away.
   But mark, how chained to the triumphal chair
The mighty phantoms of an elder day—

   "All that is mortal of great Plato[470] there
Expiates the joy and woe his master knew not;   255
   That star that ruled his doom was far too fair[471]—

[465] *Frederic*: Frederick II (Frederick the Great) of Prussia (1712–1786).

[466] *Kant*: Immanuel Kant (1724–1804), German Enlightenment philosopher.

[467] *Catherine*: Catherine II (Catherine the Great) (1729–1796), empress of Russia.

[468] *Leopold*: Leopold II (1747–1792), Holy Roman Emperor and king of Hungary and Bohemia.

[469] *demagogue . . . sage*: i.e., Voltaire and Kant, respectively.

[470] *Plato*: see footnote 428, page 325.

[471] *joy . . . fair*: Plato's master was the philosopher Socrates. Plato loved a youth named Aster, whose name means "star" in Greek.

"And Life, where long that flower of Heaven grew not,
    Conquered the heart by love which gold or pain
Or age or sloth or slavery could subdue not—

"And near [ ] walk the [ ] twain.[472]   260
The tutor and his pupil,[473] whom Dominion
    Followed as tame as vulture in a chain.—

"The world was darkened beneath either pinion
    Of him whom from the flock of conquerors
Fame singled as her thunderbearing minion;   265

    "The other long outlived both woes and wars,
Throned in new thoughts of men, and still had kept
    The jealous keys of truth's eternal doors

"If Bacon's spirit[474] [ ] had not leapt
    Like lightning out of darkness; he compelled   270
The Proteus shape[475] of Nature's as it slept

    "To wake and to unbar the caves that held
The treasure of the secrets of its reign[476]—
    See the great bards of old[477] who inly quelled

[472] *near . . .twain*: These blanks in the manuscript were filled with "him" (by Mary Shelley) and "Macedonian" (by an editor).

[473] *tutor . . . pupil*: i.e., the Greek philosopher Aristotle (384–322 B.C.) and "his pupil", the Greek king of Macedon, Alexander III (356–323 B.C.), also known as Alexander the Great, the founder of one of the largest ancient empires.

[474] *Bacon's spirit*: Francis Bacon (1561–1626), an English philosopher and advocate of the scientific method, which gave special precedent to knowledge acquired through observation and scientific experimentation, was credited by Shelley with casting off the heritage of medieval scholasticism with his scientific discoveries.

[475] *Proteus shape*: in classical mythology, an ancient sea god (the "old man of the sea") who can tell the future but will change his shape to avoid being forced to do so.

[476] *caves . . . reign*: Cf. Spenser's *Faerie Queen* (bk. 2, canto 7) and a quote (used by Bacon) from the ancient Greek philosopher Democritus (c. 460–c. 370 B.C.): "The truth of nature lieth hid in certain deep mines and caves." Francis Bacon, *The Advancement of Learning*, ed. G. W. Kitchin (London: Dent, 1973), 90.

[477] *great bards of old*: e.g., Homer.

"The passions which they sung, as by their strain			275
	May well be known: their living melody
Tempers[478] its own contagion to the vein

	"Of those who are infected with it—I
Have suffered what I wrote, or viler pain!—

	"And so my words have seeds of misery—			280
Even as the deeds of others."—"Not as theirs,"
	I said—he pointed to a company

In which I recognized amid the heirs
	Of Cæsar's crime[479] from him to Constantine.[480]
The Anarchs old whose force and murderous snares			285

	Had founded many a sceptre bearing line
And spread the plague of blood and gold abroad,
	And Gregory and John[481] and men divine

Who rose like shadows between Man and god
	Till that eclipse, still hanging under Heaven,			290
Was worshipped by the world o'er which they strode

	For the true Sun it quenched.—"Their power was
		given
But to destroy," replied the leader—"I
	Am one of those who have created, even

---

[478] *Tempers*: restrains, moderates.

[479] *Caesar's crime*: i.e., the founding of the empire—indirectly, ironically, since it was the assassination of Gaius Julius Caesar (100–44 B.C.), the Roman general and dictator in whose line the Roman Empire followed, that truly opened the door to the empire.

[480] *Constantine*: Constantine the Great (c. 272–337), effectively the first Holy Roman Emperor, who made Christianity the state religion.

[481] *Gregory and John*: i.e., papal names, referring to Pope Saint Gregory VII (c. 1015–1085) (seen by Shelley as a particular representative of papal power), and to any of the Pope Johns of history (John being one of the most popular names for popes).

"If it be but a world of agony."—   295
    "Whence camest thou and whither goest thou?
How did thy course begin," I said, "and why?

    "Mine eyes are sick of this perpetual flow
Of people, and my heart of one sad thought.—
    Speak." "Whence I came, partly I seem to know,   300

"And how and by what paths I have been brought
    To this dread pass, methinks even thou mayst guess;
Why this should be my mind can compass not;

    "Whither the conqueror hurries me still less.
But follow thou, and from spectator turn   305
    Actor or victim in this wretchedness,

"And what thou wouldst be taught I then may learn
    From thee.—Now listen … In the April prime
When all the forest tops began to burn

    "With kindling green, touched by the azure clime   310
Of the young year, I found myself asleep
    Under a mountain, which from unknown time

"Had yawned into a cavern high and deep,
    And from it came a gentle rivulet
Whose water like clear air in its calm sweep   315

    "Bent the soft grass and kept for ever wet
The stems of the sweet flowers, and filled the grove
    With sound which all who hear must needs forget

"All pleasure and all pain, all hate and love,
    Which they had known before that hour of rest: 320
A sleeping mother then would dream not of

"The only child who died upon her breast
At eventide, a king would mourn no more
     The crown of which his brow was dispossest

"When the sun lingered o'er the Ocean floor   325
     To gild his rival's new prosperity.—
Thou wouldst forget thus vainly to deplore

     "Ills, which if ills, can find no cure from thee,
The thought of which no other sleep will quell
     Nor other music blot from memory—   330

"So sweet and deep is the oblivious[482] spell.—
     Whether my life had been before that sleep
The Heaven which I imagine, or a Hell

     "Like this harsh world in which I wake to weep,
I know not. I arose and for a space   335
     The scene of woods and waters seemed to keep,

"Though it was now broad day, a gentle trace
     Of light diviner than the common Sun
Sheds on the common Earth, but all the place

     "Was filled with many sounds woven into one   340
Oblivious melody, confusing sense
     Amid the gliding waves and shadows dun;

"And as I looked the bright omnipresence
     Of morning through the orient cavern flowed,
And the Sun's image radiantly intense   345

     "Burned on the waters of the well that glowed
Like gold, and threaded all the forest maze
     With winding paths of emerald fire—there stood

[482] *oblivious*: prompting forgetfulness.

"Amid the sun, as he amid the blaze
   Of his own glory, on the vibrating   350
Floor of the fountain, paved with flashing rays,

   "A shape all light, which with one hand did fling
Dew on the earth, as if she were the Dawn
   Whose invisible rain forever seemed to sing

"A silver music on the mossy lawn,   355
   And still before her on the dusky grass
Iris[483] her many coloured scarf had drawn.—

   "In her right hand she bore a chrystal glass
Mantling with bright Nepenthe;[484]—the fierce
      splendour
   Fell from her as she moved under the mass   360

"Of the deep cavern, and with palms[485] so tender
   Their tread broke not the mirror of its billow,
Glided along the river, and did bend her

   "Head under the dark boughs, till like a willow
Her fair hair swept the bosom of the stream   365
   That whispered with delight to be their pillow.—

"As one enamoured is upborne in dream
   O'er lily-paven lakes mid silver mist
To wondrous music, so this shape might seem

   "Partly to tread the waves with feet which kist   370
The dancing foam, partly to glide along
   The airs that roughened the moist amethyst,

---

[483] *Iris*: in classical mythology, the messenger of the gods, represented in the form of the rainbow.

[484] *Nepenthe*: see footnote 53, page 209.

[485] *palms*: soles of the feet.

"Or the slant morning beams that fell among
　　The trees, or the soft shadows of the trees;
And her feet ever to the ceaseless song   375

　　"Of leaves and winds and waves and birds and bees
And falling drops moved in a measure new
　　Yet sweet, as on the summer evening breeze

"Up from the lake a shape of golden dew
　　Between two rocks, athwart the rising moon,   380
Dances i' the wind where eagle never flew.—

　　"And still her feet, no less than the sweet tune
To which they moved, seemed as they moved, to blot
　　The thoughts of him who gazed on them, and soon

"All that was seemed as if it had been not,   385
　　As if the gazer's mind was strewn beneath
Her feet like embers, and she, thought by thought,

　　"Trampled its fires into the dust of death,
As Day upon the threshold of the east
　　Treads out the lamps of night, until the breath   390

"Of darkness reillumines even the least
　　Of heaven's living eyes—like day she came,
Making the night a dream; and ere she ceased

　　"To move, as one between desire and shame
Suspended, I said—'If, as it doth seem,   395
　　Thou comest from the realm without a name,

"'Into this valley of perpetual dream,
　　Shew whence I came, and where I am, and why—
Pass not away upon the passing stream.'

"'Arise and quench thy thirst,' was her reply.   400
And as a shut lily, stricken by the wand
   Of dewy morning's vital alchemy,

"I rose; and, bending at her sweet command,
   Touched with faint lips the cup she raised,
And suddenly my brain became as sand   405

   "Where the first wave had more than half erased
The track of deer on desert Labrador,
   Whilst the fierce wolf from which they fled amazed

"Leaves his stamp visibly upon the shore
   Until the second bursts—so on my sight   410
Burst a new Vision never seen before.—

   "And the fair shape waned in the coming light
As veil by veil the silent splendour drops
From Lucifer,[486] amid the chrysolite[487]

"Of sunrise ere it strike the mountain tops—   415
   And as the presence of that fairest planet
Although unseen is felt by one who hopes

   "That his day's path may end as he began it
In that star's smile,[488] whose light is like the scent
   Of a jonquil when evening breezes fan it,   420

"Or the soft notes in which his dear lament
   The Brescian shepherd breathes,[489] or the caress
That turned his weary slumber to content.—

---

[486] *Lucifer*: Venus as morning star.

[487] *chrysolite*: a pale yellow-green gem.

[488] *his . . . smile*: i.e., below Venus (as morning and evening star).

[489] *dear . . . breathes*: Mary Shelley wrote a note to this: "The favorite song, 'Stanco di pascolar le peccorelle,' [I am weary of pasturing my sheep] is a Brescian national air." *The Complete Works of Percy Bysshe Shelley*, ed. Thomas Hutchinson, p. 513.

"So knew I in that light's severe excess
The presence of that shape which on the stream   425
   Moved, as I moved along the wilderness,

"More dimly than a day appearing dream,
   The ghost of a forgotten form of sleep,
A light from Heaven whose half extinguished beam

"Through the sick day in which we wake to weep   430
Glimmers, forever sought, forever lost.—
   So did that shape its obscure tenour keep

"Beside my path, as silent as a ghost;
   But the new Vision, and its cold bright car,
With savage music, stunning music, crost   435

   "The forest, and as if from some dread war
Triumphantly returning, the loud million
   Fiercely extolled the fortune of her star.—

"A moving arch of victory the vermilion[490]
   And green and azure plumes of Iris had   440
Built high over her wind-winged pavilion,[491]

   "And underneath ætherial glory clad
The wilderness, and far before her flew
   The tempest of the splendour which forbade

"Shadow to fall from leaf or stone;—the crew   445
   Seemed in that light like atomies[492] that dance
Within a sunbeam.—Some upon the new

   "Embroidery of flowers that did enhance
The grassy vesture of the desart, played,
   Forgetful of the chariot's swift advance;   450

---

[490] *vermilion*: red.
[491] *Iris . . . pavilion*: i.e., the rainbow, seen here as an arch of triumph for the conquering chariot of life.
[492] *atomies*: tiny dust particles.

"Others stood gazing till within the shade
   Of the great mountain its light left them dim.—
Others outspeeded it, and others made

  "Circles around it like the clouds that swim
Round the high moon in a bright sea of air,   455
   And more did follow, with exulting hymn,

"The chariot and the captives fettered there,
   But all like bubbles on an eddying flood
Fell into the same track at last and were

  "Borne onward.—I among the multitude   460
Was swept; me sweetest flowers delayed not long,
   Me not the shadow nor the solitude,

"Me not the falling stream's Lethean[493] song,
   Me, not the phantom of that early form
Which moved upon its motion,—but among   465

  "The thickest billows of the living storm
I plunged, and bared my bosom to the clime
   Of that cold light, whose airs too soon deform.—

"Before the chariot had begun to climb
   The opposing steep of that mysterious dell,   470
Behold a wonder worthy of the rhyme

  "Of him[494] who from the lowest depths of Hell
Through every Paradise and through all glory
   Love led serene, and who returned to tell

"In words of hate and awe the wondrous story   475
   How all things are transfigured, except Love;
For deaf as is a sea which wrath makes hoary

---

[493] *Lethe-wards*: Lethe is the river of the dead (of the realm of Hades), the water of which, when drunk, causes dead souls to forget their lives on earth.
[494] *him*: Dante Alighieri (1265–1321), Italian poet and author of *The Divine Comedy*.

"The world can hear not the sweet notes that move
The sphere whose light is melody to lovers—
   A wonder worthy of his rhyme—the grove   480

"Grew dense with shadows to its inmost covers,
   The earth was grey with phantoms, and the air
Was peopled with dim forms, as when there hovers

   "A flock of vampire-bats before the glare
Of the tropic sun, bringing ere evening   485
   Strange night upon some Indian isle,—thus were

"Phantoms diffused around, and some did fling
   Shadows of shadows, yet unlike themselves,
Behind them, some like eaglets on the wing

   "Were lost in the white blaze, others like elves   490
Danced in a thousand unimagined shapes
   Upon the sunny streams and grassy shelves;

"And others sate chattering like restless apes
   On vulgar paws and voluble like fire.
Some made a cradle of the ermined capes   495

   "Of kingly mantles, some upon the tiar
Of pontiffs[495] sate like vultures, others played
   Within the crown which girt with empire

"A baby's or an idiot's brow, and made
   Their nests in it; the old anatomies[496]   500
Sate hatching their bare brood under the shade

   "Of demon wings, and laughed from their dead eyes
To reassume the delegated power
   Arrayed in which these worms did monarchize

---

[495] *tiar . . . pontiffs*: a reference to the papal tiara worn by popes.
[496] *anatomies*: skeletons.

"Who make this earth their charnel.[497]—Others more   505
    Humble, like falcons sate upon the fist
Of common men, and round their heads did soar,

    "Or like small gnats and flies, as thick as mist
On evening marshes, thronged about the brow
    Of lawyer, statesman, priest and theorist,   510

"And others like discoloured flakes of snow
    On fairest bosoms and the sunniest hair
Fell, and were melted by the youthful glow

    "Which they extinguished; for like tears, they were
A veil to those from whose faint lids they rained   515
    In drops of sorrow.—I became aware

"Of whence those forms proceeded which thus stained
    The track in which we moved; after brief space
From every form the beauty slowly waned,

    "From every firmest limb and fairest face   520
The strength and freshness fell like dust, and left
    The action and the shape without the grace

"Of life; the marble brow of youth was cleft
    With care, and in the eyes where once hope shone
Desire like a lioness bereft   525

    "Of its last cub, glared ere it died; each one
Of that great crowd sent forth incessantly
    These shadows, numerous as the dead leaves blown

"In Autumn evening from a poplar tree—
    Each, like himself and like each other were,   530
At first, but soon distorted, seemed to be

[497] *charnel*: A charnel house is a vault for dead bodies.

"Obscure clouds moulded by the casual air;
And of this stuff the car's creative ray
   Wrought all the busy phantoms that were there

"As the sun shapes the clouds—thus, on the way   535
   Mask after mask fell from the countenance
And form of all, and long before the day

   "Was old, the joy which waked like Heaven's glance
The sleepers in the oblivious valley, died,
   And some grew weary of the ghastly dance   540

"And fell, as I have fallen by the way side,
   Those soonest from whose forms most shadows past
And least of strength and beauty did abide."—

   "Then, what is Life?" I said … the cripple cast
His eye upon the car which now had rolled   545
   Onward, as if that look must be the last,

And answered.… "Happy those for whom the fold
   Of

JOHN KEATS
(1795–1821)

Sonnets:

On First Looking into Chapman's Homer[1] (late 1816)

Much have I travelled in the realms of gold,[2]
  And many goodly[3] states and kingdoms seen;
  Round many western islands[4] have I been
Which bards in fealty to Apollo[5] hold.
Oft of one wide expanse had I been told   5
  That deep-browed Homer ruled as his demesne;[6]
  Yet did I never breathe its pure serene
Till I heard Chapman speak out loud and bold:
Then felt I like some watcher of the skies
  When a new planet[7] swims into his ken;[8]   10

---

[1] *Chapman's Homer*: George Chapman (c. 1559–1634), English dramatist and translator, famously translated Homer's *Iliad* and *Odyssey*. Keats' encounter with the translation and the composition of the poem (written in October 1816 and first published in December of that year) was famously captured by author Charles Cowden Clarke (1787–1877), who was a friend of Keats. Charles Cowden Clarke (1787–1877): "A beautiful copy of the folio edition of Chapman's translation of Homer had been lent me … and to work we went, turning to some of the 'famousest' passages, as we had scrappily known them in Pope's version.… Chapman supplied us with many an after-treat; but it was in the teeming wonderment of this his first introduction, that, when I came down to breakfast the next morning, I found upon my table a letter with no other enclosure than his famous sonnet, 'On First Looking into Chapman's *Homer*.' We had parted, as I have already said, at day-spring, yet he contrived that I should receive the poem from a distance of, may be, two miles by ten o'clock." Quoted in Sir Sidney Colvin, *John Keats: His Life and Poetry, His Friends, Critics, and After-Fame* (New York: Scribner's, 1925), p. 39.

[2] *realms of gold*: i.e., the world of poetic imagination.

[3] *goodly*: large, pleasing.

[4] *western islands*: In classical mythology, Odysseus, the hero of Homer's *Odyssey*, experienced many wondrous adventures through the western isles during his voyage home from the Trojan War.

[5] *Apollo*: in classical mythology, the god of poetry, music, and the sun.

[6] *demesne*: tenant or vassal holding lands (and loyal to a lord).

[7] *new planet*: The planet Uranus was discovered in 1781.

[8] *ken*: knowledge, sight.

Or like stout Cortez[9] when with eagle eyes
    He stared at the Pacific—and all his men
Looked at each other with a wild surmise—
    Silent, upon a peak in Darien.[10]

On Leaving Some Friends at an Early Hour (late 1816)

Give me a golden pen, and let me lean
    On heaped up flowers, in regions clear, and far;
    Bring me a tablet whiter than a star,
Or hand of hymning angel, when 'tis seen
The silver strings of heavenly harp atween: 5
    And let there glide by many a pearly car,
    Pink robes, and wavy hair, and diamond jar,
And half-discovered wings, and glances keen.
The while let music wander round my ears,
    And as it reaches each delicious ending,   10
        Let me write down a line of glorious tone,
And full of many wonders of the spheres:
    For what a height my spirit is contending!
    'Tis not content so soon to be alone.

On Seeing the Elgin Marbles[11] (1817)

My spirit is too weak—mortality
    Weighs heavily on me like unwilling sleep,
    And each imagined pinnacle and steep
Of godlike hardship, tells me I must die

---

    [9] *Cortez*: In fact, Vasco Núñez de Balboa (c. 1475–1519), the Spanish explorer and conquistador, discovered the Pacific Ocean, not Hernando Cortés (1485–1547), his fellow Spanish explorer and conquistador.
    [10] *Darien*: mountain range beside Panama.
    [11] *Elgin Marbles*: The Parthenon Marbles, classical Greek sculptures housed in the British Museum, were brought to England by the earl of Elgin, ambassador to the Ottoman Empire, during the early nineteenth century.

Like a sick Eagle looking at the sky.[12]   5
   Yet 'tis a gentle luxury to weep
   That I have not the cloudy winds to keep
Fresh for the opening of the morning's eye.
Such dim-conceivèd glories of the brain
   Bring round the heart an undescribable feud;   10
So do these wonders a most dizzy pain,
   That mingles Grecian grandeur with the rude
Wasting of old Time—with a billowy main[13]—
   A sun—a shadow of a magnitude.

Endymion: A Poetic Romance

Endymion (April–November 1817) is the first of Keats' attempts
at an extended, major poetic statement, and the only one of
importance he was to complete. The poem reveals the particu-
lar influence of Lemprière's *Classical Dictionary* (almost omni-
present in Keats), Spenser, Shakespeare, and the Elizabethans.
The frequency of enjambed lines in *Endymion* reflects Keats'
overt hostility to Augustan poetics; this was to change (see the
introduction to *Lamia*).

Aside from the ineffaceable beauty of the opening lines
(already characteristic of both Keats' manner and concerns),
and one or two other passages, it remains best known for
the infamous savaging it received at the hands of critics in
Blackwood's and the *Quarterly*, and the Romantic myth that
such broadsides were in some way responsible for Keats'
death. Not all reactions were unfavorable, however, and
Keats himself saw the poem as a necessary attempt rather than
an achievement.

---

[12] *sick . . . sky*: According to popular legend, the eagle could renew his youth by
flying toward the sun and then diving into a fountain. Eagles were also believed
capable of looking directly into the sun.
   [13] *billowy main*: i.e., ocean wave.

From *Endymion* (1817)

BOOK I

A thing of beauty is a joy for ever:
Its loveliness increases; it will never
Pass into nothingness; but still will keep
A bower quiet for us, and a sleep
Full of sweet dreams, and health, and quiet breathing.   5
Therefore, on every morrow, are we wreathing
A flowery band to bind us to the earth,
Spite of despondence, of the inhuman dearth
Of noble natures, of the gloomy days,
Of all the unhealthy and o'er-darkened ways   10
Made for our searching: yes, in spite of all,
Some shape of beauty moves away the pall
From our dark spirits. Such the sun, the moon,
Trees old, and young, sprouting a shady boon
For simple sheep; and such are daffodils   15
With the green world they live in; and clear rills[14]
That for themselves a cooling covert[15] make
'Gainst the hot season; the mid forest brake,[16]
Rich with a sprinkling of fair musk-rose blooms:
And such too is the grandeur of the dooms   20
We have imagined for the mighty dead;
All lovely tales that we have heard or read—
An endless fountain of immortal drink,
Pouring unto us from the heaven's brink.

    Nor do we merely feel these essences   25
For one short hour; no, even as the trees
That whisper round a temple become soon
Dear as the temple's self, so does the moon,

[14] *rills*: very small brooks.
[15] *covert*: hidden shelter.
[16] *brake*: thicket, area overgrown densely with briars.

The passion poesy, glories infinite,
Haunt us till they become a cheering light 30
Unto our souls, and bound to us so fast,
That, whether there be shine, or gloom o'ercast,
They alway must be with us, or we die.

Therefore, 'tis with full happiness that I
Will trace the story of Endymion. 35

From *To George and Tom Keats, 21–27(?) December 1817*

"Brown & Dilke walked with me & back from the Christmas pantomime. I had not a dispute but a disquisition with Dilke, on various subjects; several things dovetailed in my mind, & at once it struck me, what quality went to form a Man of Achievement especially in Literature & which Shakespeare possessed so enormously—I mean *Negative Capability*, that is when man is capable of being in uncertainties, Mysteries, doubts, without any irritable reaching after fact & reason—Coleridge, for instance, would let go by a fine isolated verisimilitude caught from the Penetralium of mystery, from being incapable of remaining content with half knowledge. This pursued through Volumes would perhaps take us no further than this, that with a great poet the sense of Beauty overcomes every other consideration, or rather obliterates all consideration."

Sonnets:

On the Sea (1817)

It keeps eternal whisperings around
    Desolate shores, and with its mighty swell
    Gluts twice ten thousand caverns, till the spell
Of Hecate[17] leaves them their old shadowy sound.

---

[17]*Hecate*: in classical mythology, goddess of the crossroads, magic, and witchcraft.

Often 'tis in such gentle temper found,   5
    That scarcely will the very smallest shell
    Be moved for days from where it sometime fell,
When last the winds of Heaven were unbound.
Oh ye! who have your eye-balls vexed and tired,
    Feast them upon the wideness of the Sea—   10
        Oh ye! whose ears are dinned with uproar rude,
    Or fed too much with cloying melody—
        Sit ye near some old cavern's mouth and brood
Until ye start, as if the sea-nymphs quired![18]

On Sitting Down to Read *King Lear* Once Again (early 1818)

O golden-tongued Romance, with serene lute!
    Fair plumèd Syren, Queen of far-away!
    Leave melodizing on this wintry day,
Shut up thine olden pages, and be mute:
Adieu! for, once again, the fierce dispute   5
    Betwixt damnation and impassioned clay
    Must I burn through, once more humbly assay[19]
The bitter-sweet of this Shakespearian fruit:
Chief Poet! and ye clouds of Albion,[20]
    Begetters of our deep eternal theme!   10
When through the old oak forest I am gone,
    Let me not wander in a barren dream,
But, when I am consumèd in the fire,
Give me new Phoenix[21] wings to fly at my desire.

[18] *quired*: choired.
[19] *assay*: attempt.
[20] *Albion*: England.
[21] *Phoenix*: in classical mythology, a sacred bird that expires in fire and is reborn from the ashes.

"Bright star! would I were steadfast as thou art" (1818)

Bright star! would I were steadfast as thou art—
    Not in lone splendour hung aloft the night
And watching, with eternal lids apart,
    Like nature's patient, sleepless Eremite,[22]
The moving waters at their priestlike task   5
    Of pure ablution[23] round earth's human shores,
Or gazing on the new soft-fallen mask
    Of snow upon the mountains and the moors—
No—yet still steadfast, still unchangeable,
    Pillowed upon my fair love's ripening breast,   10
To feel for ever its soft swell and fall,
    Awake for ever in a sweet unrest,
Still, still to hear her tender-taken breath,
And so live ever—or else swoon to death.

"Why did I laugh tonight?" (March 1819)

Why did I laugh tonight? No voice will tell:
    No God, no Demon of severe response,
Deigns to reply from Heaven or from Hell.
    Then to my human heart I turn at once—
Heart! thou and I are here sad and alone;   5
    Say, wherefore did I laugh! O mortal pain!
O Darkness! Darkness! ever must I moan,
    To question Heaven and Hell and Heart in vain.
Why did I laugh? I know this being's lease—
    My fancy to its utmost blisses spreads;   10
Yet could I on this very midnight cease,
    And the world's gaudy ensigns see in shreds.
Verse, Fame, and Beauty are intense indeed,
    But Death intenser—Death is Life's high meed.

[22] *Eremite*: hermit.
[23] *ablution*: ritual washing.

Hyperion:[24] A Fragment

Hyperion began in September 1818 and was definitively aban-
doned in April 1819 (in its original form as *Hyperion*). In
this epic, mythopoeic fragment, Keats began to construct,
or reconstruct, a myth, starting from what limited Greek
material there is upon the "Titanomachia": a great strug-
gle between the older, elemental Titans and the younger
Olympians, in which the latter gods were victorious and
systematically replaced the Titans in their roles governing
the powers of the universe. The eponymous Hyperion was
deity of the sun, until he was ousted by Apollo. In scale and
conception, the work, inevitably, invites comparison to the
great English epics of Milton—and indeed Keats consciously
turned to *Paradise Lost* for a model. In its original use of Greek
myth, it is similar to Shelley's *Prometheus Unbound.* However,
Hyperion "surveys the fallen condition of the Titans without
either a Miltonic didactic emphasis or a Shelleyan personal-
izing self-dramatization. Here is the first triumph of Keats's
earlier idea of poetry as a disinterested mode."[25]

The poem begins, in fact, toward the end of the
Titanomachia—in the throes, not of violent action, but of
change on a universal scale: Jupiter and the Olympians have
prevailed over Saturn and the Titans; only one among their
kin, Hyperion, has yet to be deposed. The Titans gather to take
counsel (Book II), attempting to reach a better understanding
of what has happened and to find a response, but only Oceanus
has an answer: he counsels acceptance of inevitable, necessary
change, on the grounds that despite their greatness, they are
being replaced by what is more excellent still. This prophetic
rationale is startling, not only in its humility and truthfulness,
but also for being a statement of the "doctrine of progress", of an
evolutionary philosophy, long before Darwin made such thought
popular. But it is in turning to Book III and Apollo undergoing

---

[24] Hyperion: in classical mythology, one of the twelve Titans.
[25] Lionel Trilling and Harold Bloom, *The Oxford Anthology of English Literature*,
vol. 4, *Romantic Poetry and Prose* (Oxford: Oxford University Press, 1973), p. 504.

his apotheosis, under the guidance of Mnemosyne (the mother of the Muses and goddess of Memory) that we begin to understand the qualities that are held up as godlike, and what must be suffered to achieve them. For to be transformed into the god of poetry, music, and prophecy, as well as of the sun, he is dying to what he was, dying to the life he had known, and attaining only through this sacrificial change the enlightenment, the knowledge of truth, and the beauty that are divine. It is such powers of sympathy, such beauty, that better befit the Olympians to rule a world of men, than their magnificent predecessors. But the poem is broken off, in part because "there were too many Miltonic inversions in it"[26]—perhaps also because of the great difficulty in exploring such themes more deeply and yet maintaining enough structural dynamism to keep it buoyant. We have some idea as to how it was originally planned in its fullness from his friend and literary associate Richard Woodhouse: "The poem, if completed, would have treated of the dethronement of Hyperion, the former God of the Sun, by Apollo—and incidentally, of those of Oceanus by Neptune, of Saturn by Jupiter, etc.—and of the war of the Giants [i.e., Titans] for Saturn's reestablishment, with other events, of which we have but very dark hints in the mythological poets of Greece and Rome. In fact, the incidents would have been pure creations of the poet's brain."[27] De Sélincourt contests this, asserting the extent to which Keats' intentions had changed: that Keats now intended to conclude *Hyperion* in four books rather than his originally intended ten, and hazarding that Apollo

> would have gone forth to meet Hyperion, who, struck by the power of supreme beauty, would have found resistance impossible. Critics have inclined to take for granted that an actual battle was contemplated by Keats, but I do not believe that such was, at least, his final intention.... A combat would have been completely alien to the whole idea of the poem as Keats

[26] Letter to John Hamilton Reynolds, September 21, 1819. *Letters of John Keats to His Family and Friends*, ed. Sir Sidney Colvin (London: Macmillan, 1891), 321.

[27] In John Keats, *The Complete Poems*, ed. John Barnard (New York: Penguin, 1978), pp. 609–10.

conceived it, and as, in fact, it is universally interpreted from the speech of Oceanus in the second book.... The poem would have closed with a description of the new age which had been inaugurated by the triumph of the Olympians, and, in particular, of Apollo the god of light and song.[28]

If Keats has left us with hardly more than the head and torso of a poem, it is one that betrays the hand of a Rodin. In the words of his sometime antagonist Byron: "His fragment of Hyperion seems actually inspired by the Titans, and is as sublime as Aeschylus."[29]

Hyperion (September–December 1818)

BOOK I

Deep in the shady sadness of a vale[30]
Far sunken from the healthy breath of morn,
Far from the fiery noon, and eve's one star,
Sat grey-haired Saturn,[31] quiet as a stone,
Still as the silence round about his lair;					5
Forest on forest hung about his head
Like cloud on cloud. No stir of air was there,
Not so much life as on a summer's day
Robs not one light seed from the feathered grass,
But where the dead leaf fell, there did it rest.					10
A stream went voiceless by, still deadened more
By reason of his fallen divinity
Spreading a shade: the Naiad[32] 'mid her reeds
Pressed her cold finger closer to her lips.

[28] Ernest de Sélincourt, *The Poems of John Keats* (New York: Dodd, Mead, 1905), pp. 488–89.

[29] George Gordon, Lord Byron, "Observations upon an Article in Blackwood's Magazine", November 12, 1821, in G.M. Matthews, ed., *Keats: The Critical Heritage* (London: Routledge & Kegan Paul, 1971), p. 128.

[30] *vale*: valley.

[31] *Saturn*: in classical mythology, the ancient god of the harvest, father of Jupiter or Jove (deposed by his rebellious sons).

[32] *Naiad*: in classical mythology, a water nymph.

Along the margin-sand large foot-marks went,   15
No further than to where his feet had strayed,
And slept there since. Upon the sodden ground
His old right hand lay nerveless, listless, dead,
Unsceptred; and his realmless eyes were closed;
While his bowed head seemed listening to the Earth,   20
His ancient mother, for some comfort yet.

It seemed no force could wake him from his place;
But there came one, who with a kindred hand
Touched his wide shoulders, after bending low
With reverence, though to one who knew it not.   25
She was a Goddess of the infant world;
By her in stature the tall Amazon[33]
Had stood a pigmy's height:[34] she would have ta'en
Achilles[35] by the hair and bent his neck;
Or with a finger stayed Ixion's wheel.[36]   30
Her face was large as that of Memphian sphinx,[37]
Pedestalled haply in a palace court,
When sages looked to Egypt for their lore.
But O! how unlike marble was that face,
How beautiful, if sorrow had not made   35
Sorrow more beautiful than Beauty's self.
There was a listening fear in her regard,
As if calamity had but begun;
As if the vanward[38] clouds of evil days

---

[33] *Amazon*: In classical mythology, the Amazons were a nation of female warriors.

[34] *pigmy's height*: i.e., very short.

[35] *Achilles*: in classical mythology, Greek military hero of the Trojan War who, in some myths, was killed by the queen of the Amazons, Penthesilea.

[36] *Ixion's wheel*: In classical mythology, Ixion was a king punished by the gods for committing murder and for his lust for the goddess Hera. He was doomed to be bound to a winged fiery wheel eternally spinning.

[37] *Memphian sphinx*: Memphis, in Egypt, was home to one of the most famous statues of the sphinx, a creature of classical mythology, part lion, part bird, and part woman.

[38] *vanward*: advanced.

Had spent their malice, and the sullen rear 40
Was with its storèd thunder labouring up.
One hand she pressed upon that aching spot
Where beats the human heart, as if just there,
Though an immortal, she felt cruel pain;
The other upon Saturn's bended neck 45
She laid, and to the level of his ear
Leaning with parted lips, some words she spake
In solemn tenor and deep organ tone—
Some mourning words, which in our feeble tongue
Would come in these like accents (O how frail 50
To that large utterance of the early Gods!):
'Saturn, look up!—though wherefore, poor old King?
I have no comfort for thee, no, not one:
I cannot say, "O wherefore sleepest thou?" 55
For heaven is parted from thee, and the earth
Knows thee not, thus afflicted, for a God;
And ocean too, with all its solemn noise,
Has from thy sceptre passed; and all the air
Is emptied of thine hoary majesty.
Thy thunder, conscious of the new command,[39] 60
Rumbles reluctant o'er our fallen house;
And thy sharp lightning in unpractised hands[40]
Scorches and burns our once serene domain.
O aching time! O moments big as years!
All as ye pass swell out the monstrous truth, 65
And press it so upon our weary griefs
That unbelief has not a space to breathe.
Saturn, sleep on—O thoughtless, why did I
Thus violate thy slumbrous solitude?
Why should I ope thy melancholy eyes? 70
Saturn, sleep on, while at thy feet I weep!'

[39] *new command*: i.e., of Jupiter.
[40] *unpractised hands*: i.e., those of Jupiter.

    As when, upon a trancèd summer-night,
Those green-robed senators of mighty woods,
Tall oaks, branch-charmèd by the earnest stars,
Dream, and so dream all night without a stir,   75
Save from one gradual solitary gust
Which comes upon the silence, and dies off,
As if the ebbing air had but one wave;
So came these words and went; the while in tears
She touched her fair large forehead to the ground,   80
Just where her falling hair might be outspread
A soft and silken mat for Saturn's feet.
One moon, with alteration slow, had shed
Her silver seasons four upon the night,
And still these two were postured motionless,   85
Like natural sculpture in cathedral cavern;
The frozen God still couchant[41] on the earth,
And the sad Goddess weeping at his feet:
Until at length old Saturn lifted up
His faded eyes, and saw his kingdom gone,   90
And all the gloom and sorrow of the place,
And that fair kneeling Goddess; and then spake,
As with a palsied tongue, and while his beard
Shook horrid with such aspen-malady:[42]
'O tender spouse of gold Hyperion,   95
Thea,[43] I feel thee ere I see thy face;
Look up, and let me see our doom in it;
Look up, and tell me if this feeble shape
Is Saturn's; tell me, if thou hear'st the voice
Of Saturn; tell me, if this wrinkling brow,   100
Naked and bare of its great diadem,

---

[41] *couchant*: a term in heraldry, meaning lying down, often with the head up.

[42] *aspen-malady*: Aspen leaves appear to tremble or shimmer in the wind.

[43] *Thea*: in classical mythology, the Titan goddess of sight and the blue sky, wife to her brother Hyperion and mother to Helios (the sun), Eos (the dawn), and Selene (the moon).

Peers like the front of Saturn. Who had power
To make me desolate? whence came the strength?
How was it nurtured to such bursting forth,
While Fate seemed strangled in my nervous[44] grasp?   105
But it is so; and I am smothered up,
And buried from all godlike exercise
Of influence benign on planets pale,
Of admonitions to the winds and seas,
Of peaceful sway above man's harvesting,   110
And all those acts which Deity supreme
Doth ease its heart of love in.—I am gone
Away from my own bosom; I have left
My strong identity, my real self,
Somewhere between the throne and where I sit   115
Here on this spot of earth. Search, Thea, search!
Open thine eyes eterne, and sphere them round
Upon all space—space starred, and lorn of light;
Space regioned with life-air; and barren void;
Spaces of fire, and all the yawn of hell.   120
Search, Thea, search! and tell me, if thou seest
A certain shape or shadow, making way
With wings or chariot fierce to repossess
A heaven he lost erewhile: it must—it must
Be of ripe progress: Saturn must be King.   125
Yes, there must be a golden victory;
There must be Gods thrown down, and trumpets blown
Of triumph calm, and hymns of festival
Upon the gold clouds metropolitan,
Voices of soft proclaim, and silver stir   130
Of strings in hollow shells; and there shall be
Beautiful things made new, for the surprise
Of the sky-children. I will give command:
"Thea! Thea! Thea! where is Saturn?"

---

[44] *nervous*: anxious, also vigorous.

This passion lifted him upon his feet,   135
And made his hands to struggle in the air,
His Druid[45] locks to shake and ooze with sweat,
His eyes to fever out, his voice to cease.
He stood, and heard not Thea's sobbing deep;
A little time, and then again he snatched   140
Utterance thus: 'But cannot I create?
Cannot I form? Cannot I fashion forth
Another world, another universe,
To overbear and crumble this to naught?
Where is another Chaos? Where?'—That word   145
Found way unto Olympus,[46] and made quake
The rebel three.[47] Thea was startled up,
And in her bearing was a sort of hope,
As thus she quick-voiced spake, yet full of awe.

'This cheers our fallen house: come to our friends,   150
O Saturn! come away, and give them heart.
I know the covert, for thence came I hither.'
Thus brief; then with beseeching eyes she went
With backward footing through the shade a space:
He followed, and she turned to lead the way   155
Through agèd boughs, that yielded like the mist
Which eagles cleave up-mounting from their nest.

Meanwhile in other realms big tears were shed,
More sorrow like to this, and such like woe,
Too huge for mortal tongue or pen of scribe.   160
The Titans fierce, self-hid, or prison-bound,
Groaned for the old allegiance once more,

---

[45] *Druid*: ancient Celtic priest, bard of nature.

[46] *Olympus*: mountain home of the gods.

[47] *rebel three*: i.e., the classical gods Jupiter, Neptune, and Pluto (three sons of Saturn who rebelled against him and now rule the heavens, the sea, and the underworld).

And listened in sharp pain for Saturn's voice.
But one of the whole mammoth-brood still kept
His sovereignty, and rule, and majesty—   165
Blazing Hyperion on his orbèd fire
Still sat, still snuffed the incense, teeming up
From man to the sun's God—yet unsecure:
For as among us mortals omens drear
Fright and perplex, so also shuddered he—   170
Not at dog's howl, or gloom-bird's hated screech,[48]
Or the familiar visiting of one
Upon the first toll of his passing-bell,[49]
Or prophesyings of the midnight lamp;
But horrors, portioned to a giant nerve,   175
Oft made Hyperion ache. His palace bright
Bastioned with pyramids of glowing gold,
And touched with shade of bronzèd obelisks,
Glared a blood-red through all its thousand courts,
Arches, and domes, and fiery galleries;   180
And all its curtains of Aurorian clouds
Flushed angerly, while sometimes eagle's wings,
Unseen before by Gods or wondering men,
Darkened the place, and neighing steeds were heard,
Not heard before by Gods or wondering men.   185
Also, when he would taste the spicy wreaths
Of incense, breathed aloft from sacred hills,
Instead of sweets, his ample palate took
Savour of poisonous brass and metal sick:
And so, when harboured in the sleepy west,   190
After the full completion of fair day,
For rest divine upon exalted couch
And slumber in the arms of melody,
He paced away the pleasant hours of ease

---

[48] *dog's . . . screech*: such noises as barking dogs and the screech of the owl (the "gloom-bird") were taken as ill omens.
[49] *familiar . . . passing-bell*: i.e., members of a family visiting and praying over someone who is dying (for whom the "passing-bell" rings).

With stride colossal, on from hall to hall;   195
While far within each aisle and deep recess,
His wingèd minions in close clusters stood,
Amazed and full of fear; like anxious men
Who on wide plains gather in panting troops,
When earthquakes jar their battlements and towers.   200
Even now, while Saturn, roused from icy trance,
Went step for step with Thea through the woods,
Hyperion, leaving twilight in the rear,
Came slope upon the threshold of the west;
Then, as was wont, his palace-door flew ope   205
In smoothest silence, save what solemn tubes,
Blown by the serious Zephyrs,[50] gave of sweet
And wandering sounds, slow-breathèd melodies—
And like a rose in vermeil tint and shape,
In fragrance soft, and coolness to the eye,   210
That inlet to severe magnificence
Stood full blown, for the God to enter in.

He entered, but he entered full of wrath;
His flaming robes streamed out beyond his heels,
And gave a roar, as if of earthly fire,   215
That scared away the meek ethereal Hours[51]
And made their dove-wings tremble. On he flared,
From stately nave to nave, from vault to vault,
Through bowers of fragrant and enwreathèd light,
And diamond-pavèd lustrous long arcades,   220
Until he reached the great main cupola.
There standing fierce beneath, he stamped his foot,
And from the basement deep to the high towers
Jarred his own golden region; and before
The quavering thunder thereupon had ceased,   225
His voice leapt out, despite of god-like curb,

---

[50] *Zephyrs*: west winds.
[51] *Hours*: the Horae, in classical mythology, winged, anthropomorphized creatures, representing the hours and seasons.

To this result: 'O dreams of day and night!
O monstrous forms! O effigies of pain!
O spectres busy in a cold, cold gloom!
O lank-eared Phantoms of black-weeded pools!   230
Why do I know ye? Why have I seen ye? Why
Is my eternal essence thus distraught
To see and to behold these horrors new?
Saturn is fallen, am I too to fall?
Am I to leave this haven of my rest,   235
This cradle of my glory, this soft clime,
This calm luxuriance of blissful light,
These crystalline pavilions, aud pure fanes,[52]
Of all my lucent empire? It is left
Deserted, void, nor any haunt of mine.   240
The blaze, the splendour, and the symmetry,
I cannot see—but darkness, death and darkness.
Even here, into my centre of repose,
The shady visions come to domineer,
Insult, and blind, and stifle up my pomp.—   245
Fall!—No, by Tellus and her briny robes![53]
Over the fiery frontier of my realms
I will advance a terrible right arm
Shall scare that infant thunderer, rebel Jove,
And bid old Saturn take his throne again.'—   250
He spake, and ceased, the while a heavier threat
Held struggle with his throat but came not forth;
For as in theatres of crowded men
Hubbub increases more they call out 'Hush!',
So at Hyperion's words the Phantoms pale   255
Bestirred themselves, thrice horrible and cold;
And from the mirrored level where he stood
A mist arose, as from a scummy marsh.
At this, through all his bulk an agony

---

[52] *fanes*: temples.
[53] *Tellus ... robes*: in classical mythology, Terra Mater, the earth goddess (surrounded by the seas).

Crept gradual, from the feet unto the crown,   260
Like a lithe serpent vast and muscular
Making slow way, with head and neck convulsed
From over-strainèd might. Released, he fled
To the eastern gates, and full six dewy hours
Before the dawn in season due should blush,   265
He breathed fierce breath against the sleepy portals,
Cleared them of heavy vapours, burst them wide
Suddenly on the ocean's chilly streams.
The planet orb of fire, whereon he rode
Each day from east to west the heavens through,   270
Spun round in sable curtaining of clouds;
Not therefore veilèd quite, blindfold, and hid,
But ever and anon the glancing spheres,
Circles, and arcs, and broad-belting colure,[54]
Glowed through, and wrought upon the muffling dark   275
Sweet-shapèd lightnings from the nadir deep
Up to the zenith[55]—hieroglyphics old
Which sages and keen-eyed astrologers
Then living on the earth, with labouring thought
Won from the gaze of many centuries—   280
Now lost, save what we find on remnants huge
Of stone, or marble swart, their import gone,
Their wisdom long since fled. Two wings this orb
 Possessed for glory, two fair argent[56] wings,
Ever exalted at the God's approach: 285
And now, from forth the gloom their plumes immense
Rose, one by one, till all outspreaded were;
While still the dazzling globe maintained eclipse,
Awaiting for Hyperion's command.
Fain would he have commanded, fain took throne   290
And bid the day begin, if but for change.

---

[54] *colure*: (an astronomical term), either of the two great meridians of the celestial sphere.

[55] *zenith*: (an astronomical term), the point in the sky directly overhead, the highest point.

[56] *argent*: silver.

He might not.—No, though a primeval God:
The sacred seasons might not be disturbed.
Therefore the operations of the dawn
Stayed in their birth, even as here 'tis told.   295
Those silver wings expanded sisterly,
Eager to sail their orb; the porches wide
Opened upon the dusk demesnes[57] of night;
And the bright Titan, frenzied with new woes,
Unused to bend, by hard compulsion bent   300
His spirit to the sorrow of the time;
And all along a dismal rack of clouds,
Upon the boundaries of day and night,
He stretched himself in grief and radiance faint.
There as he lay, the Heaven with its stars   305
Looked down on him with pity, and the voice
Of Coelus,[58] from the universal space,
Thus whispered low and solemn in his ear:
'O brightest of my children dear, earth-born
And sky-engendered, Son of Mysteries   310
All unrevealèd even to the powers
Which met at thy creating; at whose joys
And palpitations sweet, and pleasures soft,
I, Coelus, wonder how they came and whence;
And at the fruits thereof what shapes they be,   315
Distinct, and visible—symbols divine,
Manifestations of that beauteous life
Diffused unseen throughout eternal space:
Of these new-formed art thou, O brightest child!
Of these, thy brethren and the Goddesses!   320
There is sad feud among ye, and rebellion
Of son against his sire. I saw him fall,
I saw my first-born tumbled from his throne!
To me his arms were spread, to me his voice

---

[57] *demesnes*: lands, domains.
[58] *Coelus*: in classical mythology, god of the sky (also known as Uranus), father of the Titans.

Found way from forth the thunders round his head! 325
Pale wox[59] I, and in vapours hid my face.
Art thou, too, near such doom? Vague fear there is:
For I have seen my sons most unlike Gods.
Divine ye were created, and divine
In sad demeanour, solemn, undisturbed, 330
Unrufflèd, like high Gods, ye lived and ruled:
Now I behold in you fear, hope, and wrath;
Actions of rage and passion—even as
I see them, on the mortal world beneath,
In men who die. This is the grief, O Son! 335
Sad sign of ruin, sudden dismay, and fall!
Yet do thou strive; as thou art capable,
As thou canst move about, an evident God;
And canst oppose to each malignant hour
Ethereal presence. I am but a voice; 340
My life is but the life of winds and tides,
No more than winds and tides can I avail.—
But thou canst.—Be thou therefore in the van
Of circumstance; yea, seize the arrow's barb
Before the tense string murmur.—To the earth! 345
For there thou wilt find Saturn, and his woes.
Meantime I will keep watch on thy bright sun,
And of thy seasons be a careful nurse.'—
Ere half this region-whisper had come down,[60]
Hyperion arose, and on the stars 350
Lifted his curvèd lids, and kept them wide
Until it ceased; and still he kept them wide;
And still they were the same bright, patient stars.
Then with a slow incline of his broad breast,
Like to a diver in the pearly seas, 355
Forward he stooped over the airy shore,
And plunged all noiseless into the deep night.

[59] *wox*: waxed (became).
[60] *come down*: i.e., from the sky where Coelus rules.

BOOK II

Just at the self-same beat of Time's wide wings,
Hyperion slid into the rustled air
And Saturn gained with Thea that sad place
Where Cybele[61] and the bruised Titans mourned.
It was a den where no insulting light   5
Could glimmer on their tears; where their own groans
They felt, but heard not, for the solid roar
Of thunderous waterfalls and torrents hoarse,
Pouring a constant bulk, uncertain where.
Crag jutting forth to crag, and rocks that seemed   10
Ever as if just rising from a sleep,
Forehead to forehead held their monstrous horns;
And thus in thousand hugest fantasies
Made a fit roofing to this nest of woe.
Instead of thrones, hard flint they sat upon,   15
Couches of rugged stone, and slaty ridge
Stubborned with iron. All were not assembled:
Some chained in torture, and some wandering.
Coeus, and Gyges, and Briareüs,
Typhon, and Dolor, and Porphyrion,[62]   20
With many more, the brawniest in assault,
Were pent in regions of laborious breath;
Dungeoned in opaque element, to keep
Their clenchèd teeth still clenched, and all their limbs
Locked up like veins of metal, cramped and screwed;   25
Without a motion, save of their big hearts
Heaving in pain, and horribly convulsed
With sanguine fev'rous boiling gurge of pulse.

---

[61] *Cybele*: in classical mythology, the wife of Saturn (also known as Rhea) and mother of the Olympian gods.
[62] *Coeus . . . Porphyrion*: Titans and other giants who participated in the battle against the Olympians and, as punishment, were imprisoned below the earth or within mountains. Coeus was the Titan husband of Phoebe. Gyges and Briareüs were Hecatonchires ("Hundred-Handed Ones", giants who, according to some classical sources, fought with the Olympians against the Titans, but according to the Latin poet Virgil fought on the side of the Titans).

Mnemosyne[63] was straying in the world;
Far from her moon had Phoebe[64] wanderèd;   30
And many else were free to roam abroad,
But for the main, here found they covert drear.
Scarce images of life, one here, one there,
Lay vast and edgeways; like a dismal cirque
Of Druid stones,[65] upon a forlorn moor,   35
When the chill rain begins at shut of eve,
In dull November, and their chancel vault,[66]
The Heaven itself, is blinded throughout night.
Each one kept shroud, nor to his neighbour gave
Or word, or look, or action of despair.   40
Creüs[67] was one; his ponderous iron mace
Lay by him, and a shattered rib of rock
Told of his rage, ere he thus sank and pined.
 Iäpetus[68] another; in his grasp,
A serpent's plashy neck; its barbèd tongue   45
Squeezed from the gorge, and all its uncurled length
Dead—and because the creature could not spit
Its poison in the eyes of conquering Jove.
Next Cottus;[69] prone he lay, chin uppermost,
As though in pain, for still upon the flint   50
He ground severe his skull, with open mouth
And eyes at horrid working. Nearest him
Asia,[70] born of most enormous Caf,

---

[63] *Mnemosyne*: in classical mythology, the Titan goddess of memory and the mother of the nine Muses.

[64] *Phoebe*: Titan wife of Coeus.

[65] *dismal . . . stones*: i.e., ancient stone formation into a vault for the dead.

[66] *chancel vault*: i.e., like the imagined vault formed by the stones. The chancel is the space around the sanctuary in a Christian church.

[67] *Creüs*: in classical mythology, one of the Titans.

[68] *Iäpetus*: in classical mythology, Titan, known as the "Titan of Mortal Life", father of Atlas, Prometheus, Epimetheus, and Menoetius.

[69] *Cottus*: in classical mythology, one of the giants who stormed Olympus (potentially one of the Hecatonchires).

[70] *Asia*: in classical mythology (also known as Clymene), wife of the Titan Iapetus and mother of Atlas, Prometheus, Epimetheus, and Menoetius. Here associated with Caf, a mountain.

Who cost her mother Tellus keener pangs,
Though feminine, than any of her sons: 55
More thought than woe was in her dusky face,
For she was prophesying of her glory;
And in her wide imagination stood
Palm-shaded temples, and high rival fanes,[71]
By Oxus[72] or in Ganges' sacred isles.[73]   60
Even as Hope upon her anchor leans,
So leant she, not so fair, upon a tusk
Shed from the broadest of her elephants.
Above her, on a crag's uneasy shelve,
Upon his elbow raised, all prostrate else,   65
Shadowed Enceladus[74]—once tame and mild
As grazing ox unworried in the meads;
Now tiger-passioned, lion-thoughted, wroth,
He meditated, plotted, and even now
Was hurling mountains in that second war,   70
Not long delayed, that scared the younger Gods
To hide themselves in forms of beast and bird.
Nor far hence Atlas;[75] and beside him prone
Phorcus,[76] the sire of Gorgons. Neighboured close
Oceanus, and Tethys,[77] in whose lap   75
Sobbed Clymene[78] among her tangled hair.

[71] *fanes*: temples.

[72] *Oxus*: river in Persia.

[73] *Ganges'*: Ganges is a river in India, sacred to the Hindus.

[74] *Enceladus*: in classical mythology, one of the Gigantes, son of Uranus and Gaia (the earth).

[75] *Atlas*: In classical mythology, the Titan brother of Prometheus was transformed into a mountain by the Greek hero Perseus, who carried with him the head of the Gorgon Medusa, so hideous that it turned any who gazed upon it to stone.

[76] *Phorcus*: in classical mythology, sea god who married his sister and fathered the Gorgons (monstrous female creatures) and the dragon that guarded over the apples of the Hesperides.

[77] *Oceanus . . . Tethys*: in classical mythology, sea gods, parents of the Oceanides (sea nymphs).

[78] *Clymene*: in classical mythology, one of the Oceanides.

In midst of all lay Themis,[79] at the feet
Of Ops[80] the queen all clouded round from sight;
No shape distinguishable, more than when
Thick night confounds the pine-tops with the clouds—   80
And many else whose names may not be told.
For when the Muse's wings are air-ward spread,
Who shall delay her flight? And she must chant
Of Saturn, and his guide, who now had climbed
With damp and slippery footing from a depth   85
More horrid still. Above a sombre cliff
Their heads appeared, and up their stature grew
Till on the level height their steps found ease:
Then Thea spread abroad her trembling arms
Upon the precincts of this nest of pain,   90
And sidelong fixed her eye on Saturn's face.
There saw she direst strife—the supreme God
At war with all the frailty of grief,
Of rage, of fear, anxiety, revenge,
Remorse, spleen, hope, but most of all despair.   95
Against these plagues he strove in vain; for Fate
Had poured a mortal oil upon his head,
A disanointing poison, so that Thea,
Affrighted, kept her still, and let him pass
First onwards in, among the fallen tribe.   100

   As with us mortal men, the laden heart
Is persecuted more, and fevered more,
When it is nighing to the mournful house
Where other hearts are sick of the same bruise;
So Saturn, as he walked into the midst,   105
Felt faint, and would have sunk among the rest,
But that he met Enceladus's eye,

[79] *Themis*: in classical mythology, Titan mother (by Zeus) of the Parcae (the Fates) and the Horae.
[80] *Ops*: in classical mythology, Cybele, the wife of Saturn and mother of the Olympian gods.

Whose mightiness, and awe of him, at once
Came like an inspiration; and he shouted,
'Titans, behold your God!' At which some groaned;   110
Some started on their feet; some also shouted;
Some wept, some wailed, all bowed with reverence;
And Ops, uplifting her black folded veil,
Showed her pale cheeks, and all her forehead wan,
Her eye-brows thin and jet, and hollow eyes.   115
There is a roaring in the bleak-grown pines
When Winter lifts his voice; there is a noise
Among immortals when a God gives sign,
With hushing finger, how he means to load
His tongue with the full weight of utterless thought,   120
With thunder, and with music, and with pomp:
Such noise is like the roar of bleak-grown pines,
Which, when it ceases in this mountained world,
No other sound succeeds; but ceasing here,
Among these fallen, Saturn's voice therefrom   125
Grew up like organ, that begins anew
Its strain, when other harmonies, stopped short,
Leave the dinned air vibrating silverly.
Thus grew it up: 'Not
in my own sad breast,
Which is its own great judge and searcher-out,   130
Can I find reason why ye should be thus:
Not in the legends of the first of days,
Studied from that old spirit-leavèd book
Which starry Uranus with finger bright
Saved from the shores of darkness, when the waves   135
Low-ebbed still hid it up in shallow gloom—
And the which book ye know I ever kept
For my firm-basèd footstool—Ah, infirm!
Not there, nor in sign, symbol, or portent
Of element, earth, water, air, and fire—   140
At war, at peace, or inter-quarrelling
One against one, or two, or three, or all
Each several one against the other three,

As fire with air loud warring when rain-floods
Drown both, and press them both against earth's face,   145
Where, finding sulphur, a quadruple wrath
Unhinges the poor world—not in that strife,
Wherefrom I take strange lore, and read it deep,
Can I find reason why ye should be thus—
No, nowhere can unriddle, though I search,   150
And pore on Nature's universal scroll
Even to swooning, why ye, Divinities,
The first-born of all shaped and palpable Gods,
Should cower beneath what, in comparison,
Is untremendous might. Yet ye are here,   155
O'erwhelmed, and spurned, and battered, ye are here!
O Titans, shall I say, "Arise!"?—Ye groan:
Shall I say "Crouch!"?—Ye groan. What can I then?
O Heaven wide! O unseen parent dear!
What can I? Tell me, all ye brethren Gods,   160
How we can war, how engine our great wrath!
O speak your counsel now, for Saturn's ear
Is all a-hungered. Thou, Oceanus,
Ponderest high and deep, and in thy face
I see, astonied, that severe content   165
Which comes of thought and musing. Give us help!'

   So ended Saturn; and the God of the Sea,[81]
Sophist and sage from no Athenian grove,
But cogitation in his watery shades,
Arose, with locks not oozy, and began,   170
In murmurs which his first-endeavouring tongue
Caught infant-like from the far-foamèd sands.
'O ye, whom wrath consumes! who, passion-stung,
Writhe at defeat, and nurse your agonies!
Shut up your senses, stifle up your ears,   175
My voice is not a bellows unto ire.
Yet listen, ye who will, whilst I bring proof

[81] *God . . . Sea*: i.e., Oceanus.

How ye, perforce, must be content to stoop;
And in the proof much comfort will I give,
If ye will take that comfort in its truth.   180
We fall by course of Nature's law, not force
Of thunder, or of Jove. Great Saturn, thou
Hast sifted well the atom-universe;
But for this reason, that thou art the King,
And only blind from sheer supremacy,   185
One avenue was shaded from thine eyes,
Through which I wandered to eternal truth.
And first, as thou wast not the first of powers,
So art thou not the last; it cannot be:
Thou art not the beginning nor the end.   190
From Chaos and parental Darkness came
Light, the first fruits of that intestine broil,
That sullen ferment, which for wondrous ends
Was ripening in itself. The ripe hour came,
And with it Light, and Light, engendering   195
Upon its own producer, forthwith touched
The whole enormous matter into life.
Upon that very hour, our parentage,
The Heavens, and the Earth, were manifest:
Then thou first born, and we the giant race,   200
Found ourselves ruling new and beauteous realms.
Now comes the pain of truth, to whom 'tis pain—
O folly! for to bear all naked truths,
And to envisage circumstance, all calm,
That is the top of sovereignty. Mark well!   205
As Heaven and Earth are fairer, fairer far
Than Chaos and blank Darkness, though once chiefs;
And as we show beyond that Heaven and Earth
In form and shape compact and beautiful,
In will, in action free, companionship,   210
And thousand other signs of purer life;
So on our heels a fresh perfection treads,
A power more strong in beauty, born of us
And fated to excel us, as we pass

In glory that old Darkness:[82] nor are we 215
Thereby more conquered, than by us the rule
Of shapeless Chaos. Say, doth the dull soil
Quarrel with the proud forests it hath fed,
And feedeth still, more comely than itself?
Can it deny the chiefdom of green groves? 220
Or shall the tree be envious of the dove
Because it cooeth, and hath snowy wings
To wander wherewithal and find its joys?
We are such forest-trees, and our fair boughs
Have bred forth, not pale solitary doves, 225
But eagles golden-feathered, who do tower
Above us in their beauty, and must reign
In right thereof. For 'tis the eternal law
That first in beauty should be first in might:
Yea, by that law, another race may drive 230
Our conquerors to mourn as we do now.
Have ye beheld the young God of the Seas,
My dispossessor? Have ye seen his face?
Have ye beheld his chariot, foamed along
By noble wingèd creatures he hath made? 235
I saw him on the calmèd waters scud,
With such a glow of beauty in his eyes,
That it enforced me to bid sad farewell
To all my empire: farewell sad I took,

---

[82] *As Heaven and Earth . . . old Darkness:* "The great Myth of the nineteenth and early twentieth century … that picture of reality which resulted … , not logically but imaginatively, from some of the more striking and (so to speak) marketable theories of the real scientists … is implicit in nearly every modern article on politics, sociology, and ethics…. The central idea of the Myth is what its believers would call 'Evolution' or 'Development' or 'Emergence', just as the central idea in the myth of Adonis is Death and Rebirth…. The clearest and finest poetical expressions of the Myth come before the *Origin of Species* was published (1859) and long before it had established itself as scientific orthodoxy…. Almost before they spoke clearly, imagination was ripe for it. The finest expression of the Myth in English does not come from Bridges, nor from Shaw, nor from Wells, nor from Olaf Stapledon. It is this: [he quotes *Hyperion*, bk. 2, lines 206–15]. Thus Oceanus in Keats's *Hyperion*, nearly forty years before the *Origin of Species*." C. S. Lewis, "The Funeral of a Great Myth", in *Christian Reflections* (London: Fount, 1991), pp. 110–12.

And hither came, to see how dolorous fate   240
Had wrought upon ye; and how I might best
Give consolation in this woe extreme.
Receive the truth, and let it be your balm.'

Whether through posed conviction, or disdain,
They guarded silence, when Oceanus   245
Left murmuring, what deepest thought can tell?
But so it was; none answered for a space,
Save one whom none regarded, Clymene;[83]
And yet she answered not, only complained,
With hectic[84] lips, and eyes up-looking mild,   250
Thus wording timidly among the fierce:
'O Father, I am here the simplest voice,
And all my knowledge is that joy is gone,
And this thing woe crept in among our hearts,
There to remain for ever, as I fear.   255
I would not bode of evil, if I thought
So weak a creature could turn off the help
Which by just right should come of mighty Gods;
Yet let me tell my sorrow, let me tell
Of what I heard, and how it made me weep,   260
And know that we had parted from all hope.
I stood upon a shore, a pleasant shore,
Where a sweet clime was breathèd from a land
Of fragrance, quietness, and trees, and flowers.
Full of calm joy it was, as I of grief;   265
Too full of joy and soft delicious warmth;
So that I felt a movement in my heart
To chide, and to reproach that solitude
With songs of misery, music of our woes;
And sat me down, and took a mouthèd shell   270
And murmured into it, and made melody—
O melody no more! for while I sang,

---

[83]*Clymene*: in classical mythology, one of the Oceanides.
[84]*hectic*: red or purple, as in a hectic fever.

And with poor skill let pass into the breeze
The dull shell's echo, from a bowery strand
Just opposite, an island of the sea,   275
There came enchantment with the shifting wind,
That did both drown and keep alive my ears.
I threw my shell away upon the sand,
And a wave filled it, as my sense was filled
With that new blissful golden melody.   280
A living death was in each gush of sounds,
Each family of rapturous hurried notes,
That fell, one after one, yet all at once,
Like pearl beads dropping sudden from their string;
And then another, then another strain,   285
Each like a dove leaving its olive perch,
With music winged instead of silent plumes,
To hover round my head, and make me sick
Of joy and grief at once. Grief overcame,
And I was stopping up my frantic ears,   290
When, past all hindrance of my trembling hands,
A voice came sweeter, sweeter than all tune,
And still it cried, "Apollo! young Apollo!
The morning-bright Apollo! young Apollo!"
I fled, it followed me, and cried "Apollo!"   295
O Father, and O Brethren, had ye felt
Those pains of mine—O Saturn, hadst thou felt,
Ye would not call this too indulgèd tongue
Presumptuous, in thus venturing to be heard.'

So far her voice flowed on, like timorous brook   300
That, lingering along a pebbled coast,
Doth fear to meet the sea: but sea it met,
And shuddered; for the overwhelming voice
Of huge Enceladus swallowed it in wrath:
The ponderous syllables, like sullen waves   305
In the half-glutted hollows of reef-rocks,
Came booming thus, while still upon his arm
He leaned—not rising, from supreme contempt:

'Or shall we listen to the over-wise,
Or to the over-foolish, Giant-Gods?   310
Not thunderbolt on thunderbolt, till all
That rebel Jove's whole armoury were spent,
Not world on world upon these shoulders piled
Could agonize me more than baby-words
In midst of this dethronement horrible.   315
Speak! Roar! Shout! Yell! ye sleepy Titans all.
Do ye forget the blows, the buffets vile?
Are ye not smitten by a youngling arm?
Dost thou forget, sham Monarch of the Waves,
Thy scalding in the seas? What, have I roused   320
Your spleens with so few simple words as these?
O joy! for now I see ye are not lost:
O joy! for now I see a thousand eyes
Wide-glaring for revenge!'—As this he said,
He lifted up his stature vast, and stood,   325
Still without intermission speaking thus:
'Now ye are flames, I'll tell you how to burn,
And purge the ether of our enemies;
How to feed fierce the crooked stings of fire,
And singe away the swollen clouds of Jove,   330
Stifling that puny essence in its tent.
O let him feel the evil he hath done;
For though I scorn Oceanus's lore,
Much pain have I for more than loss of realms:
The days of peace and slumbrous calm are fled;   335
Those days, all innocent of scathing war,
When all the fair Existences of heaven
Came open-eyed to guess what we would speak—
That was before our brows were taught to frown,
Before our lips knew else but solemn sounds;   340
That was before we knew the wingèd thing,
Victory, might be lost, or might be won.
And be ye mindful that Hyperion,
Our brightest brother, still is undisgraced—
Hyperion, lo! his radiance is here!'   345

    All eyes were on Enceladus's face,
And they beheld, while still Hyperion's name
Flew from his lips up to the vaulted rocks,
A pallid gleam across his features stern—
Not savage, for he saw full many a God   350
Wroth as himself. He looked upon them all,
And in each face he saw a gleam of light,
But splendider in Saturn's, whose hoar locks
Shone like the bubbling foam about a keel
When the prow sweeps into a midnight cove.   355
In pale and silver silence they remained,
Till suddenly a splendour, like the morn,
Pervaded all the beetling gloomy steeps,
All the sad spaces of oblivion,
And every gulf, and every chasm old,   360
And every height, and every sullen depth,
Voiceless, or hoarse with loud tormented streams;
And all the everlasting cataracts,
And all the headlong torrents far and near,
Mantled before in darkness and huge shade,   365
Now saw the light and made it terrible.
It was Hyperion: a granite peak
His bright feet touched, and there he stayed to view
The misery his brilliance had betrayed
To the most hateful seeing of itself.   370
Golden his hair of short Numidian[85] curl,
Regal his shape majestic, a vast shade
In midst of his own brightness, like the bulk
Of Memnon's image[86] at the set of sun
To one who travels from the dusking East: 375
Sighs, too, as mournful as that Memnon's harp,
He uttered, while his hands contemplative

---

[85]*Numidian*: Numidia was an ancient West African kingdom.
[86]*Memnon's image*: the Colossi of Memnon, massive statues of Pharoah
Amenhotep III (fourteenth century B.C.). Additionally, in classical mythology,
Memnon was an Ethiopian king.

He pressed together, and in silence stood.
Despondence seized again the fallen Gods
At sight of the dejected King of Day,   380
And many hid their faces from the light:
But fierce Enceladus sent forth his eyes
Among the brotherhood; and, at their glare,
Uprose Iäpetus, and Creüs too,
And Phorcus, sea-born, and together strode   385
To where he towered on his eminence.
There those four shouted forth old Saturn's name;
Hyperion from the peak loud answered, 'Saturn!'
Saturn sat near the Mother of the Gods,
In whose face was no joy, though all the Gods   390
Gave from their hollow throats the name of 'Saturn!'

BOOK III

Thus in alternate uproar and sad peace,
Amazèd were those Titans utterly.
O leave them, Muse! O leave them to their woes;
For thou art weak to sing such tumults dire:
A solitary sorrow best befits   5
Thy lips, and antheming a lonely grief.
Leave them, O Muse! for thou anon wilt find
Many a fallen old Divinity
Wandering in vain about bewildered shores.
Meantime touch piously the Delphic harp,[87]   10
And not a wind of heaven but will breathe
In aid soft warble from the Dorian flute;[88]
For lo! 'tis for the Father of all verse.
Flush every thing that hath a vermeil hue,
Let the rose glow intense and warm the air,   15
And let the clouds of even and of morn

---

[87] *Delphic harp*: Delphi, a town on Mount Parnassus, the site of the Delphic oracle, sacred to Apollo, god of music.

[88] *Dorian flute*: Musical prowess is attributed to the classical Greek ethnic community of the Dorians (e.g., the Dorian mode of music).

Float in voluptuous fleeces o'er the hills;
Let the red wine within the goblet boil,
Cold as a bubbling well; let faint-lipped shells,
On sands, or in great deeps, vermilion turn   20
Through all their labyrinths; and let the maid
Blush keenly, as with some warm kiss surprised.
Chief isle of the embowered Cyclades,[89]
Rejoice, O Delos,[90] with thine olives green,
And poplars, and lawn-shading palms, and beech,   25
In which the Zephyr breathes the loudest song,
And hazels thick, dark-stemmed beneath the shade:
Apollo is once more the golden theme!
Where was he, when the Giant of the Sun
Stood bright, amid the sorrow of his peers?   30
Together had he left his mother fair
And his twin-sister sleeping in their bower,
And in the morning twilight wandered forth
Beside the osiers of a rivulet,
Full ankle-deep in lilies of the vale.   35
The nightingale had ceased, and a few stars
Were lingering in the heavens, while the thrush
Began calm-throated. Throughout all the isle
There was no covert, no retirèd cave
Unhaunted by the murmurous noise of waves,   40
Though scarcely heard in many a green recess.
He listened, and he wept, and his bright tears
Went trickling down the golden bow he held.
Thus with half-shut suffusèd eyes he stood,
While from beneath some cumbrous boughs hard by   45
With solemn step an awful Goddess came,
And there was purport in her looks for him,
Which he with eager guess began to read
Perplexed, the while melodiously he said:

---

[89] *Cyclades*: group of Greek islands in the Aegean Sea, southeast of mainland Greece.
[90] *Delos*: island of Delos, in the middle of the Cyclades (sacred to Dionysius).

'How cam'st thou over the unfooted sea?   50
Or hath that antique mien and robèd form
Moved in these vales invisible till now?
Sure I have heard those vestments sweeping o'er
The fallen leaves, when I have sat alone
In cool mid-forest. Surely I have traced   55
The rustle of those ample skirts about
These grassy solitudes, and seen the flowers
Lift up their heads, as still the whisper passed.
Goddess! I have beheld those eyes before,
And their eternal calm, and all that face,   60
Or I have dreamed.'—'Yes,' said the supreme shape,
'Thou hast dreamed of me; and awaking up
Didst find a lyre all golden by thy side,
Whose strings touched by thy fingers, all the vast
Unwearied ear of the whole universe   65
Listened in pain and pleasure at the birth
Of such new tuneful wonder. Is't not strange
That thou shouldst weep, so gifted? Tell me, youth,
What sorrow thou canst feel; for I am sad
When thou dost shed a tear. Explain thy griefs   70
To one who in this lonely isle hath been
The watcher of thy sleep and hours of life,
From the young day when first thy infant hand
Plucked witless the weak flowers, till thine arm
Could bend that bow heroic to all times.   75
Show thy heart's secret to an ancient Power
Who hath forsaken old and sacred thrones
For prophecies of thee, and for the sake
Of loveliness new born.'—Apollo then,
With sudden scrutiny and gloomless eyes,   80
Thus answered, while his white melodious throat
Throbbed with the syllables: 'Mnemosyne!
Thy name is on my tongue, I know not how;
Why should I tell thee what thou so well seest?
Why should I strive to show what from thy lips   85
Would come no mystery? For me, dark, dark,

And painful vile oblivion seals my eyes:
I strive to search wherefore I am so sad,
Until a melancholy numbs my limbs;
And then upon the grass I sit, and moan,   90
Like one who once had wings. O why should I
Feel cursed and thwarted, when the liegeless air
Yields to my step aspirant? Why should I
Spurn the green turf as hateful to my feet?
Goddess benign, point forth some unknown thing: 95
Are there not other regions than this isle?
What are the stars? There is the sun, the sun!
And the most patient brilliance of the moon!
And stars by thousands! Point me out the way
To any one particular beauteous star,   100
And I will flit into it with my lyre,
And make its silvery splendour pant with bliss.
I have heard the cloudy thunder. Where is power?
Whose hand, whose essence, what Divinity
Makes this alarum in the elements,   105
While I here idle listen on the shores
In fearless yet in aching ignorance?
O tell me, lonely Goddess, by thy harp,
That waileth every morn and eventide,
Tell me why thus I rave, about these groves!   110
Mute thou remainest—mute! yet I can read
A wondrous lesson in thy silent face:
Knowledge enormous makes a God of me.
Names, deeds, grey legends, dire events, rebellions,
Majesties, sovran voices, agonies,   115
Creations and destroyings, all at once
Pour into the wide hollows of my brain,
And deify me, as if some blithe wine
Or bright elixir peerless I had drunk,
And so become immortal.'—Thus the God,   120
While his enkindlèd eyes, with level glance
Beneath his white soft temples, stedfast kept
Trembling with light upon Mnemosyne.

Soon wild commotions shook him, and made flush
All the immortal fairness of his limbs—   125
Most like the struggle at the gate of death;
Or liker still to one who should take leave
Of pale immortal death, and with a pang
As hot as death's is chill, with fierce convulse
Die into life: so young Apollo anguished.   130
His very hair, his golden tresses famed
Kept undulation round his eager neck.
During the pain Mnemosyne upheld
Her arms as one who prophesied.—At length
Apollo shrieked—and lo! from all his limbs   135
Celestial....

The Eve of St Agnes[91]

The Eve of St Agnes was composed in January–February 1819
and revised in September of the same year. The poem is to
some extent an epiphenomenon of Keats' (never consum-
mated) romantic involvement with Fanny Brawne (begun in
autumn 1818).

The most popular of Keats' narrative poems, it is also his only
successful poem in the stanza of his beloved master, Spenser,
and the one that best exemplifies his maxim to "load every rift
of your subject with ore".[92] The influence of Shakespeare (espe-
cially *Romeo and Juliet*), Boccaccio, Coleridge's "Christabel",
Scott's *Lay of the Last Minstrel*, and Gothic architecture[93] are
also evident.

With its combination of richness of color and detail, medi-
evalism, sensuality, the violent and the weird, folklore, and

[91] The Eve ... Agnes: On the eve of the feast of the early Christian virgin
martyr St. Agnes (January 21), young women were known traditionally to per-
form various practices (particularly fasting to bring on a vision) to determine
who their future husbands would be.
[92] Letter to Shelley, August 16, 1820, in *Letters of John Keats to His Family and
Friends*, p. 366.
[93] Keats had recently visited Chichester Cathedral.

archaic diction, *The Eve of St Agnes*[94] both anticipated and influenced pre-Raphaelitism.

The Eve of St Agnes (early 1819)

I

St Agnes' Eve—Ah, bitter chill it was!
The owl, for all his feathers, was a-cold;
The hare limped trembling through the frozen grass,
And silent was the flock in woolly fold:
Numb were the Beadsman's[95] fingers, while he told   5
His rosary, and while his frosted breath,
Like pious incense from a censer[96] old,
Seemed taking flight for heaven, without a death,
Past the sweet Virgin's picture, while his prayer he
  saith.

II

His prayer he saith, this patient, holy man;   10
Then takes his lamp, and riseth from his knees,
And back returneth, meagre, barefoot, wan,
Along the chapel aisle by slow degrees:
The sculptured dead, on each side, seem to freeze,
Emprisoned in black, purgatorial rails;   15
Knights, ladies, praying in dumb orat'ries,
He passeth by; and his weak spirit fails
To think how they may ache in icy hoods and mails.

---

[94] Together with *La Belle Dame sans Merci* and, to a lesser extent, *Isabella* and "The Eve of St Mark".

[95] *Beadsman's*: A beadsman was a pensioner or almsman who would pray for the soul of his benefactor.

[96] *censer*: vessel for burning incense, to be swung, that the perfumed smoke may spread.

III

Northward he turneth through a little door,
And scarce three steps, ere Music's golden tongue   20
Flattered to tears this agèd man and poor;
But no—already had his deathbell rung:
The joys of all his life were said and sung:
His was harsh penance on St Agnes' Eve.
Another way he went, and soon among   25
Rough ashes sat he for his soul's reprieve,
And all night kept awake, for sinners' sake to grieve.

IV

That ancient Beadsman heard the prelude soft;
And so it chanced, for many a door was wide,
From hurry to and fro. Soon, up aloft,   30
The silver, snarling trumpets 'gan to chide:
The level chambers, ready with their pride,
Were glowing to receive a thousand guests:
The carvèd angels, ever eager-eyed,
Stared, where upon their heads the cornice rests,   35
With hair blown back, and wings put cross-wise on their
     breasts.

V

At length burst in the argent[97] revelry,
With plume, tiara, and all rich array,
Numerous as shadows haunting faerily
The brain, new-stuffed, in youth, with triumphs gay   40
Of old romance. These let us wish away,
And turn, sole-thoughted, to one Lady there,
Whose heart had brooded, all that wintry day,
On love, and winged St Agnes' saintly care,
As she had heard old dames full many times declare.   45

---

[97] *argent*: silver.

VI

They told her how, upon St Agnes' Eve,
Young virgins might have visions of delight,
And soft adorings from their loves receive
Upon the honeyed middle of the night,
If ceremonies due they did aright;   50
As, supperless to bed they must retire,
And couch supine their beauties, lily white;
Nor look behind, nor sideways, but require
Of Heaven with upward eyes for all that they desire.

VII

Full of this whim was thoughtful Madeline: 55
The music, yearning like a God in pain,
She scarcely heard: her maiden eyes divine,
Fixed on the floor, saw many a sweeping train
Pass by—she heeded not at all: in vain
Came many a tip-toe, amorous cavalier,   60
And back retired—not cooled by high disdain,
But she saw not: her heart was otherwhere:
She sighed for Agnes' dreams, the sweetest of the year.

VIII

She danced along with vague, regardless eyes,
Anxious her lips, her breathing quick and short: 65
The hallowed hour was near at hand: she sighs
Amid the timbrels, and the thronged resort
Of whisperers in anger, or in sport;
'Mid looks of love, defiance, hate, and scorn,
Hoodwinked with faery fancy—all amort,[98]   70
Save to St Agnes and her lambs unshorn,
And all the bliss to be before to-morrow morn.

[98] *amort*: dead.

IX

So, purposing each moment to retire,
She lingered still. Meantime, across the moors,
Had come young Porphyro, with heart on fire   75
For Madeline. Beside the portal doors,
Buttressed from moonlight, stands he, and implores
All saints to give him sight of Madeline
But for one moment in the tedious hours,
That he might gaze and worship all unseen;   80
Perchance speak, kneel, touch, kiss—in sooth such
    things have been.

X

He ventures in—let no buzzed whisper tell,
All eyes be muffled, or a hundred swords
Will storm his heart, Love's fev'rous citadel:
For him, those chambers held barbarian hordes,   85
Hyena foemen, and hot-blooded lords,
Whose very dogs would execrations howl
Against his lineage: not one breast affords
Him any mercy, in that mansion foul,
Save one old beldame,[99] weak in body and in soul.   90

XI

Ah, happy chance! the agèd creature came,
Shuffling along with ivory-headed wand,
To where he stood, hid from the torch's flame,
Behind a broad hall-pillar, far beyond
The sound of merriment and chorus bland: 95
He startled her; but soon she knew his face,
And grasped his fingers in her palsied hand,
Saying, 'Mercy, Porphyro! hie[100] thee from this place:
They are all here to-night, the whole blood-thirsty race!

[99] *beldame*: old woman, probably ugly.
[100] *hie*: get quickly.

XII

'Get hence! get hence! there's dwarfish Hildebrand— 100
He had a fever late, and in the fit
He cursèd thee and thine, both house and land:
Then there's that old Lord Maurice, not a whit
More tame for his grey hairs—Alas me! flit!
Flit like a ghost away.' 'Ah, gossip dear, 105
We're safe enough; here in this arm-chair sit,
And tell me how—' 'Good Saints! not here, not here;
Follow me, child, or else these stones will be thy bier.'

XIII

He followed through a lowly archèd way,
Brushing the cobwebs with his lofty plume, 110
And as she muttered, 'Well-a—well-a-day!'
He found him in a little moonlight room,
Pale, latticed, chill, and silent as a tomb.
'Now tell me where is Madeline,' said he,
'O tell me, Angela, by the holy loom 115
Which none but secret sisterhood may see,
When they St Agnes' wool are weaving piously.'

XIV

'St Agnes? Ah! it is St Agnes' Eve—
Yet men will murder upon holy days:
Thou must hold water in a witch's sieve, 120
And be liege-lord of all the Elves and Fays,
To venture so: it fills me with amaze
To see thee, Porphyro!—St Agnes' Eve!
God's help! my lady fair the conjuror plays
This very night. Good angels her deceive! 125
But let me laugh awhile, I've mickle[101] time to grieve.'

---

[101] *mickle*: much.

XV

Feebly she laugheth in the languid moon,
While Porphyro upon her face doth look,
Like puzzled urchin on an agèd crone
Who keepeth closed a wondrous riddle-book,   130
As spectacled she sits in chimney nook.
But soon his eyes grew brilliant, when she told
His lady's purpose; and he scarce could brook
Tears, at the thought of those enchantments cold,
And Madeline asleep in lap of legends old.   135

XVI

Sudden a thought came like a full-blown rose,
Flushing his brow, and in his painèd heart
Made purple riot; then doth he propose
A stratagem, that makes the beldame start:
'A cruel man and impious thou art: 140
Sweet lady, let her pray, and sleep, and dream
Alone with her good angels, far apart
From wicked men like thee. Go, go!—I deem
Thou canst not surely be the same that thou didst
    seem.'

XVII

'I will not harm her, by all saints I swear,'   145
Quoth Porphyro: 'O may I ne'er find grace
When my weak voice shall whisper its last prayer,
If one of her soft ringlets I displace,
Or look with ruffian passion in her face:
Good Angela, believe me by these tears;   150
Or I will, even in a moment's space,
Awake, with horrid shout, my foeman's ears,
And beard them, though they be more fanged than
    wolves and bears.'

XVIII

'Ah! why wilt thou affright a feeble soul?   155
A poor, weak, palsy-stricken, churchyard thing,
Whose passing-bell may ere the midnight toll;
Whose prayers for thee, each morn and evening,
Were never missed.'—Thus plaining, doth she bring
A gentler speech from burning Porphyro,
So woeful, and of such deep sorrowing,   160
That Angela gives promise she will do
Whatever he shall wish, betide her weal or woe.[102]

XIX

Which was, to lead him, in close secrecy,
Even to Madeline's chamber, and there hide
Him in a closet, of such privacy   165
That he might see her beauty unespied,
And win perhaps that night a peerless bride,
While legioned faeries paced the coverlet,
And pale enchantment held her sleepy-eyed.
Never on such a night have lovers met,   170
Since Merlin[103] paid his Demon all the monstrous
    debt.

XX

'It shall be as thou wishest,' said the Dame:
'All cates[104] and dainties shall be storèd there
Quickly on this feast-night; by the tambour frame[105]
Her own lute thou wilt see. No time to spare,   175
For I am slow and feeble, and scarce dare
On such a catering trust my dizzy head.

---

[102] *betide . . . woe*: i.e., should good or ill befall her.

[103] *Merlin*: an ancient prophet or wizard (though the precise allusion to the Demon is unclear).

[104] *cates*: choice dainty food, delicacies.

[105] *tambour frame*: embroidery hoop.

Wait here, my child, with patience; kneel in prayer
The while. Ah! thou must needs the lady wed,
Or may I never leave my grave among the dead.'   180

XXI

So saying, she hobbled off with busy fear.
The lover's endless minutes slowly passed;
The dame returned, and whispered in his ear
To follow her; with agèd eyes aghast
From fright of dim espial. Safe at last,   185
Through many a dusky gallery, they gain
The maiden's chamber, silken, hushed, and chaste;
Where Porphyro took covert,[106] pleased amain.[107]
His poor guide hurried back with agues in her brain.

XXII

Her faltering hand upon the balustrade,[108]   190
Old Angela was feeling for the stair,
When Madeline, St Agnes' charmèd maid,
Rose, like a missioned spirit, unaware:
With silver taper's light, and pious care,
She turned, and down the agèd gossip led   195
Young Porphyro, for gazing on that bed—
She comes, she comes again, like ring-dove frayed[109]
    and fled.

XXIII

Out went the taper as she hurried in;
Its little smoke, in pallid moonshine, died: 200
She closed the door, she panted, all akin
To spirits of the air, and visions wide—
No uttered syllable, or, woe betide!

[106] *took covert*: hid himself.
[107] *amain*: with great strength, speed, or haste.
[108] *balustrade*: posts supporting a railing.
[109] *frayed*: afraid.

But to her heart, her heart was voluble,
Paining with eloquence her balmy side; 205
As though a tongueless nightingale should swell
Her throat in vain, and die, heart-stiflèd, in her dell.

XXIV

A casement[110] high and triple-arched there was,
All garlanded with carven imag'ries
Of fruits, and flowers, and bunches of knot-grass,[111] 210
And diamonded with panes of quaint device,
Innumerable of stains and splendid dyes,
As are the tiger-moth's[112] deep-damasked[113] wings;
And in the midst, 'mong thousand heraldries,
And twilight saints, and dim emblazonings,[114] 215
A shielded scutcheon[115] blushed with blood of queens
and kings.[116]

XXV

Full on this casement shone the wintry moon,
And threw warm gules[117] on Madeline's fair breast,
As down she knelt for heaven's grace and boon;
Rose-bloom fell on her hands, together pressed, 220
And on her silver cross soft amethyst,

[110] *casement*: window frame.

[111] *knot-grass*: a troublesome common weed, composed of intricately branched creeping stems and small white flowers.

[112] *tiger-moth's*: The tiger moth is a large moth, brightly colored with scarlet and brown and displaying white streaks and spots.

[113] *deep-damasked*: Damask is an elaborately designed fabric, which displays a pattern visible from both sides of the fabric.

[114] *emblazonings*: i.e., heraldic devices.

[115] *shielded scutcheon*: shield displaying a coat of arms, lines in gules (red) indicating royal blood.

[116] *blood . . . kings*: i.e., the shield shows lines in red (gules) as a sign of the bearer's relationship to the royal bloodline. This entire stanza refers to marks of neo-Gothic architecture.

[117] *gules*: a term in heraldry meaning red. The light of the moon looks red when it shines on Madeline through the stained glass coat of arms in the casement.

And on her hair a glory, like a saint:
She seemed a splendid angel, newly dressed,
Save wings, for Heaven—Porphyro grew faint;
She knelt, so pure a thing, so free from mortal taint.   225

XXVI

Anon his heart revives; her vespers done,
Of all its wreathèd pearls her hair she frees;
Unclasps her warmèd jewels one by one;
Loosens her fragrant bodice; by degrees
Her rich attire creeps rustling to her knees: 230
Half-hidden, like a mermaid in sea-weed,
Pensive awhile she dreams awake, and sees,
In fancy, fair St Agnes in her bed,
But dares not look behind, or all the charm is fled.

XXVII

Soon, trembling in her soft and chilly nest,   235
In sort of wakeful swoon, perplexed she lay,
Until the poppied warmth of sleep oppressed
Her soothèd limbs, and soul fatigued away—
Flown, like a thought, until the morrow-day;
Blissfully havened both from joy and pain;   240
Clasped like a missal where swart Paynims pray;
Blinded alike from sunshine and from rain,
As though a rose should shut, and be a bud again.

XXVIII

Stolen to this paradise, and so entranced,
Porphyro gazed upon her empty dress,   245
And listened to her breathing, if it chanced
To wake into a slumbrous tenderness;
Which when he heard, that minute did he bless,
And breathed himself: then from the closet crept,

Noiseless as fear in a wide wilderness, 250
    And over the hushed carpet, silent, stepped,
And 'tween the curtains peeped, where, lo!—how fast
    she slept.

XXIX

Then by the bed-side, where the faded moon
Made a dim, silver twilight, soft he set
A table, and, half anguished, threw thereon
A cloth of woven crimson, gold, and jet— 255
O for some drowsy Morphean amulet![118]
The boisterous, midnight, festive clarion,[119]
The kettle-drum, and far-heard clarinet,
Affray his ears, though but in dying tone; 260
The hall door shuts again, and all the noise is gone.

XXX

And still she slept an azure-lidded sleep,
In blanchèd linen, smooth, and lavendered,
While he from forth the closet brought a heap
Of candied apple, quince, and plum, and gourd, 265
With jellies soother[120] than the creamy curd,
And lucent syrups, tinct with cinnamon;
Manna and dates, in argosy[121] transferred
From Fez;[122] and spicèd dainties, every one,
From silken Samarkand[123] to cedared Lebanon.[124] 270

---

[118] *Morphean amulet*: An amulet is a charm, and in classical mythology, Morpheus is the god of sleep.

[119] *clarion*: shrill war trumpet.

[120] *soother*: more soothing, sweeter.

[121] *argosy*: large merchant ship.

[122] *Fez*: in antiquity, one of the four imperial cities of Morocco, noted as a center of Islamic arts and handicrafts.

[123] *Samarkand*: in the medieval period, an Islamic imperial city, noted for its palaces, gardens, and silk industry.

[124] *cedared Lebanon*: Lebanon, a country of the Eastern Mediterranean, is specially known for its cedar trees. See Psalm 104:16.

XXXI

These delicates he heaped with glowing hand
On golden dishes and in baskets bright
Of wreathèd silver; sumptuous they stand
In the retirèd quiet of the night,
Filling the chilly room with perfume light.   275
'And now, my love, my seraph[125] fair, awake!
Thou art my heaven, and I thine eremite:[126]
Open thine eyes, for meek St Agnes' sake,
Or I shall drowse beside thee, so my soul doth ache.'

XXXII

Thus whispering, his warm, unnervèd arm   280
Sank in her pillow. Shaded was her dream
By the dusk curtains—'twas a midnight charm
Impossible to melt as icèd stream:
The lustrous salvers[127] in the moonlight gleam;
Broad golden fringe upon the carpet lies.   285
It seemed he never, never could redeem
From such a steadfast spell his lady's eyes;
So mused awhile, entoiled in woofèd fantasies.

XXXIII

Awakening up, he took her hollow lute,
Tumultuous, and, in chords that tenderest be,   290
He played an ancient ditty, long since mute,
In Provence called, 'La belle dame sans mercy',[128]
Close to her ear touching the melody—
Wherewith disturbed, she uttered a soft moan:
He ceased—she panted quick—and suddenly   295
Her blue affrayèd eyes wide open shone.
Upon his knees he sank, pale as smooth-sculptured stone.

[125] *seraph*: angel.
[126] *eremite*: hermit.
[127] *salvers*: trays (probably silver).
[128] 'La . . . *mercy*': poem by the French poet Alain Chartier (c. 1385–1430), and a poem by Keats. See p. 410.

XXXIV

Her eyes were open, but she still beheld,
Now wide awake, the vision of her sleep—
There was a painful change, that nigh expelled   300
The blisses of her dream so pure and deep.
At which fair Madeline began to weep,
And moan forth witless words with many a sigh,
While still her gaze on Porphyro would keep;
Who knelt, with joinèd hands and piteous eye,   305
Fearing to move or speak, she looked so dreamingly.

XXXV

'Ah, Porphyro!' said she, 'but even now
Thy voice was at sweet tremble in mine ear,
Made tuneable with every sweetest vow,
And those sad eyes were spiritual and clear: 310
How changed thou art! How pallid, chill, and drear!
Give me that voice again, my Porphyro,
Those looks immortal, those complainings dear!
O leave me not in this eternal woe,
For if thou diest, my Love, I know not where to go.'   315

XXXVI

Beyond a mortal man impassioned far
At these voluptuous accents, he arose,
Ethereal, flushed, and like a throbbing star
Seen mid the sapphire heaven's deep repose;
Into her dream he melted, as the rose   320
Blendeth its odour with the violet—
Solution sweet. Meantime the frost-wind blows
Like Love's alarum[129] pattering the sharp sleet
Against the window-panes; St Agnes' moon hath set.

---

[129] *alarum*: warning or call to arms.

XXXVII

'Tis dark: quick pattereth the flaw-blown[130] sleet.   325
'This is no dream, my bride, my Madeline!'
'Tis dark: the icèd gusts still rave and beat.
'No dream, alas! alas! and woe is mine!
Porphyro will leave me here to fade and pine.—
Cruel! what traitor could thee hither bring?   330
I curse not, for my heart is lost in thine,
Though thou forsakest a deceivèd thing—
A dove forlorn and lost with sick unprunèd wing.'

XXXVIII

'My Madeline! sweet dreamer! lovely bride!
Say, may I be for aye thy vassal blessed?   335
Thy beauty's shield, heart-shaped and vermeil[131] dyed?
Ah, silver shrine, here will I take my rest
After so many hours of toil and quest,
A famished pilgrim—saved by miracle.
Though I have found, I will not rob thy nest   340
Saving of thy sweet self; if thou think'st well
To trust, fair Madeline, to no rude infidel.

XXXIX

'Hark! 'tis an elfin-storm from faery land,
Of haggard seeming,[132] but a boon indeed:
Arise—arise! the morning is at hand.   345
The bloated wassaillers will never heed—
Let us away, my love, with happy speed—
There are no ears to hear, or eyes to see,
Drowned all in Rhenish[133] and the sleepy mead;
Awake! arise! my love, and fearless be,   350
For o'er the southern moors I have a home for thee.'

[130] *flaw-blown*: A flaw is a flying blast.
[131] *vermeil*: vermilion (i.e., red or orange-red).
[132] *haggard seeming*: wild appearance.
[133] *Rhenish*: Rhine wine.

XL

She hurried at his words, beset with fears,
For there were sleeping dragons all around,
At glaring watch, perhaps, with ready spears—
Down the wide stairs a darkling way they found.
In all the house was heard no human sound.   355
A chain-drooped lamp was flickering by each door;
The arras,[134] rich with horseman, hawk, and hound,
Fluttered in the besieging wind's uproar;
And the long carpets rose along the gusty floor.   360

XLI

They glide, like phantoms, into the wide hall;
Like phantoms, to the iron porch, they glide;
Where lay the Porter, in uneasy sprawl,
With a huge empty flaggon[135] by his side:
The wakeful bloodhound rose, and shook his hide,   365
But his sagacious eye an inmate owns.
By one, and one, the bolts full easy slide—
The chains lie silent on the footworn stones—
The key turns, and the door upon its hinges groans.

XLII

And they are gone—ay, ages long ago   370
These lovers fled away into the storm.
That night the Baron dreamt of many a woe,
And all his warrior-guests, with shade and form
Of witch, and demon, and large coffin-worm,
Were long be-nightmared. Angela the old   375
Died palsy-twitched, with meagre face deform;
The Beadsman, after thousand aves told,
For aye unsought for slept among his ashes cold.

[134] *arras*: tapestry, used as a wall hanging or curtain.
[135] *flaggon*: a flagon, a large wine bottle.

La Belle Dame sans Merci:[136] A Ballad (April 1819)

I

O what can ail thee, knight-at-arms,[137]
    Alone and palely loitering?
The sedge[138] has withered from the lake,
    And no birds sing.

II

O what can ail thee, knight-at-arms,   5
    So haggard and so woe-begone?
The squirrel's granary is full,
    And the harvest's done.

III

I see a lily on thy brow,
    With anguish moist and fever-dew,   10
And on thy cheeks a fading rose
    Fast withereth too.

IV

I met a lady in the meads,
    Full beautiful—a faery's child,
Her hair was long, her foot was light,   15
    And her eyes were wild.

[136]La … Merci: "The beautiful woman without pity". Keats wrote the poem on April 21, 1819, and revised it for publication in his friend Leigh Hunt's periodical, *The Indicator*, on May 10, 1820. It has been suggested that Keats, who was failing in health, was pressured into making the changes; the critical consensus (shared by this editor) is that the first draft is decidedly the better of the two versions, and it is the earlier text which is given here.

[137]*knight-at-arms*: In another version of the poem, the word "wight" is used, a Middle English word meaning "a living creature".

[138]*sedge*: low-growing plant (like a grass).

V

I made a garland for her head,
    And bracelets too, and fragrant zone;
She looked at me as she did love,
    And made sweet moan. 20

VI

I set her on my pacing steed,
    And nothing else saw all day long,
For sidelong would she bend, and sing
    A faery's song.

VII

She found me roots of relish sweet, 25
    And honey wild, and manna-dew,
And sure in language strange she said—
    'I love thee true'.

VIII

She took me to her elfin grot,
    And there she wept and sighed full sore, 30
And there I shut her wild wild eyes
    With kisses four.

IX

And there she lullèd me asleep
    And there I dreamed—Ah! woe betide!—
The latest dream I ever dreamt 35
    On the cold hill side.

X

I saw pale kings and princes too,
    Pale warriors, death-pale were they all;
They cried—'La Belle Dame sans Merci
    Thee hath in thrall!' 40

XI

I saw their starved lips in the gloam,
  With horrid warning gapèd wide,
And I awoke and found me here,
  On the cold hill's side.

XII

And this is why I sojourn here   45
  Alone and palely loitering,
Though the sedge is withered from the lake,
  And no birds sing.

Lamia[139]

Lamia was written in June–July 1819, during Keats' recasting of *Hyperion*. The Lamia has an entry in Lemprière's *Classical Dictionary*; the source of the story is Robert Burton's *Anatomy of Melancholy* (Pt. III, Sec. 2, Mem. I, Subs. I).

The influences on the versification of this "most perfect of [Keats'] free narratives"[140]—which grapples with themes central to the recently composed odes—are of considerable interest. Byron's technique inspires the asides dislocating the narrator from a facile identification with the characters and their sentiments. The handling of the heroic couplet, the presence of alexandrines and triplets, and the "varied richness of metrical control",[141] reveal the influence of Dryden, whose *Fables* Keats had been studying carefully, just as they reflect the latter's "reaction against the Miltonic mode"[142] (see the introduction to *The Fall of Hyperion*, p. 450).

---

[139] Lamia: In ancient mythology, Lamia was a queen of Libya who later became a demon that devoured children.

[140] Robert Bridges, in *The Poems of John Keats*, ed. G. Thorn Drury (London: Lawrence and Bullen, 1896), p. lxi.

[141] Upali Amarasinghe, *Dryden and Pope in the Early Nineteenth Century: A Study of Changing Literary Taste 1800–1830* (Cambridge: Cambridge University Press, 2010), p. 170.

[142] Ibid.

This move, from Milton to Dante in Dryden's company, in quest of a poetic idiom suitable for extended, and sometimes philosophical, statement—evident in the procession from *Hyperion* through the odes to *Lamia* and *The Fall of Hyperion*—foreshadows T.S. Eliot's path.[143]

Lamia (1819)

PART I

Upon a time, before the faery broods
Drove Nymph and Satyr[144] from the prosperous woods,
Before King Oberon's[145] bright diadem,
Sceptre, and mantle, clasped with dewy gem,
Frighted away the Dryads[146] and the Fauns[147]   5
From rushes[148] green, and brakes,[149] and cowslipped[150] lawns,
The ever-smitten Hermes[151] empty left
His golden throne, bent warm on amorous theft:
From high Olympus[152] had he stolen light,
On this side of Jove's[153] clouds, to escape the sight   10

---

[143] Consider, for instance, Eliot's discussion (in which Dryden subsequently features) of Poe's criticism: "Poe has a remarkable passage about the impossibility of writing a long poem—for a long poem, he holds, is at best a series of short poems strung together.... Yet it is only in a poem of some length that a variety of moods can be expressed.... A long poem may gain by the widest possible variations of intensity. But Poe wanted a poem to be of the first intensity throughout: it is questionable whether he could have appreciated the more philosophical passages in Dante's *Purgatorio*." T.S. Eliot, "From Poe to Valéry", in *To Criticize the Critic* (London: Faber, 1978), p. 34.

[144] *Satyr*: From ancient mythology, woodland creatures, half beast and half man.

[145] *King Oberon's*: Oberon is a ruler of the fairies popular in medieval and Renaissance literature, including Shakespeare's *A Midsummer Night's Dream* (c. 1590–1596).

[146] *Dryads*: in classical mythology, tree nymphs.

[147] *Fauns*: in classical mythology, rustic forest creatures, half man and half goat.

[148] *rushes*: marsh plants.

[149] *brakes*: thickets, areas overgrown densely with briars.

[150] *cowslipped*: the British primrose.

[151] *Hermes*: in classical mythology, messenger god, prone to romantic entanglements.

[152] *Olympus*: mountain home of the gods.

[153] *Jove's*: In classical mythology, Jove is the king of the gods.

Of his great summoner, and made retreat
Into a forest on the shores of Crete.[154]
For somewhere in that sacred island dwelt
A nymph, to whom all hoofèd Satyrs knelt,
At whose white feet the languid Tritons[155] poured   15
Pearls, while on land they withered and adored.
Fast by the springs where she to bathe was wont,
And in those meads where sometime she might haunt,
Were strewn rich gifts, unknown to any Muse,
Though Fancy's casket were unlocked to choose.   20
Ah, what a world of love was at her feet!
So Hermes thought, and a celestial heat
Burnt from his wingèd heels to either ear,
That from a whiteness, as the lily clear,
Blushed into roses 'mid his golden hair,   25
Fallen in jealous curls about his shoulders bare.

From vale to vale, from wood to wood, he flew,
Breathing upon the flowers his passion new,
And wound with many a river to its head
To find where this sweet nymph prepared her secret bed.   30
In vain; the sweet nymph might nowhere be found,
And so he rested, on the lonely ground,
Pensive, and full of painful jealousies
Of the Wood-Gods, and even the very trees.
There as he stood, he heard a mournful voice,   35
Such as, once heard, in gentle heart destroys
All pain but pity; thus the lone voice spake:
'When from this wreathèd tomb shall I awake!
When move in a sweet body fit for life,
And love, and pleasure, and the ruddy strife   40
Of hearts and lips! Ah, miserable me!'

[154]*Crete*: the largest of the Greek islands (believed to be the place where Jupiter was educated in a cave).

[155]*Tritons*: in classical mythology, sea-gods (part man and part fish), named after the god Triton, son and ocean messenger of Poseidon, the primary god of the sea.

The God, dove-footed, glided silently
Round bush and tree, soft-brushing, in his speed,
The taller grasses and full-flowering weed,
Until he found a palpitating snake,   45
Bright, and cirque-couchant[156] in a dusky brake.[157]

   She was a gordian[158] shape of dazzling hue,
Vermilion-spotted,[159] golden, green, and blue;
Striped like a zebra, freckled like a pard,[160]
Eyed like a peacock, and all crimson barred;   50
And full of silver moons, that, as she breathed,
Dissolved, or brighter shone, or interwreathed
Their lustres with the gloomier tapestries—
So rainbow-sided, touched with miseries,
She seemed, at once, some penanced lady elf,[161]   55
Some demon's mistress, or the demon's self.
Upon her crest she wore a wannish fire
Sprinkled with stars, like Ariadne's tiar;[162]
Her head was serpent, but ah, bitter-sweet!
She had a woman's mouth with all its pearls complete: 60
And for her eyes—what could such eyes do there
But weep, and weep, that they were born so fair,
As Proserpine still weeps for her Sicilian air?[163]
Her throat was serpent, but the words she spake
Came, as through bubbling honey, for Love's sake,   65

---

[156] *cirque-couchant*: coiled up (in a circle).

[157] *brake*: thicket, area overgrown densely with briars.

[158] *gordian*: knotted. In classical legend, the Gordian Knot was an extraordinary puzzle that Alexander the Great solved by simply cutting it.

[159] *Vermilion-spotted*: spotted with red.

[160] *pard*: leopard.

[161] *penanced . . . elf*: i.e., an elf or fairy transformed into a snake as punishment.

[162] *Ariadne's tiar*: In classical mythology, Ariadne was the daughter of King Minos of Crete and lover of the hero Theseus. She was deserted by him and taken as a bride by the god Bacchus, who gave her a crown of stars (commemorated in the heavens as the constellation Corona).

[163] *Proserpine . . . air*: In classical mythology, Proserpine (or Persephone), daughter of Demeter, goddess of the harvest, was carried off forcibly from her Sicilian home by Hades, god of the dead.

And thus—while Hermes on his pinions lay,
Like a stooped falcon ere he takes his prey—

'Fair Hermes, crowned with feathers, fluttering light,
I had a splendid dream of thee last night:
I saw thee sitting, on a throne of gold,   70
Among the Gods, upon Olympus old,
The only sad one; for thou didst not hear
The soft, lute-fingered Muses chanting clear,
Nor even Apollo when he sang alone,
Deaf to his throbbing throat's long, long melodious moan.   75
I dreamt I saw thee, robed in purple flakes,
Break amorous through the clouds, as morning breaks,
And, swiftly as a bright Phoebean dart,[164]
Strike for the Cretan isle; and here thou art!
Too gentle Hermes, hast thou found the maid?'   80
Whereat the star of Lethe[165] not delayed
His rosy eloquence, and thus inquired:
'Thou smooth-lipped serpent, surely high inspired!
Thou beauteous wreath, with melancholy eyes,
Possess whatever bliss thou canst devise,   85
Telling me only where my nymph is fled—
Where she doth breathe!' 'Bright planet, thou hast said,'
Returned the snake, 'but seal with oaths, fair God!'
'I swear,' said Hermes, 'by my serpent rod,[166]
And by thine eyes, and by thy starry crown!'   90
Light flew his earnest words, among the blossoms blown.
Then thus again the brilliance feminine:
'Too frail of heart! for this lost nymph of thine,
Free as the air, invisibly, she strays
About these thornless wilds; her pleasant days   95

[164] *Phoebean dart*: i.e., ray of sunshine (referencing Phoebus Apollo, classical god of the sun).

[165] *star of Lethe*: Lethe is the river of the dead, and Hermes, "the star of Lethe", is responsible for escorting dead souls to the afterlife, across Lethe.

[166] *serpent rod*: In classical mythology, Hermes carried the caduceus, a staff entwined by two serpents.

She tastes unseen; unseen her nimble feet
Leave traces in the grass and flowers sweet;
From weary tendrils, and bowed branches green,
She plucks the fruit unseen, she bathes unseen;
And by my power is her beauty veiled   100
To keep it unaffronted, unassailed
By the love-glances of unlovely eyes
Of Satyrs, Fauns, and bleared Silenus'[167] sighs.
Pale grew her immortality, for woe
Of all these lovers, and she grievèd so   105
I took compassion on her, bade her steep
Her hair in weïrd syrops, that would keep
Her loveliness invisible, yet free
To wander as she loves, in liberty.
Thou shalt behold her, Hermes, thou alone,   110
If thou wilt, as thou swearest, grant my boon!'
Then, once again, the charmèd God began
An oath, and through the serpent's ears it ran
Warm, tremulous, devout, psalterian.[168]
Ravished, she lifted her Circean[169] head,   115
Blushed a live damask, and swift-lisping said,
'I was a woman, let me have once more
A woman's shape, and charming as before.
I love a youth of Corinth—O the bliss!
Give me my woman's form, and place me where he is.   120
Stoop, Hermes, let me breathe upon thy brow,
And thou shalt see thy sweet nymph even now.'
The God on half-shut feathers sank serene,
She breathed upon his eyes, and swift was seen
Of both the guarded nymph near-smiling on the green. 125
It was no dream; or say a dream it was,
Real are the dreams of Gods, and smoothly pass

---

[167] *Silenus*': In classical mythology, Silenus was a fat, drunken companion and tutor of the god Dionysus.

[168] *psalterian*: like the music of a psaltery (a stringed instrument, like a harp).

[169] *Circean*: (1) powerful like the classical mythological witch Circe; (2) transformed like one of Circe's victims.

Their pleasures in a long immortal dream.
One warm, flushed moment, hovering, it might seem
Dashed by the wood-nymph's beauty, so he burned;   130
Then, lighting on the printless verdure, turned
To the swooned serpent, and with languid arm,
Delicate, put to proof the lithe Caducean charm.
So done, upon the nymph his eyes he bent
Full of adoring tears and blandishment,   135
And towards her stepped: she, like a moon in wane,
Faded before him, cowered, nor could restrain
Her fearful sobs, self-folding like a flower
That faints into itself at evening hour:
But the God fostering her chillèd hand,   140
She felt the warmth, her eyelids opened bland,
And, like new flowers at morning song of bees,
Bloomed, and gave up her honey to the lees.
Into the green-recessèd woods they flew;
Nor grew they pale, as mortal lovers do.   145

   Left to herself, the serpent now began
To change; her elfin blood in madness ran,
Her mouth foamed, and the grass, therewith besprent,[170]
Withered at dew so sweet and virulent;
Her eyes in torture fixed, and anguish drear,   150
Hot, glazed, and wide, with lid-lashes all sear,
Flashed phosphor and sharp sparks, without one cooling
   tear.
The colours all inflamed throughout her train,
She writhed about, convulsed with scarlet pain:
A deep volcanian yellow took the place   155
Of all her milder-moonèd body's grace;
And, as the lava ravishes the mead,[171]
Spoilt all her silver mail, and golden brede;[172]

---

[170] *besprent*: sprinkled over.
[171] *mead*: meadow.
[172] *brede*: a braided or woven piece of embroidery.

Made gloom of all her frecklings, streaks and bars,
Eclipsed her crescents, and licked up her stars.   160
So that, in moments few, she was undressed
Of all her sapphires, greens, and amethyst,
And rubious-argent;[173] of all these bereft,
Nothing but pain and ugliness were left.
Still shone her crown; that vanished, also she   165
Melted and disappeared as suddenly;
And in the air, her new voice luting soft,
Cried, 'Lycius! gentle Lycius!'—Borne aloft
With the bright mists about the mountains hoar
These words dissolved: Crete's forests heard no more.   170

   Whither fled Lamia, now a lady bright,
A full-born beauty new and exquisite?
She fled into that valley they pass o'er
Who go to Corinth from Cenchreas'[174] shore;
And rested at the foot of those wild hills,   175
The rugged founts of the Peræan[175] rills,[176]
And of that other ridge whose barren back
Stretches, with all its mist and cloudy rack,
South-westward to Cleone.[177] There she stood
About a young bird's flutter from a wood,   180
Fair, on a sloping green of mossy tread,
By a clear pool, wherein she passionèd
To see herself escaped from so sore ills,
While her robes flaunted with the daffodils.

   Ah, happy Lycius!—for she was a maid   185
More beautiful than ever twisted braid,
Or sighed, or blushed, or on spring-flowered lea

---

[173] *rubious-argent*: i.e., reddish-silver.
[174] *Corinth . . . Cenchreas*': Corinth is a port on the Saronic coast, and
Cenchreae is a seaport on the south side of the Isthmus of Corinth.
[175] *Peræan*: a mountainous region northwest of Corinth.
[176] *rills*: very small brooks.
[177] *Cleone*: village south of Corinth.

Spread a green kirtle[178] to the minstrelsy:[179]
A virgin purest lipped, yet in the lore
Of love deep learnèd to the red heart's core;   190
Not one hour old, yet of sciential brain
To unperplex bliss from its neighbour pain,
Define their pettish limits, and estrange
Their points of contact, and swift counterchange;
Intrigue with the specious chaos, and dispart   195
Its most ambiguous atoms with sure art;
As though in Cupid's college she had spent
Sweet days a lovely graduate, still unshent,[180]
And kept his rosy terms in idle languishment.

 Why this fair creature chose so faerily   200
By the wayside to linger, we shall see;
But first 'tis fit to tell how she could muse
And dream, when in the serpent prison-house,
Of all she list, strange or magnificent:
How, ever, where she willed, her spirit went;   205
Whether to faint Elysium,[181] or where
Down through tress-lifting waves the Nereids[182] fair
Wind into Thetis'[183] bower by many a pearly stair;
Or where God Bacchus[184] drains his cups divine,
Stretched out, at ease, beneath a glutinous[185] pine;   210
Or where in Pluto's gardens palatine[186]
Mulciber's[187] columns gleam in far piazzian line.

---

[178] *kirtle*: long, tunic-like gown.

[179] *minstrelsy*: music of medieval minstrels.

[180] *unshent*: i.e., still a maiden.

[181] *Elysium*: in classical mythology, ancient conception of the afterlife (for virtuous dead).

[182] *Nereids*: sea nymphs.

[183] *Thetis*: see footnote 81, page 219.

[184] *Bacchus*: in classical mythology, god of wine.

[185] *glutinous*: glue-like, gummy (i.e., sappy).

[186] *Pluto's . . . palatine*: In classical mythology, Pluto is the god of the underworld.

[187] *Mulciber's*: Mulciber is an alternative name associated with the classical blacksmith god Vulcan but is also the name given by John Milton to the architect of the demon city of Pandaemonium in *Paradise Lost*.

And sometimes into cities she would send
Her dream, with feast and rioting to blend;
And once, while among mortals dreaming thus, 215
She saw the young Corinthian Lycius
Charioting foremost in the envious race,
Like a young Jove with calm uneager face,
And fell into a swooning love of him.
Now on the moth-time of that evening dim 220
He would return that way, as well she knew,
To Corinth from the shore; for freshly blew
The eastern soft wind, and his galley now
Grated the quaystones with her brazen prow
In port Cenchreas, from Egina isle[188] 225
Fresh anchored; whither he had been awhile
To sacrifice to Jove, whose temple there
Waits with high marble doors for blood and incense rare.
Jove heard his vows, and bettered his desire;
For by some freakful chance he made retire 230
From his companions, and set forth to walk,
Perhaps grown wearied of their Corinth talk:[189]
Over the solitary hills he fared,
Thoughtless at first, but ere eve's star appeared
His fantasy was lost, where reason fades, 235
In the calmed twilight of Platonic shades.
Lamia beheld him coming, near, more near—
Close to her passing, in indifference drear,
His silent sandals swept the mossy green;
So neighboured to him, and yet so unseen 240
She stood: he passed, shut up in mysteries,
His mind wrapped like his mantle, while her eyes
Followed his steps, and her neck regal white
Turned—syllabling thus, 'Ah, Lycius bright,
And will you leave me on the hills alone? 245
Lycius, look back! and be some pity shown.'

[188] *Egina isle*: i.e., Aegina, one of the Saronic Islands of Greece.
[189] *Corinth talk*: i.e., lascivious conversation (drawing on Corinth's reputation as a center of immorality, contrasted in a few lines with "Platonic", i.e., nonerotic).

He did—not with cold wonder fearingly,
But Orpheus-like at an Eurydice[190]—
For so delicious were the words she sung,
It seemed he had loved them a whole summer long.   250
And soon his eyes had drunk her beauty up,
Leaving no drop in the bewildering cup,
And still the cup was full—while he, afraid
Lest she should vanish ere his lip had paid
Due adoration, thus began to adore   255
(Her soft look growing coy, she saw his chain so sure):
'Leave thee alone! Look back! Ah, Goddess, see
Whether my eyes can ever turn from thee!
For pity do not this sad heart belie—
Even as thou vanisheth so I shall die.   260
Stay! though a Naiad of the rivers, stay!
To thy far wishes will thy streams obey:
Stay! though the greenest woods be thy domain,
Alone they can drink up the morning rain:
Though a descended Pleiad,[191] will not one   265
Of thine harmonious sisters keep in tune
Thy spheres, and as thy silver proxy shine?
So sweetly to these ravished ears of mine
Came thy sweet greeting, that if thou shouldst fade
Thy memory will waste me to a shade—   270
For pity do not melt!'—'If I should stay,'
Said Lamia, 'here, upon this floor of clay,
And pain my steps upon these flowers too rough,
What canst thou say or do of charm enough
To dull the nice remembrance of my home?   275
Thou canst not ask me with thee here to roam

---

[190] *Orpheus-like ... Euridice*: In classical mythology, the musician Orpheus journeyed to the underworld to beg for the life of his wife, Euridice, and with his music persuaded the god of the underworld to let her return to life on condition that she follow him forth without his looking back—which he tragically was unable to manage.

[191] *Pleiad*: in classical mythology, one of the Pleiades, daughters of Atlas nymphs transformed after death into seven stars.

Over these hills and vales, where no joy is—
Empty of immortality and bliss!
Thou art a scholar, Lycius, and must know
That finer spirits cannot breathe below   280
In human climes, and live. Alas! poor youth,
What taste of purer air hast thou to soothe
My essence? What serener palaces,
Where I may all my many senses please,
And by mysterious sleights[192] a hundred thirsts appease?   285
It cannot be—Adieu!' So said, she rose
Tip-toe with white arms spread. He, sick to lose
The amorous promise of her lone complain,
Swooned, murmuring of love, and pale with pain.
The cruel lady, without any show   290
Of sorrow for her tender favourite's woe,
But rather, if her eyes could brighter be,
With brighter eyes and slow amenity,
Put her new lips to his, and gave afresh
The life she had so tangled in her mesh;   295
And as he from one trance was wakening
Into another, she began to sing,
Happy in beauty, life, and love, and every thing,
A song of love, too sweet for earthly lyres,
While, like held breath, the stars drew in their panting
    fires.   300
And then she whispered in such trembling tone,
As those who, safe together met alone
For the first time through many anguished days,
Use other speech than looks; bidding him raise
His drooping head, and clear his soul of doubt,   305
For that she was a woman, and without
Any more subtle fluid in her veins
Than throbbing blood, and that the self-same pains
Inhabited her frail-strung heart as his.
And next she wondered how his eyes could miss   310

[192] *sleights*: clever or skillful tricks or deception.

Her face so long in Corinth, where, she said,
She dwelt but half retired, and there had led
Days happy as the gold coin could invent
Without the aid of love; yet in content
Till she saw him, as once she passed him by,   315
Where 'gainst a column he leant thoughtfully
At Venus' temple porch, 'mid baskets heaped
Of amorous herbs and flowers, newly reaped
Late on that eve, as 'twas the night before
The Adonian feast;[193] whereof she saw no more,   320
But wept alone those days, for why should she adore?
Lycius from death awoke into amaze,
To see her still, and singing so sweet lays;
Then from amaze into delight he fell
To hear her whisper woman's lore so well;   325
And every word she spake enticed him on
To unperplexed delight and pleasure known.
Let the mad poets say whate'er they please
Of the sweets of Faeries, Peris,[194] Goddesses,
There is not such a treat among them all,   330
Haunters of cavern, lake, and waterfall,
As a real woman, lineal indeed
From Pyrrha's pebbles[195] or old Adam's seed.
Thus gentle Lamia judged, and judged aright,
That Lycius could not love in half a fright,   335
So threw the goddess off, and won his heart
More pleasantly by playing woman's part,
With no more awe than what her beauty gave,
That, while it smote, still guaranteed to save.

---

[193] *Adonian feast*: feast for Adonis (in classical mythology, the beloved of Venus and an archetype of ideal male beauty).

[194] *Peris*: Persian winged female spirit.

[195] *Pyrrha's pebbles*: In classical mythology, Pyrrha was the wife of the virtuous man Deucalion (classical counterpart to Noah), who with him was spared from death in a mighty flood. After the flood, they repopulated the earth by throwing pebbles over their shoulders: Deucalion's were transformed into men, and Pyrrha's were transformed into women.

Lycius to all made eloquent reply,   340
Marrying to every word a twinborn sigh;
And last, pointing to Corinth, asked her sweet,
If 'twas too far that night for her soft feet.
The way was short, for Lamia's eagerness
Made, by a spell, the triple league decrease   345
To a few paces; not at all surmised
By blinded Lycius, so in her comprised.
They passed the city gates, he knew not how,
So noiseless, and he never thought to know.

   As men talk in a dream, so Corinth all,   350
Throughout her palaces imperial,
And all her populous streets and temples lewd,[196]
Muttered, like tempest in the distance brewed,
To the wide-spreaded night above her towers.
Men, women, rich and poor, in the cool hours,   355
Shuffled their sandals o'er the pavement white,
Companioned or alone; while many a light
Flared, here and there, from wealthy festivals,
And threw their moving shadows on the walls,
Or found them clustered in the corniced shade   360
Of some arched temple door, or dusky colonnade.

   Muffling his face, of greeting friends in fear,
Her fingers he pressed hard, as one came near
With curled grey beard, sharp eyes, and smooth bald
   crown,
Slow-stepped, and robed in philosophic gown: 365
Lycius shrank closer, as they met and passed,
Into his mantle, adding wings to haste,
While hurried Lamia trembled: 'Ah,' said he,
'Why do you shudder, love, so ruefully?
Why does your tender palm dissolve in dew?'—   370

---

[196] *lewd*: (1) lay (not clerical); (2) lascivious (Corinth was notorious for immoral activity, particularly temple prostitution).

'I'm wearied,' said fair Lamia, 'tell me who
Is that old man? I cannot bring to mind
His features—Lycius! wherefore did you blind
Yourself from his quick eyes?' Lycius replied,
''Tis Apollonius sage,[197] my trusty guide   375
And good instructor; but tonight he seems
The ghost of folly haunting my sweet dreams.'

    While yet he spake they had arrived before
A pillared porch, with lofty portal door,
Where hung a silver lamp, whose phosphor glow   380
Reflected in the slabbèd steps below,
Mild as a star in water; for so new,
And so unsullied was the marble hue,
So through the crystal polish, liquid fine,
Ran the dark veins, that none but feet divine   385
Could e'er have touched there. Sounds Aeolian[198]
Breathed from the hinges, as the ample span
Of the wide doors disclosed a place unknown
Some time to any, but those two alone,
And a few Persian mutes, who that same year   390
Were seen about the markets: none knew where
They could inhabit; the most curious
Were foiled, who watched to trace them to their house.
And but the flitter-wingèd verse must tell,
For truth's sake, what woe afterwards befell,   395
'Twould humour many a heart to leave them thus,
Shut from the busy world, of more incredulous.

PART II

Love in a hut, with water and a crust,
Is—Love, forgive us!—cinders, ashes, dust;
Love in a palace is perhaps at last
More grievous torment than a hermit's fast.

---

[197] *Apollonius sage*: Apollonius of Tyana (c. first century), Greek philosopher.
[198] *Sounds Aeolian*: The Aeolian harp is played upon by the wind.

That is a doubtful tale from faery land,   5
Hard for the non-elect to understand.
Had Lycius lived to hand his story down,
He might have given the moral a fresh frown,
Or clenched it quite: but too short was their bliss
To breed distrust and hate, that make the soft voice hiss.   10
Besides, there, nightly, with terrific glare,
Love, jealous grown of so complete a pair,
Hovered and buzzed his wings, with fearful roar,
Above the lintel of their chamber door,
And down the passage cast a glow upon the floor.   15

    For all this came a ruin: side by side
They were enthronèd, in the eventide,
Upon a couch, near to a curtaining
Whose airy texture, from a golden string,
Floated into the room, and let appear   20
Unveiled the summer heaven, blue and clear,
Betwixt two marble shafts. There they reposed,
Where use had made it sweet, with eyelids closed,
Saving a tithe[199] which love still open kept,
That they might see each other while they almost slept;   25
When from the slope side of a suburb hill,
Deafening the swallow's twitter, came a thrill
Of trumpets—Lycius started—the sounds fled,
But left a thought, a buzzing in his head.
For the first time, since first he harboured in   30
That purple-linèd palace of sweet sin,
His spirit passed beyond its golden bourne
Into the noisy world almost forsworn.
The lady, ever watchful, penetrant,
Saw this with pain, so arguing a want   35
Of something more, more than her empery[200]
Of joys; and she began to moan and sigh

[199] *tithe*: 10 percent of an income.
[200] *empery*: empire, kingdom.

Because he mused beyond her, knowing well
That but a moment's thought is passion's passing-bell.
'Why do you sigh, fair creature?' whispered he: 40
'Why do you think?' returned she tenderly,
'You have deserted me—where am I now?
Not in your heart while care weighs on your brow:
No, no, you have dismissed me; and I go
From your breast houseless—ay, it must be so.'   45
He answered, bending to her open eyes,
Where he was mirrored small in paradise,
'My silver planet, both of eve and morn!
Why will you plead yourself so sad forlorn,
While I am striving how to fill my heart   50
With deeper crimson, and a double smart?
How to entangle, trammel up[201] and snare
Your soul in mine, and labyrinth[202] you there
Like the hid scent in an unbudded rose?
Ay, a sweet kiss—you see your mighty woes.   55
My thoughts! shall I unveil them? Listen then!
What mortal hath a prize, that other men
May be confounded and abashed withal,
But lets it sometimes pace abroad majestical,
And triumph, as in thee I should rejoice   60
Amid the hoarse alarm of Corinth's voice.
Let my foes choke, and my friends shout afar,
While through the throngèd streets your bridal car
Wheels round its dazzling spokes.'—The lady's cheek
Trembled; she nothing said, but, pale and meek,   65
Arose and knelt before him, wept a rain
Of sorrows at his words; at last with pain
Beseeching him, the while his hand she wrung,
To change his purpose. He thereat was stung,
Perverse, with stronger fancy to reclaim   70

[201] *trammel up*: enmesh, confine.
[202] *labyrinth*: in classical mythology, the elaborate maze constructed by the artisan Daedalus.

Her wild and timid nature to his aim:
Besides, for all his love, in self-despite,
Against his better self, he took delight
Luxurious in her sorrows, soft and new.
His passion, cruel grown, took on a hue 75
Fierce and sanguineous as 'twas possible
In one whose brow had no dark veins to swell.
Fine was the mitigated fury, like
Apollo's presence when in act to strike
The serpent—Ha, the serpent![203] Certes,[204] she 80
Was none. She burnt, she loved the tyranny,
And, all subdued, consented to the hour
When to the bridal he should lead his paramour.
Whispering in midnight silence, said the youth,
'Sure some sweet name thou hast, though, by my
  truth, 85
I have not asked it, ever thinking thee
Not mortal, but of heavenly progeny,
As still I do. Hast any mortal name,
Fit appellation for this dazzling frame?
Or friends or kinsfolk on the citied earth, 90
To share our marriage feast and nuptial mirth?'
'I have no friends,' said Lamia, 'no, not one;
My presence in wide Corinth hardly known:
My parents' bones are in their dusty urns
Sepulchred, where no kindled incense burns, 95
Seeing all their luckless race are dead, save me,
And I neglect the holy rite for thee.
Even as you list invite your many guests;
But if, as now it seems, your vision rests
With any pleasure on me, do not bid 100
Old Apollonius—from him keep me hid.'
Lycius, perplexed at words so blind and blank,

---

[203] *Apollo's . . . serpent*: In classical mythology, the archer god Apollo killed the
serpent Python.
[204] *Certes*: certainly.

Made close inquiry; from whose touch she shrank,
Feigning a sleep; and he to the dull shade
Of deep sleep in a moment was betrayed.   105

    It was the custom then to bring away
The bride from home at blushing shut of day,
Veiled, in a chariot, heralded along
By strewn flowers, torches, and a marriage song,
With other pageants: but this fair unknown   110
Had not a friend. So being left alone,
(Lycius was gone to summon all his kin)
And knowing surely she could never win
His foolish heart from its mad pompousness,
She set herself, high-thoughted, how to dress   115
The misery in fit magnificence.
She did so, but 'tis doubtful how and whence
Came, and who were her subtle servitors.
About the halls, and to and from the doors,
There was a noise of wings, till in short space   120
The glowing banquet-room shone with wide-archèd
    grace.
A haunting music, sole perhaps and lone
Supportress of the faery-roof, made moan
Throughout, as fearful the whole charm might fade.
Fresh carvèd cedar, mimicking a glade   125
Of palm and plantain, met from either side,
High in the midst, in honour of the bride;
Two palms and then two plantains, and so on,
From either side their stems branched one to one
All down the aislèd place; and beneath all   130
There ran a stream of lamps straight on from wall
    to wall.
So canopied, lay an untasted feast
Teeming with odours. Lamia, regal dressed,
Silently paced about, and as she went,
In pale contented sort of discontent,   135
Missioned her viewless servants to enrich

The fretted splendour of each nook and niche.
Between the tree-stems, marbled plain at first,
Came jasper panels; then anon, there burst
Forth creeping imagery of slighter trees, 140
And with the larger wove in small intricacies.
Approving all, she faded at self-will,
And shut the chamber up, close, hushed and still,
Complete and ready for the revels rude,
When dreadful guests would come to spoil her solitude. 145

The day appeared, and all the gossip rout.
O senseless Lycius! Madman! wherefore flout
The silent-blessing fate, warm cloistered hours,
And show to common eyes these secret bowers?
The herd approached; each guest, with busy brain, 150
Arriving at the portal, gazed amain,
And entered marvelling—for they knew the street,
Remembered it from childhood all complete
Without a gap, yet ne'er before had seen
That royal porch, that high-built fair demesne.[205] 155
So in they hurried all, mazed, curious and keen—
Save one, who looked thereon with eye severe,
And with calm-planted steps walked in austere.
'Twas Apollonius: something too he laughed,
As though some knotty problem, that had daffed 160
His patient thought, had now begun to thaw,
And solve and melt—'twas just as he foresaw.

He met within the murmurous vestibule
His young disciple. ''Tis no common rule,
Lycius,' said he, 'for uninvited guest 165
To force himself upon you, and infest
With an unbidden presence the bright throng
Of younger friends; yet must I do this wrong,
And you forgive me.' Lycius blushed, and led

[205] *demesne*: land, domain.

The old man through the inner doors broad-spread;   170
With reconciling words and courteous mien
Turning into sweet milk the sophist's[206] spleen.

    Of wealthy lustre was the banquet-room,
Filled with pervading brilliance and perfume:
Before each lucid panel fuming stood   175
A censer[207] fed with myrrh and spicèd wood,
Each by a sacred tripod held aloft,
Whose slender feet wide-swerved upon the soft
Wool-woofèd carpets; fifty wreaths of smoke
From fifty censers their light voyage took   180
To the high roof, still mimicked as they rose
Along the mirrored walls by twin-clouds odorous.
Twelve spherèd tables, by silk seats ensphered,
High as the level of a man's breast reared
On libbard's[208] paws, upheld the heavy gold   185
Of cups and goblets, and the store thrice told
Of Ceres' horn,[209] and, in huge vessels, wine
Came from the gloomy tun[210] with merry shine.
Thus loaded with a feast the tables stood,
Each shrining in the midst the image of a God.   190

    When in an antechamber every guest
Had felt the cold full sponge to pleasure pressed,
By ministering slaves, upon his hands and feet,
And fragrant oils with ceremony meet
Poured on his hair, they all moved to the feast   195

---

[206] *sophist's*: The sophists were classical teachers specializing in the tools of philosophy and rhetoric (often portrayed as linguistically and morally slippery characters).

[207] *censer*: See footnote 96, page 395.

[208] *libbard's*: "Libbard" is an archaic term for a leopard.

[209] *Ceres' horn*: i.e., cornucopia (in classical mythology, symbol of plenty, associated with Ceres, goddess of the harvest and of grain).

[210] *tun*: large cask or barrel.

In white robes, and themselves in order placed
Around the silken couches, wondering
Whence all this mighty cost and blaze of wealth could
    spring.

  Soft went the music the soft air along,
While fluent Greek a vowelled undersong   200
Kept up among the guests, discoursing low
At first, for scarcely was the wine at flow;
But when the happy vintage touched their brains,
Louder they talk, and louder come the strains
Of powerful instruments. The gorgeous dyes,   205
The space, the splendour of the draperies,
The roof of awful richness, nectarous cheer,
Beautiful slaves, and Lamia's self, appear,
Now, when the wine has done its rosy deed,
And every soul from human trammels freed,   210
No more so strange; for merry wine, sweet wine,
Will make Elysian shades[211] not too fair, too divine.

  Soon was God Bacchus at meridian height;
Flushed were their cheeks, and bright eyes double bright:
Garlands of every green, and every scent   215
From vales deflowered, or forest-trees branch rent,
In baskets of bright osiered gold[212] were brought
High as the handles heaped, to suit the thought
Of every guest—that each, as he did please,
Might fancy-fit his brows, silk-pillowed at his ease.   220

  What wreath for Lamia? What for Lycius?
What for the sage, old Apollonius?
Upon her aching forehead be there hung

[211] *Elysian shades*: i.e., the dead.
[212] *baskets . . . gold*: i.e., gold made to look like baskets of braided osier (or willow branches).

The leaves of willow[213] and of adder's tongue;[214]
And for the youth, quick, let us strip for him   225
The thyrsus,[215] that his watching eyes may swim
Into forgetfulness; and, for the sage,
Let spear-grass and the spiteful thistle[216] wage
War on his temples. Do not all charms fly
At the mere touch of cold philosophy?   230
There was an awful rainbow once in heaven:
We know her woof, her texture; she is given
In the dull catalogue of common things.
Philosophy will clip an Angel's wings,
Conquer all mysteries by rule and line,   235
Empty the haunted air, and gnoméd mine—
Unweave a rainbow, as it erewhile made
The tender-personed Lamia melt into a shade.

By her glad Lycius sitting, in chief place,
Scarce saw in all the room another face,   240
Till, checking his love trance, a cup he took
Full brimmed, and opposite sent forth a look
'Cross the broad table, to beseech a glance
From his old teacher's wrinkled countenance,
And pledge him. The bald-head philosopher   245
Had fixed his eye, without a twinkle or stir
Full on the alarméd beauty of the bride,
Brow-beating her fair form, and troubling her sweet pride.
Lycius then pressed her hand, with devout touch,
As pale it lay upon the rosy couch: 250
'Twas icy, and the cold ran through his veins;
Then sudden it grew hot, and all the pains

---

[213] *willow*: symbolic of deserted lovers.

[214] *adder's tongue*: a form of fern or dogtooth violet (the leaves of which resemble the forked tongue of an adder).

[215] *thyrsus*: in classical mythology, the staff covered with vines and leaves and topped with a pine cone commonly carried by the god Dionysus (or Bacchus) and his followers.

[216] *thistle*: commonly growing prickly plant.

Of an unnatural heat shot to his heart.
'Lamia, what means this? Wherefore dost thou start?
Know'st thou that man?' Poor Lamia answered not.   255
He gazed into her eyes, and not a jot
Owned they the lovelorn piteous appeal;
More, more he gazed; his human senses reel;
Some hungry spell that loveliness absorbs;
There was no recognition in those orbs.   260
'Lamia!' he cried—and no soft-toned reply.
The many heard, and the loud revelry
Grew hush; the stately music no more breathes;
The myrtle sickened in a thousand wreaths.
By faint degrees, voice, lute, and pleasure ceased;   265
A deadly silence step by step increased,
Until it seemed a horrid presence there,
And not a man but felt the terror in his hair.
'Lamia!' he shrieked; and nothing but the shriek
With its sad echo did the silence break.   270
'Begone, foul dream!' he cried, gazing again
In the bride's face, where now no azure vein
Wandered on fair-spaced temples; no soft bloom
Misted the cheek; no passion to illume
The deep-recessèd vision. All was blight;   275
Lamia, no longer fair, there sat a deadly white.
'Shut, shut those juggling eyes, thou ruthless man!
Turn them aside, wretch! or the righteous ban
Of all the Gods, whose dreadful images
Here represent their shadowy presences,   280
May pierce them on the sudden with the thorn
Of painful blindness; leaving thee forlorn,
In trembling dotage to the feeblest fright
Of conscience, for their long offended might,
For all thine impious proud-heart sophistries,   285
Unlawful magic, and enticing lies.
Corinthians! look upon that grey-beard wretch!
Mark how, possessed, his lashless eyelids stretch
Around his demon eyes! Corinthians, see!

My sweet bride withers at their potency.'   290
'Fool!' said the sophist, in an undertone
Gruff with contempt; which a death-nighing moan
From Lycius answered, as heart-struck and lost,
He sank supine beside the aching ghost.
'Fool! Fool!' repeated he, while his eyes still   295
Relented not, nor moved; 'From every ill
Of life have I preserved thee to this day,
And shall I see thee made a serpent's prey?'
Then Lamia breathed death-breath; the sophist's eye,
Like a sharp spear, went through her utterly,   300
Keen, cruel, perceant,[217] stinging: she, as well
As her weak hand could any meaning tell,
Motioned him to be silent; vainly so,
He looked and looked again a level—*No!*
'A Serpent!' echoed he; no sooner said,   305
Than with a frightful scream she vanishèd:
And Lycius' arms were empty of delight,
As were his limbs of life, from that same night.
On the high couch he lay!—his friends came round—
Supported him—no pulse, or breath they found,   310
And, in its marriage robe, the heavy body wound.

Odes

The first four odes were written April–May 1819; "To Autumn", September 1819.

This sequence of poems is arguably Keats' greatest—and certainly his completest—achievement, particularly when read as a unified tapestry. The extent to which the language, thought, and feeling in the odes are complementary was already evident to some Keats specialists over one hundred years ago.[218] Helen Vendler's work brought this appreciation to a new level, and

---

[217] *perceant*: piercing.
[218] See, for example, de Sélincourt, *Poems of John Keats*, p. ix.

her analyses of the odes in their individual, as well as complete, form are a matchless starting point for understanding their content and discourse. It is clear that Keats wrote every ode with reference to its predecessors, building a dialogue that can be fully understood only in its contrapuntal complexity when they are read as a whole. This intertextual conversation poses "questions about the conditions for creativity, the forms art can take, the hierarchy of the fine arts (including the art of poetry), the hierarchy of genres within poetry, the relation of art to the order of nature, and the relation of art to human life and death".[219]

The "Ode on Indolence" (not included here) can be seen as seminal for the rest of the series. At its core are the poet's unwillingness to be roused from indolence by a Greek triad of Love, Ambition, and Poetry; the vacillation of his mood from self-indulgence to self-reproach; the experience of the intrusive, recurrent return of figures, thoughts, patterns.

The "Ode to Psyche" "aims, whatever its sensual metaphors ..., at a complete, exclusive, and lasting annihilation of the senses in favor of the brain. The locus of reality in the ode passes from the world of myth to the world of mind.... The implicit boast of *Psyche* is that the 'working brain' can produce a flawless virtual object, indistinguishable from the 'real' object in the mythological or historical world."[220]

In the "Ode to a Nightingale",

> Keats continues his inquiries into the nature of art, both in the mind and in the various media available to the mind....
>
> In choosing music as its artifact, the *Ode to a Nightingale* decides for beauty alone, without truth-content. The representational function of both literature and the visual arts precludes their being taken as "pure" examples of aesthetic being. Questions of ideational content and of social or moral value arise perhaps inevitably in criticism of literature, painting, sculpture,

---

[219] Helen Vendler, *The Odes of John Keats* (Cambridge, Mass.: Harvard University Press, 1985), p. 6.
[220] Ibid., p. 47.

and even dance; but such questions become very nearly unintelligible when posed with respect to instrumental music.... The interesting thing about the song of Keats's nightingale is that it is vocal without verbal content, a pure vocalise.[221]

In the "Ode on a Grecian Urn",

> abandoning nonrepresentational "natural" music as his metaphor, he took as metaphor another special case, the one (because of the Elgin marbles) most in the public eye, the case of sculpture....
>
> The *Ode on a Grecian Urn* squarely confronts the truth that art is not "natural," like leaves on a tree, but artificial. The sculptor must chisel the stone, a medium external to himself and recalcitrant. In restricting itself to one sense, the *Urn* resembles *Nightingale*, but in the *Urn* the sense is sight, not hearing.... If *Nightingale* is an experiment in thinking about art in terms of pure, "natural," nonrepresentational music prolonged in time, the *Urn* is an experiment in thinking about art in terms of pure, "artificial," representational visuality extended in space (a space whose extension, in Keats's special case, rounds on itself—the urn is a self-limiting frieze)....
>
> Keats now proposes, with respect to art as he understands it and wishes to practice it, that art is a constructive and conscious shaping of a medium, and that what is created is representational, bearing some relation to "Truth." ...
>
> The actions represented on the urn excite in the beholder an empathy like that solicited in the listener by the *melos* of the nightingale, but they, unlike the birdsong, are allowed to provoke him to early questions. The constitutive trope of the *Urn* is interrogation, that trope of the perplexed mind.[222]

The "Ode on Melancholy" introduces the

> questing activity of a newly strenuous hero, who refuses the opiates of drowsiness and indolence in favor of transcendent

[221] Ibid., pp. 77–78.
[222] Ibid., pp. 116–18.

Platonic search. The protagonist in the earlier odes had been placed in a position of inactivity in the world, and had always been defined as a poet: for the first time, in *Melancholy*, the hero fares abroad, and traverses the known and unknown perilous seas, and is defined as ambitious lover and hero rather than as poet. The wakefulness rejected in *Indolence* and bitterly experienced at the end of *Nightingale* is here pursued as a positive good—pursued at first, however, too defensively and too far.

The formal pattern of the *Ode on Melancholy* in its three-stanza published form is one of desperate action and equally desperate reaction, of thesis and antithesis, followed by a third stanza which finds a synthesis both unexpected and satisfying....

We arrive at the ode *To Autumn* with the other odes (and the interlude of *The Fall of Hyperion*) in mind. Once again Keats must find a female divinity to worship.... And now that he has written about music and the visual arts and the working brain of inner Fancy and dramatic tragedy, can he find a way of writing about his own art, poetry?... What language will he find to embody the indistinguishability of Truth and Beauty, that truth he had so far been able only to assert, not to enact?

In his autumn sonnet, *When I have fears that I may cease to be*, Keats had compared his fertile brain to a field of corn; after eighteen months of meditation on that symbol ..., Keats returned to it for his finest ode, *To Autumn*. In the sonnet, ... the act of conceiving poems is paralleled to natural fruitfulness, his books are the garners into which his grain is gathered.... In the sonnet, the implications of the symbol are not worked out: Keats nowhere confronts the fact that a high pile of books will leave a field entirely bare, the last gleanings gone, the teeming brain empty and stripped. The ode *To Autumn* continues the metaphor onward to the sacrificial base of harvest, and does not avert its eyes. It contains Keats's most reflective view of creativity and art, not least because it is a poem springing from so many anterior poems.[223]

---

[223] Ibid., pp. 157–58, 233–34.

Ode to Psyche (late April 1819)

O Goddess! hear these tuneless numbers,[224] wrung
    By sweet enforcement and remembrance dear,
And pardon that thy secrets should be sung
    Even into thine own soft-conchèd[225] ear:
Surely I dreamt to-day, or did I see   5
    The wingèd Psyche[226] with awakened eyes?
I wandered in a forest thoughtlessly,
    And, on the sudden, fainting with surprise,
Saw two fair creatures, couchèd side by side
    In deepest grass, beneath the whispering roof   10
    Of leaves and tremblèd blossoms, where there ran
        A brooklet, scarce espied:
'Mid hushed, cool-rooted flowers, fragrant-eyed,
    Blue, silver-white, and budded Tyrian,[227]
They lay calm-breathing on the bedded grass;   15
    Their arms embraced, and their pinions[228] too;
    Their lips touched not, but had not bade adieu,
As if disjoined by soft-handed slumber,
And ready still past kisses to outnumber
    At tender eye-dawn of aurorean love:[229]   20
        The wingèd boy[230] I knew;
But who wast thou, O happy, happy dove?
    His Psyche true!

O latest born and loveliest vision far
    Of all Olympus' faded hierarchy!   25

---

[224] *numbers:* poetic verses.

[225] *soft-conchèd:* like a soft shell.

[226] *Psyche:* in classical mythology, the beloved of Cupid (Greek for the "soul", often associated with the butterfly).

[227] *Tyrian:* purple (from the city of Tyre, which produced a purple dye).

[228] *pinions:* wings.

[229] *aurorean love:* i.e., first love (taken from Aurora, classical goddess of the dawn).

[230] *wingèd boy:* i.e., Cupid, son of Venus.

Fairer than Phoebe's[231] sapphire-regioned star,
   Or Vesper,[232] amorous glow-worm of the sky;
Fairer than these, though temple thou hast none,
    Nor altar heaped with flowers;
Nor virgin-choir to make delicious moan   30
    Upon the midnight hours;
No voice, no lute, no pipe, no incense sweet
   From chain-swung censer[233] teeming;
No shrine, no grove, no oracle, no heat
   Of pale-mouthed prophet dreaming.   35

O brightest! though too late for antique vows,
   Too, too late for the fond believing lyre,[234]
When holy were the haunted forest boughs,
   Holy the air, the water, and the fire;
Yet even in these days so far retired   40
   From happy pieties, thy lucent[235] fans,
   Fluttering among the faint Olympians,
I see, and sing, by my own eyes inspired.
So let me be thy choir, and make a moan
    Upon the midnight hours;   45
Thy voice, thy lute, thy pipe, thy incense sweet
   From swingèd censer teeming—
Thy shrine, thy grove, thy oracle, thy heat
   Of pale-mouthed prophet dreaming.

Yes, I will be thy priest, and build a fane[236]   50
   In some untrodden region of my mind,
Where branchèd thoughts, new grown with pleasant pain,
   Instead of pines shall murmur in the wind:

[231] *Phoebe's*: In classical mythology, Phoebe is the goddess of the moon.

[232] *Vesper*: the planet Venus as the evening star.

[233] *censer*: See footnote 96, page 395.

[234] *fond … lyre*: The lyre is a harp-like instrument, and "fond" here means "caring", but a pun is also being made on "fond" for "foolish" and "lyre" for "liar".

[235] *lucent*: translucent.

[236] *fane*: temple.

Far, far around shall those dark-clustered trees
　　Fledge[237] the wild-ridgèd mountains steep by steep;　　55
And there by zephyrs,[238] streams, and birds, and bees,
　　The moss-lain Dryads[239] shall be lulled to sleep;
And in the midst of this wide quietness
A rosy sanctuary will I dress
With the wreathed trellis of a working brain,　　　　　60
　　With buds, and bells, and stars without a name,
With all the gardener Fancy e'er could feign,[240]
　　Who breeding flowers, will never breed the same:
And there shall be for thee all soft delight
　　That shadowy thought can win,　　　　　　　　　65
A bright torch, and a casement ope at night,[241]
　　To let the warm Love in!

Ode to a Nightingale (May 1819)

I

My heart aches, and a drowsy numbness pains
　　My sense, as though of hemlock[242] I had drunk,
Or emptied some dull opiate to the drains
　　One minute past, and Lethe-wards[243] had sunk:
'Tis not through envy of thy happy lot,　　　　　　　5
　　But being too happy in thine happiness—
　　　　That thou, light-wingèd Dryad[244] of the trees,
　　　　　　In some melodious plot
Of beechen green, and shadows numberless,
　　Singest of summer in full-throated ease.　　　　　10

---

[237] *Fledge*: furnish with feathers.
[238] *zephyrs*: west winds.
[239] *Dryads*: tree nymphs.
[240] *feign*: invent, create (deceptively perhaps).
[241] *casement ... night*: According to classical mythology, Cupid could come only at night to visit his beloved Psyche.
[242] *hemlock*: poisonous plant that sometimes can be used as a strong sedative.
[243] *Lethe-wards*: Lethe is the river of the dead (of the realm of Hades), the water of which, when drunk, causes dead souls to forget their lives on earth.
[244] *Dryad*: tree nymph.

II

O, for a draught of vintage! that hath been
  Cooled a long age in the deep-delvèd earth,
Tasting of Flora and the country green,
  Dance, and Provençal song,[245] and sunburnt mirth!
O for a beaker full of the warm South,   15
  Full of the true, the blushful Hippocrene,[246]
    With beaded bubbles winking at the brim,
      And purple-stainèd mouth,
That I might drink, and leave the world unseen,
  And with thee fade away into the forest dim—   20

III

Fade far away, dissolve, and quite forget
  What thou among the leaves hast never known,
The weariness, the fever, and the fret
  Here, where men sit and hear each other groan;
Where palsy shakes a few, sad, last grey hairs,   25
  Where youth grows pale, and spectre-thin, and dies;
    Where but to think is to be full of sorrow
      And leaden-eyed despairs;
Where Beauty cannot keep her lustrous eyes,
  Or new Love pine at them beyond to-morrow.   30

IV

Away! away! for I will fly to thee,
  Not charioted by Bacchus and his pards,[247]
But on the viewless[248] wings of Poesy,
  Though the dull brain perplexes and retards.

---

[245] *Provençal song*: song from Provençe, in the south of France (probably referring particularly to the love songs of the troubadours).

[246] *Hippocrene*: in classical mythology, a fountain sacred to the Muses, the water of which would grant poetic inspiration to any who drank it.

[247] *pards*: leopards. In classical mythology, Bacchus, the god of wine, is often figured as being drawn in a chariot by leopards.

[248] *viewless*: invisible.

Already with thee! tender is the night, 35
   And haply the Queen-Moon is on her throne,
      Clustered around by all her starry Fays;[249]
         But here there is no light,
Save what from heaven is with the breezes blown
   Through verdurous glooms and winding mossy ways. 40

V

I cannot see what flowers are at my feet,
   Nor what soft incense hangs upon the boughs,
But, in embalmèd darkness, guess each sweet
   Wherewith the seasonable month endows
The grass, the thicket, and the fruit-tree wild— 45
   White hawthorn, and the pastoral eglantine;[250]
      Fast fading violets covered up in leaves;
        And mid-May's eldest child,
The coming musk-rose, full of dewy wine,
   The murmurous haunt of flies on summer eves. 50

VI

Darkling[251] I listen; and, for many a time
   I have been half in love with easeful Death,
Called him soft names in many a musèd rhyme,
   To take into the air my quiet breath;
Now more than ever seems it rich to die, 55
   To cease upon the midnight with no pain,
      While thou art pouring forth thy soul abroad
        In such an ecstasy!
Still wouldst thou sing, and I have ears in vain—
   To thy high requiem become a sod. 60

[249] *Fays*: fairies.
[250] *eglantine*: sweetbriar.
[251] *Darkling*: in the dark.

VII

Thou wast not born for death, immortal Bird!
   No hungry generations tread thee down;
The voice I hear this passing night was heard
   In ancient days by emperor and clown:
Perhaps the self-same song that found a path   65
    Through the sad heart of Ruth, when, sick for home,
      She stood in tears amid the alien corn;[252]
        The same that oft-times hath
Charmed magic casements, opening on the foam
   Of perilous seas, in faery lands forlorn.[253]   70

VIII

Forlorn! the very word is like a bell
   To toll me back from thee to my sole self!
Adieu! the fancy cannot cheat so well
   As she is famed to do, deceiving elf.
Adieu! adieu! thy plaintive anthem fades   75
   Past the near meadows, over the still stream,
    Up the hill-side; and now 'tis buried deep
      In the next valley-glades:
   Was it a vision, or a waking dream?
    Fled is that music—Do I wake or sleep?   80

[252] *self-same . . . corn*: The biblical Book of Ruth tells that Ruth and her mother-in-law were forced to leave Moab during a famine and Ruth went to work in the corn fields of her kinsman Boaz, whom she later married.

[253] *forlorn*: lost, wretched.

Ode on a Grecian Urn (1819–May?)

I

Thou still unravished bride of quietness,
    Thou foster-child of silence and slow time,
Sylvan historian,[254] who canst thus express
    A flowery tale more sweetly than our rhyme:
What leaf-fringed legend haunts about thy shape   5
    Of deities or mortals, or of both,
        In Tempe or the dales of Arcady?[255]
    What men or gods are these? What maidens loth?
What mad pursuit? What struggle to escape?
        What pipes and timbrels?[256] What wild ecstasy?   10

II

Heard melodies are sweet, but those unheard
    Are sweeter; therefore, ye soft pipes, play on;
Not to the sensual ear, but, more endeared,
    Pipe to the spirit ditties of no tone:
Fair youth, beneath the trees, thou canst not leave   15
    Thy song, nor ever can those trees be bare;
        Bold Lover, never, never canst thou kiss,
Though winning near the goal—yet, do not grieve:
    She cannot fade, though thou hast not thy bliss,
        For ever wilt thou love, and she be fair!   20

III

Ah, happy, happy boughs! that cannot shed
    Your leaves, nor ever bid the Spring adieu;
And, happy melodist, unwearièd,
    For ever piping songs for ever new;

---

[254] *Sylvan historian*: literally, a historian of the woods. Greek vases were decorated with vegetation.
  [255] *Tempe . . . Arcady*: Both Tempe (a valley in Thessaly) and Arcady (in the Peloponnesus) are considered pastoral, Edenic realms.
  [256] *timbrels*: ancient percussion instrument, like a tambourine.

More happy love! more happy, happy love! 25
 For ever warm and still to be enjoyed,
  For ever panting, and for ever young—
All breathing human passion far above,
 That leaves a heart high-sorrowful and cloyed,
  A burning forehead, and a parching tongue. 30

IV

Who are these coming to the sacrifice?
 To what green altar, O mysterious priest,
Lead'st thou that heifer lowing at the skies,
 And all her silken flanks with garlands dressed?
What little town by river or sea shore, 35
 Or mountain-built with peaceful citadel,
  Is emptied of this folk, this pious morn?
And, little town, thy streets for evermore
 Will silent be; and not a soul to tell
  Why thou art desolate, can e'er return. 40

V

O Attic shape! Fair attitude! with brede[257]
 Of marble men and maidens overwrought,
With forest branches and the trodden weed;
 Thou, silent form, dost tease us out of thought
As doth eternity: Cold Pastoral! 45
 When old age shall this generation waste,
  Thou shalt remain, in midst of other woe
Than ours, a friend to man, to whom thou say'st,
 'Beauty is truth, truth beauty,—that is all
  Ye know on earth, and all ye need to know.' 50

---

[257] *brede*: a braided or woven piece of embroidery.

Ode on Melancholy (May 1819)

I

No, no, go not to Lethe,[258] neither twist
    Wolf's-bane,[259] tight-rooted, for its poisonous wine:
Nor suffer thy pale forehead to be kissed
    By nightshade,[260] ruby grape of Proserpine;[261]
Make not your rosary of yew-berries,[262]   5
    Nor let the beetle, nor the death-moth be
        Your mournful Psyche,[263] nor the downy owl[264]
A partner in your sorrow's mysteries;
    For shade to shade will come too drowsily,
        And drown the wakeful anguish of the soul.   10

II

But when the melancholy fit shall fall
    Sudden from heaven like a weeping cloud,
That fosters the droop-headed flowers all,
    And hides the green hill in an April shroud;
Then glut thy sorrow on a morning rose,   15
    Or on the rainbow of the salt sand-wave,
        Or on the wealth of globèd peonies;

---

[258] *Lethe*: See footnote 16, page 5.

[259] *Wolf's-bane*: aconite, a poisonous yellow-flowered plant (common to European mountains).

[260] *nightshade*: a genus of herbs, shrubs, and trees that bears flowers and (sometimes) poisonous red or black berries.

[261] *Proserpine*: In classical mythology, Proserpine (or Persephone), daughter of Demeter, goddess of the harvest, was carried off forcibly from her Sicilian home by Hades, god of the dead, and sealed her fate as his wife by eating the dark berries of a pomegranate. Here the reference may be simply to the poisonous effect of nightshade, which may readily bring the eater into the underworld.

[262] *yew-berries*: poisonous fruit of the yew tree, associated with mourning and often planted in graveyards.

[263] *Psyche*: i.e., soul (often figured as a butterfly). In the first stanza, Keats is admonishing the reader against indulging morbid associations with melancholy, in this instance envisioning the innocent butterfly (the Greek symbol of the soul/psyche) as a sinister death's-head moth.

[264] *downy owl*: a bird of ill omen.

Or if thy mistress some rich anger shows,
    Emprison her soft hand, and let her rave,
        And feed deep, deep upon her peerless eyes.   20

III

She dwells with Beauty—Beauty that must die;
    And Joy, whose hand is ever at his lips
Bidding adieu; and aching Pleasure nigh,
    Turning to poison while the bee-mouth sips:
Ay, in the very temple of Delight   25
    Veiled Melancholy has her sovran shrine,
        Though seen of none save him whose strenuous tongue
    Can burst Joy's grape against his palate fine;
His soul shall taste the sadness of her might,
    And be among her cloudy trophies hung.[265]   30

To Autumn (September 1819)

I

Season of mists and mellow fruitfulness,
    Close bosom-friend of the maturing sun,
Conspiring with him how to load and bless
    With fruit the vines that round the thatch-eves run;
To bend with apples the mossed cottage-trees,   5
    And fill all fruit with ripeness to the core;
        To swell the gourd, and plump the hazel shells
    With a sweet kernel; to set budding more,
And still more, later flowers for the bees,
Until they think warm days will never cease,   10
    For Summer has o'er-brimmed their clammy[266] cells.

---

[265] *cloudy . . . hung*: In ancient temples, triumphant heroes hung their trophies
in celebration.
[266] *clammy*: soft, moist, sticky.

II

Who hath not seen thee oft amid thy store?
   Sometimes whoever seeks abroad may find
Thee sitting careless on a granary floor,
   Thy hair soft-lifted by the winnowing wind;   15
Or on a half-reaped furrow sound asleep,
   Drowsed with the fume of poppies, while thy hook[267]
      Spares the next swath and all its twinèd flowers;
And sometimes like a gleaner[268] thou dost keep
   Steady thy laden head across a brook;   20
   Or by a cyder-press, with patient look,
      Thou watchest the last oozings hours by hours.

III

Where are the songs of Spring? Ay, where are they?
   Think not of them, thou hast thy music too—
While barrèd clouds bloom the soft-dying day,   25
   And touch the stubble-plains with rosy hue:
Then in a wailful choir the small gnats mourn
   Among the river sallows,[269] borne aloft
      Or sinking as the light wind lives or dies;
And full-grown lambs loud bleat from hilly bourn;[270]   30
   Hedge-crickets sing; and now with treble soft
   The red-breast whistles from a garden-croft;
      And gathering swallows twitter in the skies.

The Fall of Hyperion: A Dream

Having abandoned *Hyperion* in April 1819, Keats began
to rework his old idea radically, changing not merely the

---

[267] *hook*: a sharp sickle-like agricultural tool.
[268] *gleaner*: worker who picks up produce left by reapers.
[269] *sallows*: willows.
[270] *hilly bourn*: hills upon the horizon.

structure but the style and import of the original. So *The Fall of Hyperion* was born. Sadly it, too, was left incomplete at his death in 1821, perhaps this time simply through ill health, though other, intrinsic, factors may have been at play. In this reinterpretation of his chosen myth, Keats found a way to set forth in a more nuanced way the development of the poetic imagination, through a scenario in which the protagonist is himself "the Poet", conversing in a vision with Moneta, a Titan goddess (the same Mnemosyne who appears in *Hyperion*, here in her Roman guise) who reveals to him the history of the fall of her race, challenges him, and mentors his initiation to the true life of a poet. Starting when he finds a natural garden in a forest where a feast of fruits is laid (the experience, open to all, of nature's delights as inspiration), he thirsts to taste a draught that sends him into the visionary world, which is by contrast inclement, stark, and where stand once-glorious ruins. There he is drawn onward by the shadowy Muse of Memory, who only after testing him reveals her face, admits him to the ancient Temple of Saturn, and eventually its shrine, and shows to him her vivid memories of the overthrow of the Titans and the coming to authority of the Olympian gods (at which point this work takes up again the thread once left in *Hyperion*). Hyperion himself assumes a crucial role only toward the end of this account, as he leads the Titans in their doomed attack upon the new gods.

In this recasting, Keats appears to have turned to Dante for inspiration, both stylistically and thematically: the language is more fluid, more colloquial than in the first epic, for instance, and his use of the vision and guiding muse are clearly in the Dantean line. The personal note struck in *The Fall*, more than in its predecessor, echoes a significant altering of focus—from the theme of change itself as a dynamic force in creation, to the experience given by such painful, creative change to the receptive mind. Moneta, goddess of memory, is strikingly imprinted with the sorrow she has undergone not merely on her own behalf but in witnessing that of others; her strange beauty is almost unbearable, yet it provokes a deep thirst to know more of her mind. To become worthy of the title "poet" and of eternal fame, the protagonist must also feel deep sympathy with those he beholds—in this case the Titanic and Olympian gods. Here we have, in poetic word and practice, Keats' theory of "Negative Capability" as an essential quality of the poet, that is to say, the ability to forget oneself entirely and allow oneself to be filled with the thoughts and feelings of others—the unpleasant as much as the pleasant, the vicious with the virtuous—without attempting to reconcile or change them, but rather then to represent them in one's work. There is an implicit belief that such revelations as are thus experienced harbor beauty in themselves that goes unnoticed by those looking only for what is aesthetic or virtuous, but also that they eventually inspire sympathetic action, as well as dreams.

Though *Hyperion* used to be considered the greater of the two fragments, *The Fall* has largely overtaken it, owing to some extent to the rise in Dante's stock and the decline in Milton's[271] among critics in sympathy with literary Modernism. According to Lionel Trilling and Harold Bloom,

> Keats actively confronts his Muse, Moneta, and compels her not only to accept him as a true poet but to modify her harsh and narrow categorizations of poets and of humanist men of action. He does this not by asserting his own identity, but by finding a truer form in the merged, higher identity of a more humanistic poethood than the world has known.... Moneta presides over a ruined shrine of all the dead faiths, and the lesson Keats searches out in her countenance is that tragedy is not enough, though he still desires to be a tragic poet. The burden of history, of the fused but broken splendor of past poetic achievements, is heroically taken on by Keats as a necessary prelude to a new level of achievement he believes he can attain. He did not live to do so, but this fragment persuades us that he was the chosen man to make the attempt.[272]

---

[271] Some critics have denied Keats' wholesale change of allegiance, pointing out that Keats studied Dante before writing the first *Hyperion* and that though *The Fall* was certainly purged of many Miltonisms, many were retained and still others introduced.

[272] Trilling and Bloom, *Oxford Anthology of English Literature*, 4:543–44.

The Fall of Hyperion: A Dream (July–September 1819)

CANTO I

Fanatics have their dreams, wherewith they weave
A paradise for a sect; the savage too
From forth the loftiest fashion of his sleep
Guesses at Heaven: pity these have not
Traced upon vellum[273] or wild Indian leaf[274]   5
The shadows of melodious utterance.
But bare of laurel they live, dream, and die;
For Poesy alone can tell her dreams,
With the fine spell of words alone can save
Imagination from the sable charm   10
And dumb enchantment. Who alive can say,
'Thou art no Poet—may'st not tell thy dreams'?
Since every man whose soul is not a clod
Hath visions, and would speak, if he had loved,
And been well nurtured in his mother tongue.   15
Whether the dream now purposed to rehearse
Be Poet's or Fanatic's will be known
When this warm scribe my hand is in the grave.

Methought I stood where trees of every clime,
Palm, myrtle, oak, and sycamore, and beech,   20
With plantain,[275] and spice-blossoms, made a screen—
In neighbourhood of fountains, by the noise
Soft-showering in mine ears, and, by the touch
Of scent, not far from roses. Turning round,
I saw an arbour with a drooping roof   25
Of trellis vines, and bells, and larger blooms,
Like floral censers, swinging light in air;
Before its wreathèd doorway, on a mound
Of moss, was spread a feast of summer fruits,

---

[273] *vellum*: high-quality parchment (traditionally made of skins).
[274] *wild . . . leaf*: handmade paper from India, probably with an imprint of leaves displayed on it.
[275] *plantain*: a tree producing a kind of banana.

Which, nearer seen, seemed refuse of a meal   30
By angel tasted, or our Mother Eve;[276]
For empty shells were scattered on the grass,
And grape-stalks but half bare, and remnants more,
Sweet-smelling, whose pure kinds I could not know.   35
Still was more plenty than the fabled horn[277]
Thrice emptied could pour forth at banqueting
For Proserpine[278] returned to her own fields,
Where the white heifers low. And appetite
More yearning than on earth I ever felt
Growing within, I ate deliciously;   40
And, after not long, thirsted, for thereby
Stood a cool vessel of transparent juice,
Sipped by the wandered bee, the which I took,
And, pledging all the mortals of the world,
And all the dead whose names are in our lips,   45
Drank. That full draught is parent of my theme.
No Asian poppy, nor elixir fine
Of the soon-fading jealous Caliphat;[279]
No poison gendered in close monkish cell,
To thin the scarlet conclave[280] of old men,   50
Could so have rapt unwilling life away.
Among the fragrant husks and berries crushed,
Upon the grass I struggled hard against
The domineering potion; but in vain—
The cloudy swoon came on, and down I sunk,   55
Like a Silenus[281] on an antique vase.

---

[276] *meal . . . Eve*: In John Milton's *Paradise Lost*, Eve prepares a meal (bk. 5, lines 303–7, 326–28).

[277] *fabled horn*: i.e., cornucopia. In classical mythology, it is a symbol of plenty, associated with Ceres, goddess of the harvest and of grain.

[278] *Proserpine*: in classical mythology, daughter of Demeter (or Ceres), goddess of the harvest, carried off forcibly by Hades, god of the dead, and allowed to return home to her mother six months out of the year.

[279] *Caliphat*: caliph, Islamic religious leader (ruling over a caliphate).

[280] *scarlet conclave*: The conclave of cardinals (robed in scarlet) meets to elect a new pope (a gathering that is here suspected of being full of intrigue and "poison").

[281] *Silenus*: in classical mythology, companion and tutor of the god Dionysus.

How long I slumbered 'tis a chance to guess.
When sense of life returned, I started up
As if with wings; but the fair trees were gone,
The mossy mound and arbour were no more.   60
I looked around upon the carvèd sides
Of an old sanctuary with roof august,[282]
Builded so high, it seemed that filmèd clouds
Might spread beneath, as o'er the stars of heaven.
So old the place was, I remembered none   65
The like upon the earth: what I had seen
Of grey cathedrals, buttressed walls, rent towers,[283]
The superannuations[284] of sunk realms,
Or Nature's rocks toiled hard in waves and winds,
Seemed but the faulture[285] of decrepit things   70
To that eternal domèd monument.
Upon the marble at my feet there lay
Store of strange vessels and large draperies,
Which needs had been of dyed asbestos[286] wove,
Or in that place the moth could not corrupt,[287]   75
So white the linen; so, in some, distinct
Ran imageries from a sombre loom.
All in a mingled heap confused there lay
Robes, golden tongs, censer and chafing-dish,
Girdles, and chains, and holy jewelleries—   80

     Turning from these with awe, once more I raised
My eyes to fathom the space every way—
The embossèd[288] roof, the silent massy range
Of columns north and south, ending in mist
Of nothing, then to eastward, where black gates   85
Were shut against the sunrise evermore.

[282] *old . . . august*: a discarded temple.
[283] *rent towers*: towers pulled down.
[284] *superannuations*: antiquated structures.
[285] *faulture*: weakness, like a geological fault (a term coined by Keats).
[286] *asbestos*: natural mineral that could be made into an incombustible fabric.
[287] *that place . . . corrupt*: i.e., Heaven. See Matthew 6:19–20.
[288] *embossèd*: molded or carved in relief.

Then to the west I looked,[289] and saw far off
An Image, huge of feature as a cloud,
At level of whose feet an altar slept,
To be approached on either side by steps,   90
And marble balustrade, and patient travail
To count with toil the innumerable degrees.
Towards the altar sober-paced I went,
Repressing haste, as too unholy there;
And, coming nearer, saw beside the shrine   95
One ministering; and there arose a flame.
When in mid-May the sickening East wind
Shifts sudden to the south, the small warm rain
Melts out the frozen incense from all flowers,
And fills the air with so much pleasant health   100
That even the dying man forgets his shroud—
Even so that lofty sacrificial fire,
Sending forth Maian incense,[290] spread around
Forgetfulness of everything but bliss,
And clouded all the altar with soft smoke,   105
From whose white fragrant curtains thus I heard
Language pronounced: 'If thou canst not ascend
These steps, die on that marble where thou art.
Thy flesh, near cousin to the common dust,
Will parch for lack of nutriment—thy bones   110
Will wither in few years, and vanish so
That not the quickest eye could find a grain
Of what thou now art on that pavement cold.
The sands of thy short life are spent this hour,
And no hand in the universe can turn   115
Thy hourglass, if these gummèd leaves be burnt
Ere thou canst mount up these immortal steps.'
I heard, I looked: two senses both at once,
So fine, so subtle, felt the tyranny

[289] *Then . . . looked*: In Greek temples, worshippers faced west.
[290] *Maian incense*: i.e., the scent of spring flowers. In classical mythology, Maia, one of the Pleiades and mother of Hermes, ruled over the spring.

Of that fierce threat, and the hard task proposed.   120
Prodigious seemed the toil; the leaves were yet
Burning—when suddenly a palsied chill
Struck from the pavèd level up my limbs,
And was ascending quick to put cold grasp
Upon those streams that pulse beside the throat.   125
I shrieked; and the sharp anguish of my shriek
Stung my own ears—I strove hard to escape
The numbness, strove to gain the lowest step.
Slow, heavy, deadly was my pace: the cold
Grew stifling, suffocating, at the heart;   130
And when I clasped my hands I felt them not.
One minute before death, my iced foot touched
The lowest stair; and as it touched, life seemed
To pour in at the toes: I mounted up,
As once fair Angels on a ladder[291] flew   135
From the green turf to Heaven. 'Holy Power,'
Cried I, approaching near the hornèd shrine,
'What am I that should so be saved from death?
What am I that another death come not
To choke my utterance sacrilegious here?'   140
Then said the veilèd shadow: 'Thou hast felt
What 'tis to die and live again before
Thy fated hour. That thou hadst power to do so
Is thy own safety; thou hast dated on[292]
Thy doom.' 'High Prophetess,' said I, 'purge off,   145
Benign, if so it please thee, my mind's film.'[293]
'None can usurp this height,' returned that shade,
'But those to whom the miseries of the world
Are misery, and will not let them rest.
All else who find a haven in the world,   150
Where they may thoughtless sleep away their days,

[291] *ladder*: i.e., Jacob's ladder, from earth to Heaven, seen by the Old Testament patriarch Jacob in a dream. See Genesis 28:12.
[292] *dated on*: postponed.
[293] *High . . . film*: He asks the prophetess to explain and clarify.

If by a chance into this fane they come,
Rot on the pavement where thou rotted'st half.'
'Are there not thousands in the world,' said I,
Encouraged by the sooth[294] voice of the shade,   155
'Who love their fellows even to the death;
Who feel the giant agony of the world;
And more, like slaves to poor humanity,
Labour for mortal good? I sure should see
Other men here: but I am here alone.'   160
'They whom thou spak'st of are no visionaries,'
Rejoined that voice—'They are no dreamers weak,
They seek no wonder but the human face;
No music but a happy-noted voice—
They come not here, they have no thought to come—   165
And thou art here, for thou art less than they—
What benefit canst thou do, or all thy tribe,
To the great world? Thou art a dreaming thing,
A fever of thyself. Think of the Earth;
What bliss even in hope is there for thee?   170
What haven? Every creature hath its home;
Every sole man hath days of joy and pain,
Whether his labours be sublime or low—
The pain alone; the joy alone; distinct:
Only the dreamer venoms all his days,   175
Bearing more woe than all his sins deserve.
Therefore, that happiness be somewhat shared,
Such things as thou art are admitted oft
Into like gardens thou didst pass erewhile,
And suffered in these temples; for that cause   180
Thou standest safe beneath this statue's knees.'
'That I am favoured for unworthiness,
By such propitious parley medicined
In sickness not ignoble, I rejoice—
Ay, and could weep for love of such award.'   185
So answered I, continuing, 'If it please,

---

[294] *sooth*: (1) soothing; (2) truthful.

Majestic shadow, tell me: sure not all
Those melodies sung into the world's ear
Are useless: sure a poet is a sage,
A humanist, physician to all men.   190
That I am none I feel, as vultures feel
They are no birds when eagles are abroad.
What am I then? Thou spakest of my tribe:
What tribe?'—The tall shade veiled in drooping white
Then spake, so much more earnest, that the breath   195
Moved the thin linen folds that drooping hung
About a golden censer from the hand
Pendent.—'Art thou not of the dreamer tribe?
The poet and the dreamer are distinct,
Diverse, sheer opposite, antipodes.   200
The one pours out a balm upon the world,
The other vexes it.' Then shouted I,
Spite of myself, and with a Pythia's[295] spleen,
'Apollo! faded, far-flown Apollo!
Where is thy misty pestilence[296] to creep   205
Into the dwellings, through the door crannies,
Of all mock lyrists, large self-worshippers
And careless hectorers in proud bad verse.
Though I breathe death with them it will be life
To see them sprawl before me into graves.   210
Majestic shadow, tell me where I am,
Whose altar this; for whom this incense curls;
What image this, whose face I cannot see,
For the broad marble knees; and who thou art,
Of accent feminine so courteous?'   215

Then the tall shade, in drooping linens veiled,
Spake out, so much more earnest, that her breath
Stirred the thin folds of gauze that drooping hung

[295] *Pythia's*: In classical mythology, Pythia was the priestess of Apollo at
Delphi, and her name was associated with the monster Python, slain by Apollo.
[296] *pestilence*: In classical mythology, Apollo was the god with mastery over
the plagues.

About a golden censer from her hand
Pendent; and by her voice I knew she shed   220
Long-treasured tears. 'This temple, sad and lone,
Is all spared from the thunder of a war
Foughten long since by giant hierarchy
Against rebellion;[297] this old image here,
Whose carvèd features wrinkled as he fell,   225
Is Saturn's; I Moneta,[298] left supreme
Sole priestess of his desolation.'
I had no words to answer, for my tongue,
Useless, could find about its roofèd home
No syllable of a fit majesty   230
To make rejoinder to Moneta's mourn.
There was a silence, while the altar's blaze
Was fainting for sweet food:[299] I looked thereon,
And on the pavèd floor, where nigh were piled
Faggots of cinnamon, and many heaps   235
Of other crispèd spice-wood—then again
I looked upon the altar, and its horns
Whitened with ashes, and its languorous flame,
And then upon the offerings again;
And so by turns—till sad Moneta cried: 240
'The sacrifice is done, but not the less
Will I be kind to thee for thy goodwill.
My power, which to me is still a curse,
Shall be to thee a wonder; for the scenes
Still swooning vivid through my globèd brain,   245
With an electral changing misery,
Thou shalt with those dull mortal eyes behold,
Free from all pain, if wonder pain thee not.'
As near as an immortal's spherèd words
Could to a mother's soften, were these last: 250

---

[297] *thunder . . . rebellion*: i.e., in classical mythology, the battle between the Olympian gods and the Titans.

[298] *Moneta*: Here Keats conflates two goddesses of classical mythology: Moneta, an epithet of Juno, queen of the gods, and Mnemosyne, goddess of memory.

[299] *altar's . . . food*: i.e., the fire is dying because no sacrifices have been made.

And yet I had a terror of her robes,
And chiefly of the veils, that from her brow
Hung pale, and curtained her in mysteries
That made my heart too small to hold its blood.
This saw that Goddess, and with sacred hand   255
Parted the veils. Then saw I a wan face,
Not pined by human sorrows, but bright-blanched
By an immortal sickness which kills not;
It works a constant change, which happy death
Can put no end to; deathwards progressing   260
To no death was that visage; it had passed
The lily and the snow; and beyond these
I must not think now, though I saw that face—
But for her eyes I should have fled away.
They held me back, with a benignant light,   265
Soft-mitigated by divinest lids
Half-closed, and visionless entire they seemed
Of all external things—they saw me not,
But in blank splendour beamed like the mild moon,
Who comforts those she sees not, who knows not   270
What eyes are upward cast. As I had found
A grain of gold upon a mountain side,
And twinged with avarice strained out my eyes
To search its sullen entrails rich with ore,
So at the view of sad Moneta's brow   275
I ached to see what things the hollow brain
Behind enwombèd; what high tragedy
In the dark secret chambers of her skull
Was acting, that could give so dread a stress
To her cold lips, and fill with such a light   280
Her planetary eyes; and touch her voice
With such a sorrow—'Shade of Memory!'[300]
Cried I, with act adorant[301] at her feet,

---

[300] '*Shade of Memory!*': i.e., Mnemosyne, in classical mythology, the Titan
goddess of memory and the mother of the nine Muses.
[301] *adorant*: adoring.

'By all the gloom hung round thy fallen house,
By this last temple,[302] by the golden age,   285
By great Apollo, thy dear foster child,
And by thyself, forlorn divinity,
The pale Omega[303] of a withered race,
Let me behold, according as thou said'st,
What in thy brain so ferments to and fro.'   290
No sooner had this conjuration passed
My devout lips, than side by side we stood
(Like a stunt bramble by a solemn pine)
Deep in the shady sadness of a vale,
Far sunken from the healthy breath of morn,   295
Far from the fiery noon and eve's one star.
Onward I looked beneath the gloomy boughs,
And saw, what first I thought an image huge,
Like to the image pedestalled so high
In Saturn's temple. Then Moneta's voice   300
Came brief upon mine ear: 'So Saturn sat
When he had lost his realms.' Whereon there grew
A power within me of enormous ken
To see as a God sees, and take the depth
Of things as nimbly as the outward eye   305
Can size and shape pervade. The lofty theme
At those few words hung vast before my mind,
With half-unravelled web. I set myself
Upon an eagle's watch, that I might see,
And seeing ne'er forget. No stir of life   310
Was in this shrouded vale, not so much air
As in zoning of a summer's day
Robs not one light seed from the feathered grass,
But where the dead leaf fell there did it rest.
A stream went voiceless by, still deadened more 315
By reason of the fallen divinity

---

[302] *last temple*: In classical mythology, Moneta is seen as the last of the Titans, foster mother of Apollo.

[303] *Omega*: i.e., the last (from the final letter of the Greek alphabet).

Spreading more shade; the Naiad[304] 'mid her reeds
Pressed her cold finger closer to her lips.
Along the margin-sand large footmarks went
No farther than to where old Saturn's feet   320
Had rested, and there slept—how long a sleep!
Degraded, cold, upon the sodden ground
His old right hand lay nerveless, listless, dead,
Unsceptred; and his realmless eyes were closed,
While his bowed head seemed listening to the Earth,   325
His ancient mother, for some comfort yet.

   It seemed no force could wake him from his place;
But there came one who, with a kindred hand
Touched his wide shoulders, after bending low
With reverence, though to one who knew it not.   330
Then came the grieved voice of Mnemosyne,
And grieved I hearkened. 'That divinity
Whom thou saw'st step from yon forlornest wood,
And with slow pace approach our fallen King,
Is Thea,[305] softest-natured of our brood.'   335
I marked the goddess in fair statuary
Surpassing wan Moneta by the head,
And in her sorrow nearer woman's tears.
There was a listening fear in her regard,
As if calamity had but begun;   340
As if the vanward clouds of evil days
Had spent their malice, and the sullen rear
Was with its storèd thunder labouring up.
One hand she pressed upon that aching spot
Where beats the human heart, as if just there,   345
Though an immortal, she felt cruel pain;
The other upon Saturn's bended neck

---

[304] *Naiad*: sea nymph.
[305] *Thea*: in classical mythology, the Titan goddess of sight and the blue sky, wife to her brother Hyperion and mother to Helios (the sun), Eos (the dawn), and Selene (the moon).

She laid, and to the level of his hollow ear
Leaning with parted lips, some words she spake
In solemn tenor and deep organ tune,   350
Some mourning words, which in our feeble tongue
Would come in this-like accenting—how frail
To that large utterance of the early Gods!—
'Saturn! look up—and for what, poor lost King?
I have no comfort for thee, no—not one;   355
I cannot cry, *Wherefore thus sleepest thou?*
For Heaven is parted from thee, and the Earth
Knows thee not, so afflicted, for a God;
And Ocean too, with all its solemn noise,
Has from thy sceptre passed, and all the air   360
Is emptied of thine hoary Majesty.
Thy thunder, captious at the new command,
Rumbles reluctant o'er our fallen house;
And thy sharp lightning, in unpractised hands,
Scorches and burns our once serene domain.   365
With such remorseless speed still come new woes
That unbelief has not a space to breathe.
Saturn! sleep on. Me thoughtless, why should I
Thus violate thy slumbrous solitude?
Why should I ope thy melancholy eyes?   370
Saturn, sleep on, while at thy feet I weep.'

      As when, upon a trancèd summer night,
Forests, branch-charmèd by the earnest stars,
Dream, and so dream all night without a noise,
Save from one gradual solitary gust,   375
Swelling upon the silence; dying off;
As if the ebbing air had but one wave—
So came these words, and went; the while in tears
She pressed her fair large forehead to the earth,
Just where her fallen hair might spread in curls,   380
A soft and silken mat for Saturn's feet.
Long, long those two were postured motionless,
Like sculpture builded-up upon the grave

Of their own power. A long awful time
I looked upon them: still they were the same;   385
The frozen God still bending to the earth,
And the sad Goddess weeping at his feet;
Moneta silent. Without stay or prop,
But my own weak mortality, I bore
The load of this eternal quietude,   390
The unchanging gloom, and the three fixèd shapes
Ponderous upon my senses a whole moon.
For by my burning brain I measured sure
Her silver seasons shedded on the night,
And ever day by day methought I grew   395
More gaunt and ghostly. Oftentimes I prayed
Intense, that death would take me from the vale
And all its burthens. Gasping with despair
Of change, hour after hour I cursed myself—
Until old Saturn raised his faded eyes,   400
And looked around and saw his kingdom gone,
And all the gloom and sorrow of the place,
And that fair kneeling Goddess at his feet.
As the moist scent of flowers, and grass, and leaves,
Fills forest dells with a pervading air   405
Known to the woodland nostril, so the words
Of Saturn filled the mossy glooms around,
Even to the hollows of time-eaten oaks,
And to the windings of the foxes' hole,
With sad low tones, while thus he spake, and sent   410
Strange musings to the solitary Pan:[306]

   'Moan, brethren, moan; for we are swallowed up
And buried from all godlike exercise
Of influence benign on planets pale,
And peaceful sway above man's harvesting,   415
And all those acts which deity supreme

---

[306] *Pan*: in classical mythology, the Satyr god of the wilderness, shepherds, and huntsmen (sometimes conflated with Faunus).

Doth ease its heart of love in. Moan and wail.
Moan, brethren, moan; for lo! the rebel spheres
Spin round, the stars their ancient courses keep,
Clouds still with shadowy moisture haunt the earth, 420
Still suck their fill of light from sun and moon,
Still buds the tree, and still the sea-shores murmur.
There is no death in all the universe,
No smell of death—there shall be death—moan, moan,
Moan, Cybele,[307] moan; for thy pernicious babes 425
Have changed a God into a shaking palsy.
Moan, brethren, moan, for I have no strength left,
Weak as the reed—weak—feeble as my voice—
O, O, the pain, the pain of feebleness.
Moan, moan, for still I thaw—or give me help: 430
Throw down those imps, and give me victory.
Let me hear other groans, and trumpets blown
Of triumph calm, and hymns of festival,
From the gold peaks of heaven's high-pilèd clouds—
Voices of soft proclaim, and silver stir 435
Of strings in hollow shells; and let there be
Beautiful things made new for the surprise
Of the sky-children—' So he feebly ceased,
With such a poor and sickly sounding pause,
Methought I heard some old man of the earth 440
Bewailing earthly loss; nor could my eyes
And ears act with that pleasant unison of sense
Which marries sweet sound with the grace of form
And dolorous accent from a tragic harp
With large-limbed visions. More I scrutinized: 445
Still fixed he sat beneath the sable trees,
Whose arms spread straggling in wild serpent forms,
With leaves all hushed; his awful presence there
(Now all was silent) gave a deadly lie
To what I erewhile heard—only his lips 450

---

[307] *Cybele*: in classical mythology, the wife of Saturn and mother of the Olympian gods (who rebelled against and overthrew Saturn).

Trembled amid the white curls of his beard.
They told the truth, though, round, the snowy locks
Hung nobly, as upon the face of heaven
A midday fleece of clouds. Thea arose,
And stretched her white arm through the hollow dark,   455
Pointing some whither; whereat he too rose
Like a vast giant, seen by men at sea
To grow pale from the waves at dull midnight.
They melted from my sight into the woods;
Ere I could turn, Moneta cried: 'These twain   460
Are speeding to the families of grief,
Where roofed in by black rocks they waste, in pain
And darkness, for no hope.'—And she spake on,
As ye may read who can unwearied pass
Onward from the antechamber of this dream,   465
Where even at the open doors awhile
I must delay, and glean my memory
Of her high phrase—perhaps no further dare.

CANTO II

'Mortal, that thou mayst understand aright,
I humanize my sayings to thine ear,
Making comparisons of earthly things;
Or thou mightst better listen to the wind,
Whose language is to thee a barren noise,   5
Though it blows legend-laden through the trees—
In melancholy realms big tears are shed,
More sorrow like to this, and such-like woe,
Too huge for mortal tongue, or pen of scribe.
The Titans fierce, self-hid or prison-bound,   10
Groan for the old allegiance once more,
Listening in their doom for Saturn's voice.
But one of our whole eagle-brood still keeps
His sovereignty, and rule, and majesty;
Blazing Hyperion on his orbèd fire   15
Still sits, still snuffs the incense teeming up

From man to the sun's God—yet unsecure.
For as upon the earth dire prodigies
Fright and perplex, so also shudders he:
Nor at dog's howl or gloom-bird's even screech,   20
Or the familiar visitings of one
Upon the first toll of his passing-bell:
But horrors, portioned to a giant nerve,
Make great Hyperion ache. His palace bright,
Bastioned with pyramids of glowing gold,   25
And touched with shade of bronzèd obelisks,
Glares a blood-red through all the thousand courts,
Arches, and domes, and fiery galleries;
And all its curtains of Aurorian clouds
Flush angerly: when he would taste the wreaths   30
Of incense breathed aloft from sacred hills,
Instead of sweets, his ample palate takes
Savour of poisonous brass and metals sick.
Wherefore, when harboured in the sleepy West,
After the full completion of fair day,   35
For rest divine upon exalted couch
And slumber in the arms of melody,
He paces through the pleasant hours of ease
With strides colossal, on from hall to hall;
While far within each aisle and deep recess   40
His wingèd minions in close clusters stand
Amazed, and full of fear; like anxious men,
Who on a wide plain gather in sad troops,
When earthquakes jar their battlements and towers.
Even now, while Saturn, roused from icy trance,   45
Goes, step for step, with Thea from yon woods,
Hyperion, leaving twilight in the rear,
Is sloping to the threshold of the West—
Thither we tend.'—Now in clear light I stood,
Relieved from the dusk vale. Mnemosyne   50
Was sitting on a square-edged polished stone,
That in its lucid depth reflected pure
Her priestess-garments. My quick eyes ran on

From stately nave to nave, from vault to vault,
Through bowers of fragrant and enwreathèd light   55
And diamond-pavèd lustrous long arcades.
Anon rushed by the bright Hyperion;
His flaming robes streamed out beyond his heels,
And gave a roar, as if of earthly fire,
That scared away the meek ethereal Hours,   60
And made their dove-wings tremble. On he flared ...

"This living hand, now warm and capable" (late 1819)

This living hand, now warm and capable
Of earnest grasping, would, if it were cold
And in the icy silence of the tomb,
So haunt thy days and chill thy dreaming nights
That thou would wish thine own heart dry of blood
So in my veins red life might stream again,
And thou be conscience-calmed—see here it is—
I hold it towards you.

Contemporary Criticisms

Keats as Sonneteer and Balladeer

Raimund Borgmeier
University of Giessen, Germany

It may perhaps be surprising that the Romantic poets were thinking in terms of literary genres at all. Of course, for a poet of the classicist period, genres were fundamental. Alexander Pope, for example, consciously followed his model Virgil by first writing pastorals, then didactic poems, and finally turning to the climax of the epic. But if you are convinced that "all good poetry is the spontaneous overflow of powerful feelings", as William Wordsworth expressed it,[1] or that a poet can be "certain of nothing but the holiness of the Heart's affection and the truth of Imagination",[2] as John Keats wrote in one of his letters, literary genres should be rather unimportant. That this was not so, I would like to show in the case of Keats by looking at his dealing with the literary forms of the sonnet and the ballad, both being very important for his poetry.

The sonnet seems to be a particularly unlikely literary genre for Romantic poetry. It makes high demands on the poet and his technical competence: no matter how much he has to say, the poet must restrict himself to fourteen lines, and, according to the original conception, has to present his ideas in the form of a thesis, which is expressed in the first part of the poem, the octave, and an antithesis, which follows in the second part, the sestet. In addition, there is a demanding rhyme scheme, in the original form *abbaabba* for the octave, and *cdecde* or *cdcdcd* for the sestet, in the later Shakespearean or English form *abab cdcd efef gg*.

[1] Quoted in *English Literary Criticism: Romantic and Victorian*, ed. Daniel Hoffman and Samuel Hynes (London: Peter Owen, 1966), p. 16.

[2] John Keats, Letter 31, in *The Letters of John Keats*, selected by Frederick Page (London; New York: Oxford University Press, 1954), p. 48. All subsequent quotations of Keats' letters are from this edition.

Nevertheless, the sonnet had a great fascination for the Romantic poets and for Keats in particular. It was a very ancient form and was reminiscent of the poetry of bygone eras, most of all the age of Shakespeare. That Milton, greatly admired by the Romantics, liked the sonnet very much and that the classicists, as, for example, Pope, decidedly disliked it made the form all the more attractive.

These literary associations find expression in Keats' early sonnets.[3] In the sonnet "Written on the Day That Mr. Leigh Hunt Left Prison" (which happened in February 1815), for instance, he says about this fellow poet and man of letters (who later on became his friend):

> In Spenser's halls he strayed, and bowers fair,
>   Culling enchanted flowers; and he flew
> With daring Milton through the fields of air.[4]

Similarly, Keats concludes Sonnet 9 in the series of "Sonnets" in his first volume of *Poems* (published 1817) with a sestet, in which he praises his intimate relationship with the sonnet writers of the past, experienced during a hiking tour:

> For I am brimfull of the friendliness
>   That in a little cottage I have found;
> Of fair-hair'd Milton's eloquent distress,
>   And all his love for gentle Lycid drown'd
> Of lovely Laura in her light green dress,
>   And faithful Petrarch gloriously crown'd.[5]

It is characteristic of the Romantic attitude that the experience of reading is personalized and presented as an encounter with real people.

---

[3] See Timothy Hilton, *Keats and His World* (London: Thames and Hudson, 1971), p. 24.

[4] John Keats, "Written on the Day That Mr. Leigh Hunt Left Prison", in *John Keats: Complete Poems*, ed. Jack Stillinger (Cambridge, Mass.; London: Belknap Press of Harvard University Press, 1982), p. 6.

[5] John Keats, "Keen, fitful gusts are whisp'ring here and there", in *Complete Poems*, p. 34.

Keats wrote as many sonnets as some well-known Elizabethan sonneteers, like Samuel Daniel or Michael Drayton.[6] Walter Jackson Bate counts altogether sixty-six sonnets by Keats,[7] Lawrence John Zillman lists sixty-seven sonnets,[8] and Keats composed these sonnets in all the phases of his poetical development, from the very beginning until the end of his brief career as a poet.

Therefore, it cannot be regarded as a coincidence that the very first poem that Keats managed to publish was a sonnet:

> O Solitude! if I must with thee dwell,
>   Let it not be among the jumbled heap
>   Of murky buildings; climb with me the steep,—
> Nature's observatory—whence the dell,
> Its flowery slopes, its river's crystal swell,
>   May seem a span; let me thy vigils keep
>   'Mongst boughs pavillion'd, where the deer's swift
>   leap
> Startles the wild bee from the fox-glove bell.
> But though I'll gladly trace these scenes with thee,
>   Yet the sweet converse of an innocent mind,
>   Whose words are images of thoughts refin'd,
> Is my soul's pleasure; and it sure must be
>   Almost the highest bliss of human-kind,
> When to thy haunts two kindred spirits flee.[9]

Keats wrote this sonnet in November 1815, shortly after his twentieth birthday (October 31). He sent the text to Leigh Hunt, who printed it in his magazine *Examiner* in May 1816.

---

[6] See Maurice Evans, ed., *Elizabethan Sonnets* (London: Dent, Rowan, and Littlefield, 1977). Daniel's sonnet cycle contains fifty-five sonnets; Drayton's, sixty-three.

[7] Walter Jackson Bate, *John Keats* (New York: Oxford University Press, 1966), p. 298. See also Christoph Bode, *John Keats: Play On* (Heidelberg: Winter, 1996), p. 35.

[8] Lawrence John Zillman, *John Keats and the Sonnet Tradition: A Critical and Comparative Study* (1939; repr., New York: Octagon, 1970), pp. 155–88.

[9] John Keats, "O Solitude! if I must with thee dwell", in *Complete Poems*, pp. 13–14.

In the following year, Keats included the poem as number 7 of the seventeen sonnets in his volume of *Poems*.[10]

The basic theme of this sonnet, the commendation of solitude, which is personified and addressed as a divine power in a kind of secular prayer, is a favorite Romantic idea. It is also not unusual that solitude may serve the poet to escape from the ugly sphere of the town ("the jumbled heap", "murky buildings") and achieve a communion with nature, depicted here with the sensuous details typical of Keats' poetry. That Keats chooses a vantage point to view nature ("[n]ature's observatory") may remind his readers that a longer poem in his first collection began with the line "I stood tip-toe upon a little hill." But when we come to the sestet, the argumentation takes a surprising turn and we are perhaps made aware that right from the beginning the speaker has only expressed a qualified praise of solitude: "if I *must* with thee dwell" (my italics). In the sestet, he argues, to put it simply, that enjoying nature on your own is good, but sharing the experience of nature with someone you can talk to about important and complex topics ("thoughts refin'd") must be extremely and absolutely delightful ("Almost the highest bliss of human-kind").[11] He leaves it open whether the "two kindred spirits" in the final line are lovers or just friends. Perhaps "the sweet converse of an innocent mind" in line 10 makes it likelier that the speaker is thinking of a woman, but this is not certain. The last word of the poem ("flee"), at any rate, once more emphasizes that leaving the town and seeking nature together is to be understood as a form of escape—an essentially Romantic view.

As far as the form is concerned, this is a Petrarchan sonnet, the octave having the rhyme scheme *abbaabba*, and the sestet,

---

[10] For the publication history, see Bate, *Keats*, p. 63, or Bode, *Keats: Play On*, p. 11.

[11] The preference of togetherness to complete solitude in Keats' sonnet appears to be the opposite of what one usually finds in Wordsworth's poetry, e.g., in his famous "Daffodils", where the poet emphasizes his solitude, although we know from the reports of his sister, Dorothy, that he had the original experience represented in the poem together with her.

cddcdc. There is a clear caesura between the two parts, marked by "But" in line 9. The sestet can really be understood as an antithesis to the octave since it makes it clear that the poet gives togetherness or relative solitude in nature preference to complete solitude, which he seemed to opt for in the octave.

Nature is also the theme in other sonnets, for example, in "On the Sea", where Keats praises the sea for its varying manifestations, sometimes restless and stormy, sometimes gentle and smooth, and invites those who suffer from the trouble and unrest of life in the city to come to the sea to be cured. Some sonnets are love poems, like "To G. A. W. [Georgiana Augusta Wylie]", in which the poet asks at what time the beloved lady is "most lovely", a question that cannot be answered, of course.[12] Other sonnets are occasional poems, written as a reaction to special experiences, as, for instance, "On Seeing the Elgin Marbles", or "On Leaving Some Friends at an Early Hour".

Following the example of Milton, Keats, in many of his sonnets, addresses a certain person: a relative, as in "To My Brother George"; a friend, as in "To a Friend Who Sent Me Some Roses"; or an admired lady who remains nameless, as in "To —". In a number of sonnets, poets whom Keats esteems particularly are addressed: "To Homer", "To Chatterton", "To Lord Byron". Sometimes, a sonnet is both an occasional poem and one that pays tribute to a great poet, as "On Visiting the Tomb of Burns" or "Sonnet Written in the Cottage Where Burns Was Born" ["This mortal body of a thousand days"], or "On Sitting Down to Read *King Lear* Once Again", in which Shakespeare is praised as "Chief Poet". Zillman lists twenty-one of Keats' sonnets in which individual poets or poets in general are mentioned.[13] Poetry and Keats' own vocation as a poet can be seen as a pervasive theme throughout the sonnets.

---

[12] John Keats, "To G. A. W. [Georgiana Augusta Wylie]", in *Complete Poems* (Boston and New York: Houghton Mifflin, 1900), p. 429.

[13] See Zillman, *Keats and Sonnet Tradition*, p. 84.

Significantly, the poem that for a long time was considered to be the last one Keats wrote is also, as mentioned before, a sonnet. According to Bate:

> It was usually entitled "The Last Sonnet" because Keats wrote his revised (and distinctly improved) version of it on a blank page of his copy of Shakespeare's poem[s] in early autumn, 1820, while he and Severn were on the boat to Italy.[14]

In November, the two friends reached Rome, where Keats died on February 23, the following year. "Bright Star" is certainly an outstanding example of Keats' art as a sonnet writer:

> Bright star! would I were steadfast as thou art—
>   Not in lone splendour hung aloft the night
> And watching, with eternal lids apart,
>   Like nature's patient, sleepless Eremite,
> The moving waters at their priestlike task
>   Of pure ablution round earth's human shores,
> Or gazing on the new soft-fallen mask
>   Of snow upon the mountains and the moors—
> No—yet still steadfast, still unchangeable,
>   Pillowed upon my fair love's ripening breast,
> To feel for ever its soft swell and fall,
>   Awake for ever in a sweet unrest,
> Still, still to hear her tender-taken breath,
> And so live ever—or else swoon to death.[15]

It appears convincing when Bate compares this sonnet to Keats' odes and suggests:

> We should note something about this sonnet that reminds us, in miniature, of the structure of two of the great odes—the

---

[14] Bate, *Keats*, p. 618.

[15] John Keats, "Bright star! would I were steadfast as thou art", in *The Romantic Poets*, ed. Joseph Pearce and Robert Asch, vol. 2, *Byron, Shelley, and Keats*, Ignatius Critical Editions (San Francisco: Ignatius Press, 2024), p. 363. All subsequent quotations of Keats' poetry from this edition will be cited in the text.

"Nightingale" and, even more, the "Grecian Urn"—whether the poem was written as an anticipation or as an echo. It is that process of symbolic debate in which a dominant symbol or concept, after being postulated at the start, becomes the motif in a counterpoint of withdrawal, qualification, and partial return.[16]

The wish to be like the bright star (we may think of the polestar mentioned in Shakespeare's famous Sonnet 116) expressed in the opening line is immediately retracted in the "[n]ot" of the following line. But we tend to neglect or disregard this retraction since the poet, in the rest of the octave, depicts what the star watches with such intensity. This is an extreme form of "[n]ature's observatory", as we found it in the first printed sonnet, an ideal vantage point. And both the process of the observation and the object of the observation are seen in religious terms: the star is personified "[l]ike nature's patient, sleepless Eremite" (line 4), which means that he is dedicated with all his energy to a holy duty; and he watches "[t]he moving waters at their priestlike task/Of pure ablution round earth's human shores" (lines 5–6), which signifies that the tides carry out a purifying assignment like a religious ritual. They, as forces of nature, heal what has suffered from "human" interference. Also the "mask/Of snow", in lines 7 and 8, appears to represent a positive metamorphosis of the places of nature ("the mountains and the moors"), which are made special in this way and removed even further from the intervention of man.

The "No", at the beginning of the sestet, emphasizes once more the initial retraction. This time, the speaker makes it clear that he qualifies his wish to be like the star to a more moderate proportion. It may remind one of the love poems of Donne that the poet here gives up the great cosmos and opts for the cosmos of love instead. In the love relationship, he wishes time and change to be suspended so that the present moment of happiness would last forever; this word ("for ever") occurs twice, in lines 11 and 12. And "still", which means *in*

---

[16] Bate, *Keats*, p. 619.

spite of what has just been said in line 9, in the final couplet gets the old meaning of *always and forever*. In the breathing of the beloved woman, the poet wants to experience on a small scale something that resembles the tides, "the moving waters" (line 5) of the octave, something that is in motion and permanent at the same time. The alternative to living like this forever, as it is put in the final words of the poem, "swoon to death", the wish to escape from ordinary consciousness, is something one frequently comes across in Keats' poetry.

As far as the rhyme scheme is concerned, this is a Shakespearean sonnet with three quatrains and a final couplet (*ababcdcdefefgg*); but, as one often finds in Shakespeare's sonnets, the argumentative structure is the classic one of an octave and a sestet (8 + 6 lines)—the octave looking at the large sphere of the cosmos, the sestet concentrating on the restricted cosmos of love. Keats started to use the Shakespearean form of the sonnet, as "a deliberate Shakespearean imitation", as Bate puts it,[17] at the end of January 1818. His first sonnet using this rhyme scheme was "When I have fears that I may cease to be". Bate gives a brief survey of Keats' use of the different forms:

> By the end of January 1818 he had written at least forty-one sonnets, all in the Petrarchan form. But from now on until the end he was to write little more than half that number—a total of twenty-five. Of these a fifth—dashed down on the spur of the moment when he reverted to old habit—are Petrarchan. Of two others, one is unrhymed ... and the second deliberately experimental. ... The remaining eighteen are either basically or entirely Shakespearean.[18]

So only slightly more than a quarter of Keats' sonnets are written in the Shakespearean or English form, which is remarkable and demonstrates, among other things, Keats' brilliance in versification since the Petrarchan form is, of course, technically much more demanding than the English one.

17 Ibid., p. 291.
18 Ibid., p. 298.

That Keats achieved a high level of poetic proficiency as a sonnet writer early on in his career becomes especially manifest in his famous sonnet "On First Looking into Chapman's Homer", which he wrote in September 1816:

> Much have I travelled in the realms of gold,
>   And many goodly states and kingdoms seen;
>   Round many western islands have I been
> Which bards in fealty to Apollo hold.
> Oft of one wide expanse had I been told
>   That deep-browed Homer ruled as his demesne;
>   Yet did I never breathe its pure serene
> Till I heard Chapman speak out loud and bold:
> Then felt I like some watcher of the skies
>   When a new planet swims into his ken;
> Or like stout Cortez when with eagle eyes
>   He stared at the Pacific—and all his men
> Looked at each other with a wild surmise—
>   Silent, upon a peak in Darien. (See p. 357.)

We know the circumstances under which this sonnet was written.[19] Keats' friend Cowden Clarke had been lent a folio edition of Chapman's translation of Homer, and he and Keats enthusiastically read to each other passages from the *Odyssey*. This lasted the whole night. After they had parted "at day-spring", as Clarke said, Keats walked home; within less than two hours, he had written the sonnet and sent it to Clarke,[20] who received it before ten o'clock. Before, Keats had known Homer only from the translation of Alexander Pope, who had turned the epic into a smooth and elegant text, as the neo-classic age favored it. The translation of the Elizabethan poet, playwright, and scholar George Chapman, however, was much more bold and vigorous, and Keats was delighted and expressed his reaction in the sonnet.

Again, the experience of reading is conveyed in a personal way as a journey and an encounter with real people. Instead of

[19] See ibid., pp. 84–89.
[20] Ibid., p. 87.

saying that he has read many poetical texts before, but not the real Homer, the speaker reports about his travels "in the realms of gold" (line 1). This image is particularly appropriate here because it creates the association of the world of classical mythology, and the speaker himself appears, as it were, in the role of Ulysses, Homer's hero, who has to make long voyages to many different coasts and islands before he finally reaches his goal. Homer is seen as an awe-inspiring, old, and wise ("deep-browed" [line 6]) ruler in this ancient world, and Chapman as a kind of pilot who directs the way to this wonderful land, whose almost divine character the poet can now enjoy ("breathe its pure serene" [line 7]).

In the sestet, Keats introduces new images to represent the effect that the discovery of this fascinating text has had on him. First, in lines 9 and 10, he compares his experience to the discovery of a new planet by an astronomer (he was thinking of the discovery of the planet Uranus by Herschel in 1781). In the final four lines, he compares this experience with the situation of the Spanish conquerors who discovered the New World and saw, for the first time, a new ocean, the Pacific. (Apparently, it was Tennyson who first observed that here Keats made a mistake because it was Balboa, not Cortez, who, in 1513, discovered the Pacific Ocean[21]—but this slight error in no way diminishes the quality of this fine sonnet.)

Robin Mayhead is right when he draws particular attention to the concluding line, where "the effect of breathless, awe-struck silence is obtained through Keats's resourceful use of verse-structure." He analyzes further:

> The secret is in the dramatic pause after "wild surmise". Three factors contribute to this: the drama of the imagined situation

[21] See Bode, *Keats: Play On*, p. 22. As Bode points out, scholars have researched Keats' previous reading, which led to this sonnet, diligently; see Robert C. Evans, "Keats's Approach to the Chapman Sonnet", *Essays & Studies* 16 (1931): 26–52; Joseph Warren Beach, "Keats's Realms of Gold", *PMLA* 49 (1934): 246–57; Claude Lee Finney, *The Evolution of Keats's Poetry*, 2 vols. (1936; repr., New York: Russell & Russell, 1963); Bernice Slote, "Of Chapman's Homer and Other Books", *College English* 23, no. 4 (1962): 256–60; Carl Woodring, "On Looking into Keats's Voyagers", *Keats-Shelley Journal* 14 (1965): 15–22.

itself; the position of the words at the end of a line; and the fact that "surmise" rhymes heavily with two previous words. The resulting impression is that of a wide-eyed catch of the breath, after which the isolated "Silent" comes out with superb appropriateness.[22]

Why Mayhead, however, thinks that this fine sonnet "has probably had rather more than its fair due of praise"[23] is difficult to understand. On the contrary, it seems that this early poem does not in the least have the looseness and the lack of concentration otherwise to be found so often in Keats' early poetry. It appears as if the form of the sonnet helped the poet to achieve concentration and compactness. This is also the conclusion that Zillman reaches in his elaborate study: "In many ways ... the quatorzains [i.e., sonnets] seem to have been the training ground where Keats prepared himself for the perfection found in the odes."[24]

During his period of maturity, in 1819, when he composed the great odes, Keats also wrote sonnets, for example, "To Sleep". It would be interesting to compare this sonnet with its Elizabethan models, for example, Sir Philip Sidney's "Come Sleep, O Sleep! the certain knot of peace" or Samuel Daniel's "Care-charmer Sleep, son of the sable Night", to see how much Keats is on a par with the early masters he admired so much.

At the same time, in May 1819, Keats wrote an exceptional sonnet, which he sent in a letter to his brother George and his sister-in-law Georgiana:

> If by dull rhymes our English must be chain'd,
> And, like Andromeda, the sonnet sweet
> Fetter'd, in spite of pained loveliness,
> Let us find out, if we must be constrain'd,
> Sandals more interwoven and complete
> To fit the naked foot of Poesy:

[22] Robin Mayhead, *John Keats* (Cambridge: Cambridge University Press, 1967), p. 27.

[23] Ibid., p. 26.

[24] Zillman, *Keats and Sonnet Tradition*, p. 151.

> Let us inspect the lyre, and weigh the stress
> Of every chord, and see what may be gain'd
> By ear industrious and attention meet;
> Misers of sound and syllable, no less
> Than Midas of his coinage, let us be
> Jealous of dead leaves in the bay wreath crown;
> So, if we may not let the muse be free,
> She will be bound with garlands of her own.[25]

Here the poet looks, with clearly ironical overtones, at the situation of the poet and his dealing with language, with syllables, stresses, and rhymes. On the one hand, the poet wants to be free in his expressions; on the other hand, he is bound by the constraints of the poetical tradition. In his letter, Keats explained his dissatisfaction with the traditional form of the sonnet in simple prose:

> I have been endeavouring to discover a better Sonnet Stanza than we have. The legitimate [the Petrarchan form] does not suit the language over-well from the pouncing rhymes—the other kind [the Shakespearean form] appears too elegiac—and the couplet at the end of it has seldom a pleasing effect—I do not pretend to have succeeded—it will explain itself.[26]

In the sonnet, the poet deliberates how best to deal with the traditional form by personifying the sonnet as a lovely young woman. She is first named "Poesy" (line 6) and finally "the muse" (line 13). The poet considers how to treat her and what outfit she should be given. He starts with the premise that constraint is necessary ("If …") and deduces from that a series of suggestions: "Let us [line 4] … Let us [line 7] … let us [line 11] …" The last two lines then represent a kind of summary by repeating the premise in a different way ("if …") and presenting the inevitable consequence: "She will be …"

[25] John Keats, "If by dull rhymes our English must be chain'd", in *Complete Poems*, p. 278.
[26] Letter 123, p. 271.

The personification leads us into the mythological world of classical antiquity. This is first established by the comparison with Andromeda, who had to be chained because she was intended to serve as an offering to pacify a wild monster (and was liberated by Perseus). Also, the outfit she should have belongs to this world: "[s]andals", "the lyre", "the bay wreath crown", "garlands"—all these belong to the classical picture of "the muse".

That we should not take these considerations completely seriously is made clear, above all, by the fact that the poet, who, of course, has to be careful with every syllable he uses, compares himself to Midas, a comical figure of classical mythology who suffers from extreme greed and has foolishly wished that everything he touches would turn into gold. But there are other signals of irony before, starting with "*dull* rhymes" (my italics). Then, in line 3, "pained loveliness" presents the young woman as slightly coquettish. The exaggerated emphasis of the endeavors of the poor poet in line 9 ("By ear industrious and attention meet") also serves to mark this as meant ironically. That there are possibly "dead leaves" in "the bay wreath crown" worn by the muse contributes a similar facetious touch. Finally, the plural used in the considerations is certainly not the plural of majesty but an expression of familiar, ironical companionship with the reader, beginning with "our English".

The message is, of course, in spite of the irony, a serious one: that traditional forms in poetry should not be used in a hackneyed manner but with consideration and suitable variation. And fittingly enough, Keats realizes this also in the form of this sonnet, which has neither the Petrarchan nor the Shakespearean form but an unusual rhyme scheme (*abcabdcabcdede*). Once more, Keats shows in this sonnet that he is capable of giving expression to what he wants *and* continuing the tradition of the sonnet in a poetically convincing manner, and so, in a way, he may overcome the proverb that he quotes as a motto to his sonnet "On Fame": "You cannot eat your cake and have it too."

Keats turns to the ballad for different reasons. He was, of course, familiar with the poetry of Wordsworth and Coleridge,

who had entitled their pioneering collection *Lyrical Ballads*
(1798), and he obviously knew their high esteem of the genre.
For them, the ballad was genuine poetry, written by the people,
and it is no coincidence that, toward the end of his Preface to
Lyrical Ballads (1800), Wordsworth quotes a stanza from a bal-
lad and contrasts it positively with a stanza of classicist poetry,
which he finds trivial and unpoetical.[27]

Keats, however, does not seem to have a particularly high
opinion of the street ballad, for in one of his letters (July 22,
1820), while he is staying in the North London suburb of
Kentish Town, he complains, "I … generally take two half
hour walks a day up and down the terrace which is very much
pester'd with cries, ballad singers, and street music."[28] Yet one
of his poems bears the generic subtitle *A Ballad* (see pp. 410–
12), and it has become rightly famous: *La Belle Dame sans Merci*
is a perfect imitation of the traditional ballad and is deservedly
ranked with Keats' great odes.

Like "Edward" or "Lord Randal", Keats' ballad consists
exclusively of direct speech (without *inquit* formulae). The first
three stanzas are spoken by the narrator, who asks a medieval
knight whom he has met in an autumnal setting what he is
suffering from. The remaining nine stanzas are the answer of
the knight; he tells about his encounter with a beautiful elfin
lady: how she took him with her to fairyland, how they made
love, and how he was finally frustrated.

Formally, Keats uses the well-known ballad stanza (with
the rhyme scheme *abcb*). There is, however, one variation: the
last line of each four-line stanza has only two, instead of three,
stresses, which retards it and gives it a particular emphasis, as
in stanzas 7 and 8:

> She found me roots of relish sweet,
>   And honey wild, and manna-dew,
> And sure in language strange she said—
>   'I love thee true'.

[27] See Hoffman and Hynes, *English Literary Criticism*, pp. 32–33.
[28] Letter 222, p. 416.

> She took me to her elfin grot,
>> And there she wept and sighed full sore,
> And there I shut her wild wild eyes
>> With kisses four. (See p. 411.)

In the long letter of February 14–May 3, 1819, where Keats communicates the text of his ballad for the first time, he jokes about the question of "why four Kisses" and gives the facetious answer, "I was obliged to choose an even number that both eyes might have fair play";[29] but numbers like this, with their potentially mystical significance, are precisely what one would expect to find in a ballad of tradition. Also the loving attention to concrete detail, as one observes in this passage, seems characteristic of the traditional ballad world. Repetition, like "her wild wild eyes", is a typical stylistic device of the ballad. Incremental repetition effectively shapes the first two stanzas of the ballad, which both begin with "O, what can ail thee, knight-at-arms ... ?" (see p. 410).

A kind of repetition is also used, with great poignancy, to create an impressive frame for the poem and link the opening and final stanzas, as well as to give the story a special emphasis. At the beginning, the narrator poses the question:

> O what can ail thee, knight-at-arms,
>> Alone and palely loitering?
> The sedge has withered from the lake,
>> And no birds sing. (See p. 410.)

The relationship between the sad figure of the knight and his autumnal surroundings remains ambivalent. We may wonder whether there is a relation of correspondence (that deserted nature corresponds to his sorrowful appearance) or of contrast (in view of the inhospitable state of nature he should not be there).

This is specified by the knight's final answer in the concluding stanza, which uses the same words but adds an important logical conjunction:

[29] Letter 123, p. 164.

And this is why I sojourn here
  Alone and palely loitering,
Though the sedge is withered from the lake,
  And no birds sing. (See p. 412.)

With his "Though", the knight makes it clear that, after his return from fairyland, he is completely alienated from the real world.

La Belle Dame sans Merci[30] not only bears the salient generic features of the popular ballad but also has a close resemblance to a specific ballad. Like Keats' poem, "Thomas Rymer" (Child 37)[31] tells the story of a man who meets the queen of Elfland, accompanies her to her country, and finally returns to his own world. It is perhaps the ballad-like openness of Keats' poem that has been a challenge and invitation for critics to offer the most diverse interpretations. From understanding it as "a poetological poem", as "a tale about how to eat wisely, or not too well", and to seeing it as a case of "sexual harassment", wildly different readings have been suggested.[32]

Even if one is not prepared to accept any of such bold attempts, *La Belle Dame sans Merci* certainly does more than merely tell a story about a strange adventure, like "Thomas Rymer". It deals with a theme that is also Keats' central concern in the odes, namely, the experience of the disintegration of the self, the reaching for the absolute, the encounter with the ideal.[33] That this is only a partial and temporary possibility for the individual is particularly expressed in stanza 9, where the knight complains:

[30] This is also the title of a poem, in rhyme royal and octaves, translated from Alain Chartier, attributed at one time to Chaucer.

[31] Child 37 is a reference to the Child ballad, named after the American scholar Francis James Child, who edited the canonical collection *The English and Scottish Popular Ballads* (1882–1898) in five volumes with 305 ballads and their numerous variants.

[32] All these examples were quoted in Bode, *Keats: Play On*, pp. 164–66 (some quotations translated).

[33] This direction is pointed out in a highly intelligent interpretation of this ballad, by Earl R. Wasserman in his *Finer Tone: Keats' Major Poems* (Baltimore; London: John Hopkins Press, 1953), pp. 65–83.

And there she lullèd me asleep
  And there I dreamed—Ah! woe betide!—
The latest dream I ever dreamt
  On the cold hill side. (See p. 411.)

So Keats, like Coleridge and Wordsworth before him,[34] uses the form of the ballad with great skill for his own purposes.[35] Both as sonneteer and as balladeer, he is outstanding among the English Romantic poets.

---

[34] See my essay "'A Still More Naked and Simple Style'—the English Romantic Poets and the Ballad", in *The Romantic Poets*, ed. Joseph Pearce and Robert Asch, vol. 1, *Blake, Wordsworth, and Coleridge*, Ignatius Critical Editions (San Francisco: Ignatius Press, 2014), pp. 445–59.

[35] Another short poem, "Song" ("The stranger lighted from his steed"), can also be regarded as a ballad (see *Complete Poems*, pp. 175–76).

"Close Reading" and the Political Lyrics of Percy Shelley

Robert C. Evans
Auburn University at Montgomery

I

"Close reading" is an analytical method often associated with critical "formalism" or with Anglo-American "New Criticism", an approach especially influential from the 1940s through the 1960s. Close reading involves looking at a text as if every single word or even every syllable is potentially significant, in several senses of that word. Since the 1960s, however, "formalism" has come under repeated attack—an ironic tribute to the enormous influence it once exercised and indeed still exercises, especially in the classroom. Close reading, however, was not a radically new invention; it was, rather, merely a re-articulation of concerns at least as old as Aristotle—concerns unlikely to die as long as readers remain truly interested in the nitty-gritty rhetorical details of literary works.

In fact, such attention to almost microscopic detail need not be associated simply with formalism. Any interpretive method can benefit by examining works of literature closely rather than making broad-brush generalizations or forcing texts to fit into preconceived patterns of meaning. One great merit of close reading is that it resists any impulse to turn literature into mere propaganda. Of all critical approaches, close reading is perhaps the least reductive, always capable of surprising us and helping us perceive the true riches of a text rather than simply finding in it some easy-to-paraphrase (and usually very simple and even sometimes trite) "message".

II

Close reading can be especially valuable in dealing with political poems—poems that almost seem to demand focus on their content. Such poems can easily be read as mere reductive propaganda. Yet anyone who wants to express a clear political position might just as easily compose an essay, pen a manifesto, or hang up a placard. Why write a poem? Of all the genres, poetry is, after all, perhaps *the* most literary. Poetry, that is, is usually so far divorced from "normal" ways of writing (because of such factors as rhyme, meter, or merely the existence of distinct lines) that it almost inevitably calls attention to itself *as* language. If we think of literature as writing that invites close attention to itself *as* writing—as skillfully manipulating the various devices of language—then poetry can seem the most literary writing of all. Yet if we think of political propaganda as writing whose *message* is crucial, political poetry can seem a strange mixing of apparently opposed impulses.

III

Among all the writers in English who have expressed strong religious or political ideas, Percy Bysshe Shelley is a conspicuous example of a poet whose works have often suffered by being treated merely as political messages.[1] Right from the start, Shelley's poems were often judged for their ideas alone rather than for their poetic success. In fact, some of Shelley's political poems were so politically offensive that they could not be published in his lifetime. Yet even admirers of Shelley's political verse have frequently admired it more for its ideas than for its literary skill and artistic craft. Admittedly, the lengthier political poems have often been examined closely, but the shorter political lyrics have often been ignored. Sometimes, quite frankly, they are not especially impressive poems. Close reading, however, can help us perceive more clearly both the weaknesses and the strengths of Shelley's political lyrics.

Some of these poems do admittedly make for awkward reading, whether read closely or simply skimmed. Yet reading such poems closely allows us to see precisely where various problems

---

[1] See, for example, Donald H. Reiman, "Shelley's Reputation Before 1960: A Sketch", in *Shelley's Poetry and Prose*, 2nd ed., ed. Donald H. Reiman and Neil Fraistat (New York: Norton, 2002), pp. 539–49.

arise. And reading them closely also allows us, sometimes, to perceive competence or even talent where we might originally have perceived simple clumsiness. Take, for instance, these lines from Shelley's "A New National Anthem":

> Lips, touched by seraphim
> Breathe out the choral hymn
> God save the Queen!
> Sweet as if angels sang,
> Loud as that [trumpet's] clang
> Wakening the world's dead gang,
> God save the Queen! (lines 36–42)[2]

The reference to a trumpet's "clang" sounds awkward today, but a check of the *Oxford English Dictionary* (*OED*) shows that in Shelley's era a "clang" could mean a "loud resonant metallic sound (esp. of trumpet, arms, large bell, some birds)".[3] In addition, a quick check of Google Books shows that "clang" was in fact often used, by major authors (including Shakespeare), in precisely this way. Similarly, the reference to the world's dead "gang" sounds odd, especially since that term often had (and still has) highly negative connotations. Perhaps Shelley meant to suggest a "gang" of prisoners or slaves (one of the word's meanings at the time, according to the *OED*). This "gang" might therefore seem a group of oppressed victims. Yet "gang" seems awkward—a choice dictated mainly and merely, it would seem, by the need to rhyme.

In contrast, more can be said for the poem's opening:

> God! prosper, speed, and save,
> God! raise from England's grave
> Her murdered Queen. (lines 1–3)

[2] All quotations from Shelley's poetry, except where otherwise noted, are from the Longman edition: *The Poems of Shelley 1819–20*, ed. Jack Donovan et al. (Harlow, U.K.: Longman, 2011). In line 40, the word "trumpet's" is usually the word that precedes "clang" in printed versions of this text, and Donovan et al. suggest that it probably was Shelley's final choice (see p. 345).

[3] *The Oxford Dictionary of Current English*, 5th ed. (London: Oxford University Press, 1964), s.v. "clang".

These lines seem relatively variously effective. First, they obviously echo, in phrasing and rhythms, the British national anthem. Indeed, the first line is, if anything, even more emphatic than the opening of the original. Shelley includes three strong verbs, but while the first two are predictably positive, the third is a bit unsettling, so that even the poem's first line catches us somewhat by surprise. The next two lines are even more ironic and grow in intensity and seriousness. Shelley creates suspense: Who, exactly, is this "Queen"? Why does she need to be saved, and how resurrected? How and by whom has she been murdered? Not until line 5 do we discover that she is "Liberty", Britain's "Immortal Queen" (line 7).

Various other aspects of this poem are effective, including the compelling, imperative vividness of line 8 ("See, she comes throned on high"), the skillful repetition in line 11 ("Millions on millions wait") and the syntactical repetition in lines 15 and 18. In general, however, this is not an especially successful poem *as a poem*. Thus, when Shelley describes the awaiting millions as "[f]irm, rapid, [and] elate", the first two adjectives (and the second especially) seem puzzling. Perhaps "[f]irm" refers to the millions' steadiness and constancy, and perhaps "rapid" refers to their quick understanding. But the phrasing here and elsewhere seems merely competent, and sometimes not even that. Sometimes, it seems clichéd (thus love is said to have "[r]ained down from Heaven above" [line 19]) and sometimes awkward (as in "Wilder her enemies/In their own dark disguise" [lines 22–23]), where "Wilder" means "bewilder" and where the rhyme seems forced. As propaganda, this poem may have stirred those already inclined to agree with its sentiments, but probably few would claim that it is especially skillful as a work of art.

IV

Conversely, a nice example of a poem that actually benefits from being read closely is part of the following fragment:

What men gain fairly—that should they possess,
And children may inherit idleness
From him who earns it … this is understood—
Private injustice may be general good.
But he who gains by base and armèd wrong
Or guilty fraud, or base compliances
With those whom force or falsehood has made strong
May be despoiled; even as a stolen dress
Is stripped from a convicted thief; and he
Left in the nakedness of infamy.

Even here, unfortunately, problems arise. The opening line is clear, but lines 2–4 seem vague. The second and third presumably mean that a productive person may have unproductive children, although the referent of "it" in line 3 is unclear, and the logical connection between lines 1 and 2 is obscure. Presumably, line 4 suggests that motives traditionally considered unjust when practiced by individuals (such as greed or self-interest) may, nonetheless, benefit society at large.

Even in these lines, however, some phrasing seems praiseworthy. Thus, the two halves of line 1 are nicely balanced, helping the speaker seem reasonable and fair. Moreover, here, unlike in line 3, the pronoun's meaning is absolutely clear. Effective alliteration appears in "men" and "gain" and also in "that" and "they", thus enhancing the line's balance. Similarly balanced are "[p]rivate injustice" and "general good"—balance again reinforced by alliteration, particularly in "injustice" and "general".

The poem becomes even better, however, from this point forward. Thus, line 5's particular phrasing is strong, partly because it moves from the general, somewhat vague adjective "base" to the more precise and threatening "armèd", while "gains" echoes "gain" in line 1 for further balance. The final five lines are also skillful. Balanced phrasing continues in line 6, with one adjective/noun pairing set off against another. The word "guilty" is somewhat ironic, since the guilt implied is social guilt (determined by others) rather than private guilt (resulting from conscientious self-reflection). It is precisely because of the absence of the first kind of guilt that the second kind exists: if more people *felt* guilty, guilty *conduct* would be less likely.

In line 8, the word "[m]ay" can suggest either that those guilty of social injustice may, *perhaps*, find themselves violently dispossessed or that they may be despoiled in the sense that society will or should *approve* of such treatment. Ironically, then, despoilers "may" themselves be "despoiled", a word appropriately suggesting the idea of clothing being removed (*OED*). The word thus foreshadows the ensuing simile of stolen clothing being stripped from a convicted thief. Indeed, that simile is much more precise, graphic, and specific than any earlier phrasing. The text thus becomes increasingly vivid. The verb "stripped" is especially strong, while "stolen dress" and "convicted thief" provide another example of rhetorical balance. Balance is also achieved in the final line, where the concrete noun "nakedness" is balanced by the abstract noun "infamy". That word brings the text to a strong conclusion, while Shelley also, in the final three lines, shows his talent for enjambment and, in the final line itself, skillfully alliterates *f*'s and *n*'s.

Ironically, "[w]hat men gain fairly" is effective political verse partly because it *is* a fragment: unlike "A New National Anthem", it is potently brief (10 lines versus 42). Its second half is especially strongly written, whatever one's own political or economic views. Paradoxically, the more effective political poetry is as *poetry*, the more effective it is also likely to be as propaganda. Badly written political verse is especially likely to win the derision of readers who do not already agree with its ideas.

V

One example of a political poem by Shelley that achieves mixed success is "To S[idmouth] and C[astlereagh]". This work attacks the contemporary home and foreign secretaries—politicians whom Shelley detested. It opens by comparing them to "[t]wo empty ravens [that] wind their clarion,/Yell by yell, and croak for croak,/When they scent the noonday smoke/Of fresh human carrion" (lines 2–5). The paired ideas of ravens with a trumpet ("clarion") can seem awkward, as can the idea of ravens yelling. Meanwhile, the reference to "smoke" (rather than stench) seems dictated mostly by the need to rhyme. Arguments might conceivably be made on behalf of all these phrasings, but that is precisely part of the point of close reading: to examine poems word by word to determine how particular phrasing either succeeds or fails. A close reader would welcome any explanation that might make these apparently awkward word choices seem convincing and assured.

Admirers of Shelley appear to have much to defend in the present poem. The next stanza, for instance, calls the politicians a pair of "gibbering night-birds" who "flit/From their bower of deadly yew/Through the night to frighten it" (lines 6–8). While most of this phrasing is unobjectionable (and "gibbering" seems effective), the reference to "it" seems strained. Is Shelley suggesting that the night-birds frighten night itself? In that case, the personification seems lax and exaggerated. He next asserts that the night-birds fly "[w]hen the moon is in a fit" (line 9)—phrasing that seems imprecise and confusing, unless we assume that clouds are passing rapidly in front of the moon, making it seem full of erratic change. Here and elsewhere, Shelley's personifications often cause problems, so that readers strain to comprehend meaning rather than instantly recognizing its power.

Thus, the ensuing comparison of the politicians to a "shark and dogfish" (line 11) seems effective, but the assertion that they "wait/*Under* an Atlantic isle" (lines 11–12; my italics) seems woefully imprecise. The sharks wait "[f]or the Negro ship, whose freight/Is the theme of their debate" (lines 13–14)—phrasing that seems effective until line 14 arrives, with its especially unfortunate noun "debate". Yet Shelley immediately redeems himself when he vividly describes the sharks "[w]rinkling their red gills the while" (line 15).

Indeed, the whole final stanza seems variously effective. There Shelley compares the politicians to

> two vultures sick for battle,
> Two scorpions under one wet stone,
> Two bloodless wolves whose dry throats rattle,
> Two crows perched on the murrained cattle,
> Two vipers tangled into one. (lines 16–20)

Much is admirable here. Thus, the vultures are "sick" for battle in which others will be victims, not themselves. Meanwhile, line 17 is especially vivid and striking: Shelley seems to be creating powerful imagery rather than repeating tired clichés. Moreover, the reference to "murrained" cattle inventively transforms the noun "murrain" (referring to disease or infection) into an adjective. Finally, he ends by making the two politicians seem inseparably toxic. The final word— "one"—is especially potent after the many earlier beginning references to "[t]wo". Indeed, this kind of repetition (known as "anaphora") gives the final stanza relentless rhythmical force, so that the concluding reference to "one" seems all the more abrupt and surprising.

"To S[idmouth] and C[astlereagh]" thus illustrates both some of the strengths and also some of the weaknesses of Shelley's political lyrics. Sometimes his imagery can seem tired, vague, inconsistent, or imprecise. At other times, however, his language can seem sharp and vivid. Only close examination of each political poem *as* a poem can reveal either the true effectiveness or ineffectiveness of Shelley the political poet.

VI

One poem worth examining more closely is titled "To —— [the Lord Chancellor]". It attacks Lord Chancellor Eldon, an ally of the politicians just discussed. Eldon, a leading judge, had ruled against Shelley in a child custody case, so the poet had personal reasons to despise him. All that really matters to a formalist close reader, however, is the poem's poetic effectiveness, and there is much to be said for it in this respect. Thus, it opens with particular vigor:

> Thy country's curse is on thee, darkest Crest
> Of that foul, knotted, many-headed worm
> Which rends our mother's bosom!—Priestly Pest!
> Masked Resurrection of a buried form! (lines 1–4)

The powerfully alliterative first line contributes to the poem's success, while the piled, ever-lengthening list of adjectives in line 2 effectively delays the abrupt appearance of the striking noun "worm". This worm, or snake, "rends" (tears, lacerates, or wounds severely) "our mother's bosom", thus figuratively destroying the source of England's life, while "our" implies that Shelley speaks not just for himself but also for other victims of injustice. Meanwhile, the abrupt exclamation "Priestly Pest!" (line 3) implies emotions so strong that the speaker cannot contain them in conventional sentence structure. The alliterating *p*'s, of course, add to the exclamation's power, while "Pest" itself is variously relevant, suggesting pestilence or plague, a noxious person or nuisance, and an infectious insect or invasive weed (*OED*). Far less clear in meaning, however, is the stanza's final line: "Masked Resurrection of a buried form!" (line 4). What this means, precisely, is not immediately clear. Such phrasing typifies Shelley's unfortunate tendency to lapse into language that sometimes seems vague and imprecise.

He quickly recovers, however, in stanza 2:

> Thy country's curse is on thee—Justice sold,
> Truth trampled, Nature's landmarks overthrown,
> And heaps of fraud-accumulated gold
> Plead, loud as thunder, at destruction's throne.
>   (lines 5–8)

This is variously effective. The opening words, for instance, echo the poem's very beginning, and the phrasing is also potent, thanks to such touches as the extreme brevity of "Justice sold,/Truth trampled"; the inventiveness of "fraud-accumulated"; and the emphatic positioning of "Plead" with its metrical emphasis. The exact meaning of "Nature's land-marks overthrown" would have been clearer to Shelley's con-temporaries than to us today, but the general idea that Eldon behaves unnaturally and even disturbs the natural order is effectively suggested.

In general, in fact, this poem is clear and rhetorically potent. Thus, Shelley mimics an unhurried pace in the words "sure slow Fate" (line 9), where all three syllables receive equal metrical emphasis. Effective phrasing also appears in the allit-erative "thine and thee" (line 12); in the abrupt outburst of "O" at the start of line 13; and in the meaningful switch from a general emphasis on "Thy country's curse" to a personal emphasis on "a father's curse" (line 13). Especially effective is the speaker's hope that a "leaden cowl" will "weigh thee down to thy approaching doom" (line 16). Here the first three syllables, rather than being read as "WEIGH thee DOWN", almost demand to be read as "WEIGH THEE DOWN". Thus, the accumulated heavy accents mimic the weight the phrase describes. In addition, line 16 also benefits musically from the alliteration of "thee" and "thine" (which themselves echo and reverse "thine and thee" from four lines earlier) and also of "down" and "doom". Finally, the key word "doom" is effec-tively placed at the very end of the stanza.

The poem continues for twelve more stanzas, each effective (for the most part) in its own ways, particularly through the use of anaphora and other forms of repetition and also through strik-ing alliteration and assonance, as in such phrases (my italics) as "hopes *l*ong cherished and too *l*ately *l*ost" (line 18); "un*t*imely *n*ight" (line 23); and "un*p*ractised *a*ccents" (line 25). This is a lengthy poem that both invites and rewards close attention. It brims with literary skill and thus makes a reader want to con-tinue reading.

VII

One justly famous political lyric by Shelley is "England in 1819". Even this work, however, has not often received the kind of close attention it deserves.[4]

> An old, mad, blind, despised, and dying King; *a*
> Princes, the dregs of their dull race, who flow *b*
> Through public scorn,—mud from a muddy spring; *a*
> Rulers who neither see nor feel nor know, *b*
> But leechlike to their fainting country cling *a*
> Till they drop, blind in blood, without a blow. *b*
> A people starved and stabbed in th'untilled field; *c*
> An army, which liberticide and prey *d*
> Makes as a two-edged sword to all who wield; *c*
> Golden and sanguine laws which tempt and slay; *d*
> Religion Christless, Godless—a book sealed; *c*
> A senate, Time's worst statute, unrepealed— *c*
> Are graves from which a glorious Phantom may *d*
> Burst, to illumine our tempestuous day. *d*[5]

In reprinting the poem, I have marked its highly unusual rhyme scheme. Shelley is here breaking all the rules of rhyming normally associated with conventional English sonnets. The poem *does* have fourteen lines, and the first four do rhyme in typically Shakespearean fashion. The rhymed closing couplet also recalls Shakespeare, but the intervening rhymes are highly unusual. It is as if, to describe England's breakdown, Shelley chose a breakdown in traditional form.

This sonnet is highly effective for many reasons, including the first line's piled, rhythmically emphasized adjectives; its

---

[4] A splendid exception is Stephen Burt's very recent analysis of the poem in Stephen Burt and David Mikics, *The Art of the Sonnet* (Cambridge, Mass.: Belknap Press of Harvard University Press, 2010), pp. 230–33. I did not discover Burt's reading of the sonnet until after completing my own and am pleased to see that our readings complement each other, without much overlap.

[5] Percy Bysshe Shelley, "England in 1819", in *The Romantic Poets*, ed. Joseph Pearce and Robert Asch, vol. 2, *Byron, Shelley, and Keats*, Ignatius Critical Editions (San Francisco: Ignatius Press, 2024), p. 193.

combination of alliteration and assonance; its skillful postpone-
ment of the crucial noun "King"; and the way all the adjectives
seem highly ironic modifiers of that noun. The decay of the
king symbolizes the decay of the kingdom, and although four
of the five adjectives might suggest some sympathy for him as a
person, the adjective "despised" suggests that he should not be
overly pitied.

In line 2, the king's sons are described as "dregs", a noun with
variously relevant connotations. It could refer, for instance (see
OED), to last remains, to small remnants, or to residue (espe-
cially the kind that sink to the bottom of a liquid). Yet "dregs"
could also suggest feces, excrement, refuse, and rubbish, as well
as any corrupt or defiling matters and even the morbid con-
sequences of a disease. The reference to "dregs", therefore, is
even more effective than it might initially seem, and so is the
adjective "dull", whose meanings are also variously appropriate.
Such meanings include unintelligent, mentally slow, stupid,
lacking wit, fatuous, foolish, inert, sluggish, inactive, lacking
vivacity, depressed, listless, melancholy, boring, and tedious.

The verb "flow" may seem inappropriate to "dregs" (can
dregs move swiftly?), and the idea of dregs flowing "[t]hrough
public scorn" may seem to mix vivid imagery with a mere dry
abstraction. But at least the reference to "public scorn" echoes
the adjective "despised" in the opening line (thus reinforc-
ing the poem's unity), and that phrase also calls attention to
Shelley's own sonnet as a specific instance of such scorn (and
also designed to provoke it). The royal heirs are "mud from a
muddy spring"—a vivid image, made especially emphatic by
the repetitive phrasing, thus suggesting intense pollution of a
potential source of national vitality.

England's political leaders are then termed "[r]ulers" (thus
emphasizing their mere power rather than any more positive
connotations), and then the poem offers a striking list of
emphatic monosyllabic verbs that echo the list of emphatic
adjectives with which the poem began. These "[r]ulers ... nei-
ther see nor feel nor know": they lack perception, emotions,

and intellect. All these verbs thus build on meanings earlier implied by "dull". These "[r]ulers" should represent the nation's interests but instead merely suck its blood with a strength that paradoxically weakens the nation.

Indeed, they are described as leeches: blind, unintelligent parasites driven by mere appetite. At least real leeches, in Shelley's day, were thought to have some beneficial medicinal uses, but these human leeches lack any positive traits. They merely "drop" (a metrically emphasized verb), "blind in blood, without a blow" (a nice example of alliteration). The language here, as throughout the poem, is crisp, clear, and straightforwardly simple. The speaker's tone is simultaneously passionate and lucid. Meanwhile, the fact that the leeches fall "without a blow" suggests their own ultimate weakness as well as the present weakness of the political opposition.

Having first discussed the nation's "[r]ulers", Shelley next describes a "people starved and stabbed in th'untilled field"—a line splendidly combining alliteration and assonance while also using the "untilled field" to symbolize infertility and death. Literally, of course, this phrase alludes to the famous massacre of political protestors in a field in Manchester in 1819, but the "field" here is both figurative and literal. Yet despite the deaths of fifteen people in Manchester from saber-swinging cavalry, Shelley suggests that the army, if it ever shifted its allegiance to the oppressed, might very well turn into a "two-edged sword"—not only a vivid phrase but probably also an allusion to biblical imagery implying divine retribution (see, for instance, Hebrews 4:12). The reference to the army's "prey" seems confusing until we discover that this noun could refer to "something taken in war or by pillage; booty, plunder" (*OED*). The army, then, is for the time being associated with the earlier leeches, both surviving on valuables taken from others.

The reference to "[g]olden and sanguine laws which tempt and slay" is less clear than the rest of the poem (who is tempted and how?). Yet the idea that laws have led to bloodshed is obviously paradoxical, and the adjective "[g]olden" can also be interpreted as an ironic allusion to the biblical "golden rule" (see Matthew 7:12).[6] If this latter reading is persuasive, then the phrasing contributes to the heavy emphasis on religious allusions and references in the sonnet's second half. Thus, Shelley contends that in contemporary England "[r]eligion" is "Christless, Godless—a book sealed". He thereby implicitly contrasts the Heavenly King and his self-sacrificing Son to the earthly king and his self-interested heirs. Likewise, Shelley tries to shame contemporary Christians by suggesting that the contemporary church is Christian only in name, not in the truest senses. The national Church shows neglect of, or even contempt for, Christ, like the neglect and contempt the rulers feel toward the English people. The Church is "Godless", not merely because God is absent from it and from its conduct, but also because its conduct is wicked, impious, and evil.

Shelley's reference to "a book sealed" alludes to printed copies of the official Anglican "Book of Common Prayer of 1662 [which was] certified under the Great Seal" of the kingdom (*OED*). Yet the phrase probably also suggests that the Bible itself is now a book obscured "beyond a person's capacity to understand" (*OED*) by a Church hierarchy more interested in retaining power than in honestly sharing the potentially revolutionary Word of God.[7] Meanwhile, the word "senate" symbolically links the British Parliament, probably ironically, with the main pillar of the republic of ancient Rome. Only when we arrive at line 13 does the long-delayed and crucial verb "[a]re" appear, so that the poem achieves and sustains enormous suspense before it powerfully concludes.

---

[6] Stephen Burt's comments on "[g]olden" are typically suggestive and thorough: "English laws do not represent justice: 'golden' is sarcastic in one sense (the laws violate ordinary morality), straightforward in another (the laws serve the rich), and allusive in a third (laws protecting private property make it into an idol like the Golden Calf)." See Burt and Mikics, *Art of the Sonnet*, p. 132.

[7] The editors of the Longman edition quote a particularly relevant biblical passage (Isaiah 29:11): "And the vision of all is become unto you as the words of a book that is sealed, which men deliver to one that is learned, saying, Read this, I pray thee: and he saith, I cannot, for it is sealed" (p. 191).

Appropriately enough, the word "graves" both echoes and brings to a culmination all the earlier references to death. Yet no sooner does Shelley emphasize that grim word than he shifts to an appealing but mysterious alternative: the possibility that "a glorious Phantom may/Burst" from the graves "to illumine our tempestuous day" (lines 13–14). Although the word "Phantom" often has negative connotations, Shelley seems to have used it to suggest an appealing apparition, spirit, or ghost. Several critics have found this reference vague or weak.[8] A passage in Shelley's prose suggests that the "Phantom" may have been meant to suggest a resurgent spirit of Liberty, in which case the phrasing would answer the earlier reference to "liberticide" (line 8).[9] Perhaps there is even a hint of some kind of spiritual revelation; in any case, the word "glorious" anticipates both "illumine" and the final word, "day", so that a poem previously filled with darkness now seems filled with literal and symbolic light.

Even "[b]urst", so emphatically placed at the beginning of the line and so heavily stressed by the meter, could imply sudden illumination, suggesting something abruptly made radiant. And the word is also, of course, wonderfully onomatopoeic. Yet the final couplet's emphasis on light is also carefully qualified by the adjective "tempestuous", suggesting such connotations as dark, stormy, violent, turbulent, and passionate. Shelley himself, of course, is passionate in this poem, but the simple word "may" also suggests a passion checked by reason. His hopes are qualified by a realistic sense of what may—or may not—be possible. Thus, a poem partly designed to provoke splendid transformation is mainly an ardent wish. The speaker implicitly identifies himself with his readers: he speaks of "our" tempestuous day, suggesting a particular moment in human history as well as his fellowship with other oppressed people of his time and place.

---

[8] F. R. Leavis, for example, famously referred to "the pathetic weakness of the final couplet". See F. R. Leavis, *Revaluation* (London: Chatto and Windus, 1947), p. 228.

[9] See the Longman edition, p. 192.

However much one may agree or disagree with Shelley's specific political stance in this work, most people who read the poem closely would be hard-pressed to deny its power and effectiveness simply *as* a poem and therefore (paradoxically) also as a piece of potent political propaganda. "England in 1819", like many of Shelley's political lyrics, benefits from close attention to the specific details of Shelley's art.

Clipping an Angel's Wings:
Science, Poetry, and the Late Romantics

Amy Fahey
Thomas More College of Liberal Arts

> We shall find the Cube of the Rainbow
> Of that there is no doubt
> But the Arc of a Lover's conjecture
> Eludes the finding out.
>
> — Emily Dickinson*

> The impulses to awe, reverence and wonder which led Blake to mysticism … are precisely those that lead others of us to science…. The mystic is content to bask in the wonder and revel in a mystery that we were not "meant" to understand. The scientist feels the same wonder but is restless, not content; recognizes the mystery as profound, then adds, "But we're working on it."
>
> — Richard Dawkins

At the close of John Keats' "Ode on a Grecian Urn", the urn proclaims to mankind, "'Beauty is truth, truth beauty,—that is all/Ye know on earth, and all ye need to know.'"[1] These memorable lines help contribute to our conception of the English Romantic poets as "poets of Nature", or at least "poets of Beauty", who reaffirmed the beauty and mystery of the created world at a time when most of Western thought had embraced the empirical suppositions of the eighteenth-century Enlightenment rationalists or the disastrous materialist views

---

* Letter from Emily Dickinson to Sarah Tuckerman, January 1880.

[1] John Keats, "Ode on a Grecian Urn", in *The Romantic Poets*, ed. Joseph Pearce and Robert Asch, vol. 2, *Byron, Shelley, and Keats*, Ignatius Critical Editions (San Francisco: Ignatius Press, 2024), p. 447, lines 49–50. Subsequent citations of poetry by Byron, Shelley, and Keats from this edition will be cited in the text.

of the French revolutionaries. Indeed, Hans Eichner suggests that "Romanticism is, perhaps predominantly, a desperate rear-guard action against the spirit and the implications of modern science."[2] Equally well-known lines, like William Wordsworth's accusation in his Preface to *Lyrical Ballads* that "we murder to dissect",[3] or William Blake's criticism of rationalist thought in "Mock on Mock on Voltaire Rousseau" ("The Atoms of Democritus/And Newton's Particles of light/Are sands upon the Red sea shore/Where Israel's tents do shine so bright"[4]), seem to confirm the perception that the Romantic poets were critical of man's desire to master nature, that they viewed the prevailing rationalist scientific method as antithetical to the sense of mystery and beauty they so frequently sought to convey in their poetry, and that they saw a direct correlation between the rationalist impulse to conquer nature in the name of human progress and the industrialization of the English countryside (one thinks of the "dark Satanic Mills" of Blake's "Jerusalem"[5]). As M. H. Abrams, in his classic study on Romantic poetry, *The Mirror and the Lamp*, reminds us, the exclusive claims to truth proposed by both the scientist and the poet often led to a combative opposition: "To some writers, it seemed that poetry and science are not only antithetic, but incompatible, and that if science is true, poetry must be false, or at any rate, trivial."[6] We thus frequently find poets like William Wordsworth, Percy Bysshe Shelley, and John Keats making impassioned arguments in defense of poetry over scientific reasoning.

Yet the English Romantic poets were acutely conflicted in their understanding of the relationship between modern

[2] Hans Eichner, "The Rise of Modern Science and the Genesis of Romanticism", *PMLA* 97 (1982): 8, 17.

[3] William Wordsworth, "Preface to the Second Edition of the *Lyrical Ballads*", in *English Romantic Writers*, ed. David Perkins (New York: Harcourt, 1967), p. 329.

[4] William Blake, "Mock on Mock on Voltaire Rousseau", in *The Romantic Poets*, ed. Joseph Pearce and Robert Asch, vol. 1, *Blake, Wordsworth, and Coleridge*, Ignatius Critical Editions (San Francisco: Ignatius Press, 2014), p. 58, lines 9–12.

[5] William Blake, "And did those feet in ancient time" [also known as the hymn "Jerusalem"], from *Milton*, in *Romantic Poets*, vol. 1, p. 79, line 8.

[6] M. H. Abrams, *The Mirror and the Lamp: Romantic Theory and the Critical Tradition* (New York: Norton & Company, 1958), p. 299.

science and their own poetic endeavors. Wordsworth, in the same Preface in which he criticizes the scientist's relentless desire for discrete knowledge, looks optimistically toward a day when the scientist and the poet will be united in their endeavors: "If the labours of Men of science should ever create any material revolution ... the Poet will sleep then no more than at present; he will be ready to follow the steps of the Man of science.... He will be at his side, carrying sensation into the midst of the objects of the science itself."[7] And the same Blake who excoriates Newton declares at the end of his apocalyptic vision in "Jerusalem" that within the "innumerable Chariots of the Almighty" that appear in Heaven, the scientists are reconciled with the poets "Bacon & Newton & Locke, & Milton & Shakespeare & Chaucer".[8] Indeed, it is possible to delineate a convergence of scientific and poetic thought during the Romantic Age, at a time when both pursuits tend toward an almost utopian vision of man's potential, whether conceived intellectually, materially, or both. As the German Romantic philosopher Friedrich Schelling headily announced to his university students in 1802:

> At the present time, everything in science and art seems to be tending toward unity, when matters that long seemed remote from each other are now recognized to be quite close, and a new more universal vision, encompassing almost all disciplines, is taking shape. An epoch such as our own is surely bound to give birth to a new world.[9]

Closer to home, Romantic scientist and aspiring (if unimpressive) poet Sir Humphry Davy, conducting electrochemical experiments in the early 1800s, could declare to his

---

[7] William Wordsworth, "Preface to *Lyrical Ballads*", in *Romantic Poets*, vol. 1, p. 100.

[8] William Blake, *Jerusalem: The Emanation of the Giant Albion* (Princeton, N.J.: Princeton University Press, 1991), p. 294.

[9] F. W. J. Schelling, *On University Studies*, trans. E. S. Morgan, ed. Norbert Guterman (Athens: Ohio University Press, 1966), p. 7, quoted in Mark Kipperman, "Coleridge, Shelley, Davy, and Science's Millenium", *Criticism*, Summer 1998, p. 409.

sympathetic friend Samuel Taylor Coleridge that he had made "some important galvanic discoveries which seem to lead to the door of the temple of the mysterious god of Life".[10]

If the perception of the English Romantics as starry-eyed friends of science is as problematic as the conception of them as simply idealized "poets of Nature" or "poets of Beauty", it is largely because they were such deeply conflicted souls. This is particularly true of the later Romantics—Shelley, Byron, and Keats—who present neither a monolithic nor an internally coherent conception of the relationship between scientific and poetic thought. It is worth reconsidering, though, from the vantage of our present day, in which it could be said that science has once again claimed primacy over poetry and the arts, what the Romantic poets have to say about the relationship between scientific rationalism and poetic understanding. Were they reactionary critics of the Enlightenment? Were they visionary synthesizers of science and poetry? For the purposes of this study, we will focus our gaze on the three late Romantic poets represented in this volume—Shelley, Byron, and Keats—for they were arguably the most complex and ambiguous in their articulation of the relationship between science and poetry.

Percy Bysshe Shelley: The Poet as Mad Scientist

Thomas Jefferson Hogg (1792–1862) befriended the young Shelley while the two were students at Oxford and later wrote a biographical sketch of the poet. In it, Hogg includes a description of the seventeen-year-old Shelley's living quarters at University College, Oxford:

> Books, boots, papers, shoes, philosophical instruments, clothes, pistols, linen, crockery, ammunition, and phials innumerable, with money, stockings, prints, crucibles, bags, and boxes, were

[10]Quoted in Trevor Levere, *Poetry Realized in Nature: Samuel Taylor Coleridge and Early Nineteenth-Century Science* (Cambridge: Cambridge University Press, 1981), p. 32.

scattered on the floor in every place; as if the young chemist, in order to analyze the mystery of creation, had endeavoured first to re-construct the primeval chaos.... An electrical machine, an air-pump, the galvanic trough, a solar microscope, and large glass jars and receivers, were conspicuous amidst the mass of matter.... Two piles of books supported the tongs, and these upheld a small glass retort above an argand lamp. I had not been seated many minutes before the liquor in the vessel boiled over, adding fresh stains to the table, and rising in fumes with a most disagreeable odor. Shelley snatched the glass quickly and dashing it in pieces among the ashes under the grate, increased the unpleasant and penetrating effluvium.[11]

We needn't be surprised if the description seems more like that of Dr. Frankenstein's laboratory than the college dorm room of one of England's most renowned poets, for as philosopher-mathematician Alfred North Whitehead once observed, if Shelley "had been born a hundred years later, the twentieth century would have seen a Newton among chemists".[12] Perhaps if Shelley had pursued his early passion for science with the same expansive energy he soon came to expend on English verse, he might well have hailed scientists as the "unacknowledged legislators of the World".[13] Yet although Shelley's initial interest in chemistry was quickly superseded by his passion for poetry, his engagement with science remained intense, running more like an electrical current than an eddying stream through much of his verse. Indeed, in his Preface to *Prometheus Unbound*, Shelley metaphorically harnesses the incredible force of lightning—such a powerful reality in the early eighteenth-century era of electrical experimentation— and employs it as a metaphor for the mind's poetic potency. Shelley suggests that poets can influence one another through

---

[11] Thomas Jefferson Hogg, *The Life of Percy Bysshe Shelley*, 4 vols. (London: Edward Moxon, 1858), 1:69–70.

[12] Alfred North Whitehead, *Science and the Modern World* (New York: Macmillan, 1925), p. 85.

[13] Percy Bysshe Shelley, *A Defence of Poetry*, in Perkins, *English Romantic Writers*, p. 1087.

"the uncommunicated lightning of their own mind"; the poetic mind, like a bolt of lightning, is figured as a harbinger or forerunner of some greater power yet to be realized: "The cloud of mind is discharging its collected lightning," the poet buoyantly declares, "and the equilibrium between institutions and opinions is now restoring, or is about to be restored."[14] Yet like other Romantic poets, Shelley's utopian pronouncements, while informed by and somewhat in sympathy with modern scientific experimentation, are yet tempered by a desire to preserve beauty and mystery.

The beauty and mystery of life are conveyed in poetry by the use of figurative language. Yet metaphor and simile are alien tools to the empirical scientist;[15] the interest in data and observation requires that we describe what something *is* with exactitude and precision, while metaphorical language suggests that life, even observable reality, is often fraught with mystery and can sometimes only be got at through comparison or approximation. "The kingdom of heaven is like a grain of mustard seed" (Matthew 13:31), Christ proclaims in one of his many parables; it is also "like leaven" (13:33) or like a "pearl of great value" (13:46), and we understand that there are intangible realities that necessitate the language of resemblance rather than unequivocal definition. The Romantic poets' use of metaphor also posits an organic relationship between man and nature; we can comprehend the richness of the comparison only if there is some fundamental sympathy between the perceiving mind and the created object. Yet some during Shelley's day proclaimed that modern science had made the use of figurative language irrelevant, rendering the profession

---

[14] Percy Bysshe Shelley, Preface to *Prometheus Unbound*, in Perkins, *English Romantic Writers*, p. 982.

[15] Consider, for instance, the following quote by John Locke: "Our Observation employ'd either about external, sensible objects; or about the internal operations of our Minds, perceived and reflected by ourselves, is that, which supplies our Understandings with all the material of thinking." John Locke, *An Essay concerning Human Understanding* (1690), ed. Peter Nidditch (1975), Book 2, Chapter 1, Section 2, 104.

of poet a useless and outdated one. This is the argument of Thomas Love Peacock in his *Four Ages of Poetry*, a work that so incensed Shelley that he wrote *A Defence of Poetry* in response. Peacock writes:

> A poet in our times is a semi-barbarian in a civilized community. He lives in the days that are past. His ideas, thoughts, feelings, associations, are all with barbarous manners, obsolete customs, and exploded superstitions. The march of his intellect is like that of a crab, backward.... The philosophic mental tranquility which looks round with an equal eye on all external things, collects a store of ideas, discriminates their relative value, assigns to all their proper place, and from the materials of useful knowledge thus collected, appreciated, and arranged, forms new combinations that impress the stamp of their power and utility on the real business of life, is diametrically the reverse of that frame of mind which poetry inspires, or from which poetry can emanate.[16]

He then asserts that on the "modern Parnassus", it is not the poets who sit at the top but the "mathematicians, astronomers, chemists",[17] and other modern scientists, who look down derisively on the pathetic poets.

Shelley was certainly not inspired by Peacock to eschew traditional forms of poetic language for a more precise, scientific verse. Still, it is interesting to trace the use of figurative language in his poetry to see where it leads us. Shelley begins his poem "To a Sky-Lark", for instance, comfortably at home in this poetic realm of metaphor: "Hail to thee, blithe Spirit!/Bird thou never wert—" (see p. 256, lines 1–2). He continues to describe the bird through poetic analogy: she is "[l]ike a cloud of fire" (see p. 256, line 8), "[l]ike an unbodied joy whose race is just begun" (see p. 256, line 15), and "[l]ike a star of Heaven" (see p. 256, line 18). The poet then announces at the poem's

---

[16] Thomas Love Peacock, *The Four Ages of Poetry*, in Perkins, *English Romantic Writers*, pp. 763–64.
[17] Ibid.

midpoint something he has already begun to suggest: "What thou art we know not" (see p. 257, line 31). In the absence of concrete knowledge, the speaker can only answer the poetic question, "What is most like thee?" (see p. 257, line 32). The resemblances continue to flow: the skylark is "like a Poet hidden" (see p. 257, line 36), "like a high-born maiden" (see p. 257, line 41), "[l]ike a glow-worm golden" (see p. 258, line 46), "[l]ike a rose embowered" (see p. 258, line 51). The accumulation of such disparate, though lyrical, images, however, does not really enlarge our understanding of the bird; instead, it seems to render the bird even more intangible, and we feel as if we had a better grasp of the skylark when she was simply conceived of as the "blithe Spirit" of the opening stanza. The creation of this feeling of frustration is, I would suggest, part of the poet's intention, since the analogies are meant to reinforce the inaccessibility of the elusive bird and to increase the reader's irritation at not being able to grasp the skylark. The comparisons having failed, the poem then takes a dramatic turn: instead of continuing to describe the skylark through imprecise analogies, the poet issues an imperative request for something discursively knowable: "Teach us, Sprite or Bird,/What sweet thoughts are thine" (see p. 258, lines 61–62). In these lines, Shelley reveals that while his method is "poetic", employing rich and figurative language, his desire could well be described as "scientific", driven by the progressive quest for detailed knowledge. The poem can be said to proceed, then, by manipulating the reader's desire away from the imprecision of metaphor toward something more palpable.

The Romantic poets were highly interested in song and its power to evoke mystery; we need think only of the highland lass of Wordsworth's "The Solitary Reaper", the Abyssinian maid of Coleridge's "Kubla Khan", or the nightingale of Keats' "Ode to a Nightingale". The speakers in all these poems recognize the beautiful and impenetrable mystery of the singer's song; in Wordsworth's "The Solitary Reaper", for instance, the voice of the highland lass singing her Gaelic work songs is more remote and mysterious than that of the nightingale or cuckoo, and the poet asks with a passionate lyrical intensity: "Will no one tell me what she sings?"[18] Yet unlike the speaker of "To a Sky-Lark", the speaker of "The Solitary Reaper" is ultimately content to remain in uncertainty, speculating that "[p]erhaps" her song may be of "old, unhappy, far-off things",[19] or of "[s]ome natural sorrow, loss, or pain",[20] but not troubling overmuch about the exact nature and meaning of the song ("Whate'er the theme, the Maiden sang …"[21]). Indeed, the meaning of the song is enlarged, rather than diminished, by its fundamental inscrutability and by the imaginative associations—the "perhaps"—which the song produces in the listener; in other words, it is the *recollection* of the song, imprecise though it necessarily is, that constitutes much of its poetic meaning. Wordsworth's speaker stops short, then, of desiring complete knowledge and mastery; rather, the value of the experience is to be found in the lingering memory of the solitary reaper's song, and the beauty of the emotions and associations it evokes in the poet. As Wordsworth himself defined it, the poetry arises from "the spontaneous overflow of powerful feelings; it takes its origin from emotion recollected in tranquility".[22]

The speaker of "To a Sky-Lark", however, is not content to remain in ignorance of the skylark and her song, nor does the string of associations the bird evokes advance its meaning; rather, the speaker is convinced that the bird must possess a knowledge, or "skill" ("[t]hings more true and deep/Than we mortals dream" [see p. 259, lines 83–84]), which would benefit mankind and, more specifically, would render the poet a figure of power: "Better than all measures/Of delightful sound—/Better than all treasures/That in books are found—/Thy skill to poet were …" (see p. 259, lines 96–100).

[18] William Wordsworth, "The Solitary Reaper", in *Romantic Poets*, vol. 1, p. 258, line 17.

[19] Ibid., pp. 258–59, lines 18–19.

[20] Ibid., p. 259, line 23.

[21] Ibid., line 25.

[22] Wordsworth, "Preface to *Lyrical Ballads*", in *Romantic Poets*, vol. 1, p. 106.

The speaker's restless desire will not be sated by anything but knowledge of the bird's song, and the poem closes with a frenzied, quasi-prophetic imperative:

> Teach me half the gladness
>   That thy brain must know,
> Such harmonious madness
>   From my lips would flow
> The world should listen then—as I am listening now.
>   (See p. 260, lines 101–5.)

The poet's gaze has now been narrowed even further, so that the petitioning "[t]each *us*" (see p. 258, line 61; my italics) of earlier in the poem is replaced by the almost Promethean cry of "[t]each *me*" (see p. 260, line 101; my italics), with the express purpose of exerting influence over humanity. Indeed, it is this Promethean—one might almost say Nietzschean—will-to-power that permeates much of Shelley's poetry, from his verse play *Prometheus Unbound*, to shorter lyrics like the "Hymn to Intellectual Beauty" or the "Ode to the West Wind".

In what way, though, is the speaker's restless craving for knowledge of a skylark's song related to the modern scientific project? Readers of Shelley often point to a famous passage in the prose work alluded to above, *A Defence of Poetry*, as confirmation of his opposition to a scientific desire for mastery:

> Our calculations have outrun our conceptions; we have eaten more than we can digest. The cultivation of those sciences which have enlarged the limits of the empire of man over the external world, has, for want of the poetical faculty, proportionally circumscribed those of the internal world; and man, having enslaved the elements, remains himself a slave.[23]

Read quite carefully, however, the passage is not an overt condemnation of the empirical method; it is, rather, a profession that science, when not subject to the creative power of the

---

[23] Shelley, *Defence of Poetry*, p. 1084.

poet, leads to enslavement. This is a powerful and persuasive argument, particularly in our present age of rapid biotechnical innovation, when, as Paul Cantor has noted, "human beings lose control of the products of their technological imagination, and perhaps end up serving the very forces that were meant to serve them."[24] But in assigning poets the central role as what he calls the "unacknowledged legislators of the world",[25] Shelley arguably perverts a proper understanding of poetry's domain. By annexing to the poet the chief power to influence the course and outcome of human affairs, Shelley, I would suggest, ends up committing the very error he ascribes to the modern scientist. The Romantic poet, in other words, has bit off more than he can chew. Severed from any proper understanding of man's end—as Shelley unfortunately was—the poet's insatiable appetite for knowledge and power becomes as flawed and dangerous as that of the mad scientist; indeed, as Jacques Maritain, in his study *Creative Intuition in Art and Poetry*, suggests, poetry thus cut off from any teleological purpose necessarily results in the inversion of "poetic knowledge into absolute knowledge", making poetry "contrary to its nature, a means of science". Maritain continues:

> Poetry thus out of joint will develop a monstrous appetite for knowledge, a vampire's appetite which will drain man body and soul. It will claim for itself all the living springs and the gift of heroic life, it will wish to be all things and to provide all things—act, holiness, transubstantiation, and miracle; it will assume the burden of humanity.[26]

Shelley's poetic vision, shot through as it is with flashes of insight regarding the beauty of the created world and man's moral condition, is nevertheless polluted by the unholy desire,

---

[24] Paul Cantor, "The Scientist and the Poet", *New Atlantis*, Winter 2004, p. 85.

[25] Shelley, *Defence of Poetry*, p. 1087.

[26] Jacques Maritain, *Creative Intuition in Art and Poetry* (New York: Pantheon Books, 1955), p. 186.

like Dr. Victor Frankenstein, to assume absolute power over humanity.

George Gordon, Lord Byron: Science and Poetry in the Hands of an Angry God

Mary Shelley, writing in the Introduction to her pioneering work of science fiction, *Frankenstein*, speaks of the frequent discourse between Byron and her poet-husband Shelley regarding current and exciting scientific discoveries:

> Many and long were the conversations between Lord Byron and Shelley, to which I was a devout but nearly silent listener.... They talked of the experiment of Dr. [Erasmus] Darwin ... who preserved a piece of vermicelli in a glass case, till by some extraordinary means it began to move with voluntary motion. Not thus, after all, would life be given. Perhaps a corpse would be reanimated; galvanism had given token of such things: perhaps the component parts of a creature might be manufactured, brought together, and endued with vital warmth.[27]

If in private conversation Byron displayed an active interest in the scientific advances of his day, his poetry betrays a much more jaundiced view toward the prospects for man's improvement through science. Science, declares the "First Destiny" in Byron's verse drama *Manfred*, is "but an exchange of ignorance for that/Which is another kind of ignorance" (Act 2, Scene 4, line 63).[28] Manfred, the dark hero of the play, announces in his opening soliloquy that he has essayed the realms of "philosophy and science, and the springs of wonder", but "they avail not", since that "all-nameless Hour" when he committed the unpardonable sin for which he has been exiled from human company. Manfred, like Byron's Childe Harold and the great Romantic hero Prometheus (and like the Satan of

[27] Mary Shelley, Introduction to *Frankenstein* (Boston: Severs, Francis, 1869), p. 11.
[28] George Gordon, Lord Byron, "Manfred: A Dramatic Poem", in Perkins, *English Romantic Writer*, pp. 810–28. All quotations from *Manfred* are from this source.

Milton's *Paradise Lost* before them), exemplifies the qualities of reckless boldness and an almost self-destructive desire for mastery that we have since come to associate with the "Byronic hero", a figure whose potential contributions to humanity have been rendered void by his commission of a sin that has made him an alien in his own land. Like the "First Destiny" who declares that science is but yet another form of ignorance, Byron frequently presents us in his poetry with a misanthropic vision of the role of science in human affairs.

From a young age, George Gordon, Lord Byron, was steeped in the Calvinist doctrine of his Scottish forebears. Born with a club foot, Byron was repeatedly warned by his Scots Presbyterian mother and his Scottish nurses that his deformity was an indication of his sinfulness. Though marked out with a sense of damnation at an early age, Byron attempted to reject this stigma, but instead of embracing a faith that conceived of man as both tainted by original sin yet made in the image and likeness of a benevolent Creator, he chose to pursue the reckless life of an enlightened liberal voluptuary. Yet in his poetry (and arguably in his life), Byron was never able fully to overcome the dim view of human nature promulgated by the doctor of Geneva.

Thus, the narrator of *Don Juan* reflects sardonically on man's pursuit of scientific progress:

> Man's a strange animal, and makes strange use
>   Of his own nature, and the various arts,
> And likes particularly to produce
>   Some new experiment to show his parts; ...
> This is the patent age of new inventions
>   For killing bodies and for saving souls
> All propagated with the best intentions.[29]

When the narrator announces that mankind is operating with "the best intentions" in his scientific experimentation, he does

---

[29] George Gordon, Lord Byron, *Don Juan*, canto 1, stanza CXVII, lines 1017–20, 1049–50, in Perkins, *English Romantic Writers*, p. 847.

so with more than a hint of sarcasm. As he continues to tell us, the same humanity who is struggling to find cures for terminal illnesses is indiscriminately killing on the battlefield (Byron was horrified by Waterloo), or busy spreading further deadly illnesses through sexual promiscuity. The narrator continues by cataloguing recent inventions and experiments that have been hailed as stages on the upward ascent to the perfection of mankind: vaccination for smallpox, galvanism, Davy's lantern (a safety lamp for coal miners invented by Sir Humphry Davy), but the value of each of these is quickly undercut. The smallpox is being replaced by the "great" pox—the sexually transmitted disease syphilis. Galvanism (moving the muscles of dead bodies by passing an electrical current through them), which "has set some corpses grinning",[30] has failed to bring the dead back to life.

Byron's reference to the invention of a safety lamp for miners is often read as evidence of his knowledge and approval of current scientific advances. But the poet quickly declares that "Davy's lantern" is a way "to benefit mankind, as true,/Perhaps, as shooting them at Waterloo".[31] Read closely, the passage suggests that the invention of the lantern—which historians of science actually agree made possible the exploration of deeper and more dangerous mines, resulting in an increase in mining fatalities—merely rendered it, as with the "advances" of modern warfare, easier and more efficient for more men to be killed.[32] Byron thus presents us with a catalogue of scientific achievement that he quickly discredits by illustrating that man, instead of producing material improvement through science, merely creates new problems for himself. "What wondrous new machines have late been spinning! ... Man's a phenomenon, one knows not what,/And wonderful beyond

---

[30] Ibid., canto 1, stanza CXXX, I. 1034, p. 848.

[31] Ibid., canto 1, stanza CXXXII, I. 1055–56, p. 848.

[32] See, for instance, Mark Kipperman, "Coleridge, Shelley, Davy, and Science's Millennium", *Criticism* 40 (Spring 1998): 430. See also Christopher Lawrence, "Humphry Davy and Romanticism", in *Romanticism and the Sciences*, ed. Andrew Cunningham and Nicholas Jardine (Cambridge: Cambridge University Press, 1990), p. 224.

all wondrous measure",[33] the poet jubilantly declares, but the sarcasm is unmistakable in his description of the inextricable link between man's efforts at self-preservation and his relentless pursuit of self-destruction. It is tempting to see in Byron's assessment a bold critique of the ideology of Enlightenment or French materialist thinkers, who heralded the possibility of the physical, moral, and social perfection of humanity. And indeed, that is one likely target of the poet's critical venom. But because Byron's strong sense of man's imperfection is not balanced by the Christian recognition of man as *imago Dei*, the critique ends in *Don Juan* with a kind of flippant nihilism: "[W]e die, you know—and then—/What then?—I do not know,/no more do you—And so good night."[34]

Certainly when contrasted with Shelley's excessive optimism regarding the potential for man to overcome societal ills through "intellectual beauty", Byron's cynicism appears acute. In canto 4 of *Childe Harold's Pilgrimage*, Byron engages in an extended meditation on the ruins of Venice and Rome; the outcast narrator of the poem reflects that all of man's dreams of progress and mastery have come to naught but destruction and ruin. "Mankind have felt their strength", he had declared in canto 3, but "they might have used it better"[35]: instead of emancipating man from ignorance and submission, as the French Revolution had promised, they have merely tricked ambition and pride in a new garb and have hastened the demise of human civilization in the process. In Byron's ruminations on ruin, we can detect a kind of nascent environmentalism, with the poet suggesting that man's footprint on the earth (carbon or otherwise) inevitably signifies destruction: "A world is at our feet as fragile as our clay" (see p. 57, canto 4, stanza 78, line 702). Byron engages in an extended panegyric to the ocean, a realm made more precious because unlike the earth, man cannot manipulate, and therefore cannot spoil, it: "Man

---

[33] Lord Byron, *Don Juan*, canto 1, stanza CXXXII, ll. 1038; canto 1, stanza CXXXIII, ll. 1057–58, in Perkins, *English Romantic Writers*, p. 848

[34] Ibid., canto 1, stanzas CXXXIII–CXXXIV, ll. 1064–66, p. 848.

[35] George Gordon, Lord Byron, *Childe Harold's Pilgrimage*, canto 1, stanza LXXXIII, ll. 780–81, in Perkins, *English Romantic Writers*.

marks the earth with ruin—his control/Stops with the shore" (see p. 74, canto 4, stanza 179, lines 1605–6). In his reflections on the ruin and destruction brought about by human selfishness in *Childe Harold*, and especially in the grim doomsday scenario of his bleak dream-poem "Darkness", Byron more than suggests that the quest for knowledge and mastery will end not in a Heaven on earth, but in the eventual destruction of the earth itself. Indeed, in an intellectual and poetic world that was busy trumpeting human progress, it is significant that "less" is a suffix frequently employed by Byron in his poetry: Rome is "[c]hildless and crownless, in her voiceless woe;/… The very sepulchres lie tenantless" (see p. 57, canto 4, stanza 79, lines 704, 708); in "Darkness", the earth is "seasonless, herbless, treeless, manless, lifeless"; [36] Manfred in the poem of the same name compares himself to "blasted pines": "barkless, branchless,/A blighted trunk upon a cursed root" (Act 1, scene 2, lines 70–72). The accumulated effect of this negation is one of incredible loss rather than gain; it also affirms Byron's view that man leaves the earth more impoverished than he found it.

If *Don Juan* and *Childe Harold* present us with the futility of scientific progress in the face of a humanity marked out for ruin and failure, does Byron then embrace the Romantic idealization of man's relationship to nature as an elevating force? Prior to debunking the myth of scientific progress in the first canto of *Don Juan*, the narrator had given us a catalogue of "sweet" images calculated to play upon the Romantic notion of nature's beauty and empathy:

> 'Tis sweet to hear
> At midnight on the blue and moonlit deep
> The song and oar of Adria's gondolier,
> By distance mellowed, o'er the waters sweep;
> 'Tis sweet to see the evening star appear;
> 'Tis sweet to listen as the night-winds creep
> From leaf to leaf; 'tis sweet to view on high
> The rainbow, based on ocean, span the sky.…

---

[36] George Gordon, Lord Byron, "Darkness", I. 71, in Perkins, *English Romantic Writers*, p. 795.

'Tis sweet to be awakened by the lark,
     Or lulled by falling waters; sweet the hum
Of bees, the voice of girls, the song of birds,
     The lisp of children, and their earliest words.[37]

The soothing, stereotypically Romantic list continues for some length, but the attentive reader begins to sense the mockery and satire lurking beneath the cloying accumulation. True to form, Byron abandons the dulcet tones of the lulling waters and the lisping children, giving us the mirror image of a "sweetness" borne not of nature's beauty and harmony but of man's avaricious and grasping human nature:

Sweet is the vintage, when the showering grapes
     In Bacchanal profusion reel to earth,
Purple and gushing: sweet are our escapes
     From civic revelry to rural mirth;
Sweet to the miser are his glittering heaps,...
     Sweet is revenge—especially to women,
Pillage to soldiers, prize-money to seamen....
     Sweet is a legacy, and passing sweet
The unexpected death of some old lady
     Or gentleman of seventy years complete....
'Tis sweet to win, no matter how, one's laurels,
     By blood or ink.[38]

In this undercutting of the Romantic notion of "emotion recollected in tranquility", as Wordsworth would have it,[39] Byron suggests a kind of pointlessness to the Romantic poetic endeavor; like the pursuit of scientific knowledge, the pursuit of beauty will inevitably lead one back to a grasping, morally disfigured humanity.

Unlike some other Romantic writers, then, Byron does not frame the relationship between scientific knowledge and poetic apprehension as an irreconcilable competition between

[37] Lord Byron, *Don Juan*, canto 1, stanza CXXII, ll. 969–76, p. 847.
[38] Ibid., stanzas CXXIV–CXXVI, ll. 985–1002, p. 847.
[39] Wordsworth, "Preface to *Lyrical Ballads*", in *Romantic Poets*, vol. 1, p. 106.

two opposing ways of viewing reality, nor does he envision a future where they are united in their effort to advance human civilization. Instead, he ultimately lumps them together as twin images of man's futile (and futile because doomed) pursuit for self-perfection; both are inherently flawed because man is an inescapably flawed creature. Byron's presentation of man's wretchedness does not take the form of a fire-and-brimstone excoriation worthy of a Jonathan Edwards or Calvin himself; instead, the poet even undercuts this "dark view" of human progress by presenting us with a devil-may-care attitude bordering on nihilism. Byron's narrators often make grand claims about man's capacity for mastery and power, including his ability to conquer nature and penetrate mysteries through science. Yet these bold assertions are repeatedly undercut by the poet's relentless fatalism; similarly, while Byron gives us glimpses of a nature full of wonder and mystery, that sublime vision is inevitably torn out from under us by recalling us to the beholders' fundamental iniquity. What could be a useful and legitimate critique of scientific rationalism, then, ends up sounding like nothing more than the teeming malignancy of a poetic mind obsessed with the failures of an ignorant and irredeemable humanity.

John Keats on "Cold and Enfeebling" Science

Poet and social critic T. S. Eliot considered the letters of John Keats "the most notable and the most important ever written by any English poet".[40] In what is perhaps the most famous, if possibly the most obscure, epistolary pronouncement by a poet in the English language, Keats complains in a December 1817 letter to his brothers, George and Tom, about poets—like Coleridge—who are "incapable of remaining content with half knowledge". He enumerates a quality he thinks is indispensible to literary genius, "& which Shakespeare possessed so

[40] T. S. Eliot, *The Use of Poetry and the Use of Criticism: Studies in the Relation of Criticism to Poetry in England*, Charles Eliot Norton Lectures, 1933 (Harvard: Harvard University Press, 1986), p. 92.

enormously—I mean *Negative Capability*, that is when man is capable of being in uncertainties, Mysteries, doubts, without any irritable reaching after fact & reason".[41] What Keats proposes here can be considered the opposite extreme from the desire for knowledge articulated in Shelley's "To a Sky-Lark"; it is, fundamentally, a poetic vision openly at odds with the analytical imperative of empirical science. Throughout his letters and his verse, Keats repeatedly prophesies the loss of mystery brought about through the rise of scientific rationalism. "Kean! Kean!" Keats warns the noted Shakespearean actor of his day in a review for the journal *Champion*, "have a carefulness of thy health … a pity for us in these cold and enfeebling times! … for romance lives but in books. The goblin is driven from the heath, and the rainbow is robbed of its mystery!"[42]

If we are tempted to view Keats as a young Romantic dreamer, content to remain in an idealized world where "a thing of beauty is a joy forever", and perhaps willfully ignorant of the ways of modern science, we need only remind ourselves of a few key facts regarding Keats' early life. Having lost both parents by the age of thirteen, Keats was soon apprenticed to an apothecary and surgeon. His friend Charles Cowden Clarke noted the "clarity and technical precision"[43] with which Keats could talk about human anatomy and other medical concerns.

---

[41] John Keats, *Letters*, in Perkins, *English Romantic Writers*, p. 1209. Keats' understanding of "Negative Capability", though variously defined by literary theorists, is perhaps best summarized by Walter Jackson Bate in his study *Major British Writers*: "Our life is filled with change, uncertainties, mysteries; no one complete system of rigid categories will explain it fully…. We must … resist the temptation to make up our minds on everything, and to have always ready a neat answer. If we discard a momentary insight, for example, because we cannot fit it into a static category or systematic framework, we are selfishly asserting our own 'identity.' A great poet is less concerned with himself, and has his eyes on what is without. With him, 'the sense of Beauty'—the capacity to relish concrete reality in its full, if elusive, meaning—'overcomes every other consideration.' In fact, it goes beyond and 'obliterates' the act of 'consideration'—of deliberating, analyzing, and piecing together experience into a logical structure." Quoted in ibid., p. 361.

[42] John Keats, "Mr. Kean", *The Champion* (December 2, 1817): 405.

[43] Walter Jackson Bate, *John Keats* (Cambridge, Mass.: Harvard University Press, 1963), p. 65.

Yet early on, Keats expressed impatience with the endless sci-
entific lectures he was compelled to attend. As Keats confesses
to Clarke, "The other day ... during the lecture, there came
a sunbeam into the room, and with it a whole troop of crea-
tures floating in the ray; and I was off with them to Oberon
and fairyland."[44] When, shortly after receiving his license to
practice as a physician and surgeon, he left his position as a
wound dresser at Guy's Hospital in order to pursue the career of
poet, his friends and acquaintances were shocked by what they
considered his foolhardy abandonment of a promising medical
career. Keats' contemporary John Taylor recounts the young
man's announcement to his guardian Richard Abbey:

> He communicated ... that he did not intend to be a Surgeon—
> Not intend to be a Surgeon! Why what do you mean to be? I
> mean to rely upon my Abilities as a Poet—John, you are either
> Mad or a Fool, to talk in so absurd a Manner. My mind is made
> up, said the youngster very quietly.... Seeing nothing could
> be done Abby called him a Silly Boy, & prophesied a speedy
> Termination to his inconsiderate Enterprise.[45]

Though Abbey's prophecy proved famously off the mark, both
material and critical success eluded Keats during his short life-
time. Nonetheless, he never abandoned his early insistence on
the primacy of poetic truth over scientific knowledge.

If Keats was by far the most skeptical of the Romantic poets
regarding the compatibility of science and poetry, this does not
mean that he totally eschewed the language of modern science
in his poetry. Rather, in his first and perhaps most famous sonnet,
"On First Looking into Chapman's Homer", Keats appropriates
the language of discovery as an apt metaphor for the reader's
apprehension of poetic beauty. The poem is ostensibly about
the young Keats' revelatory introduction to Homer through the
Elizabethan translation of George Chapman; reading Chapman,

---

[44] Quoted in Joseph Epstein, "The Medical Keats", *Hudson Review* 52:1 (Spring
1999): 52.

[45] Ibid., p. 54.

the poet declares, is like discovering a new world, and the poet compares himself to astronomer William Herschel when he identifies the "new" planet Uranus, or Spanish explorer Cortez (Keats' mistake for Balboa) when he first catches sight of the Pacific. But the end result of Keats' "voyage" is not an expression of mastery, or even a frustrated desire for complete knowledge; rather, it is a feeling of awe, a kind of hushed reverence in the face of something yet mysterious and greater than oneself. Cortez and his men, as Keats reminds us in his sonnet "On First Looking into Chapman's Homer", are left "[s]ilent, upon a peak in Darien" (see p. 358, line 14).

Keats' most well-known poetic pronouncement on modern science comes from his late poem *Lamia*. The poem, about a serpent transformed into a beautiful maiden who deceives a young suitor, is arguably not Keats' greatest work. But by raising important questions about the relationship between illusion and reality, Keats suggests in *Lamia* that the desire to penetrate the mysteries of reality ends up emptying life of richness and meaning.

> Do not all charms fly
> At the mere touch of cold philosophy?
> There was an awful rainbow once in heaven:
> We know her woof, her texture; she is given
> In the dull catalogue of common things.
> Philosophy will clip an Angel's wings,
> Conquer all mysteries by rule and line,
> Empty the haunted air, and gnomèd mine—
> Unweave a rainbow, as it erewhile made
> The tender-personed Lamia melt into a shade.
> (See p. 434, lines 229–38.)

The allusion to the "awful rainbow" that can be unwoven by "cold philosophy" (read as "cold science"—the two terms were often used interchangeably during this period) is a reference to Sir Isaac Newton, who in the late seventeenth century discovered the refraction of white light into the spectrum of colors. Keats was not the only Romantic thinker to take Newton to task for his role in destroying mystery through science; there is also the account of the legendary "immortal dinner", told and retold by generations of readers, in which Keats, along with Wordsworth, Coleridge, and other Romantic luminaries, was present at the dinner party of Charles Lamb. The tipsy Lamb chided painter Benjamin Haydon for including the head of Sir Isaac Newton in his painting *Jerusalem*, for, as he and Keats agreed, Newton "had destroyed all the poetry of the rainbow by reducing it to the prismatic colors". Keats then joined in a toast of "confusion to mathematics",[46] which, though perhaps half in jest, nevertheless reinforces our sense of the poet's sympathetic privileging of mystery over empirical precision. Once science has done its work, Keats insists, the world becomes but a "dull catalogue of common things".

Many readers—including most scientists—would object strongly to Keats' condemnation of rational science and would vehemently dispute the claim that taking apart something or rationally explaining it inevitably diminishes its beauty and mystery as a poetic object. Indeed, M. H. Abrams dubs as "Keats' fallacy" the Romantic assumption that "scientific description discredits the phenomena for which it is intended to account."[47] But lurking behind the supposedly benign desire to describe can be the more menacing desire to manipulate, control, and master matter, often for ends that are contrary to natural and revealed law. In our own day, we all too frequently witness the transformation of scientific inquiry from a type of knowledge to a totalizing worldview, and the scientist's insatiable desire to explain reality ultimately leaves room for nothing beyond dull, inert matter. Richard Dawkins, emeritus professor in the Public Understanding of Science at Oxford University, sums up the modern scientist's end game in his book *Unweaving the Rainbow: Science, Delusion, and the Appetite for Wonder* (the main title is taken, of course, from Keats' *Lamia*): "I believe that an orderly universe, one

[46] For one account, see ibid., pp. 269–73.
[47] Abrams, *Mirror and the Lamp*, p. 312.

indifferent to human preoccupations, in which everything has an explanation even if we have a long way to go before we find it, is a more beautiful, more wonderful place than a universe tricked out with capricious, *ad hoc* magic."[48] Dawkins' other works, like *The Selfish Gene*, *The God Delusion*, and *The Blind Watchmaker: Why the Evidence of Evolution Reveals a World Without Design*, similarly reflect a belief in a world that can be somehow at once mysterious and rational, yet ultimately without purpose. Of course, in redefining the poetic categories of wonder and mystery for science, Dawkins, like Thomas Peacock before him, makes the poet at best irrelevant, at worst the handmaiden of a perverted science. The modern scientist's reduction of poetry to a mere cog in the evolutionary wheel, however, is not simply absurd; it is, as Keats presciently warned us, incredibly dangerous.

Conclusion

As Shakespeare's Hamlet famously declares to his rational-minded friend from Wittenberg, "There are more things in heaven and earth, Horatio,/Than are dreamt of in your philosophy" (Act 1, scene 5, lines 166–67).[49] Romantic poetry frequently recalls us to "more things", to the mystery and beauty of the human mind and the created world. But as southern literary critic Allen Tate has observed, the philosophy of Romanticism, while positing the "organic relation of man and nature", fails to root this relation in "an order which goes beyond individual perception—in short, religious order".[50] As we see in the works of Shelley, Byron, and Keats, without this deeper grounding, any attempt to synthesize, order, or otherwise discriminate between the claims of science and poetry is

---

[48] Richard Dawkins, *Unweaving the Rainbow: Science, Delusion, and the Appetite for Wonder* (Boston: Houghton Mifflin, 1998), p. 17.

[49] William Shakespeare, *Hamlet*, ed. Joseph Pearce, Ignatius Critical Editions (San Francisco: Ignatius Press, 2008).

[50] Allen Tate, *Essays of Four Decades* (Wilmington, Del.: ISI Books, 1999), p. 161.

destined to disappoint. The works of the later Romantics may help inoculate us against a rigidly empirical, scientific attitude toward nature and reality; they may caution us against a utopian belief in self-perfection or a dystopian view of man's inescapable doom; and they may, in some notable instances, lead us to contemplate truth and beauty. But they are by no means a complete cure for the disease of modern rationalism. For that, one must turn to something yet higher than either science or poetry.

Shake Your Chains to Earth like Dew:
Shelley and the Industrial Revolution

James E. Hartley
Mount Holyoke College

When first coming to the Romantic poets, it is not uncommon to experience a bit of disorientation. You might expect the Romantic poets to be, well, romantic. Knowing, for example, that Jane Austen is the greatest Romantic novelist, it is reasonable to expect stories of love and beautiful people. Similar expectations are formed by tales of young women swooning over the brooding Lord Byron or the youthful John Keats.

Imagine the shock, then, when picking up a volume of English Romantic poetry and flipping open at random to discover the following:

> I met a Murder on the way—
> He had a mask like Castlereagh—
> Very smooth he looked, yet grim;
> Seven bloodhounds followed him:
>
> All were fat; and well they might
> Be in admirable plight,
> For one by one, and two by two,
> He tossed them human hearts to chew
> Which from his wide cloak he drew.[1]

It's hard to imagine a passage like that in *Pride and Prejudice*. The disconnect here between what we might expect would be in English Romantic poetry and what we actually find when we read Lord Byron, Percy Bysshe Shelley, and John Keats is part of the larger problem with the word "Romantic". In his

[1] Percy Bysshe Shelley, "The Mask of Anarchy", in *Percy Bysshe Shelley: The Major Works*, eds. Zachary Leader and Michael O'Neill (Oxford: Oxford University Press, 2003), p. 400, lines 5–14.

531

excellent survey of Romanticism, Jacques Barzun notes that while everybody assumes we all know what the word means when we see it, there is actually a surprisingly large range of meanings for that one word.[2] Barzun provides a list of ninety different passages in which people have used the word to mean different, and oftentimes directly opposite, things.

Given, then, that "Romantic" does not necessarily mean what we thought it meant, what enables us to lump together a set of poets as the English Romantic poets? There are sharp differences between these poets, perhaps best embodied in Shelley's remark about William Wordsworth: "What a beastly and pitiful wretch that Wordsworth! That such a man should be such a poet!"[3] What unites William Blake, William Wordsworth, Samuel Coleridge, Lord Byron, Percy Bysshe Shelley, and John Keats is primarily what they are not; the Romantic era can be defined as being a reaction to the excesses of the Enlightenment.

The Enlightenment began with Rene Descartes' declaration in *Discourse on Method* (1637), "I think, therefore I am." For the next century and a half, a host of luminaries worked out the nature of the world by rigorously applying the power of reason. For example, Descartes, followed by the French *philosophes*, reasoned out the nature of God and the universe. In England, Locke (*Second Treatise*) thought about the political system, and Smith (*Wealth of Nations*) did the same for the economy. Newton (*Principia Mathematica*) demonstrated that the same force explains why objects fall to the ground and how planets move in the solar system, developing calculus along the way.

Reading through a catalogue of Enlightenment discoveries, it is not hard to become excited about the achievements of the human mind. And yet, there is something a bit disquieting

---

[2] Jacques Barzun, *Classic, Romantic and Modern* (Garden City, N.Y.: Anchor Books, 1961).

[3] Michael Henry Scrivener, *Radical Shelley: The Philosophical Anarchism and Utopian Thought of Percy Bysshe Shelley* (Princeton, N.J.: Princeton University Press, 1981), p. 219.

about the whole Enlightenment enterprise, something indefinably wrong. Wordsworth, in his remarkable poem "Tintern Abbey", identifies the problem. He begins by recognizing the "beauteous forms" of nature:

> To them I may have owed another gift,
> Of aspect more sublime; that blessed mood,
> In which the burthen of the mystery,
> In which the heavy and weary weight
> Of all this unintelligible world,
> Is lightened.[4]

Enlightenment thinkers sought to make everything in the world intelligible, yet Wordsworth here notes that the beauty of nature convinced him that they failed. How?

> And I have felt
> A presence that disturbs me with the joy
> Of elevated thoughts; a sense sublime
> Of something far more deeply interfused,
> Whose dwelling is the light of setting suns,
> And the round ocean, and the living air,
> And the blue sky, and in the mind of man,
> A motion and a spirit, that impels
> All thinking things, all objects of all thought,
> And rolls through all things.[5]

There is something, in other words, beyond and before reason, something that is more fundamental than Descartes' thinking things, something that we know, not through cold calculation, but that we know nonetheless. The Romantic era is the revolt against the idea that reason is all there is. The Romantics are united by their exploration of the rediscovery of the idea that there are more things in Heaven and earth than are dreamt of by the *philosophes*.

---

[4] William Wordsworth, "Tintern Abbey", in *The Romantic Poets*, ed. Joseph Pearce and Robert Asch, vol. 1, *Blake, Wordsworth, and Coleridge*, Ignatius Critical Editions (San Francisco: Ignatius Press, 2014), p. 126, lines 37–42. All subsequent quotations of "Tintern Abbey" are from this edition.

[5] Ibid., p. 128, lines 94–103.

Shelley echoes Wordsworth's argument in his own master-piece "Hymn to Intellectual Beauty", in which he begins by declaring the presence of something vaguely indescribable:

> The awful shadow of some unseen Power
>   Floats though unseen amongst us,—visiting
>   This various world with as inconstant wing
> As summer winds that creep from flower to flower,—
> Like moonbeams that behind some piny mountain
>   shower,
>   It visits with inconstant glance
>   Each human heart and countenance;
> Like hues and harmonies of evening,—
>   Like clouds in starlight widely spread,—
>   Like memory of music fled,—
>   Like aught that for its grace may be
> Dear, and yet dearer for its mystery.[6]

We learn through the poem that this unseen power, which expresses itself through the hues and harmonies of evening or the memory of music fled, is beauty, intellectual beauty as the title says. This spirit of beauty appeared to the poet in dramatic fashion ("Sudden, thy shadow fell on me;/I shrieked, and clasped my hands in ecstasy!"[7]) and gives him great hope:

>   never joy illumed my brow
>   Unlinked with hope that thou wouldst free
>   This world from its dark slavery,
>   That thou—O awful Loveliness,
> Wouldst give whate'er these words cannot express.[8]

What words cannot express, that inexpressible knowledge, is a spirit that hovers about us, periodically illuminating us through means unrelated to articulated reasoning. But, despite

---

[6] Percy Bysshe Shelley, "Hymn to Intellectual Beauty", in *Percy Bysshe Shelley: The Major Works*, lines 9–12.

[7] Ibid., lines 59–60.

[8] Ibid., lines 69–72.

how essential this intellectual beauty is ("Thou—that to human thought art nourishment"[9]), there is a constant danger of its retreat from the world, a danger that the poet declares he will dedicate his powers to preventing.

Like Wordsworth, Shelley is here arguing for a knowledge that is certain, but not reasoned, a knowledge that it is the poet's task to convey through arguments that appeal to the imagination. "Reason is the enumeration of quantities already known; Imagination the perception of the value of those quantities, both separately and as a whole.... Reason is to Imagination as the instrument to the agent, as the body to the spirit, as the shadow to the substance."[10] Notice carefully the relative positions of reason and imagination in Shelley's argument. It is no wonder, then, that he would declare of poets:

> Poets are the hierophants [priests] of an unapprehended inspiration, the mirrors of the gigantic shadows which futurity casts upon the present, the words which express what they understand not; the trumpets which sing to battle, and feel not what they inspire: the influence which is moved not, but moves. Poets are the unacknowledged legislators of the World.[11]

Poets legislate for the world because they alone see beyond the superficial, see beyond the reasoned world. Poets see something deeper than those things the Enlightenment thinkers spent their lives discovering.

Yet, while Shelley echoes Wordsworth's revolt against the excesses of Enlightenment reasoning, in looking forward, the two poets are hardly of one mind. Shelley wrote several poems expressing disdain for Wordsworth, none more clear

---

[9] Ibid., line 44.
[10] Percy Bysshe Shelley, *A Defence of Poetry*, in *Percy Bysshe Shelley: The Major Works*, pp. 674–75.
[11] Percy Bysshe Shelley, *A Defence of Poetry*, in *The Romantic Poets*, ed. Joseph Pearce and Robert Asch, vol. 2, *Byron, Shelley, and Keats*, Ignatius Critical Editions (San Francisco: Ignatius Press, 2024), p. 330. All quotations of Shelley's works from this edition will be cited in the text.

than "To Wordsworth". In that poem, Shelley notes a deplorable change:

> In honored poverty thy voice did weave
> Songs consecrate to truth and liberty,—
> Deserting these, thou leavest me to grieve,
> That having been, that thou shouldst cease to be.[12]

He repeated the same complaint in "Verses Written on Receiving a Celandine in a Letter from England" ("A deathless Poet whose young prime/Was as serene as thine;/But he is changed and withered now,/Fallen on a cold and evil time;/His heart is gone—his flame is dim,/And Infamy sits mocking him"[13]), in the extended satire "Peter Bell the Third", and in "An Exhortation" ("Yet dare not stain with wealth or power/A poet's free and heavenly mind"[14]).

The conflict between Wordsworth and Shelley arises from their different reaction to one of the most obvious manifestations of the Enlightenment: the birth of the Industrial Revolution. Neither of these poets liked what they saw, but while Wordsworth yearned for a return to an earlier aristocratic age, Shelley rejected the earlier age too. Indeed, Shelley was rootless: "Man's yesterday may ne'er be like his morrow;/Nought may endure but Mutability" ("Mutability"; see p. 191, lines 15–16). When faced with the modern world, Shelley found nothing but unfulfilled promise:

> he sought,
> For his lost heart was tender, things to love
> But found them not, alas; nor was there aught
> The world contains, the which he could approve.
> ("Lift Not the Painted Veil"; see p. 192, lines 7–10)

---

[12] Percy Bysshe Shelley, "To Wordsworth", in *Percy Bysshe Shelley: The Major Works*, p. 91, lines 11–14.

[13] Percy Bysshe Shelley, "Verses Written on Receiving a Celandine in a Letter from England", in *Percy Bysshe Shelley: The Major Works*, p. 113, lines 27–32.

[14] Percy Bysshe Shelley, "An Exhortation", in *Percy Bysshe Shelley: The Major Works*, p. 112, lines 15–16.

To see the cause of Shelley's despair, we need to look closer at the Industrial Revolution itself.

The Industrial Revolution began in the eighteenth century as technological improvements in agriculture meant that fewer workers were needed on farms to provide food for the nation and technological improvements in manufacturing created a demand for workers in factories. Perhaps the single most important invention was the steam engine, which allowed factories to be located anywhere, and thus clusters of factories cropped up in cities. The result was a massive migration from the countryside to the cities, accompanied, not surprisingly, by great social disorder. Working conditions in the early factories were poor, and housing conditions in the rapidly expanding cities were even poorer:

> On 8 November 1816 John Quincy Adams, then the American Minister in London, found, while walking through Brentford, an exhausted man in the street who told him he had not eaten for two days. "The number of these wretched objects I meet in my daily walks is distressing," he recorded. "Not a day passes but we have beggars come to the house, each with a different, hideous tale of misery. The extremes of opulence and want are more remarkable and more constantly obvious in this country than in any other I ever saw."[15]

By the mid-1810s, Luddite riots were occurring throughout England, in which disenchanted workers deliberately sabotaged factories. Political agitation spread.

In 1819, a great clash occurred at St. Peter's Field near Manchester. Faced with a government that seemed indifferent to the plight of the factory workers, a gathering was organized to demand increased representation of the lower classes in the political realm. The government, led by Castlereagh and Sidmouth, concerned about this large assembly, alerted the local magistrates. There is debate among historians about the

[15] Paul Johnson, *The Birth of the Modern: World Society 1815–1830* (New York: HarperCollins, 1991), p. 361.

details, but the end result was shocking. The militia charged the crowd, wounding hundreds and killing several.[16]

Shelley's reaction to what became known as Peterloo was strong: "The torrent of my indignation has not yet done boiling in my veins."[17] He rapidly composed "The Mask of Anarchy", which begins by noting he was asleep in Italy when the news came; the sleep here is a figurative ploy, indicating that not just Shelley but also the reader had been paying too little attention to what was occurring in England. The poem shows the true state of things as the poet meets Murder, Fraud, Hypocrisy, and Anarchy, all of which are revealed to be masks worn by members of the English ruling class. This army of destruction is marching through England, seizing both "Bank and Tower",[18] thereby controlling the sources of power for both commerce (Bank of England) and government (Tower of London). This parade of tyranny is stopped by Hope, who, though looking like Despair, rises up and with a simple message vanquishes the evil powers. That message is an immediate appeal to the workers of England, a call to freedom from the slavery in which they toil.

The workers in England are nothing but tools, small cogs in the giant machine of industry, all toiling for the benefit of the rulers of society. Hope calls on the workers to rise up and declare themselves free, free from the hunger and war and meaningless toil for others' benefit, free to enjoy the benefits of wisdom, peace, love, science, poetry, and thought. The poem ends with this message of hope ringing out through the land.

"The Mask of Anarchy" was not Shelley's first poem about the undesirable effects of the Industrial Revolution. One of his earliest poems, "Zeinab and Kathema", observes, "Here, woe on all but wealth has set its foot,/Famine, disease and crime

---

[16] As is usual in such cases, there is dispute about the numbers, but to give an idea about the probable range, between fifty thousand and eighty thousand protestors gathered, eleven to fifteen people died, and four hundred to eight hundred were wounded.

[17] Richard Holmes, *Shelley: The Pursuit* (London: Weidenfeld and Nicolson, 1974), p. 529.

[18] Shelley, "Mask of Anarchy", in *Percy Bysshe Shelley: The Major Works*, p. 402, line 83.

even wealth's proud gates pollute."[19] Later, "Queen Mab" takes direct aim at the economy described by Adam Smith: "The harmony and happiness of man/Yields to the wealth of nations."[20]

> Commerce! beneath whose poison-breathing shade
> No solitary virtue dares to spring,
> But poverty and wealth with equal hand
> Scatter their withering curses, and unfold
> The doors of premature and violent death,
> To pining famine and full-fed disease,
> To all that shares the lot of human life,
> Which poisoned body and soul, scarce drags the chain,
> That lengthens as it goes and clanks behind.[21]

These miseries are all driven by "tyrants" who, "by the sale of human life,/Heap luxuries to their sensualism" and reduce their "hosts of blind and unresisting dupes...."[22]

> to perform
> A task of cold and brutal drudgery;—
> Hardened to hope, insensible to fear,
> Scarce living pulleys of a dead machine.
> Mere wheels of work and articles of trade,
> That grace the proud and noisy pomp of wealth![23]

Shelley later wrote several other works in which he catalogued the horror of the Industrial Revolution, arguing that "Hell is a city much like London."[24] The most extended treatment of the theme is in his prose work *A Philosophical View of Reform*. In it, Shelley describes the Industrial Revolution:

[19] Percy Bysshe Shelley, "Zeinab and Kathema", in *Percy Bysshe Shelley: The Major Works*, p. 6, lines 101–2.

[20] Percy Bysshe Shelley, "Queen Mab", in *Percy Bysshe Shelley: The Major Works*, p. 40, lines 79–80.

[21] Ibid., p. 39, lines 44–52.

[22] Ibid., p. 40, lines 64–65.

[23] Ibid., p. 40, lines 73–78.

[24] Percy Bysshe Shelley, "Peter Bell the Third", in *Percy Bysshe Shelley: The Major Works*, p. 423, line 147.

One of the vaunted effects of this system is to increase the national industry. That is, to increase the labours of the poor and those luxuries of the rich which they supply. To make a manufacturer work sixteen hours where he only worked eight. To turn children into lifeless and bloodless machines at an age when otherwise they would be at play before the cottage doors of their parents. To augment indefinitely the proportion of those who enjoy the profit of the labour of others as compared with those who exercise this labour.[25]

And later, he adds:

For fourteen hours' labour which they do perform, they receive—no matter in what nominal amount—the price of seven. They eat less bread, wear worse clothes, are more ignorant, immoral, miserable and desperate. This, then, is the condition of the lowest and largest class, from whose labour the whole materials of life are wrought, of which the others are only the receivers or the consumers.[26]

Shelley believed that the horrors of the Industrial Revolution were the deliberate result of Enlightenment thinking. The problem was that "poets have been encouraged to resign the civic crown to reasoners and mechanists",[27] but the rise of the latter produced much ill.

Whilst the mechanist abridges, and the political economist combines, labour, let them beware that their speculations, for want of a correspondence with those first principles which belong to the imagination, do not tend, as they have in modern England, to exasperate at once the extremes of luxury and want. They have exemplified the saying, "To him that hath, more shall be given; and from him that hath not the little that he hath shall be taken away". The rich have become richer,

[25] Percy Bysshe Shelley, *A Philosophical View of Reform*, in *Percy Bysshe Shelley: The Major Works*, p. 651.

[26] Ibid., pp. 653–54.

[27] Shelley, *Philosophical View of Reform*, in *Percy Bysshe Shelley: The Major Works*, p. 693.

and the poor have become poorer; and the vessel of the state is driven between the Scylla and Charybdis of anarchy and despotism. Such are the effects which must ever flow from an unmitigated exercise of the calculating faculty.[28]

With this backdrop, it is easy to see why so much of Shelley's poetry is violent at its core. His description of England in "Lines Written during the Castlereagh Administration" begins with this chilling image:

> Corpses are cold in the tomb—
> Stones on the pavement are dumb—
> Abortions are dead in the womb
> And their mothers look pale, like the death-white shore
> Of Albion, free no more.[29]

And then three stanzas later we hear death, destruction, sin, and, most tellingly, wealth in a "festival din".[30] Similarly, in the sonnet "England in 1819", we find "[a] people starved and stabbed in th'untilled field" (see p. 193, line 7). In "To S and C", Shelley describes these government officials as

> two vultures sick for battle,
> Two scorpions under one wet stone,
> Two bloodless wolves whose dry throats rattle,
> Two crows perched on the murrained cattle,
> Two vipers tangled into one.[31]

Ultimately, Shelley preaches revolution, a revolution of those who are working in the factories and cities of the Industrial Revolution. There is nothing subtle about this call for revolution in poems like "What Men Gain Fairly", but nowhere is it more explicit than in that clarion call "A Song to the Men of England", worth repeating in its entirety here:

---

[28] Ibid., p. 694.
[29] Percy Bysshe Shelley, "Lines Written during the Castlereagh Administration", in *Percy Bysshe Shelley: The Major Works*, p. 443, lines 1–5.
[30] Ibid., p. 443, line 16.
[31] Percy Bysshe Shelley, "To S and C", in *Percy Bysshe Shelley: The Major Works*, p. 444, lines 16–20.

Men of England, wherefore plough
For the lords who lay ye low?
Wherefore weave with toil and care
The rich robes your tyrants wear?

Wherefore feed and clothe and save
From the cradle to the grave,
Those ungrateful drones who would
Drain your sweat—nay, drink your blood?

Wherefore, Bees of England, forge
Many a weapon, chain and scourge,
That these stingless drones may spoil
The forced produce of your toil?

Have ye leisure, comfort, calm,
Shelter, food, love's gentle balm?
Or what is it ye buy so dear
With your pain and with your fear?

The seed ye sow, another reaps:
The wealth ye find, another keeps:
The robes ye weave, another wears:
The arms ye forge, another bears.

Sow seed—but let no tyrant reap:
Find wealth—let no imposter heap:
Weave robes—let not the idle wear:
Forge arms—in your defence to bear.

Shrink to your cellars, holes, and cells—
In hall ye deck, another dwells.
Why shake the chains ye wrought? Ye see
The steel ye tempered glance on ye.

With plough and spade and hoe and loom
Trace your grave and build your tomb
And weave your winding-sheet—till fair
England be your Sepulchre.[32]

[32] Percy Bysshe Shelley, "Men of England: A Song", in *Percy Bysshe Shelley: The Major Works*, p. 442, lines 1–32.

If Shelley's complaint about the nature of the Industrial Revolution sounds familiar, it is because we have heard the voice of Shelley's followers many times. Consider the repeated stanza in "The Mask of Anarchy":

> Rise like Lions after slumber
> In unvanquishable number,
> Shake your chains to Earth like dew
> Which in sleep had fallen on you—
> Ye are many—they are few.[33]

Compare that to this:

> But with the development of industry the proletariat not only increases in number; it becomes concentrated in greater masses, its strength grows, and it feels that strength more.... All previous historical movements were movements of minorities, or in the interest of minorities. The proletarian movement is the self-conscious, independent movement of the immense majority, in the interests of the immense majority.... The Communists disdain to conceal their views and aims. They openly declare that their ends can be attained only by the forcible overthrow of all existing social conditions. Let the ruling classes tremble at a Communistic revolution. The proletarians have nothing to lose but their chains. They have a world to win.[34]

That is, of course, from Marx and Engels' "Manifesto of the Communist Party", written three decades after Shelley completed his poem.

The correlation between Shelley and Marx was noted by Marx's daughter and her husband in *Shelley's Socialism*. Their most intriguing observation is a statement attributed to Marx (but never published elsewhere):

> As Marx, who understood the poets as well as he understood the philosophers and economists, was wont to say: "The real

---

[33] Shelley, "Mask of Anarchy", in *Percy Bysshe Shelley: The Major Works*, p. 404, lines 151–55.

[34] Karl Marx and Friedrich Engels, "Manifesto of the Communist Party", in *The Marx-Engels Reader*, 2nd ed., ed. Robert C. Tucker (1848; repr., New York: W. W. Norton, 1978), pp. 400, 482, 500.

difference between Byron and Shelley is this; those who under-
stand them and love them rejoice that Byron died at thirty-six,
because if he had lived he would have become a reactionary
bourgeois; they grieve that Shelley died at twenty-nine, because
he was essentially a revolutionist, and he would always have
been one of the advanced guard of socialism."[35]

They go on to provide a litany of examples from Shelley's writ-
ings that the late nineteenth-century socialists echoed, con-
cluding, "We claim him as a socialist."[36]

In some ways, Shelley was every bit as ambitious as Marx.
Much of Shelley's poetry was deliberately written in a style
designed to have mass appeal. He proposed to his publisher
the idea of a volume entitled *Popular Songs*, which would have
included nothing but his poems preaching revolution.[37] It is
not hard to see how much of Shelley's poetry would have the
sort of effect he desired. "A Song to the Men of England" in
its brute simplicity is a brilliant call to arms, in refrains easily
remembered.[38] The volume *Popular Songs* was never published,
presumably because Shelley's publisher thought it would have
been too dangerous to bring out such a volume in an era where
people were routinely jailed for political protests.

While Shelley is clearly protesting against his world, what is
he arguing should replace it? What, in other words, is Shelley's
ultimate aim? Consider another aspect of Romantic poetry, a
constant appeal to nature. For example, in "Tintern Abbey",
the deeper understanding dwells in the setting sun, round
ocean, living air, and blue sky; Wordsworth is

[35] Edward Aveling and Eleanor Marx Aveling, *Shelley's Socialism* (1888; repr.,
London: Journeyman Press, 1979), p. 16.

[36] Ibid., p. 38.

[37] Shelley never outlined the exact contents of his proposed volume, and
since the volume was never published, there is no way to know what it would
have included. Holmes suggests that the contents would have been "The Mask
of Anarchy", "Lines Written during the Castlereagh Administration", "Men of
England: A Song", "To S and C", "What Men Gain Fairly", "A New National
Anthem", "Sonnet: England in 1819", and "Ballad of the Starving Mother", with
perhaps "Ode to Liberty" and "Ode to the West Wind" thrown in for good mea-
sure. See Holmes, *Shelley*, p. 593.

[38] So memorable is it, in fact, that Orwell parodied it nicely in *Animal Farm*.

> well pleased to recognize
> In nature and the language of the sense,
> The anchor of my purest thoughts, the nurse,
> The guide, the guardian of my heart, and soul
> Of all my moral being.[39]

The glories of the natural world are the source of inspiration for the insights available to the mind.

Shelley, too, looks to nature, but notice what it is that he finds so worthy there. Toward the end of "To a Sky-Lark", after repeatedly evoking lofty thoughts about the beauty of the world, Shelley describes our state:

> We look before and after,
>   And pine for what is not—
> Our sincerest laughter
>   With some pain is fraught—
> Our sweetest songs are those that tell of saddest
>   thought. (See p. 259, lines 86–90.)

That catalogue of woe is introduced by the odd phrase about how we look before and after. The source of that phrase is Hamlet's exclamation:

> Sure he that made us with such large discourse,
> Looking before and after, gave us not
> That capability and godlike reason
> To fust in us unus'd.
>   (*Hamlet*, Act 4, scene 4, lines 36–39)[40]

Our *godlike* reason, our ability to think about the past and the future, our large capacity to puzzle out the world, must, Hamlet declares, serve some purpose and is the very thing that elevates man above the beasts. Shelley is here declaring that Hamlet was wrong, that there is something "[b]etter than all treasures/That in books are found" ("To a Sky-Lark"; see p. 259, lines 98–99), that our ability to reason

---

[39] Wordsworth, "Tintern Abbey", p. 128, lines 108–12.

[40] William Shakespeare, *Hamlet*, ed. Joseph Pearce, Ignatius Critical Editions (San Francisco: Ignatius Press, 2008).

leads to naught but pain. To find happiness, we must emulate the skylark, who "[h]igher still and higher/From the earth thou springest" (see p. 256, lines 6–7) and from great heights, shucking off the petty cares and toils of this world, sings his beautiful songs. Nature is liberating.

This equating of nature with liberation is amplified in "Adonais", Shelley's elegy for Keats. Again after some magnificent description of the natural world, Shelley declares that Keats is "made one with Nature" (see p. 317, line 370):

> Peace, peace! he is not dead, he doth not sleep—
> He hath awakened from the dream of life—
> 'Tis we, who lost in stormy visions, keep
> With phantoms an unprofitable strife,
> And in mad trance, strike with our spirit's knife
> Invulnerable nothings.—*We* decay
> Like corpses in a charnel; fear and grief
> Convulse us and consume us day by day,
> And cold hopes swarm like worms within our living
> clay.
>
> He has outsoared the shadow of our night;
> Envy and calumny and hate and pain,
> And that unrest which men miscall delight,
> Can touch him not and torture not again;
> From the contagion of the world's slow stain
> He is secure, and now can never mourn
> A heart grown cold, a head grown grey in vain;
> Nor, when the spirit's self has ceased to burn,
> With sparkless ashes load an unlamented urn.
> (See p. 316, lines 343–60.)

Keats, having liberated himself from our earthbound cares, is at one with nature, free from fear and grief. Nature, in other words, is a desired state because it is free, free from all the restrictions and problems that man through his reason has bound our lives. Nature does what it wants; it sings through a skylark high above the earth; it "wields the world with never

wearied love,/Sustains it from beneath, and kindles it above"
(see p. 317, lines 377–78).

Again, the contrast with Wordsworth is instructive. In
"Tintern Abbey", Wordsworth begins with a hearkening back
to the past, evoking nature as a way to remind us of the glories
of an earlier, seemingly simpler, time. But it is not the serenity of
nature that appeals to Shelley; it is the wild chaos, the free-
dom and liberation that nature represents. While Wordsworth
would like to reverse the Industrial Revolution, bringing us
back to a past world more in tune with nature, Shelley wants
to move beyond the factories and the cities to a world in which
restrictions have been abolished. It is thus not a surprise to
see where Shelley locates his ringing call for freedom in "The
Mask of Anarchy".

> "Let a great Assembly be
> Of the fearless and the free
> On some spot of English ground
> Where the plains stretch wide around.
>
> "Let the blue sky overhead,
> The green earth on which ye tread,
> All that must eternal be
> Witness the solemnity.
>
> "From the corners uttermost
> Of the bounds of English coast;
> From every hut, village, and town
> Where those who live and suffer moan
> For others' misery or their own,
>
> ....
> "Let a vast Assembly be,
> And with great solemnity
> Declare with measured words that ye
> Are, as God has made ye, free—"[41]

---

[41] Shelley, "Mask of Anarchy", in *Percy Bysshe Shelley: The Major Works*,
pp. 407–9, lines 262–74, 295–98.

The people leave the places of civilization, the towns and workhouses and prisons and palaces, head for the open fields, with blue sky and green earth, to declare their goals. They will shake their chains to earth and be free.

Once man has become liberated, what comes next? What is the nature of this world to which Shelley aspires? On this he is silent. He sees the Industrial Revolution, hates what he sees, and imagines smashing it. And what will follow? What does freedom bring?

Shelley doesn't say, and it isn't clear he ever really bothered to think seriously about such things. The closest Shelley comes to a positive description of what should be done is in *A Philosophical View of Reform*, where he suggests improving the justice system and abolishing the national debt, the standing army, sinecures, and tithes. Those things may or may not be desirable, but it is impossible to see how they solve the fundamental economic problem. "We derive tranquility and courage and grandeur of soul from contemplating an object [equality of possessions] which is, because we will it, and may be, because we hope and desire it, and must be, if succeeding generations of the enlightened sincerely and earnestly seek it."[42] Somehow, someway, if we all just want it enough, Liberty will provide for us all in the end.

In an evaluation of Shelley's poetic gifts, Symonds, an early biographer, notes that his poetry is not without faults:

> The most prominent of these are haste, incoherence, verbal carelessness, incompleteness, a want of narrative force, and a weak hold on objective realities. Even his warmest admirers, if they are sincere critics, will concede that his verse, taken altogether, is marked by inequality. In his eager self-abandonment to inspiration, he produced much that is unsatisfying simply because it is not ripe. There was no defect of power in him, but a defect of patience; and the final word to

---

[42] Shelley, *Philosophical View of Reform*, in *Percy Bysshe Shelley: The Major Works*, p. 664.

be pronounced in estimating the larger bulk of his poetry is the word immature.[43]

That evaluation holds not only for the style of Shelley's poetry but also for its content. Throughout his work, Shelley is screaming revolt against the world as it is. He sees the world industrializing and protests that the world is not good, but he has no practical positive vision of how to change that world. It is no slight to Shelley's amazing poetical gift to note that his political vision is, in a word, immature. He proudly claimed that poets are the legislators of the world, but he has no legislation to offer. Perhaps, what Shelley should have said was that poets like him are the acknowledged critics of the world and left the hard work of legislating to those whose thoughts dwell in less lofty realms.

[43] John A. Symonds, *Shelley* (New York: Harper & Brothers, 1901), pp. 185–86.

Lord Byron Learns to Laugh: The Perfecting and Exorcising of the Byronic Hero

Louis Markos
Houston Baptist University

The story is told a hundred different ways in a hundred different cultures. The young, untested hero travels blissfully along the road in search of adventure and meets, instead, the devil. And there, at the crossroads, he sells his soul for a "year at the top". It matters little what his dearly bought year will bring him—fame, fortune, desire, talent. It matters even less whether his initial motivation seems honorable: to unlock the secrets of immortality (like Dr. Frankenstein) or to release mankind from his bestial side (like Dr. Jekyll) or to bring about world peace (like Captain Nemo). Indeed, he may not even meet the devil himself. What he encounters at the crossroads may simply be the lure of forbidden knowledge—and of the power that such knowledge always promises to bring.

These Faustian heroes (anti-heroes?) have always been with us, but their numbers vastly increased, and have continued to increase, since the French Revolution inspired (infected?) the Western world with a belief that man's potential is unlimited and that he is the maker of his own destiny. In the wake of the Revolution, the British Romantic poet Lord Byron wrote a dozen or so popular verse romances about young heroes who commit an unforgivable sin and, as a result, become lonely wanderers and outcasts who can no longer dwell within the circle of humanity. Though these "oriental tales" have been all but forgotten today—their exotic titles include *The Prisoner of Chillon*, *The Corsair*, *Lara*, *The Giaour*, *The Bride of Abydos*, and *The Siege of Corinth*—their moody, passionate, tormented protagonists captured the imagination of Europe and ensured that such figures would henceforth bear the generic title of Byronic hero.

The life cycle of the Byronic hero always begins with the breaching of some type of taboo (Adam eating the forbidden fruit; Cain killing his brother; Prometheus stealing the fire; Oedipus marrying his mother; the Ancient Mariner shooting the albatross), an act that, whether nobly or basely motivated, manifests itself ultimately as an act of rebellion and defiance. He soon discovers that the fruit is sour and that his action has made him both a curse and a contagion, but he has progressed too far in his sin to go back and, in any case, is too proud to seek forgiveness (Macbeth, Heathcliff, Ahab, Dorian Gray). For Christians, the ultimate example of this figure is Satan, the fallen archangel who is not only himself the great Byronic hero but who would tempt all of us to become little Byronic heroes. Perhaps the Byronic hero reaches its fullest embodiment in Satan's legendary, mythopoeic counterpart: Count Dracula, the Prince of Darkness who lives on the borders of society, feeds on human blood, and fears the Cross. Indeed, popular culture in America is overrun with Byronic heroes: from the Mummy and the Wolfman to the Highlander and Darth Vader to the innumerable dark, vigilante-like superheroes who populate the pages of comic books and graphic novels and who have come to dominate movie screens since the late 1990's. It is not too much to say that our modern—and now postmodern—age is obsessed with the Byronic hero, with his willingness to risk all for forbidden knowledge, his self-inflicted torment and agony, his tragic greatness.

Ironically, although our age remains fixated on the seductive qualities of the Byronic hero, its creator managed, in the space of three short years, to internalize, then perfect, then exorcise his own melancholy creation.

Let's see how he did it.

Wanderers o'er Eternity

While constructing the ultimately forgettable plots of his oriental tales, Byron (1788–1824) worked steadily on a travel poem inspired by his own "grand tour" of the Mediterranean world in 1810–1811. Though not strictly autobiographical, *Childe Harold's Pilgrimage*—as Byron would come to call it— helped seal Byron's status as a national celebrity and as the supreme European embodiment of Romanticism. Written in the demanding form of the Spenserian stanza (Keats would later write *The Eve of St. Agnes* and Shelley *Adonais* in this same form), *Childe Harold's Pilgrimage*, published in two cantos in 1812, transported its British readers to distant, sun-drenched lands and demonstrated to the world Byron's metrical skills and his gift for evoking time and place, color and mood.

Riding high on the success of *Childe Harold I* and *II*, not to mention the continued success of his oriental tales (when *The Corsair* was published in 1814, it sold thirteen thousand copies in a single day), Byron cemented his good fortune by marrying Anne Isabella Milbanke on January 2, 1815. In December, Lady Byron gave birth to a daughter, Augusta Ada. Fortune seemed to smile on the young poet, promising him many years of fame, fortune, and happiness.

And then disaster struck. News leaked out that Byron's legendary amorous intrigues had included an incestuous affair with his half sister Augusta. A bitter divorce ensued, and Byron, but a scarce four months after the birth of Ada, found himself on a boat, sailing for the Continent. Never again would he lay eyes upon his daughter or his native land. Guilty of a taboo sin, the once-famous, now-ostracized Bryon would spend his remaining eight years as a wanderer, his pride, remorse, and shame cutting him off from home and family. He had become himself a Byronic hero.

Almost immediately, Byron set to work on a third installment of his travel poem (*Childe Harold's Pilgrimage III*), which was written, carried to England (by Shelley), and published by the end of 1816. Though the public might have accepted Byron's claim that the Harold of I and II was not autobiographical, even a casual reading of Part III leaves no doubt that Harold has become little more than a mask for the self-exiled poet. The opening stanzas of the poem are spoken by a narrator

who is unambiguously Byron; yet, when the poem shifts from
the narrator's voice to that of Harold, there is no change what-
soever in tone, mood, or perspective.

The poem begins with the forlorn and heartfelt cry of a
father ripped away from his child:

> Is thy face like thy mother's, my fair child!
> ADA! sole daughter of my house and heart?
> When last I saw thy young blue eyes they smiled,
> And when we parted,—not as now we part,
> But with a hope.—
> 　　　　　　　　Awaking with a start,
> The waters heave around me; and on high
> The winds lift up their voices: I depart,
> Whither I know not; but the hour's gone by,
> When Albion's lessening shores could grieve or
> 　　glad mine eye.[1]

Not only is he parted from Ada, but his recollection of their
final parting has itself become nothing more than a dream
to trouble his present weariness. We imagine the speaker as
one doomed forever to roam the seas, cut off from Albion
(England), unable to find rest or peace. And, though the
speaker/Harold will soon stand upon solid ground, the image
of Byron—who has so come to embody, "channel", and inter-
nalize his "fictional" Byronic hero that I will henceforth use his
name—remains with the reader throughout the poem. In fact,
in the final lines of stanza 2, Byron himself fixes the image of
his sea-swept self in our mind:

> Still must I on; for I am as a weed,
> Flung from the rock, on Ocean's foam, to sail
> Where'er the surge may sweep, the tempest's breath
> 　　prevail. (See p. 21, stanza 2, lines 16–18.)

---

[1] George Gordon, Lord Byron, *Childe Harold's Pilgrimage: Canto the Third*, in
The Romantic Poets, ed. Joseph Pearce and Robert Asch, vol. 2, *Byron, Shelley,
and Keats*, Ignatius Critical Editions (San Francisco: Ignatius Press, 2024), p. 20,
stanza 1, lines 1–9. Subsequent citations of *Childe Harold's Pilgrimage: Canto the
Third* from this edition will be cited in the text.

As is the case with all Byronic heroes, Byron's choices and actions, intended to raise him above the realm of fate and destiny, have left him a victim of those very forces he thought to transcend.

In a slow succession of melancholy stanzas, Byron finds in himself all the qualities that mark the Byronic hero. He is what we might call, paradoxically, a "young old man": one who has "grown aged in this world of woe,/In deeds, not years" (see p. 22, stanza 5, lines 37–38). Not yet thirty, Byron feels within that he has suffered through ages of woe, a suffering that sets him apart from his peers. It is a suffering from which he cannot escape, for, like all Byronic heroes, he is burdened by a crushing overself-consciousness:

> Yet must I think less wildly:—I *have* thought
> Too long and darkly, till my brain became,
> In its own eddy boiling and o'erwrought,
> A whirling gulf of phantasy and flame:
> And thus, untaught in youth my heart to tame,
> My springs of life were poison'd. 'Tis too late!
> (See p. 22, stanza 7, lines 55–60.)

Like Hamlet, he has thought too much and brooded too long. Possessing once "the native hue of resolution", he has allowed what could have brought him healthful action to be "sicklied o'er with the pale cast of thought" (*Hamlet*, Act 3, scene 1, lines 84–85).[2] He has not only poisoned the well springs of his own mind; he is a prisoner in that well.

Perhaps he might be drawn out of that well by a faithful friend, but he has isolated himself from the human world around him. Harold (that is, Byron) knows himself "the most unfit/Of men to herd with Man; with whom he [holds]/Little in common."[3] No, not among his fellow men, but only among the forces of nature does he find a spirit kindred to his own:

---

[2] All citations from *Hamlet* are from William Shakespeare, *Hamlet*, ed. Joseph Pearce, Ignatius Critical Editions (San Francisco: Ignatius Press, 2008).

[3] In George Gordon, Lord Byron, *Childe Harold's Pilgrimage: Canto the Third*, in *English Romantic Poetry and Prose*, ed. Russell Noyes (New York: Oxford University Press, 1956), p. 800, stanza 12, lines 100–102.

Where rose the mountains, there to him were
    friends;
Where roll'd the ocean, thereon was his home;
Where a blue sky, and glowing clime, extends,
He had the passion and the power to roam;
The desert, forest, cavern, breaker's foam,
Were unto him companionship; they spake
A mutual language, clearer than the tome
Of his land's tongue, which he would oft forsake
For Nature's pages glass'd by sunbeams on the lake.[4]

There is a type of power and sublimity in nature that Byron does not find in human society, though he does encounter it amid the ruins of mighty empires—especially those of ancient Greece and Rome—and in meditating upon heroic, if tragic, men like Napoleon.

Indeed, later in the poem, Byron—writing one year after Waterloo—describes Napoleon as though he were himself a supreme embodiment of the Byronic hero. First lifted up and then abandoned by Fortune, Napoleon "stood unbow'd beneath the ills upon him piled" (see p. 30, stanza 39, line 351). His final downfall proceeded not from the armies of Wellington but from his own inner contradictions and extremes. He was too great, too fiery, too ethereal for this mundane world o'er which he towered like a "headland rock" (see p. 31, stanza 41, line 361):

But quiet to quick bosoms is a hell,
And *there* hath been thy bane; there is a fire
And motion of the soul which will not dwell
In its own narrow being, but aspire
Beyond the fitting medium of desire;
And, but once kindled, quenchless evermore,
Preys upon high adventure, nor can tire
Of aught but rest; a fever at the core,
Fatal to him who bears, to all who ever bore.

---

[4] In ibid., pp. 800–801, stanza 13, lines 109–17.

> This makes the madmen who have made men mad
> By their contagion; Conquerors and Kings,
> Founders of sects and systems, to whom add
> Sophists, Bards, Statesmen, all unquiet things
> Which stir too strongly the soul's secret springs,
> And are themselves the fools to those they fool.
> (See p. 31, stanzas 42–43, lines 370–84.)

Unlike the angels, who are pure spirit, and the beasts, who are pure body, we, the noble yet fallen human race, are the amphibians of the universe. It is our burden to reconcile body and soul, physical and spiritual, to know both our limits and our potential. The Byronic hero, to his glory and his ultimate destruction, refuses to effect such a reconciliation. Whether we call him Napoleon or Byron, Ahab or Heathcliff, Dr. Jekyll or Dorian Gray, his soul rests uneasy in its shell of clay. All within is passion and fire, a fever that first infects itself and then brings contagion to the world.

It is best then, Byron warns us, that we stay away from such men, lest we, too, become infected by their madness. Later in the poem, Byron even seems to use this warning to defend himself from the charge of misanthropy:

> To fly from, need not be to hate, mankind:
> All are not fit with them to stir and toil,
> Nor is it discontent to keep the mind
> Deep in its fountain, lest it overboil
> In one hot throng, where we become the spoil
> Of our infection. (See p. 36, stanza 69, lines 653–58.)

If I have separated myself from home and country, Byron seems to be saying, it is only because I do not wish to bring further torment to those I love. As the vampire cannot walk in the day, so the Byronic hero can never truly become a part of society. We must realize, asserts Byron, calling back his initial metaphor of the ship lost at sea, that there live among us "wanderers o'er Eternity/Whose bark drives on and on, and anchor'd ne'er shall be" (see p. 37, stanza 70, lines 669–70). Is it not better for such that they dwell alone and apart, neither hurting nor taking hurt from society? "Is it not better thus our lives to wear,/Than join the crushing crowd, doomed to inflict or bear?"[5]

And so Byron, like *both* Dr. Frankenstein and his creature, flees the cities of men to seek the more companionable forms of nature. For him, the "[h]igh mountains are a feeling, but the hum/Of human cities torture."[6] His sensitive soul cannot bear the unnatural noises of the city, whether they rise up from the din of industrialization or the din of gossip. As the canto draws to a close, Byron, still adrift in melancholy and remorse, at least takes consolation in the fact that he has not bowed down to the city-world he despises:

> I have not loved the world, nor the world me;
> I have not flattered its rank breath, nor bowed
> To its idolatries a patient knee,
> Nor coin'd my cheek to smiles, nor cried aloud
> In worship of an echo: in the crowd
> They could not deem me one of such; I stood
> Among them, but not of them.[7]

Speaking the very language of Christ (see John 14–17), but in a fully secularized form, Byron depicts himself as one who has forsaken the vanity and falseness of the world to pursue a higher ideal. What sets him apart, however, from the Christian saint is that the ideal to which he sanctifies himself is an internal, finally self-centered one, rather than one that inheres in the Creator and Savior of mankind. Indeed, it would not be a stretch to say that the Byronic hero, in all his various forms, is someone who seeks transcendence apart from God and is thus shipwrecked back upon his own lonely self.

That Byron himself was aware of this can be seen in the fact that he no sooner completed *Childe Harold's Pilgrimage III*

---

[5] In ibid., p. 809, stanza 71, lines 678–79.
[6] In ibid., p. 809, stanza 72, lines 682–83.
[7] In ibid., p. 815, stanza 113, lines 1049–55.

than he began to compose a reworking of the Faust legend, *Manfred* (1817), that would mark his fullest and most perfect embodiment of the Byronic hero. In this overwhelmingly intense closet drama (that is, a play that, like Milton's *Samson Agonistes*, is meant to be read rather than acted), Byron found a way to fuse completely the dramatic elements of his oriental tales with the brooding autobiographical angst of *Childe Harold III*.

Sorrow Is Knowledge

In the opening scene of the play, we discover Manfred alone at midnight in a Gothic castle poised atop the higher Alps. He begins by speaking his first of many soliloquies, a speech that immediately establishes him as an isolated and introspective Byronic hero:

> The lamp must be replenish'd, but even then
> It will not burn so long as I must watch.
> My slumbers—if I slumber—are not sleep,
> But a continuance of enduring thought,
> Which then I can resist not: in my heart
> There is a vigil, and these eyes but close
> To look within; and yet I live, and bear
> The aspect and the form of breathing men.
> But grief should be the instructor of the wise;
> Sorrow is knowledge: they who know the most
> Must mourn the deepest o'er the fatal truth,
> The Tree of Knowledge is not that of Life.
>   (Act 1, scene 1, lines 1–12)[8]

Byron presents us here with one of the most enduring images in literature of Romantic overself-consciousness. Manfred's life has become a perpetual vigil of sleepless thought. However, unlike the mature Wordsworth of the "Intimations Ode", who

[8] George Gordon, Lord Byron, *Manfred*, in *English Romantic Poetry and Prose*, ed. Russell Noyes (New York: Oxford University Press, 1956). All citations of *Manfred* are from this edition.

560 *Louis Markos*

proclaims in the final stanza of the poem that he is one who "hath kept watch o'er man's mortality",[9] Manfred's watch has brought him neither peace nor comfort nor even a deeper wisdom. Rather, like the Solomon of the early chapters of Ecclesiastes, he has learned that all is vanity. Line 10, in fact, offers a direct allusion to Ecclesiastes 1:18: "For in much wisdom is much vexation, and he who increases knowledge increases sorrow."

Manfred, like Adam (the first mortal Byronic hero), has learned the bitter truth that the Tree of Knowledge brings not life but a continuance of grief, remorse, and unhealthy introspection. In vain, Manfred goes on to muse—echoing once more the cadences of Ecclesiastes—why he has sought relief in learning, in charity, in revenge; for all these have "avail'd not" (Act 1, scene 1, lines 17, 19, 21). By the end of Solomon's melancholy "soliloquy", the Preacher finds relief in God, but this is a relief that Manfred cannot embrace, that he will not even consider embracing. Rather, rejecting both the aid of his fellow men and the consolations of religion, Manfred calls upon the spirits of earth, sea, and air that haunt "the tops / Of mountains inaccessible" (Act 1, scene 1, lines 32–33) to hear his complaint and to provide him with solace.

Compelled by the magical powers of the Faustian Manfred, seven spirits attend upon his call, the seventh of whom embodies the (astrological) star under which Manfred was born. In describing the nature of his star, the spirit provides as well a picture of Manfred himself:

> The star which rules thy destiny
> Was ruled, ere earth began, by me:
> It was a world as fresh and fair
> As e'er revolved round sun in air;
> Its course was free and regular,
> Space bosom'd not a lovelier star.

[9] William Wordsworth, "Ode: Intimations of Immortality from Recollections of Early Childhood", in *The Romantic Poets*, ed. Joseph Pearce and Robert Asch, vol. 1, *Blake, Wordsworth, and Coleridge*, Ignatius Critical Editions (San Francisco: Ignatius Press, 2014), p. 177, line 198.

The hour arrived—and it became
A wandering mass of shapeless flame,
A pathless comet, and a curse,
The menace of the universe;
Still rolling on with innate force,
Without a sphere, without a course,
A bright deformity on high,
The monster of the upper sky!
And thou! beneath its influence born—
Thou worm! whom I obey and scorn
     (Act 1, scene 1, lines 110–25)

Manfred, like Lucifer (the first immortal Byronic hero), began as a creature fair and bright; his mind, his actions, and his course were beautiful, measured, and free—until corruption was found in him. The star, the angel, the man: all fell out of their proper path to become a monster, a chaos, a blight to all who came within their orbit. Driven ever onward by an innate force and compulsion, Manfred becomes a wanderer on the earth, even as his once fortunate star has itself become a cosmic outcast.

But with his pain and his solitude has come an inner power that makes him the equal of the spiritual forces with whom he communes. Though they despise the pretensions of this earth-born, clay-bound mortal ("Thou worm!"), they find in him a strength they cannot resist. We as readers are in many ways repelled by Manfred and his towering hubris, yet we, too, cannot help but be drawn to the almost tangible energy of his defiance. Here and throughout the play, Manfred hurls down his gauntlet before fearsome spirits, witches, and demons whose mere presence would make the strongest man tremble. In the face of their haughty scorn, Manfred asserts his own gleam of divine fire:

The mind, the spirit, the Promethean spark,
The lightning of my being, is as bright,
Pervading, and far-darting as your own,
And shall not yield to yours, though coop'd in clay!
     (Act 1, scene 1, lines 154–57)

It must be remembered that the fire Prometheus stole from the gods provided mankind not only with protection, warmth, and light but also, at least in the minds of the British Romantics, with that revolutionary energy that tears down all thrones, boundaries, and veils, an energy that William Blake embodied in a mythical being he named Orc. Shelley himself was drawn to the orcic energy unleashed by Prometheus—a figure whom he saw as combining the defiance of Satan with the self-sacrifice of Christ—and he incorporated it into his own Manfred-like closet drama, *Prometheus Unbound* (1819). When Shelley's wife, Mary, wrote her own meditation on the Byronic hero, *Frankenstein* (1818), she significantly offered *The Modern Prometheus* as an alternate title to her novel.

For the rebellious Blake, Byron, and Shelley, not to mention the Byronic hero, man must ever strive to transcend the limits of his "clay-coop", a finally impossible goal that sets up an agonizing struggle between body and soul that is as prone to draw them up to the realm of the angels as drag them down to the level of the beasts. So Hamlet, agonizing over the claims of flesh and spirit, hails man as being "in action … like an angel" and "in apprehension … like a God", but also as nothing more than a "quintessence of dust" (*Hamlet*, Act 2, scene 2, lines 304–5, 307). In contrast, Wordsworth and Coleridge, who slowly matured into an orthodox Christian faith, were able to accept and embrace their ontological status as enfleshed souls who were, like Christ himself, fully physical and fully spiritual. Alas, the Byronic hero, unable to embrace this incarnational vision, finds himself in perpetual war with his own creaturely condition. In the end, he can find companionship only among spirits who despise him and among sublime, inaccessible landscapes that know him not.

Poised atop one of these landscapes, Manfred demands of the spirits that they grant him a boon. The spirits believe that Manfred will ask for power or wealth or kingly sway, but he will have none of it. He desires but one gift: "forgetfulness", "oblivion" (*Manfred*, Act 1, scene 1, lines 136, 144), an end to his lifelong vigil. But this is the one thing that the immortal spirits

have not the power to give. Instead, the seventh spirit appears
to Manfred in the form of a beautiful woman. Manfred's "heart
is crushed" (Act 1, scene 1, line 191) at the sight, and he falls
into a swoon, during which time a vengeful spirit speaks an apt
curse over this upstart worm he abhors:

> By thy cold breast and serpent smile,
> By thy unfathom'd gulfs of guile,
> By that most seeming virtuous eye,
> By thy shut soul's hypocrisy;
> By the perfection of thine art
> Which pass'd for human thine own heart;
> By thy delight in others' pain,
> And by thy brotherhood of Cain,
> I call upon thee! and compel
> Thyself to be thy proper Hell!
> (Act 1, scene 1, lines 242–51)

Like Achilles, Oedipus, Napoleon, and Samson, it is Manfred
in the end who will rain down destruction upon himself; it is
he who shall be his own executioner. Like the jealousy that
destroys the noble Othello, the poison that kills Manfred shall
flow from within his own twisted soul. As the spirit exclaims
just before the previously quoted passage: "In proving every
poison known,/I found the strongest was thine [Manfred's]
own." (Act 1, scene 1, lines 240–41).

The spirit is right to invoke the name of Cain, for, like Cain,
Manfred bears a mark that preserves his life while simultane-
ously preventing him from participating in human love and
companionship (see Genesis 4:1–16). Manfred defies anyone
to judge him, not because he fears judgment per se, but because
he has already judged and condemned himself. His hell resides
within his own mind, but it is a real hell. "The mind is its own
place", proclaims the Satan of *Paradise Lost*, "and in itself/Can
make a Heaven of Hell, a Hell of Heaven."[10] Or again to quote

---

[10] John Milton, *Paradise Lost*, ed. Scott Elledge (New York: Norton, 1993),
Book 1, lines 254–55.

the melancholy Hamlet: "[F]or there is nothing either good or bad, but thinking makes it so" (*Hamlet*, Act 2, scene 2, lines 248–50). Like the Mephistopheles of Marlowe's *Doctor Faustus*, Manfred carries hell around with him, and that is why only forgetfulness, oblivion, annihilation can save him, so he thinks, from his self-imposed prison. Truly he is his own worst enemy.

In the next scene of the play, Manfred climbs to the top of the Jungfrau, intent on throwing himself from the cliff. At the last moment, however, he is stopped by a chamois hunter who takes the distraught Manfred to his Alpine cottage. When the hunter suggests to Manfred the "aid of holy men, and heavenly patience" (*Manfred*, Act 2, scene 1, line 34), Manfred refuses both, explaining that he is not of the same "order" (Act 2, scene 1, line 38) as the hunter and that it is his burden to bear alone a punishment that he alone can bear. For a moment, Manfred envies the hunter his simple, pious, healthful life, but he knows it is not one that he can share. Like Harold, he is a "young old man" whose soul has already been "scorch'd" (Act 2, scene 1, line 73).

As Manfred prepares to leave the cottage, the hunter, bewildered by the weight of guilt his guest bears upon his brow, asks how one so gentle in thought and speech could ever have visited vengeance on his enemies. "Oh! no, no, no!" Manfred responds,

> My injuries came down on those who loved me—
> On those whom I best loved: I never quell'd
> An enemy, save in my just defence—
> But my embrace was fatal.
>   (Act 2, scene 1, lines 83–87)

Although the Byronic hero is generally doomed to wander the earth companionless and alone, for some, like Manfred, this doom is increased tenfold when they meet one with whom they can share their outcast state. For a time, it seems that joy and redemption are within reach, but in the end, the Byronic hero, unable to resolve the extremes of his own fiery nature, inevitably causes the death of the very one he loves.

In the next scene of the play, during which Manfred, still hungry for oblivion, seeks the aid of the Witch of the Alps, we finally learn the identity of this beloved creature whom Manfred loved and destroyed and for whom he suffers his weary penance:

> She was like me in lineaments; her eyes,
> Her hair, her features, all, to the very tone
> Even of her voice, they said were like to mine;
> But soften'd all, and temper'd into beauty.
> (Act 2, scene 2, lines 199–202)

A quick glance back at my analysis of *Childe Harold's Pilgrimage III* will leave little doubt that the woman Manfred here describes is his sister, and that his fatal romance represents that same breaking of a taboo sin (incest) that so haunted Byron and compelled him to fashion his two most perfect Byronic heroes: Harold and Manfred. (It is also the same sin around which Wagner patterned much of his excessively Byronic *Ring Cycle*, the parents of Siegfried being Siegmund and his sister Sieglinde.) As Manfred describes her—her name is Astarte, and it is she whose form the seventh spirit took, causing Manfred to swoon—she is his female counterpart, what Jung would call his anima or inner feminine side. Unfortunately for Manfred, he proves to be no more able to reconcile his flesh and spirit than his masculine and feminine side. Though he does not physically kill Astarte, he, like Heathcliff, breaks his lover's heart, leading her to what is essentially a suicidal death.

In the scene that follows, Manfred attends a lurid Walpurgis Night, where he convinces the spirits to call up before him the phantom of Astarte. They do so, but, to Manfred's despair, Astarte remains silent, refusing, like Dido in *Aeneid VI*, to respond to his desperate pleas for forgiveness and rest. Finally, after an agonizing speech from Manfred—which Emily Brontë clearly echoes in the parting dialogue between Heathcliff and Catherine in *Wuthering Heights* (1847)—Astarte speaks, but only to prophesy Manfred's coming death and to bid him farewell.

In the third and final act of the play, Manfred waits, in his castle and the nearby mountains, for the death prophesied by Astarte to claim him. Two times a brave and pious abbot, whom Byron treats with surprising respect, meets with Manfred and implores him to be reconciled with "the true church, and through the church to heaven" (Act 3, scene 1, line 51). Though Manfred shows reverence for the man and his calling, his reply is firm and unequivocal:

> I hear thee. This is my reply: whate'er
> I may have been, or am, doth rest between
> Heaven and myself; I shall not choose a mortal
> To be my mediator. (Act 3, scene 1, lines 52–55)

The Byronic hero, in his pride and isolation, knows nothing of mediators: he is ever his own judge, jury, and hangman. Indeed, as he explains to the abbot several lines later, he is already "self-condemn'd" (Act 3, scene 1, line 77).

And Manfred carries his rejection of all mediation or judgment right through to the last moments of his life. When the spirit comes to claim Manfred's soul, informing him that his hour has come and that he must now depart with him, Manfred resists in an act of defiance that the reader cannot help but cheer:

> I knew, and know my hour is come, but not
> To render up my soul to such as thee:
> Away! I'll die as I have lived—alone.
>   (Act 3, scene 4, lines 88–90)

The spirit remonstrates that Manfred's crimes have rendered him forfeit, but Manfred cries out with his last breath:

> Thou hast no power upon me, *that* I feel;
> Thou never shalt possess me, *that* I know:
> What I have done is done; I bear within
> A torture which could nothing gain from thine ...
> *Thou* didst not tempt me, and thou couldst not
>   tempt me;

I have not been thy dupe, nor am thy prey—
But was my own destroyer, and will be
My own hereafter.—Back, ye baffled fiends!
The hand of death is on me—but not yours!
(Act 3, scene 4, lines 125–28, 137–41)

And with that, the spirit, whom Byron identifies in his stage direction as a "demon", disappears. Moments later, Manfred succumbs to death. His last quizzical line, spoken to the aston‐ished abbot, is this: "Old man! 'tis not so difficult to die" (Act 3, scene 4, line 151). Whether the tone of this parting line is angry or sad, stoic or triumphant, Byron does not say. It is enough that Manfred has stayed true to his Byronic code. What we feel for him in the end is less pity than a sense of awed sadness; for here was one like King Saul: a glorious ruin who should have been destined for greatness, but who could not overcome his own pride, intransigence, and despair.

I Do Not Know, No More Do You

As far as we know, Byron, like Manfred, went to his early death without seeking the reconciliation of the Church. And yet, though Byron seems to have shared to the end his hero's refusal of all mediation—whether human or divine—he did find an aesthetic way to shuffle off the excessive melancholy and isola‐tion of Harold and Manfred.

And he did so swiftly.

Within a year of the publication of *Manfred*, Byron began work on a new poem, written not in the dark, gloomy mode of Shelley and Keats but in the bright, satirical mode of Pope and Swift. From the almost stifling seriousness of *Childe Harold III* and *Manfred*, Byron threw himself into writing the first two cantos of *Don Juan* (1819, with successive cantos to follow), an uproariously funny mock epic that parodies the very angst of the former two poems. Composed in the Italian ottava rima form—with playful, multisyllabic rhymes that would later influence the librettos of W.S. Gilbert—*Don Juan* offers its readers a tour de force of romance, intrigue, and adventure.

Its titular character, almost an inversion of the Byronic hero, far from being smoldering and defiant, is almost feminized by Byron, who allows his supposed lothario to be dragged passively from one passionate affair to the next. Far from tormenting himself over lost companionship and love, Juan has barely enough time to straighten his tie before he is cast into a new illicit entanglement.

With the very opening of canto 1, the reader discovers he is in a very different world from that of *Manfred*. Though Byron clearly patterns the marital misery of Juan's parents (Don José and Donna Inez) on his own troubles with Lady Byron, he treats the tragic situation with an aloof air of humor that allows him to laugh at, rather than anguish over, his own unhappy divorce. Thus, in describing the fashionable snobbery and insufferable prudishness of Donna Inez/Lady Byron, Byron offers a series of hilarious, unforgettable lines that allow him to exorcise his former demons of despair through high comedy:

> Some women use their tongues—she look'd a lecture,
> Each eye a sermon, and her brow a homily.
>   (stanza 15, lines 113–14)[11]

> To others' share let "female errors fall,
> For she had not even one—the worst of all.
>   (stanza 16, lines 127–28)

> But—Oh! ye lords of ladies intellectual,
> Inform us truly, have they not hen-peck'd you all?
>   (stanza 22, lines 175–76)

Only a year earlier, Byron's meditations on his failed marriage would have provoked in him a further bout of "Byronism"; here, through the mediation of laughter, he is able to let go of feelings that would have driven him further into isolation.

---

[11] George Gordon, Lord Byron, *Don Juan*, in *English Romantic Poetry and Prose*, ed. Russell Noyes (New York: Oxford University Press, 1956). All citations of *Don Juan* are from this edition.

He is even able now to laugh at the very thing that made his divorce so much crueler than it needed to be:

> Don José and his lady quarrell'd—why,
>   Not any of the many could divine,
> Though several thousand people chose to try.
>   (stanza 23, lines 177–79)

Were it not for the grotesque, tabloid-like gossip that swirled around the private lives and hardships of Lord and Lady Byron, the couple might have been able to engineer a less bitter settlement, and Byron might have been able to remain in Britain and participate in the life of his daughter. But that was not to be: a sad truth that made a self-exiled wanderer of the Byron of *Childe Harold III* but a bemused observer of the Byron of *Don Juan*.

In the closing stanzas of canto 1, Byron presents himself not as a border figure doomed to expiate for eternity his taboo guilt but as a former rake turned gentleman-wit:

> But now at thirty years my hair is grey
>   (I wonder what it will be like at forty?
> I thought of a peruke the other day—)
> My heart is not much greener.
>   (stanza 213, lines 1697–700)

> No more—no more—Oh! never more, my heart,
>   Canst thou be my sole world, my universe!
> Once all in all, but now a thing apart,
> Thou canst not be my blessing or my curse.
>   (stanza 215, lines 1713–16)

> My days of love are over; me no more
>   The charms of maid, wife, and still less of widow,
> Can make the fool of which they made before.
>   (stanza 216, lines 1721–23)

The thirty-year-old Byron has put aside the amours of his youth, not because he has experienced a religious conversion, but because he is simply too tired for all that trouble and strife.

He is, like Harold and Manfred, a "young old man", but now he looks back on his youthful experiences, not as a cursed wizard might regret his too-early tutelage in the dark arts, but as a worldly-wise CEO might reminisce about his "frat-boy" adventures. Besides, he goes on to reveal, he has decided to take up a new "profession": "So for a good old-gentlemanly vice,/I think I must take up with avarice" (stanza 216, lines 1727–28). Rather than muse despondently with Harold and Manfred on the vanities of this world, he will simply take them up as a new pastime.

Freed from the guilt and overself-consciousness of his Byronic heroes—both fictional and autobiographical—Byron announces to the world that he is through, at least for now, with remorse and self-pity. Life is just too short. And besides, when it comes down to it, is all that forbidden knowledge stuff really worth the bother?

In what may be the single most shocking moment in *Don Juan I*—a canto filled with shocks of every conceivable kind—the narrator, who is clearly Byron, begins to ponder, in true Harold/Manfred mode, the mysteries and vagaries of life. Line by line he slowly builds to a philosophical pronouncement of prophetic power, and then—well, read for yourself:

> Few mortals know what end they would be at,
>   But whether glory, power, or love, or treasure,
> The path is through perplexing ways, and when
> The goal is gain'd, we die, you know—and then—
>
> What then?—I do not know, no more do you—
>   And so good night.
>   (stanzas 133–34, lines 1061–66)

Had there been the slightest inkling in *Childe Harold III* or *Manfred* of such a resolution to the riddles and terrors of death, those noble and titanic works would have exploded like a pierced balloon. For the Byronic hero can bear any physical, emotional, or spiritual torment, can suffer any blow—except laughter. "The best way to drive out the devil, if he will not yield to texts of Scripture," advises Luther in a quote that C. S. Lewis used as one of the epigraphs to his *Screwtape Letters*, "is to jeer and flout him, for he cannot bear scorn."[12]

Perhaps, then, G. K. Chesterton was correct when he named, in the final sentence of *Orthodoxy*, the one quality that Jesus hid from the world. As Jesus never, despite the intense isolation and rejection he suffered while on earth, allowed himself to sink into Byronic self-pity, it is instructive that Chesterton believed that the one quality Jesus cloaked in silence, the one thing too great for him to reveal while on earth, was his mirth.

[12] C. S. Lewis, *The Screwtape Letters* (New York: Macmillan, 1980), p. 5.

John Keats' Five Spring Odes and "To Autumn": The Drama of the Soul's Priest, Poet, and Prophet

Russell Elliott Murphy
University of Arkansas at Little Rock

It is a philosophical given that the mind cannot know a thing in terms of what it is, only in terms of what it is like, and that becomes even more true when it comes to knowing that elusive and insubstantial "thing" that humans call the soul. Suffice it to say that, when it comes to the poets of the English Romantic movement who flourished for little more than three decades during the late eighteenth and early nineteenth centuries, their search for poetic likenesses for the soul, and for the soulfulness of beauty, composes a major part of their creative endeavors. Indeed, in the cases of the three younger among English Romanticism's major figures— George Gordon, Lord Byron (1788–1824), Percy Bysshe Shelley (1792–1822), and John Keats (1795–1821)—their attempts to express the ineffable is a key to their themes, one that will never fail to yield satisfactorily convincing results.

"What thou art we know not", Shelley will say to the "blithe Spirit" that he hails the skylark as in his ode of that name.[1] "What is most like thee?" (see p. 257, line 32) he therefore continues, and he then provides a parade of simile upon simile in couplet after couplet, all in a valiant effort to find that exact image—the *bon mot* of poetic currency—that will paint the precise word picture, insisting as he does so that, whatever else the skylark might be, "[b]ird thou never wert" (see p. 256, line 2).

---

[1] Percy Bysshe Shelley, "To a Sky-Lark", in *The Romantic Poets*, ed. Joseph Pearce and Robert Asch, vol. 2, *Byron, Shelley, and Keats*, Ignatius Critical Editions (San Francisco: Ignatius Press, 2024), pp. 257, 256, lines 31, 1. All quotations from "To a Sky-Lark" are from this edition and will be cited in the text.

Shelley's essential meaning is hard to miss: as the spirit's surrogate, the skylark can be known only for what it is not, never for its very self.

The poet presently under consideration, John Keats, was another who famously used a bird to represent (although to "body forth" might be much more to the point) the soul in a poem of his. Indeed, it is one of his most significant poems, if not as well one of the most celebrated poems in the English language from that era, his "Ode to a Nightingale". Since this essay will be discussing not only this poem but an entire series of odes by Keats that are ostensibly associated closely with it, a working definition of that poetic genre would first be in order.

For English speakers, it can safely be said that an ode is an effusion, a veritable explosion of entangled thoughts and feelings and sensations. As a poetic genre, the ode has become most commonly associated with the poetry of these same English Romantic poets, as well as with two equally renowned elder compatriots of theirs, William Wordsworth (1770–1850) and Samuel Taylor Coleridge (1772–1834).

In general terms, the ode is *the* poetic form that these poets were wont to use whenever the power of a thought or feeling, and sometimes both, is so overpowering that no other mode of expression can contain it or otherwise do it justice.

From the point of view of formal considerations, however, the ode is really a poetic sleight of hand. While a poet like Keats may resort to the ode in the hope of creating and sustaining the illusion that the poet-speaker can barely contain himself or his feelings, the ode, as a composition, is in fact a very carefully measured and calculated poetic undertaking that has been complexly and carefully constructed to give the impression that it is "but a moment's thought". Indeed, in Keats' capable hands, the ode adheres to rigid rhythmic requirements and rhyme schemes that themselves could never possibly have resulted from the poet's madly surrendering sense and form to the kind of unbridled emotional enthusiasms and confusions to which the typical ode seems to be giving voice.

The merest glance at "Ode to a Nightingale" would establish the validity of this observation instantly for even the most novice of readers. Each of that poem's eight stanzas is composed of exactly ten pentameter lines and, with only a very slight variation in stanza 2, each conforms as well to the same rhyme scheme: *ab ab cde cde*. No poet can achieve such formal control without the expenditure of a painstaking and highly conscious attention to detail, one that would seem to belie the poem's appearance of being "unpremeditated art" enabling a "spontaneous overflow of powerful feeling", borrowing phrases from Shelley ("To a Sky-Lark", see p. 256, line 5) and Wordsworth,[2] respectively.

Since a heightened emotionalism is the effect that the poet wishes to create in an ode, readers are very often overcome by and sometimes even put out by the poetry's apparently irrational effusions, failing to notice or acknowledge the intense and intentional self-control that the poet has exercised in shaping them.

That is really quite unfortunate, because, again contrary to the conventional wisdom, the English Romantics, and Keats virtually foremost among them, were devoted to trying to capture the very essence of lived experience and to express it with a virtually scientific precision.

Yes, scientific. Their fabled idealism, which by now has made the word "Romantic" synonymous with "impractical" or "unrealistic" or "illogical", is founded in fact on their adamant refusal to admit to themselves that the apprehension of beauty and truth, even as transitory as those experiences may sometimes seem to be, is no less substantial and real an experience, as experience, than any other human experience.

In their poetry, then, they set out to prove as much, even if only for themselves. Most assuredly, and as the rest of this essay hopes to demonstrate, that is the case with John Keats

---

[2] William Wordsworth, "Preface to *Lyrical Ballads*", in *The Romantic Poets*, ed. Joseph Pearce and Robert Asch, vol. 1, *Blake, Wordsworth, and Coleridge*, Ignatius Critical Editions (San Francisco: Ignatius Press, 2014), pp. 90, 106.

as he composed, during the spring and then fall of 1819, five odes—"To Psyche", "To a Nightingale", "On a Grecian Urn", "On Melancholy", and "On Indolence"—and their coda, "To Autumn".

* * * * *

While the exact order of their composition is not known, it is universally accepted that the first five of these odes were composed in April and May of 1819, while "To Autumn", appropriately enough, was composed right at the very end of the summer of that same year, on September 19, to be precise. Whether it was intended or not, and more to the point, these six odes are linked by a common theme, and that theme is itself one of the most common in all of literature and religion and philosophy, among virtually every known human culture since time immemorial. It is the theme—or perhaps it is only the expression of its hope—that there is something substantial that endures the legendary ravages of time, a something that must last not so much *in* as *because of* its very changelessness.

The individual soul's craving not only to guess at but actually to behold that changelessness has been a constant source of inspiration, in the arts, of its greatest agony or drama, and in these six poems of the young John Keats that drama is again played out in a manner that is not tragic and may even be true to life itself.

So then, proceeding on the basis of the order of the odes as they are listed above, an ordering somewhat established by Keats' scholar Jack Stillinger[3] in his still-definitive Belknap Press edition of the *Complete Poems* (1978), that drama unfolds exactly as if it were a five-act play in which the

---

[3] Because of thematic and stylistic considerations, Stillinger argues for the omission of "Indolence" from among the so-called Five Great Odes, although he sees its composition falling within the same period (March 19 through June 9, 1819) as the four other odes that Keats composed during the spring of 1819 (471). Its placement in my listing here as the fifth of the spring odes, to which grouping "To Autumn" acts as a thematic coda, is coordinate instead with M. H. Abrams' ordering of the odes in the *Norton Anthology of English Literature* and forms the basis for this present reading of the five spring odes and "To Autumn" that follows.

poet-speaker sets off on a quest to discover Truth and Beauty not as merely ideals but as the very stuff of life itself.

His will not be an effort to convince but to experience, and in his experiencing these ideals, and his expression of those experiences as poetry, lies all the validity of the remarkable conclusion that he arrives at in one last and truly final act or coda, "To Autumn".

* * * * *

An appreciation of the historical background to the ancient Roman myth of Psyche is necessary for an understanding of the terms of the quest as the poet-speaker will set them forth in the drama's first act, "Ode to Psyche". To know something of the fourth-century A.D. Roman poet Apuleius' delightful fable about a young woman named Psyche and her lover, Cupid, the son of the goddess Venus and himself the god of Love (as his original Greek name, Eros, more readily attests) is, as it were, not merely to know something of the language in which the information contained in the ode is being conveyed, but to gain an invaluable insight into Keats' thematic goal.

While a reader today might think of an ancient Roman myth as a relatively erudite subject, a reasonably educated person in Keats' time would have been well-versed in the classics. So, then, Keats is dealing with a common cultural currency as he resorts to classical allusions throughout the odes, even if references to Lethe and Bacchus and, yes, Psyche might seem to be rather rare coins nowadays. In fact, a letter of Keats' dated "Friday, April 30" of 1819 confirms that he was not only well aware of the late origins of the so-called myth of Psyche but also inspired by it. Much more to the point of the poem itself, the poetic climax rests upon that very fact, identifying Psyche as "latest born"[4] and, so, one who thus arrived upon the scene "too late for antique vows"

---

[4] John Keats, "Ode to Psyche", in *Romantic Poets*, vol. 2, p. 440, line 24. With the exception of "On Indolence", all references to the texts of the odes are from this edition and will be cited in the text.

(see p. 441, line 36). "I am more orthodox than to let a hea-
then Goddess be so neglected", Keats will boastfully conclude
his comments.[5]

In order to appreciate the terms of the unfolding drama as
set out in "Psyche", then, since the poet-speaker quite openly
dedicates himself to serve the "Goddess" as her priest, the cul-
tus that the poet-speaker envisions as hers needs an explication
that only a knowledge of Apuleius' original fable can provide.
Ostensibly, the Roman poet's tale, rife with high (melo)drama
and suspense, has all the earmarks of one of the many retellings
of classical myths famously penned by the Roman poet Ovid
during the reign of Augustus, itself, in retrospect, imperial
Rome's last heyday of its foundations in so-called pagan beliefs.
Apuleius, however, is writing more than 150 years after Ovid.

Briefly, then, Psyche, whose name in Greek means "but-
terfly", is a mortal, a young woman of such stunning beauty
that no man dares approach her except to gaze on her perfec-
tion.[6] Envied, if not despised, by Venus, and beloved of her
son, Cupid, Psyche undergoes much travail before Cupid con-
vinces Jove, the father of gods and men, to permit Cupid to
marry Psyche, who is herself, by that act, now one with the
gods themselves living on Olympus. With Psyche an immortal
herself now, her beauty is no longer a threat to Venus, and so,
the goddess placated, all's well that ends well, as the Bard says.

Apuleius' motives for telling such a story should seem to
be clear by now, offering as he does a pagan myth to compete
with the Christian Gospels that tell of the Son of Divine Love
sacrificing himself so that the human soul might itself finally
inherit the place eternally reserved for it in Heaven.

As Keats knows, however, Apuleius' religio-cultural rescue
mission came too late. Though Apuleius' Psyche was literally,

---

[5] *Letters of John Keats to His Family and Friends*, ed. Sidney Colvin (New York:
Barnes & Noble Digital Edition, 2011), p. 330.

[6] For the details of this summary of Apuleius' tale, I am relying upon the
lengthy synopsis of the story presented by Edith Hamilton in her widely read and
enduring work *Mythology: Timeless Tales of Gods and Goddesses* (1942; repr., New
York: Grand Central Books, 1999), 121–34.

in Keats' words, the "latest born and loveliest vision far / Of all Olympus' faded hierarchy" (see p. 440, lines 24–25), Keats must nonetheless tell the stillborn goddess a bitter truth: "[T]emple thou hast none, / Nor altar heaped with flowers; / Nor virgin-choir to make delicious moan / Upon the midnight hours" (see p. 441, lines 28–31).

If "Ode to Psyche" constitutes this first act in an unfolding drama of the human soul's longing for something that is everlasting, then the poet-speaker of the ode establishes at the outset the same truth to which his fellow poet Apuleius nearly two millennia earlier had himself borne witness: that Psyche, the soul, lives eternally, and she lives enfolded forever in the arms of her beloved, who is none other than the God of Love himself. Indeed, the poet-speaker literally stumbles upon that truth:

> I wandered in a forest thoughtlessly,
>   And, on the sudden, fainting with surprise,
> Saw two fair creatures, couchèd side by side.
> ....
>   The wingèd boy I knew;
> But who wast thou, O happy, happy dove?
>   His Psyche true! (See p. 440, lines 7–9, 21–23.)

Furthermore, in this transitory world where nothing endures for more than an instant—a sad fact that Act 2, the "Nightingale" ode, will shortly be reminding readers—the poet-speaker is more than just a witness to the human soul's eternal union with the never-ending love that it seeks. Rather, the soul, Psyche, is found savoring that moment of eternal bliss eternally: as the two "lay calm-breathing on the bedded grass" (see p. 440, line 15), "[t]heir lips touched not, but had not bade adieu" (see p. 440, line 17). They live, in other words, the inmost, utmost human wish, and that is each and every individual's most outlandish wish that, in the presence of the sensations of a perfect bliss, the moment might not ever pass.

Psyche's and Cupid's certainly will not. Instead of envying them their perfect bliss, however, the poet-speaker bends his knee to them, if not indeed to her alone, to plead to the neglected goddess: "[L]et me be thy choir" (see p. 441, line 44), pledging that "I will be thy priest" (see p. 441, line 50).

So ends Act 1, and the curtain comes down.

* * * * *

If Keats' "Ode to Psyche" celebrates the imagination's power to overcome the limits of time and space as much as it also laments the passage of time, Act 2, "Ode to a Nightingale", opens with the newly ordained priest of Psyche reveling in a timeless moment in which the very beauty that the poet-speaker had vowed to serve at the close of Act 1 is now intoxicating his own soul with the beauty of the song of the nightingale:

> My heart aches, and a drowsy numbness pains
>   My sense, as though of hemlock I had drunk.
> . . . .
>   One minute past, and Lethe-wards had sunk:
> 'Tis not through envy of thy happy lot,
>   But being too happy . . .
>   That thou . . .
> . . . .
>   Singest of summer in full-throated ease.
>   (See p. 442, lines 1–2, 4–7, 10.)

In obvious terms, as it opens, the "Nightingale" ode finds the poet-speaker caught up in the throes of the very sort of ecstasy that he had just finished imagining Psyche and her Cupid sharing. Nor would it be a digression to note at this juncture that the very word "ecstasy" refers to one's being beside or outside oneself, as in the phrase "to be beside oneself with joy".

Such a moment is more than the poet-speaker feels himself capable of bearing—"too happy"—and yet, as the second stanza opens, he wishes for a glass of wine, a sparkling Burgundy perhaps, one "that hath been / Cooled a long age in the deep-delvèd earth" (see p. 443, lines 11–12), in order to enhance this heady experience of an escape from the dull tedium of common human existence.

If one were to wonder why the poet-speaker might crave such an escape, he provides the reasons in the very next stanza. By numbing his senses with wine, he might thereby be able to "quite forget/... The weariness, the fever, and the fret/Here" (see p. 443, lines 21, 23–24). In case there be any doubt, he then goes on to make it abundantly clear that "here" is the unfolding of the day-to-day, with its ceaseless passing of all that is most cherished—youth, beauty, love—amid its sorrows and despairs, until "palsy shakes a few, sad, last grey hairs" (see p. 443, line 25) and death provides the only genuine relief.

Thus, a new resolve is boldly, powerfully, and most masterfully and beautifully expressed in stanza 4. Forsaking the artificial inebriation that might be supplied by alcohol, analogized in the Roman god of wine, Bacchus, the poet-speaker determines that he need only mount on "the viewless wings of Poesy" (see p. 443, line 33)—the poetical imagination—to join his spirit to the nightingale's.

Once he thus lets go, as it were, he is, rather than here, *there*.

> Though the dull brain perplexes and retards.
> Already with thee! tender is the night.
> (See pp. 443–44, lines 34–35.)

The poet-speaker's fear that the "dull brain" might itself undermine the genuine ecstasy of the moment demonstrates Keats' penchant for trying to engage experience without the intervening intrusion of the mind. Very early on in "To Psyche", for example, the poet-speaker notes that he is wandering "thoughtlessly" (see p. 440, line 7); similarly, in his "Ode on a Grecian Urn", the upcoming Act 3 of the unfolding drama, he will comment toward the end on how the urn "dost tease us out of thought" (see p. 447, line 44). Here in the "Nightingale" ode, as already noted, he speaks of releasing himself into an imaginative flight, in spite of the "dull brain", with its logical capacity to dismiss the perplexing as nonsense.

Each of these instances in which the poet-speaker patently resists the temptation to succumb to cold logic iterates a poetical skill that Keats calls elsewhere, in a December 22, 1817, letter to his brothers, George and Thomas, *Negative Capability*. "With a great poet," Keats insists, "the sense of Beauty ... obliterates all consideration."[7]

Keats cites Shakespeare as a prime example of a poet who "possessed ... [such a talent] enormously", citing his own contemporary, Coleridge, as a poet who, at the opposite extreme, is "incapable of remaining content with half knowledge". Rather, to possess this supreme poetic gift one must be "capable of being in uncertainties, mysteries, doubt, without any irritable reaching after fact and reason".[8]

To puzzle out the concept any further would be to give the lie to the emphatic simplicity with which Keats proposes it. For the next stanza and a half, the poet-speaker, then, swept up by the sheer beauty of the moment, streams the synaesthestic breezes of smell and sound and sight ("the sense of Beauty ... obliterates all consideration") until, as the sixth stanza opens, he reflects for a moment on how much he wishes that now he might happily and willingly die "[w]hile thou [the nightingale] art pouring forth thy soul abroad/In such an ecstasy!" (see p. 444, lines 57–58). Doing so, however, tricks him into paradox, paradox into associative logic, and associative logic into the discursive logic of the "dull brain", whose voice of busy common sense and irritable reaching after fact and logic will thus end up winning the day, or, as it were, the night.

For that commonplace human desire, in the throes of great joy, to wish that one were dead ("I'm so happy I could die!") makes him aware of the bitter irony that he would then no longer be able to hear the song whose very beauty moves him to wish that he might "cease upon the midnight" hour (see p. 444, line 56):

> Still wouldst thou sing, and I have ears in vain—
>   To thy high requiem become a sod.
>   (See p. 444, lines 59–60.)

No sooner does the poet-speaker start thinking of death than the jig is up for his gossamer vision. In the final two

---

[7] *Letters*, p. 81.
[8] Ibid., p. 82.

stanzas it devolves until, living creature that it is, even the nightingale moves on, taking her song with her. Even the associative value of words betrays the delicate balance of thought and feeling: "[F]orlorn", he says at the end of stanza 7 (see p. 445, line 70), thinking of the long passed. "Forlorn!" he says as stanza 8 opens (see p. 445, line 71), thinking now, however, of how it refers to the sadness of loss as well. For "the very word is like a bell/To toll me back from thee to my sole self!" (see p. 445, lines 71–72).

> Was it a vision, or a waking dream?
> Fled is that music—Do I wake or sleep?
> (See p. 445, lines 79–80.)

In sum, the poet-speaker, who envied Psyche and her Cupid for their not having ever to part, finds, as cold reality settles in, that he must bid his own adieu to a moment that had seemed to bring an eternal bliss, bidding adieu as well to its source, the singing nightingale, who has flown away.

* * * * *

No wonder, then, as "Ode on a Grecian Urn" (Act 3) opens, that the poet-speaker finds himself pondering now an idyll that will not fly away, a scene carved upon a marble urn and told by a "[s]ylvan historian, who canst thus express/A flowery tale more sweetly than our rhyme" (see p. 446, lines 3–4).

The poet-speaker, on his quest for one experience in the here and now of creation that will last, having learned that "the fancy cannot cheat so well/As she is famed to do, deceiving elf" ("Nightingale", see p. 445, lines 73–74), has turned his back on the tedium of cold logic to realize that "[h]eard melodies are sweet, but those unheard/Are sweeter" ("Grecian Urn", see p. 446, lines 11–12). Instead of pinning his hopes for an eternal bliss on things that are themselves of this transient world, such as the nightingale's song and the nightingale itself, the poet-speaker will himself reside in a world of pure imagination as it is depicted in its frozen perfection on the urn, a world where lovers may not ever kiss, but "[s]he cannot fade" (see p. 446, line 19), and where a happy melodist is "piping songs for ever new" (see p. 446, line 24), since they can never cease to be anywhere except in this state of a perpetually static becoming.

"[T]herefore, ye soft pipes"—and are these the piper's or the poet-speaker's veins and arteries?—"play on … to the spirit ditties of no tone" (see p. 446, lines 12, 14). In this new world nothing ever fades and nothing ever dies, and everything, hovering just on the brink of fulfillment, never decays into it either, as had happened with the unraveling of the poet-speaker's experience of ecstasy in the "Nightingale" ode as the bird flew off and words failed.

Indeed, the world of the urn has by now become so real for him that he begins to imagine details behind the surface, scenes not depicted but implied. If, then, there is this procession of priest and the faithful accompanying the sacrificial heifer garlanded for the festival yet to come, there must somewhere be as well a village "emptied of this folk, this pious morn" (see p. 447, line 37). So the poet-speaker thinks then how "not a soul to tell/Why thou art desolate, can e'er return" (see p. 447, lines 39–40).

Whatever else it may have been, the "Cold Pastoral" (see p. 447, line 45) of the "silent form" of the urn that "dost tease us out of thought/As doth eternity" (see p. 447, lines 44–45) had been real while it lasted, until the word "desolate" (see p. 447, line 40) intruded its ugly head. And so, as if seizing upon the very principle of Negative Capability that he had himself enunciated, the poet-speaker achieves his own measure of that skill by practicing what he preaches and acquiescing to the experience for its sake and its sake alone. Thus, he resists the temptation to reach after fact or reason. Instead, yielding to the realization that beauty experienced is no less "true" an experience than any other experience, he can formulate an irresistibly irrefutable conclusion based on what he just now has learned from his refusal to succumb to despair. And so, while he may not have proved it to anyone else's satisfaction, the experience of the urn has convinced him that "[b]eauty is truth, truth beauty", and "that is all / Ye know on earth, and all ye need to know'" (see p. 447, lines 49–50).

* * * * *

The philosopher or religionist would rest upon his laurels with that successful formulation of a truth that only genuine speculation can arrive at. Keats is too honest a poet, however, and his poetry too honest a poetry, for it to end there. He was not exploring the expoundable, after all, in these first three odes or acts; he was trying to experience firsthand the inexpressible. Finding its expression, even if only for an instant, may satisfy others, but it cannot satisfy the poet who knows that every success is only an invitation to further seeking.

He can, as Act 3 ends, insist against the intrusion of time and its accompanying processes of decay into the moment, but even that moment of resistance and insight cannot itself last for long. So, then, it is quite in keeping with this spirit of unflinching honesty that Act 4, "Ode on Melancholy", should find the poet-speaker, rather than enjoying the fruits of his labors, suffering instead the awful coming down from the heady experience of that perfect insight upon which the "Grecian Urn" had ended.

Now he knows that he who would "burst Joy's grape against his palate" ("Melancholy", see p. 449, line 28) must indeed find that beauty and truth are things that must, like the morning rose or rainbow or all else, die. There is no end, only endings:

> She dwells with Beauty—Beauty that must die;
>   And Joy, whose hand is ever at his lips
> Bidding adieu. (See p. 449, lines 21–23.)

The moment of the bittersweet revealed, Keats recognizes that it is not Bacchus or the dull brain that one must fear in pursuing the moment of utter surrender to beauty and to truth; it is Melancholy—a sad bitterness—that waits on the other side of the ecstatic experience to catch the seeker in his net as the vision all comes crashing down, and the seeker along with it.

And, too, a quest that had begun with the poet-speaker swearing to build a temple to Psyche in some untrodden region of his mind now finds himself hung among Melancholy's trophies in "the very temple of Delight" (see p. 449, line 25), betrayed by his own naïve enthusiasms. For "the melancholy fit shall fall" (see p. 448, line 11)—it always does—and shroud the soul in dark despair, as if the wages of caring are only more care.

* * * * *

"Ode on Indolence"[9] is, then, a suitable Act 5 upon which the drama might end. One need not be a linguist to know that the Latin verb *indolere* upon which the English noun is based means, quite literally, not to be feeling pain. If the bittersweet bane of Melancholy is all that finally awaits this self-anointed priest of Psyche, who has found himself driven by despair into seeking the extremes of meaning and joy, why should he not content himself with the happy medium of not really caring anymore about such extremes?

Tired of being a "pet-lamb in a sentimental farce" (line 54), the poet has learned his true métier: "I yet have visions for the night" (line 57). Why not, he appears to conclude, sit back and idly enjoy what one could be or do or think or feel, rather than bothering to pursue some phantom prize, be it love or ambition or poetry, or truth and beauty.

Embarrassed by his previous naïveté, he sends these personal demons of his that are passing like "figures on a marble urn" (line 5)—an all-too-familiar imaginative venue for him by now—packing, and the poet-speaker who had once bemoaned bidding things adieu now says adieu with heart and fervor and relish: "Vanish, ye phantoms, from my idle spright,/Into the clouds, and never more return!" (lines 59–60).

If this sequence of odes were indeed a play, the audience may have wound up feeling that they did not get their money's

---

[9] John Keats, "Ode on Indolence", in *John Keats: Complete Poems*, ed. Jack Stillinger (Cambridge, Mass.: Belknap Press of Harvard University Press, 1978), pp. 284–86. All references to the text of this ode will be from this edition.

worth. Here was a protagonist who had witnessed the fabled wonders of an equally fabled Seventh Heaven and had not only survived the experience but also come back with the grist of an unassailably valid insight in his teeth, only to collapse finally into an exhausted defeatism.

As the disheartened audience trudges out of the auditorium, however, the house lights flash, calling them back to their seats. The curtain rises on one last act, a coda as it were, the ode "To Autumn".

The poet-speaker stands in a field at the end of the day and at the end of the season. The theme of the moment is closings, with all of nature bidding its own farewell as another year comes to an end. Every instinct to resist the inevitable, instincts that the poet-speaker had called upon and virtually exhausted in the five spring odes, has come to no avail, as it must.

The forlorn desolation that had contaminated the bitter-sweet bliss of "Ode to a Nightingale" and "Ode on a Grecian Urn" is now the only reality that there is. Wherever one might look, there are the "stubble-plains" ("Autumn", see p. 450, line 26). Our poet-speaker nostalgically wonders, thinking perhaps of that evening when a bird's singing had stolen his heart, "Where are the songs of Spring?" (see p. 450, line 23). It is in the pain of recollection and the preparation for lamentation, however, that the poet-speaker calls upon Negative Capability, that capacity to let beauty obliterate all other considerations. For there is still beauty here, even in this desolate vista, to which he says, as to himself: "Think not of them ["the songs of Spring"], thou hast thy music too—" (see p. 450, line 24).

He has learned to fall silent, like the urn, and to listen, to be still and still moving. And as he quiets the longing of his soul to contemplate once more all the beauty that has now apparently passed away and tries instead to hear the songs of autumn, he hears, in quick succession, "a wailful choir [of] the small gnats mourn" (see p. 450, line 27), "full-grown lambs loud bleat" (see p. 450, line 30), "[h]edge-crickets sing" (see p. 450, line 31), "[t]he red-breast whistles" (see p. 450, line 32), and "gathering swallows twitter" (see p. 450, line 33)—all of these sounds of nature most commonly associated with *the songs of spring*!

The very music that he had thought was gone is still there. The scene changes, but the song remains, and it is the same song. In the unceasing changelessness of change itself, and in the essential sameness of human experience, he has found his truth, he has found his beauty, and he has found his peace, and that, he has demonstrated in truthful ways, is all that any-one ever seeks and can ever find, once he learns to fall silent and listen.

Shelley has called the poet the priest and prophet of human-ity, the one who preserves its most sacred traditions and pro-claims its most heartfelt hopes and fears. He has called poets "the unacknowledged legislators of the World" (see p. 330), who, for each generation, give words to the innermost laws of our being, the indomitable rules of civility and concern for others by which we each, as isolated individuals, truly live.

In these five spring odes and their coda, "To Autumn", Keats fulfilled his own obligation to be priest and prophet and poet, the one who explores the fringes of experience only to discover that they lie at the very soul of our being, joys that awaken without warning out of the most insignificant events and take the individual by wondrous storm, trivializing every-thing else in their path.

These six odes of Keats are themselves now an enduring human record of that commonplace truth. What more could one ask?

CONTRIBUTORS

Robert Asch is the editor of the Saint Austin Press and co-editor of the *St. Austin Review*. His books include *Lionel Johnson: Poetry and Prose* (Saint Austin) and *The Romantic Poets*, volume I (Ignatius Press). He lives in Preston, England, with his wife and children.

Raimund Borgmeier is Emeritus Professor of English literature at the University of Giessen, Germany. He has worked and published on Shakespeare, the poetry of the eighteenth century and the Romantic movement, and Victorian and contemporary fiction (including science fiction and crime fiction). Several times, he was visiting professor at the University of Wisconsin, both in Madison and Milwaukee.

Robert C. Evans is the I. B. Young Professor of English at Auburn University at Montgomery. He is widely published and is especially interested in close reading and critical pluralism. He has received grants from the National Endowment for the Humanities and from the Folger, Newberry, and Huntington Libraries, among others.

Amy Fahey holds a doctorate in English and American literature from Washington University in St. Louis, and an M.Phil. in medieval literature from the University of St. Andrews, Scotland. She has taught literature courses at the Thomas More College of Liberal Arts and Christendom College.

James E. Hartley is professor of economics at Mount Holyoke College, where he teaches Macroeconomic Theory, Money and Banking, and Principles of Economics, among other economics courses. Outside the Economics Department, he has also taught multiple courses using the Great Books, including Western Civilization: An Introduction through the Great

Books, Leadership and the Liberal Arts, Is Business Moral? (developed with a grant from the National Endowment for the Humanities), Reflections on War, C. S. Lewis, and numerous tutorials and reading groups on the Western Canon.

Louis Markos is professor of English and Scholar in Residence at Houston Christian University, and he holds the Robert H. Ray Chair in Humanities. His twenty-five books include *Eye of the Beholder: How to See the World like a Romantic Poet*; *Heaven and Hell: Visions of the Afterlife in the Western Poetic Tradition*; *Pressing Forward: Alfred, Lord Tennyson and the Victorian Age*; *Literature: A Student's Guide*; *From Achilles to Christ*; and *The Myth Made Fact: Reading Greek and Roman Mythology through Christian Eyes*.

Russell Elliott Murphy is professor emeritus with the Department of English at the University of Arkansas at Little Rock. Among his many publications are *Structure and Meaning*, *Critical Companion to T. S. Eliot*, *The Meaning of Byzantium in the Poetry and Prose of W. B. Yeats*, and *Spent*, a novel. Since 1987, he has been the editor and publisher of the *Yeats Eliot Review*.

Joseph Pearce is the acclaimed author of numerous literary studies, including *Literary Converts*, *The Quest for Shakespeare*, and *Shakespeare on Love*, as well as popular biographies of Oscar Wilde, J. R. R. Tolkien, C. S. Lewis, G. K. Chesterton, and Aleksandr Solzhenitsyn. He is the general editor of the Ignatius Critical Editions series.